FRANZ LISZT

FRANZ LISZT
MUSICIAN, CELEBRITY, SUPERSTAR

OLIVER HILMES

TRANSLATED BY STEWART SPENCER

YALE UNIVERSITY PRESS
NEW HAVEN AND LONDON

First published in English by Yale University Press in 2016

Originally published under the title *Liszt Biographie eines Superstars* by
Oliver Hilmes © 2011 by Siedler Verlag, a division of Verlagsgruppe Random
House GmbH, Munich

For information about this and other Yale University Press publications, please contact:

U.S. Office: sales.press@yale.edu   yalebooks.com
Europe Office: sales@yaleup.co.uk   yalebooks.co.uk

Set in Minion Pro by IDSUK (DataConnection) Ltd
Printed and bound by CPI Group (UK) Ltd, Croydon, CR0 4YY

Library of Congress Cataloging-in-Publication Data

Franz Liszt : biography of a superstar / Oliver Hilmes ; translation,
    Stewart Spencer.
Franz Liszt. English
New Haven : Yale University Press, [2016] | "Originally
    published under the title Liszt: Biographie eines Superstars by Oliver
    Hilmes " 2011 By Siedler Verlag, a division of Verlagsgruppe Random House
    GmbH, Munich." | Includes bibliographical references and index.
LCCN 2015034552 | ISBN 9780300182934 (hardback) | ISBN 9780300228755 (paper)
LCSH: Liszt, Franz, 1811-1886. | Composers—Biography. |
Biographies. lcgft
LCC ML410.L7 H5513 2016 | DDC 780.92—dc23
LC record available at http://lccn.loc.gov/2015034552
A catalogue record for this book is available from the British Library.

10 9 8 7 6 5 4 3 2 1

CONTENTS

List of Illustrations   *vi*

Acknowledgements   *vii*

Prologue   *viii*

1   Childhood and Adolescence (1811–27)   1

2   Rehearsing and Studying (1827–35)   29

3   Années de pèlerinage (1835–9)   53

4   Living Like a Lord (1839–47)   71

5   Weimar (1847–61)   101

6   Rome (1861–8)   179

7   La vie trifurquée (1869–86)   224

   Postlude   307

Notes   *314*

Bibliography   *335*

Index   *340*

LIST OF ILLUSTRATIONS

Chapter frontispieces and plates 4, 7 and 16 taken from Robert Bory, *La vie de Franz Liszt l'image*, Paris, 1936.

1. Adam, Liszt's father (© Sammlung Rauch).
2. Carl Czerny (© akg-images/De Agostini Picture Lib./A. Dagli Orti).
3. Antonio Salieri (© akg-images).
4. Beethoven's famous kiss of consecration.
5. Liszt (© akg-images).
6. Marie d'Agoult (© akg-images).
7. Aurore Dupin, Baroness Dudevant (George Sand).
8. Liszt the young seducer (© Getty Images).
9. Liszt at thirty (© Getty Images).
10. Liszt at the piano (© akg-images).
11. Salon of Delphine Gay de Girardin (© ullstein bild – Granger, NYC).
12. Liszt the court Kapellmeister (© Getty Images).
13. Princess Carolyne von Sayn-Wittgenstein (© Interfoto/Sammlung Rauch).
14. The Altenburg in Weimar (© Klassik Stiftung Weimar/Wilhelm Höffert).
15. Daniel, Cosima, Blandine and Anna Liszt with Madame Patersi de Fossombroni (© Richard Wagner Museum, Bayreuth).
16. Agnes Street-Klindworth.
17. Abbé Liszt (© bpk/Jozséf Heller).
18. Liszt with Hans and Cosima von Bülow and Count Leo Festetics (© Richard Wagner Museum, Bayreuth).
19. Liszt in Paris (© Bibliothèque nationale de France/Nadar).
20. Fiftieth anniversary festival committee (© Magyar Nemzeti Múzeum/ Ferencz Kozmata).
21. Liszt on his seventy-third birthday (© Fotoatelier Louis Held, Inh. Stefan Renno, Weimar).
22. Liszt caricature (© ullstein bild – Granger, NYC).

ACKNOWLEDGEMENTS

IN THE COURSE OF my work I have received help from many quarters and should like to take this opportunity to express my heartfelt thanks to everyone who assisted me, especially the staff of the various archives, collections and libraries that I consulted. I am particularly grateful to Evelyn Liepsch of the Goethe- und Schiller-Archiv in Weimar for generously placing at my disposal the archive's extensive holdings.

Two of the world's leading Liszt scholars, Serge Gut and Alan Walker, willingly shared their knowledge with me, and for that I am deeply grateful.

I should also like to thank Thomas Rathnow and Tobias Winstel of Siedler Verlag and my Munich copy-editor Fritz Jensch. My agent Barbara Wenner was always at hand, offering both advice and practical help. Regina Bouchehri and Dorothee Hütte prepared the countless translations from French-language sources. Marie-Luise Adlung and Stephanie Kotyla transcribed unpublished manuscripts that were often hard to decipher. To all of them I extend my warmest thanks.

I am additionally grateful to many individuals who helped me in ways too numerous to list: Cameron Carpenter, Nicolas Dufetel, Maren Goltz, Klára Hamburger, Maximilian Lautenschläger, Elisabeth Maier, Rosemary Moravec-Hilmar, Dirk Mühlenhaus, Angelika Pöthe, Judith Schepers, Alexander Seitz and Hubert Wolf.

I should finally like to thank my parents Ilona and Wilfried Hilmes and, last but by no means least, Peter Franzek.

PROLOGUE

THE WORD 'SUPERSTAR' IS likely to put modern readers in mind of the Beatles, the Rolling Stones and other pop stars like Michael Jackson and Madonna, while lovers of classical music will think of figures such as Maria Callas, Vladimir Horowitz, Herbert von Karajan, Lang Lang, Anna Netrebko and Luciano Pavarotti.

Superstars are loved by their fans for their talents, while as people they are worshipped to distraction. When Horowitz announced his comeback in May 1965 after a twelve-year absence from the concert platform, music lovers queued for days outside New York's Carnegie Hall in the hope of buying a ticket for his recital. Rioting broke out immediately before the concert, the streets around the venue had to be closed, and when the sixty-one-year-old pianist finally appeared, he triggered a reaction that bordered on religious ecstasy. The event was phenomenally successful; it is no surprise that during his lifetime Horowitz earned several million dollars. Only one classical musician was more successful in this respect: the business-minded Herbert von Karajan, whose fortune at the time of his death in July 1989 has been conservatively estimated at £350 million. According to one business magazine, his widow, Eliette, was twenty-fourth in a list of the hundred wealthiest Austrians in 2005.

Glossy magazines and gossip columns have always been hand in glove with the world's superstars. Their co-dependence is an example of give and take, the magazines in question cultivating the superstars' image, while the latter show their gratitude by giving exclusive interviews and providing exclusive photographs. Thanks to glossy magazines, Maria Callas became a style icon of the 1960s, while Karajan enjoyed being seen as a restless, testosterone-fuelled jet-setter at the controls of sports cars and private aeroplanes. And yet this mixture of music, media and money is by no means new. In 2011 the world marked the 200th anniversary of the birth and the 125th anniversary of the death of a man who, while not exactly inventing these mechanisms, was arguably the first to deploy them with such unparalleled virtuosity: Franz Liszt.

Franz Liszt was a superstar, a genius and a European celebrity – he was utterly exceptional. Even as a child prodigy he cast a spell on audiences in Vienna, Paris and London. Later he travelled the length and breadth of Europe, taking his career to dizzying heights. The popular press of the time reported at length on his concerts and at even greater length on the numerous escapades that fuelled their feverish interest in him. There were times when the enthusiasm triggered by his public appearances bordered on delirium, and he became a figure on whom contemporaries projected all manner of erotic fantasies and secret desires.

Within a period of only eight years, Liszt gave around a thousand recitals – an incredible total. In the process he effectively invented the profession of the international concert pianist and was the first to perform the whole of the known keyboard repertory from Bach to his own contemporary Chopin – and he did so, moreover, from memory. As a composer and orchestrator, too, Liszt was a revolutionary, writing pioneering works that opened up new worlds of expression. For the music critic Klaus Umbach, Liszt was like a giant redwood among the progenitors of classical music, 'and most of those who seek to appear as his equals today and who want to be taken seriously are no more than bonsais artificially induced into seeming bigger than they are, while supported by a booming culture industry that gives the artist its blessing but for which no idiocy is beneath it.'[1]

But Liszt was also a man who kept reinventing himself. In 1847 he abandoned his calling as an itinerant virtuoso and settled in the small town of Weimar, where he made a new career for himself as a conductor, journalist, organizer, teacher and theatre administrator. If this particular change of direction still made sense to observers, they were left shaking their heads in disbelief when, only a few years later in April 1865, Liszt entered the four minor orders, becoming a Catholic abbé and for a time taking up residence within the precincts of the Vatican – not that this required him to forgo the company of beautiful women. He spent the remaining years of his life as the leading piano teacher of his age, commuting between Rome, Weimar and Budapest.

How can all these different aspects of the man be reconciled? Did Liszt himself see no contradiction between his life as a God-fearing Catholic and a man of the world whose lifestyle, embracing a whole series of scandalous love affairs, could scarcely be squared with the sexual mores of the Church of Rome?

It is difficult for us to form a picture of Liszt. Numerous photographs – several of them reproduced in the following pages – depict him at various stages in his life. The images from his years as a virtuoso have a positively iconic air to them, showing a young man with striking features, his long hair brushed carefully backwards. He is fashionably dressed, while the mysterious expression on his face is nothing if not seductive. Here the young Liszt is the very embodiment of the Romantic virtuoso. On photographs taken during his later years we see an older man whose snowy white mane of hair is in curious contrast to his cassock. All of these photographs have two things in common: not only do they give the impression that they are staged, which they undoubtedly were, but they also suggest that Liszt was a master of disguise, a man who wore many different masks.

Liszt's enigmatic ambiguity is in marked contrast to the unambiguous impression left by the man who in 1870 was to become his son-in-law: Richard Wagner. 'Mine is a different kind of organism,' Wagner insisted. 'I have sensitive nerves, I must have beauty, radiance and light. The world owes me a living! I can't live the miserable life of an organist like your Master Bach! Is it such an outrageous demand to say that I deserve the little bit of luxury that I can bear? I, who can give pleasure to thousands?'[2]

Liszt would never have put his name to such an expression of egoism and self-infatuation or, at best, he would have used the subjunctive in setting forth his demands. It is no accident that he always preferred to speak and write in French: in the gallant convolutions of the language of diplomacy he could conceal his true identity in ways that avoided detection. But when were his actions 'authentic'? And when did he show the world merely another of his masks?

Liszt's music is no less fascinating than the man himself: he wrote not only masterful studies for the piano but also ravishing show-stoppers, subtle travelogues and highly virtuosic transcriptions as well as works which, composed towards the end of his life, are altogether breathtaking, ultramodern miniatures that point the way forward to the twentieth century. His orchestral works were equally important and include a number of full-length symphonic poems. But he also wrote organ music, songs, oratorios, Masses and even an opera. Their musical language is often heroic, with a dandy-like triumphalism and condescension, while in other pieces it is poetically naïve, erotic and delicate. The works of his final years are notable for their disturbing austerity.

Liszt's piano works demand an artistry that separates the wheat from the chaff, which explains why they have always figured prominently in the recital programmes of pianists of the stature of Busoni, Horowitz, Brendel, Barenboim, Martha Argerich and Arcadi Volodos, all of whom at some point in their careers have turned their hand to the B minor Sonata, the 'Paganini' Studies and the First Mephisto Waltz.

Liszt's other works have tended to be overshadowed by his piano pieces. His orchestral music, for example, is seriously under-represented in the world of music today, a situation attributable in part to the fashionable predilections of a younger generation of conductors. But there is another – historical – reason for this neglect: the wedding of Liszt's daughter, Cosima, to his friend Richard Wagner in August 1870 was to have unfortunate repercussions for him. In establishing the Bayreuth Festival, the unscrupulously ambitious Wagners exploited their eminent kinsman for their own financial ends, and even after Wagner's death in 1883, Liszt continued to play the part of their 'lapdog', as he described himself in a moment of self-mockery. As Cosima emerged from the shadows and took on the role of the all-powerful matriarch of Bayreuth, so Liszt came to be seen by Wagnerians in general as little more than the man who had helped their idol on his way. That he was himself a composer of genius was all too easily forgotten.

'Liszt didn't exist in my youth,' recalls Richard Wagner's great-great-granddaughter, Nike:

> Worse, he existed only as a figure of mild amusement who interested no one – whenever family members referred to him, it was by the ironical title of 'the abbé'. I can still see my father Wieland falling asleep at a performance of *Die heilige Elisabeth* that he had had to attend as a family representative. If ever there were piano recitals featuring works by Liszt in the Margraves' Opera House or the Bayreuth Stadthalle, the family was conspicuous by its absence, an absence due as much as anything to sheer ignorance.

The reasons for the Wagner family's rejection of Liszt were entirely worldly, revolving as they did around hierarchies, vanity and, not least, money. Too much rivalry within the house would have been bad for business, Cosima would have thought. According to Nike Wagner, 'The musical hierarchy had to be maintained in spite of the close-knit relationships. In turn, this meant securing the "top place" within the history of music.'[3]

In fact, Wagner owed his friend and father-in-law more than he could ever express. Liszt encouraged him whenever he could and on several occasions rescued him from the brink of financial ruin. And that was not everything, for in a private moment we find Wagner admitting to Hans von Bülow that 'I have become a totally different fellow in matters of harmony as a result of getting to know Liszt's compositions.'[4] And in conversation with his second wife, Wagner even admitted to receiving stolen goods, claiming that he had 'stolen much' from Liszt: 'R. calls his symphonic poems *un repaire des voleurs* [a thieves' den], which makes us laugh heartily.'[5]

Even today many Wagnerians feel uncomfortable at the notion that their idol could have helped himself to ideas derived from the works of the much-ridiculed abbé and to have done so to such an extent. Some years ago Sir Simon Rattle took part in a platform discussion on Wagner in Amsterdam, provoking a certain disquiet when he described the

Bayreuth composer as 'one of the great magpies. If you know *Walküre* –
well, it's a shock to listen to the Liszt *Faust Symphony* and to hear how
much Wagner just stole from it.'[6] Not everyone in the hall was keen to
hear this. Ultimately, a monumental figure like Liszt needs no one to
defend his honour. But it remains one of the biographer's tasks to show
him in his true light.

Liszt's birth a little over two hundred years ago marked the start of one
of the great romances of the nineteenth century. His life takes readers
across the whole of Europe. We shall meet emperors, kings and other
crowned heads, we shall visit the pope in the Vatican and encounter
leading musicians, painters and writers, ambitious cardinals, unscrupulous spies and shady fraudsters. We shall also note with a certain amusement how Liszt became entangled in amorous intrigues. Many aspects
of Liszt's three score and fifteen years were not only grandiose, they
were also scandalous, while we might find others both bewildering and
disturbing. Yet others – such as those surrounding the 'Wittgenstein
Affair' – are as gripping as any detective story.

So who was this superstar who revolutionized music and seduced
women? The best stories are still those told by real life.

Oliver Hilmes
Berlin, January 2011

Génie oblige!

CHILDHOOD AND ADOLESCENCE
(1811–27)

The Comet

TUESDAY, 22 OCTOBER 1811 was a day like any other. The *Pressburger Zeitung* carried a brief front-page report on a visit that Emperor Franz I of Austria had paid to the Hungarian town of Komárom, although this was hardly news, not least because the reasons for the emperor's visit were withheld. On the second page, however, we find a news item from Vienna:

> On the afternoon of the 15th Herr Degen took off in his flying machine in the presence of a large crowd of onlookers. He reached a respectable height and descended to the ground, unharmed, between Trautmannsdorf and Bruck an der Leytha towards half past six in the evening.[1]

This was certainly more newsworthy: the reckless adventures of the clockmaker and pioneer of flying Jacob Degen fascinated the public of the day, whose eyes were generally raised skywards in 1811.

On 25 March the French astronomer Honoré Flaugergues had chanced upon a heavenly body that quickly became famous as the 'Great Comet of 1811' and which was visible to the naked eye for nine months of the year. Its vast nebulous haze even exceeded the sun in size.

Contemporaries were fascinated by this eerily beautiful natural spectacle, and many ascribed sinister powers to it. If a region was visited by
a particularly severe storm, then the comet was to blame. 'When the
magnificent Great Comet was seen in the spring,' recalled the poet
Hoffmann von Fallersleben,

> many were filled with fear and terror and prophesied a bloody and
> cruel war that would be followed by the overthrow of all that currently
> existed in the world. But each evening we children would delight in
> its glorious light, preferring to see in it the harbinger of a warm
> summer that would grant us long and cloudless days for our games.[2]

The summer of 1811 was indeed exceptionally hot, and this, too, was
ascribed to the comet. And when the grapes were harvested and proved
to be particularly plentiful and of high quality, the resultant product was
described as 'comet wine'.

Obscure prophets, clairvoyants and astrologers all had a field day,
and the Hungarian village of Raiding was no exception. Here the twenty-
three-year-old Anna Liszt was awaiting the birth of her first child. When
gypsies arrived in the village and predicted the birth of a famous man,
Anna saw in this a sign from heaven. Thus, at least, runs the legend.

Franz Liszt saw the light of the world on Tuesday, 22 October 1811, the
very day on which the *Pressburger Zeitung* was reporting the clockmaker's
ascent in his ornithopter. The boy was the only child of Adam and Anna
Liszt, who had married just nine months earlier, on 11 January 1811.
Raiding was then a part of the kingdom of Hungary, a country with a long
and turbulent history. Independent until 1526, it had then been overrun,
at least in part, by the Turks, but from 1699 it was wholly under the control
of the Habsburg Empire. From then on the official language was German,
with the result that whole generations of Hungarians never learnt to speak
their country's language. This was true of Adam Liszt and his family:
while self-evidently regarding themselves as Hungarians, they equally
self-evidently did not speak a word of Hungarian.

In 1811 Raiding consisted of some eighty-five buildings and 630
inhabitants. As an official in the service of Prince Nicholas II Esterházy,

Adam Liszt enjoyed a certain standing in the village. He had been working as the intendant or bookkeeper of the Esterházy sheepfolds since 1809, an important position at that time. With its various outbuildings, the Liszts' home was an impressive structure – not at all the modest cottage that it is sometimes described as having been. In short, Adam had done well for himself – not that this had brought him any happiness.

Adam Liszt was born in the village of Edelsthal on 16 December 1776. His father, Georg Adam, was a schoolteacher and had set great store by a good education for his numerous children, sending Adam to the Royal Catholic Grammar School at Pressburg (now Bratislava), which was still a part of Hungary at this date. Adam was evidently destined for the priesthood for at the age of eighteen he entered the Franciscan order as a novice at the Monastery of Malacka. But his life in the service of God ended only two years later when he was dismissed 'by reason of his inconstant and changeable nature'.[3] He then began to study philosophy only to have to break off after six months as he lacked the funds to pay his fees. Finally, on 1 January 1798, he entered the service of Nicholas II as a clerk. Presumably this was not an entirely voluntary career choice, but one way or another he had to earn a living.

Adam's great passion was music. As a youth he had received music lessons from his father, and later even studied composition in Pressburg. He was a gifted amateur in the best sense of the term and an accomplished performer on the piano, violin, cello and guitar. In 1805, after numerous requests for a transfer, he was offered a new position in Eisenstadt, where his contact with the court orchestra was a dream come true for him. Eisenstadt was the home of the Esterházys, for whom music had long played an important role. Their court orchestra was world famous and for decades had been conducted by Joseph Haydn. Since 1804 the post of Kapellmeister had been filled by Johann Nepomuk Hummel. Although Adam continued to be employed as a clerk, he sometimes helped out in the orchestra, was on friendly terms with many of the musicians and is even said to have played cards with the elderly Haydn. The years between 1805 and 1808 were arguably among the happiest of Adam Liszt's life.

Adam's superiors regarded him as hard-working, and it was out of gratitude that they transferred him to Raiding. The position of intendant of the sheepfolds undoubtedly represented a step up the career ladder for Adam, but tragically he himself could never see it in those terms. For him, it meant only a deterioration in his situation. In Eisenstadt he had come at least a little closer to realizing his dream of becoming a professional musician, but in October 1808 he was forced to leave for the provinces. Although Raiding was only thirty-five miles from Eisenstadt, in Adam's eyes it was worlds away from the scene of his greatest happiness. He grew depressed and increasingly disenchanted with his life.

During the summer of 1810 he met the twenty-two-year-old Anna Lager in Mattersdorf some twenty miles north of Raiding. She was visiting her brother at the time. Anna Lager came from a modest background and was the ninth child of the second marriage of a baker from Krems. She was only nine when she lost both her parents, her education still far from complete. Forced to leave school, she worked as a chambermaid in Vienna before meeting Adam Liszt, her elder by twelve years. They seem to have taken a liking to one another, and on 11 January 1811 they were married in the Catholic church at Unterfrauenhaid some two miles to the north-west of Raiding. Nine and a half months later their only child, Franz, was born. His baptismal certificate gives the Latin form of his name, Franciscus.

As a child, Liszt was often unwell, and on one occasion his parents even feared the worst and ordered a coffin, only for their son to recover. He attended the local school, where in winter the schoolmaster Johann Rohrer often had to contend with classes of over sixty. During the summer months that figure would fall to around thirty as the children had to help out in the fields or in their parents' businesses. Although attendance was theoretically compulsory until the age of twelve, many children simply absented themselves. Unable to speak Hungarian, Rohrer taught in German, for the most part limiting himself to reading, writing and arithmetic. In later life, Liszt repeatedly expressed his regret that his schooling had been so incomplete and that he had never been taught history, geography or foreign languages. If in the course of time he sought to make good these deficiencies, it was entirely through his own resources. Apart from German, he learnt Italian and English, but his preferred language was always French.

Adam Liszt often played the piano and sometimes performed chamber music with visiting friends from Eisenstadt, with the result that in spite of his rural surroundings, Liszt grew up in a musical atmosphere. On one occasion Adam is said to have played a piece by Ferdinand Ries, after which his son spontaneously sang one of its themes from memory. He was around six at the time. Adam taught him the rudiments of piano playing and harmony, while encouraging him to improvise at the keyboard. Other formative influences included the church services that Liszt and his family attended every Sunday. Here he fell under the spell of the legends about saints and martyrs, while the ritual associated with the Catholic Mass likewise drew him into its sway. Even if he later adopted a liberal interpretation of the Church's views on sexual morality, he still remained strangely attracted to the Catholic religion. But he was also fascinated by the groups of gypsies that passed through the region: they often came to Raiding and performed their music on the fiddle, double bass, clarinet and cimbalom (a kind of dulcimer). Liszt would listen as if intoxicated to music that veered between profound melancholy and sheer high-spirited exuberance.

Occasionally Liszt would accompany his father on his tours of inspection of the Esterházys' estates, and whenever they visited a house with a piano, he would sit down at the instrument and play, either performing pieces that he had already memorized or improvising his own music and impressing his hosts in the process. By now Adam Liszt was convinced that his son was exceptionally gifted but that he himself had reached the limits of his abilities as a teacher. If the boy's talent was to be fostered, then he would need to have proper lessons. Adam and Anna Liszt were prepared to give up their lives in Raiding in order to achieve this aim. Their only son, who had been born at the time of the Great Comet and who had escaped from the jaws of death while still in his infancy, seemed to them to have been singled out by destiny. Adam hoped that his son would be able to achieve what he himself had failed to do and become a musician.

Planning a Career

'Your Serene Highness,' Adam Liszt wrote to Prince Nicholas Esterházy in July 1819,

> you have deigned to honour with your especial attention the musical talents of my 7½-year-old son and graciously advised me to submit in writing the most humble request for your august support that I addressed to you in person, together with the plan that might best lead to the realization of that goal. I now make so bold as to comply in all humility with that request.

Adam's awkwardly worded letter represented a bold move on his part, for he ought in fact to have submitted his petition to his immediate superior in Eisenstadt. For a royal vassal to pass over all the intermediary authorities and appeal directly to his master was certainly unconventional. But Adam Liszt had ambitious plans for his son, as he went on to explain: Vienna was 'the home of music', and so Franz would have to go there to be taught by a 'great master of music'. Adam reckoned that this would cost at least 1,500 florins a year – seven times his annual income as the intendant of the prince's sheepfolds. 'I therefore make so bold as to submit, in all humility, the following proposal for Your Highness's kind consideration, a proposal which is less expensive but which will certainly achieve the greatest success in the swiftest possible time.' Nicholas was invited to transfer Adam to Vienna and appoint him to a post 'consonant with my well-known abilities and character'. He was also asked to lend the money needed to pay for Franz's music lessons: 'The rest, however large the sum involved, I shall gladly endeavour to meet from my own pocket, without ever becoming a burden to Your Highness.'[4]

Although Prince Nicholas asked his advisers to assess the merits of the proposal, he eventually turned it down, arguing that there were currently no free positions in Vienna. But Adam refused to give up and invited Nicholas to Raiding to hear his highly gifted son in person. The encounter took place on 21 September 1819 in the course of one of the prince's hunting parties. Although the boy's playing seems to have impressed the prince, he was still unwilling to lose his valued book-keeper, leaving Adam frustrated. Franz, he argued, was at a critical juncture in his development and was merely wasting his time in Raiding. A good six months later, on 13 April 1820, he appealed to Nicholas again, claiming that Franz had made enormous progress in the meantime, but this would have been even greater 'if my son had not been inhibited in his hard work by frequent illnesses and by a lack of teaching and scores'. Two years earlier Adam had paid 400 florins for a piano, but his house was so damp that the instrument had become unplayable. Now he even had to sell his gold watch in order to be able to afford a new piano. The family was on the verge of financial ruin. In his despair Adam once again raised the possibility of a transfer to Vienna,

> but if such an appointment should be impossible, then, at the end of May and with Your Highness's gracious permission, I would resign my post for a year and convert my furniture and cattle into ready money and leave for Vienna in order that initially, at least, I might take personal charge of planning the course of so costly an undertaking.

There was a certain low cunning to Adam's request for financial help, 'for a servant in the employment of the princes of Esterházy can scarcely go begging in this case'.[5]

Adam's plan worked, at least in part. Nicholas agreed to his employee's unpaid leave of absence for twelve months and also gave him an extra allowance of 200 florins, a sum which, although the equivalent of Adam's entire annual income, was no more than a drop in the ocean when set against the cost of such an exercise. As a result, further sources of income needed to be found before the Liszts could leave for Vienna in the spring of 1822. One such opportunity arose on 26 November 1820, when the nine-year-old Liszt gave a recital at the Pressburg home of one of Prince Nicholas's relatives, Count Michael Esterházy, a recital attended by many members of the local aristocracy. The event must have been an enormous success, for two days later the *Pressburger Zeitung* carried a front-page report:

This artist's extraordinary dexterity, together with the speed and skill which he brought to bear when performing at sight everything, however difficult, that was placed before him, gave rise to universal admiration and justifies the highest hopes for his future.[6]

A star was born. Even while Liszt and his father were still in Pressburg, a group of Hungarian aristocrats declared their willingness to support the young virtuoso with an annual subsidy of 600 florins payable for the next six years. Although this did not solve the family's most pressing financial problems, it did at least allow them to plan their move to Vienna.

Vienna

For Adam Liszt, Vienna was the city of his dreams. Everything that he hoped to achieve for himself and his son now seemed to be within his reach. When the family arrived in the city in the spring of 1822, they were already expected. Three years earlier Adam had called on the famous pianist Carl Czerny and presented his son to him. Czerny had asked 'Franzi', as he affectionately called the boy, to provide a sample of his skills as a pianist:

> He was a pale, sickly-looking child who, while playing, swayed about on the stool as if drunk, so that I kept thinking he would fall off. His playing was also quite irregular, untidy, confused, and he had so little idea of fingering that he threw his fingers quite arbitrarily all over the keyboard. But in spite of this, I was astonished at the talent that Nature had bestowed on him.

But if Liszt's playing was still ungainly and awkward when he was reading from a score, his ability to improvise on a given theme left Czerny profoundly impressed: 'Without the slightest knowledge of harmony, he still brought a touch of genius to his playing.' Adam asked Czerny to take on the boy if and when the family moved to Vienna. 'I told him I would be glad to, of course, and at the same time gave him instructions as to the manner in which he should continue with the boy's education.'[7] Three years later, in 1822, Czerny proved as good as his word.

Carl Czerny was a leading figure in the world of music at this time. Born in Vienna in 1791, he had studied with Beethoven, Clementi, Hummel and Antonio Salieri and was widely regarded as the most famous piano teacher of his day. He was also a prolific composer of countless marches, rondos, scherzos, capriccios and *variations brillantes*, many of them in the *galant* style of an earlier period. Since he rarely appeared in public, most of his works fell into neglect even during his lifetime – he died in 1857. Many can have received no more than a handful of performances since then. Only his collections of studies have retained their timeless significance. He began to give lessons at the age of only fifteen and went on to create more than twenty extensive sets of studies for the piano, his *School of Velocity* op. 299 being his best known. His creed as a teacher is easy to summarize: for him, hard work was everything – practising at the piano was first and foremost a question of application. He reduced the learning process to mechanical routine – in his *Forty Daily Studies* op. 337, for example, he demanded that a certain exercise be repeated up to thirty times a day. Many of these studies are as dry as dust – not that this prevented them from becoming best-sellers. Whole generations of pianists on every continent have studied the instrument according to the 'Czerny method'. And entire generations of pupils have lost all pleasure in playing the piano in consequence.

This was not the case with Liszt, however. For him, his lessons with his famous teacher were of fundamental importance. If his playing had initially been youthfully impetuous, 'irregular', 'untidy' and 'confused', Czerny was able in the course of time to impose a greater degree of order on it. Liszt never forgot the debt that he owed to Czerny, and in 1851 he dedicated his *Études d'exécution transcendante* to him, adding a note to the title page: 'To Carl Czerny in token of my gratitude, respect and friendship.'

In Czerny the young Liszt found the perfect teacher. But his presence in Vienna was not the only thing that drew Adam Liszt to the city. In his letter to Prince Nicholas Esterházy, he had spoken of an 'enterprise' or business that he wanted to build up. The term was not chosen at random, for this was the Biedermeier Age, a period from 1815 to 1848 that was ushered in by Napoleon's defeat at Waterloo and by the resultant sense that a new era was dawning throughout Europe. The Congress of Vienna that was convened under the chairmanship of Austria's foreign minister, Klemens Wenzel von Metternich, set out to impose a new order on the continent as a whole, and the relationships between the different states were now realigned in an attempt to establish a new balance of power. Central to the talks, however, was a restitution of the old order or *ancien régime*, the absolutist form of government that the French Revolution had been intended to sweep away once and for all.

Four years later, in the summer of 1819, Metternich pushed through the Carlsbad Decrees in the face of widespread opposition and inaugurated a period of strict press censorship. In Austria and Prussia in particular, liberals, nationalists and what were regarded as freethinkers were spied on and persecuted. Political reaction caused people to withdraw into themselves, resulting in the emergence of 'Biedermeier man', someone who sought happiness in the confines of family life and in the undemanding comforts within his own four walls. It was a socio-historical development that also affected literature, the visual arts, the theatre, architecture and, finally, music. Domestic music-making became increasingly important, and all who could afford to do so paid for their children to have music lessons. Instrument building flourished, and the piano became the focus of every middle-class drawing room. The middle classes replaced the aristocracy as the backbone of the country's musical life, leading in turn to the creation of private concert organizations and music societies.

Child prodigies like the young Liszt were in particular demand in the Vienna of this period. 'Among the astonishing number of local pianists whom we saw in Vienna's concert halls in the years between 1815 and 1830', the music critic Eduard Hanslick recalled, 'the vast majority were women and children.' The youngest of these pianistic prodigies – the son of a cavalry captain called Braun – was a mere four years old when he made his debut in 1815, but he was the exception. 'Yet it remains a fact that in earlier times Vienna was a very important starting point for child prodigies who were far from all being little Mozarts, Hummels and Clementis!'[8]

Adam's decision to head for Vienna seems to have been based on cold calculation, for here, he believed, he would find a market for his wares, the wares in question being a child prodigy: his son. What he was attempting to do was no different in essence from what today's classical music managers are trying all the time to achieve: to identify needs and to supply those needs with the most suitable performers. Liszt's lessons with Czerny and his marketing by his father were merely two sides of the same coin.

Life in Vienna was prohibitively expensive at this time. The family could not afford an apartment in the inner city and so they initially took rooms at an inn in Mariahilf. During the day Czerny was generally so busy that it was only in the evening that he could find the time to teach his new pupil. Adam would then accompany his son on foot to the Krugerstraße, where the unmarried Czerny lived with his parents. The two worked together almost every day: 'I never had such an eager, inspired and hard-working pupil,' Czerny recalled. 'Since he had to study each piece very quickly, he was finally so adept at sight-reading that he was capable of playing even substantial and difficult pieces at sight, as if he had been studying them for a long time.' Liszt retained this astonishing ability until the end of his life – Wagner, for example, was scarcely able to believe his eyes and ears when Liszt sat down at the piano and sight-read one of his – Wagner's – monumental orchestral scores. Czerny also recalled that 'the young Liszt's abiding cheerfulness and good spirits, coupled with the exceptional development of his talent, meant that my parents loved him like a son, while I myself loved him like a brother. Not only did I teach him without taking any remuneration, I also gave him all the scores that he needed.'[9]

For his lessons in the theory of music, Liszt turned to Antonio Salieri, a musician ill judged by history and especially by Miloš Forman in his film *Amadeus* (1984), based on Peter Shaffer's play of the same name, which presents a highly distorted view of Salieri as a person, depicting him as a composer who, lacking in talent and fuelled by envy, drove his great rival Mozart to his death. There is not a grain of truth to this claim. Salieri, who was born in Legnago in 1750, was widely respected and famous all over Europe. Court Kapellmeister in Vienna from 1788, he wrote more than forty operas, as well as countless secular and sacred choral works and numerous concertos and symphonies. He was also valued as a teacher whose pupils included Beethoven, Cherubini, Meyerbeer, Schubert – and Liszt.

The now septuagenarian Salieri taught Liszt harmony, composition and score-reading, and the boy evidently made such rapid progress that Salieri and Czerny entered their pupil in a kind of competition for composers. The composer and publisher Anton Diabelli had invited several contemporary musicians to write a variation on a waltz of his own composition. Among the fifty who responded were Czerny, Hummel, Schubert and Simon Sechter. With its rapid scales and broken chords, Liszt's contribution resembles nothing so much as a virtuoso study. The volume appeared in print at the end of 1823. The names of the fifty composers were arranged in alphabetical order, Liszt appearing in twenty-fourth position as 'Liszt Franz (boy of 11) born in Hungary'. It was his first published work.

Both Czerny and Salieri taught their young charge for nothing. When Salieri noticed that Liszt arrived for his lessons tired and sweating after walking from Mariahilf to the inner city, he wrote to Prince Esterházy and asked him to make arrangements for the family to move closer to the centre. Salieri's word evidently carried weight, for in October 1822 the Liszts were able to move to the Krugerstraße. The daily routine of a child prodigy was organized along strict lines, and Liszt attended lessons with Salieri in the Seilergasse almost every morning, with further lessons with Czerny following in the evening. In between he practised the piano and worked on his composition exercises. There was no time for children's games, and since he did not attend school, he had very little contact with other children.

Czerny was keen to ensure that his best pupil did not appear in public prematurely: first he had to study conscientiously and work on his technique. But by 1 December 1822 the boy was ready, and he gave his first concert in Vienna. On the programme was a piano concerto by Hummel and a free improvisation. He shared the platform with a singer and a violinist. Such motley programmes were the norm at this time, and – inconceivably from today's point of view – a movement from one work might be presented alongside one from another piece. That Sunday Liszt captured the hearts of his audience, and the reviewer of the Leipzig *Allgemeine musikalische Zeitung* wrote rapturously about the 'young Hercules' who had 'fallen from the clouds and compels us to the highest admiration':

> For his age, this boy's achievements border on the incredible, and one is tempted to doubt the sheer physical possibility when one hears the young giant, with unabated force, thunder out Hummel's composition, so difficult and so fatiguing, especially in the last movement; but feeling, expression, shading and all the finer nuances are also present, just as this musical prodigy is said to be able to sight-read everything placed before him and even now to be without equal in his ability to play from a full score.[10]

Just over a week later Liszt gave a second concert, this time performing a piece by Ferdinand Ries. According to the same journal, the young pianist was 'a hero steeled in battle' and 'earned the most worthwhile fruits of his astonishing talent'.[11] Those were big words.

By the time Liszt appeared in the Small Redoutensaal in the Hofburg on 13 April 1823, his career, although still in its infancy, was at a crossroads. The programme was made up of the usual mixture of orchestral works, piano pieces and vocal music, ending with a free fantasy on a theme provided by the audience. But the concert also gave rise to a legend that has dogged writings on Liszt ever since, for among the audience supposedly was none other than the fifty-two-year-old Beethoven, who at the end of the improvisation is said to have gone over to the eleven-year-old Liszt and implanted a kiss on his forehead. The tale of Beethoven's *Weihekuß*, or 'kiss of consecration', is an appealing one, but it is almost certainly untrue, for there is no clear proof that Beethoven, now completely deaf, had attended the concert. There is also no first-hand evidence to support an alternative version of the legend, whereby Liszt and Czerny visited Beethoven at home.[12] Towards the end of his life, Liszt himself gave contradictory accounts of the alleged incident, suggesting that this affecting little tale is not to be taken entirely seriously. None the less, there is no doubt that reports of the ostensible *Weihekuß* were an important catalyst in Liszt's career.

The Liszts had been living in Vienna for less than a year when the boy gave his farewell recital in the city's Redoutensaal. Adam Liszt was pleased with his son's progress over the preceding months: Franz had worked hard and given his first tumultuously acclaimed concerts, so that his name was now on everyone's lips. The successes enjoyed by 'little Hercules' were such as to add fuel to Adam's ambitions, with the result that Vienna suddenly seemed too small for him. Munich and Stuttgart beckoned, as – even more so – did London and Paris. There, in the big wide world, Adam reckoned that there was money aplenty to be earned. Franz was now the family's breadwinner.

We do not know what Liszt thought about his father's plans, but Czerny was certainly against them: 'Unfortunately his father wanted to derive great pecuniary advantage from him, and the boy was working well and just starting to compose when he went off on tour, first to Hungary and ultimately to Paris and London and so on, where he caused the greatest stir, as all the papers of the time can attest.'[13] Czerny's objections went unheard.

Le petit Litz

The firm that Adam Liszt built up in Vienna could well have been called 'Adam Liszt & Son'. By the time his twelve months' leave of absence was over, there could no longer be any question of a return to Raiding. The former accountant of the Esterházy sheepfolds had become an independent concert promoter. But it is to Adam Liszt's credit that he was not simply out to make money as quickly as possible. Viennese audiences had seen countless child prodigies who after the initial enthusiasm had worn off had proved a disappointment and whose careers had then petered out. Adam was bound, therefore, to want his son to continue to receive a sound education, for only in this way could Liszt remain successful in the longer term. Only then could the firm of Adam Liszt & Son prosper.

He needed allies, and in early August 1823 he turned to Metternich, no less:

Inasmuch as my boy's talent for music continues to make progress and shows more and more charm and originality, it is my most ardent wish and also the advice of other experts that we should pursue his education abroad and in this way gradually guide the talented young artist to the peak of Mount Parnassus. To that end I should very much like to set out with the boy at the beginning of September and travel to Munich (where I plan to give a concert in order to cover the costs of the journey, at least in part), thence to Paris in order for him to continue his studies in composition at the city's Conservatory of Music. We would remain there for a whole year, before travelling to London and back, either through Germany or Italy. In short, we would remain away for at least two years in all.

There is something a little odd about Adam's announcement in the first-person singular that he would be giving a concert in Munich – after all, it was his son who would be doing the honours. But the letter expresses the self-confidence of an ambitious entrepreneur. To that extent it is unsurprising that he had the nerve to consult the all-powerful Metternich. Since, he went on, he had no 'personal acquaintances of any standing' in Munich or Paris or London, he asked Metternich to 'take pity on me with regard to my poor but talented boy and provide me with the necessary letters of recommendation'.[14]

Enlisting the help of a man like Metternich proved to be a master-stroke, for Metternich had served as Austrian ambassador in Paris from 1806 to 1809 and knew the local conditions. Since the time of the Congress of Vienna he had been regarded as Europe's leading statesman, and by 1821 he had risen to the eminence of Austrian chancellor. A letter of recommendation in his hand or at least from his office would open all doors to high society from London to St Petersburg. Metternich immediately instructed one of his top-ranking diplomats, Franz Joseph von Bretfeld, to draft a reply:

This boy's talent is a most unusual phenomenon far in advance of his age, and in every respect it deserves encouragement in order that its originality is not prevented from developing. So I have no hesitation in agreeing to this request, and I recommend this promising young artist to Your Excellency for your kind acceptance [. . .] and ask that you provide him with all the protection necessary for him to achieve the aim of his journey and also that you cover any other expenses that he may incur.[15]

This letter was sent as a circular to the Austrian embassies in Paris and London as well as to the consulate in Munich. In every case Adam's plans were seen as enjoying the ultimate seal of approval. His journey could begin.

The Liszts left Vienna by mail coach on 20 September 1823. Their first stop was Munich, where Liszt gave three acclaimed concerts at the Court Theatre. He was the talk of the town and even hailed as a new Mozart. 'The court was present on each occasion,' Adam wrote to his friend Ludwig Hofer,

and twice we enjoyed the distinction of being presented to the King, who [. . .] embraced my son and kissed him, saying: 'Come here, my lad, I've just got to kiss you.' That we were very content you can gather from the fact that we spent a whole month there and left heavy-hearted.

News of Liszt's phenomenal success soon spread to Augsburg, the next stage on his journey, and here, too, the audience's enthusiasm knew no bounds:

We left Augsburg after thirteen days and travelled to Stuttgart, where my son performed the very next day at the Royal Court and was received with tremendous acclaim. A week later we gave a public concert at the Royal Court Theatre. From there we travelled to Strasbourg, where we gave one private and one public concert at the theatre.[16]

Liszt's recitals were financially as well as artistically successful, and at the end of the brief tour Adam could report a profit of 921 florins,[17] more than four times his annual income as an accountant for the Esterházy sheepfolds.

When Adam, Anna and Franz Liszt arrived by mail coach in Paris on 11 December 1823, they entered an entirely new world. Paris then had a population of some three-quarters of a million – by way of comparison, the population of Vienna in 1810 had been no more than 225,000. In spite of this, Paris still had a medieval air to it, a jumble of narrow streets criss-crossing its twelve arrondissements. (Not until the 1850s was the city's prefect Georges Eugène Haussmann to begin his *grands travaux* with the aim of redeveloping the city and transforming it almost overnight into a modern metropolis.) The Liszts found much that was alien to them on their arrival: the city's vast size, the customs of its inhabitants and, not least, the language. And yet they lacked nothing in confidence as they embarked on their conquest of the capital. Still flush with funds, they were able to afford four rooms at the well-appointed Hôtel d'Angleterre, two overlooking the road, two facing the inner courtyard. The rooms cost 120 francs a month, on top of which they also had to pay 65 francs for heating and service. Adam reckoned that meals would cost an extra 14 francs a day. All in all, he calculated that the family's needs amounted to 605 francs a month. It was with evident pride that he wrote to Hofer: 'That's a lot of money, don't you agree?'[18] It was a case of pride coming before a fall.

Within days of their arrival in Paris, father and son had made their way to the city's Conservatoire, an institution which, founded in 1795, had an outstanding reputation, with a teaching staff that included such eminent musicians as the violinist Rodolphe Kreutzer, the opera composer Adrien Boieldieu and the musicologist François-Joseph Fétis. In charge was the sixty-three-year-old Luigi Cherubini. Adam presumably thought that his son's enrolment was a mere formality, but he was to be disabused when Cherubini drew his attention to one of the institution's regulations that prevented foreign pianists from studying there. Not even Metternich's recommendation could induce Cherubini to relent. He had taken up his post only the previous year and evidently did not want to commit any bureaucratic errors. 'What a thunderbolt! I trembled in every limb,' Liszt himself recalled many years later. 'My groans and lamentations were unceasing.' His parents tried in vain to console him, but 'the wound was too deep and continued to bleed for a very long time'.[19]

Adam now tried to find private teachers for his son and succeeded in persuading the flautist and composer Antoine Reicha to teach him theory, while Ferdinando Paer agreed to give him composition lessons. It was Metternich who, once again, was largely to thank for Paer's involvement: even before the Liszts had arrived in Paris, he had already asked the Italian composer to keep a watchful eye on the boy. 'I am very happy to do everything possible for Herr Liszt,' Paer had dutifully replied:

> He bears a strong resemblance to the divine Mozart, and I even think that at the same age the latter was not as advanced as Liszt, nor had he revealed as much imagination. I have offered to give him some advice on composition; I shall also arrange for him to perform for their Highnesses the Duchesse de Berry and the Duc d'Orléans; and, finally, I shall not hesitate to be of use to him wherever I can in order to comply with Monseigneur's request.[20]

The lessons with Reicha and Paer did not follow any prescribed pattern but represented an occasional collaboration, with the two older men keeping a benevolent eye on their young charge, an arrangement that we would nowadays describe as 'coaching'. Liszt had no further piano lessons in Paris. By the time he left Czerny, the training of the most famous pianist of the nineteenth century was largely complete, even though he was not yet twelve years old. For the rest, Liszt was entirely self-taught; or, to strike a more rhapsodic note, the rest was genius.

In Paris the Liszts got to know the piano manufacturer Sébastien Érard and his family. Sébastien (1752–1831) and his elder brother Jean-Baptiste (1749–1826) ran a piano-making business, Érard Frères, and were regarded as instrument makers of genius. Among their various inventions was the double-escapement action that made it possible for the hammers to return to their original position immediately after striking the string, which in turn allowed the same note to be repeated at a speed hitherto unattainable, inspiring Liszt in no small way.

The Liszts and the Érards were soon in regular contact and quickly became friends. Adam and Franz often visited the Maison Érard in the rue du Mail, where the boy was allowed to try out all manner of instruments. Since Sébastien and Adam were both astute businessmen, they instinctively saw a chance to pool their resources. From now on the Érard brothers would place their pianos at Liszt's disposal, allowing them to market the lad as an exclusive Érard artist. And both Sébastien and Adam did all they could to publicize their product, with the result that it was not long before French high society was completely in thrall to the prodigy.

By March 1824 – only three months after his arrival in the city – Liszt had already given thirty-eight recitals, all of them soirées in the salons of wealthy aristocrats and members of the bourgeoisie. Guests were invited to hand over a not inconsiderable sum of money in order to hear the boy play, and we know from a letter from Adam Liszt to Ludwig Hofer that he demanded between 100 and 150 francs per head:

> I set this rate right at the outset & we never go below it, people are very happy to pay it, they also have to collect us & take us home by coach. In order to protect our health & not disrupt my boy's studies, I have to turn down a good many invitations. On one occasion my boy played at the home of Madame la Duchesse de Berry, where the whole of the royal family & other dignitaries were present & where my boy improvised on four different themes that were given to him. You can deduce the applause he received from the fact that people have been talking about nothing but prodigies and miracles. Nothing like this has been seen in Paris. The way we've been honoured is indescribable, everyone has been pushing & shoving, & persons of the very highest rank have condescended to speak to us.

Little Liszt was now a top earner. On 8 February 1824 he gave a concert that netted a profit of 2,000 francs. Whereas Adam had had to sell a gold watch only a few years earlier to buy a piano for his son, he was now juggling with figures several times that amount. A month later he played his trump card. Thanks to the support of the Duchesse de Berry, Marie Caroline Ferdinande Louise de Bourbon, who was completely besotted with Liszt, Adam had free use of the Théâtre Italien, where he organized a concert on 7 March at his own expense and even engaged an orchestra, which accompanied Liszt in Hummel's B minor Concerto and Czerny's Variations for piano and orchestra. On this occasion, the net proceeds, after all expenses had been deducted, amounted to 4,711 francs. Adam was in his element:

> A pity the theatre is so small and that the boxes had already been retained by the subscribers themselves eight days earlier, so that I wasn't able to sell them to outsiders, who would have paid much more for them. But I'm altogether satisfied, as was everyone who was present.

This concert has gone down in the annals not only on account of its financial success but also because of the 'public triumph' that, according to Adam, his son enjoyed on this occasion:

> As soon as he appeared, there was almost no end to the applause, & after every passage the enthusiasm found expression in the liveliest amazement, after every piece he was called back on stage two or three times & applauded. The gentlemen in the orchestra struck their bows mercilessly against the backs of their double basses, cellos, violas & violins, the wind players fell back on shouting & everyone was utterly entranced.

Audiences at this date would burst into spontaneous applause even during a piece, especially at particularly virtuosic passages, and Liszt evidently gave his listeners every reason for such acclaim.

Adam Liszt's most important ally was the press, and no fewer than fourteen journalists reported on the spectacle at the Théâtre Italien. Their resultant reviews were so many hymns of praise to the young virtuoso, adding in the process to the myth that was already building up around him. As Adam noted, 'He is generally called "the prodigy", a new Mozart in youthful guise.'[21]

One particularly impressive report appeared in *Le Drapeau Blanc* and was the work of the journalist Alphonse Martainville:

I cannot help it: since yesterday evening I have become a believer in the transmigration of souls. I am convinced that the soul and spirit of Mozart have passed into the body of the young List [*sic*], and never has an identity revealed itself by plainer signs. The same country, the same wonderful talent in childhood, and in the same art. [. . .] In taking the name of Liszt, Mozart has lost none of that charming exterior which always enhances the interest that a child can inspire in us by dint of his precocious talent. The features of our little prodigy express spirit and cheerfulness; the boy reveals the greatest charm, and the delight and admiration that he awakens in his audience as soon as his fingers glide across the keys seem to him an amusement that gives him the greatest pleasure. He is a delightful child.

Finally Martainville came to the concert itself:

To give an idea of the impressive achievement that his listeners were able to observe for themselves, I will mention only the effect of his playing on the orchestra of the Italian Opera, the best in France, if not in Europe: eyes, ears and soul were captivated by the magical instrument of the young virtuoso, and for a moment they forgot that they, too, were actors in this concert, so that at the return of the ritornello every instrument remained silent. By their laughter and clapping, the audience showed that it forgave this brief inattentiveness, which was perhaps the most flattering acknowledgement that the little prodigy's talent has ever received. [. . .] The warmest applause and repeated cheers echoed throughout the hall; the acclaim and enthusiasm showed no sign of abating; and the delicate hands of the members of the fairer sex who were among the audience applauded tirelessly. The happy child thanked them with a smile.[22]

A child prodigy, a genius, a new Mozart – the whole of Paris was infatuated with the boy. A lithograph was produced, and countless copies were run off, while the original was displayed in the Louvre. Years later Heinrich Heine coined the term 'Lisztomania' to refer to this state of collective rapture, but it already applied to the situation in the 1820s.

Only with the correct spelling of Liszt's name were there still problems, as various wayward versions continued to appear in the press. One of them even became a kind of trademark: Le petit Litz.

A Time of New Departures

'It's also uncertain if we'll be going to London this year,' Adam Liszt wrote to his friend Ludwig Hofer, 'as we've got bookings until 20 April & by then it seems to me to be too late. Nor can I tell you anything certain about our return to our fatherland as we're thinking of travelling to England, Holland, Switzerland & Germany.'[23] Then suddenly things moved very quickly. If Adam Liszt had been uncertain of his plans even as late as the middle of March, within weeks he and his son had boarded a ship for England. The Érards had a branch in London and had organized a number of concerts for Liszt. One of Sébastien's nephews, Pierre, accompanied the party, bringing with him a new piano. The fact that Liszt, not yet thirteen years old, was already able to travel with his own instrument in spite of the considerable logistical complications that this entailed is a further sign of the status that he now enjoyed as a result of his phenomenal success. The little group arrived in London on 1 May, and in the course of the next three months Liszt performed both in private, including at a formal dinner at the widely respected Royal Society of Musicians, and in public. Everywhere he was announced as 'the incomparable Master Liszt'. At the end of July he also had the honour of being received at Windsor by King George IV, playing for the royals for over two hours, and, as a sign of particular distinction, he and his father were allowed to spend the night there.

Adam demanded increasingly exorbitant fees: for a concert in Manchester, for example, he asked £100 – about £40,000 at today's prices. The programmes consisted for the most part of potpourris of works by Hummel, Czerny and Beethoven, but audiences also expected Liszt to improvise for them. Often he shared the platform with other performers. At his concert in Manchester on 4 August 1824, for example, his fellow performer was a four-year-old prodigy billed as 'The Infant Lyra', who played a miniature harp. The playbill fails to give her full name, but it seems from the reviews of the time that she completely upstaged the young Liszt, whose fee in the circumstances may have seemed like compensation for the indignity he had suffered.

On their return to Paris, the Liszts took rooms at the Hôtel de Strasbourg near the Église Saint-Eustache. It was during this period that Liszt turned his hand increasingly to composition and wrote his earliest piano works, including his *Huit variations* and *Sept variations brillantes sur un thème de Rossini*. He also began work on a one-act opera, *Don Sanche, ou Le château d'amour*, on which he was helped by Paer. When the work was staged at the Opéra in the middle of October 1825, the critics were polite but dismissive. As the French musicologist Serge Gut pointed out in his recent study of the composer, this was a genre 'in which Liszt never really distinguished himself, and the work is indeed of no great significance.'[24] Although Liszt continued to flirt with the medium, *Don Sanche* remains his only completed opera.

Throughout the Paris period, Adam Liszt remained in contact with Czerny, the proud father reporting in detail on his son's latest feats, quoting from newspaper articles and repeatedly working out how profitable was the progress that Liszt had made. Meanwhile, Czerny counselled caution and kept asking that Adam should not overtax his son: 'However much he may compose, he should never neglect his playing but seek to achieve the greatest pitch of perfection.'[25] Elsewhere we find him writing, 'As for his studies, he should redouble his efforts and not allow himself to be misled by exaggerated praise (which is always more harmful than censure).'[26] Czerny did not need to worry, Adam reassured him. 'He knows no passion other than composition, this alone gives him pleasure and contentment.' And he went on, 'He spends two hours practising every day and an hour reading – all the rest of the time that we're at home is given over to composition.'[27] It wasn't easy being a child prodigy.

During the spring of 1825 the Liszts undertook their second tour of England, and Franz again appeared on repeated occasions in London and Manchester and was once more received by King George IV. On one particular occasion, when Liszt and his father were invited to attend a musical soirée, a remarkable incident took place. The piano had been tuned a semitone lower than usual at the request of the Italian castrato Giovanni Battista Velluti. But the next item on the programme was a fantasy for flute and piano. Since the flautist was unable to flatten his flute, his accompanist, Cipriani Potter, would have had to transpose their duet up from C major to C sharp major, involving a risk he was unwilling to take. Pianist and flautist became embroiled in a discussion that went on for several minutes, during which time the audience grew increasingly restless. Liszt finally resolved the situation by sitting down at the piano himself and playing the piece in the transposed key, even though he had never seen it before. As Adam Liszt explained afterwards in another of his letters to Czerny, 'I do not need to tell you the enthusiasm and the amazement that this incident – a mere trifle for Franzi – caused on the part not only of the two artists themselves but also of the distinguished company that had gathered to hear them.'[28]

Although much shorter than the previous year's tour, this visit to England proved tiring, and before father and son returned to Paris in the middle of July, they spent a few weeks recovering from their exertions in the northern French resort of Boulogne-sur-Mer. 'We enjoyed ourselves very much,' Adam told Czerny, 'and went for long walks on the sea front morning and night, collecting shells and watching the ships come and go.' Even on holiday he remained a businessman at heart and arranged for Liszt to give a concert 'that not only covered all our expenses during our stay but produced an additional profit of 600 francs.'[29]

As for Anna Liszt, she spent all of this time in the background, almost invisible to her potential biographer. We know next to nothing about her early years in Paris, not least because her husband rarely mentions her in his letters. The family's move from Raiding to Vienna had not been easy for her, and she had often felt homesick in the strange, large city. She was a simple soul and had already had problems with the German language, but now she was required to learn French. One can well imagine that dealing with even straightforward day-to-day tasks was often an enormous challenge for her. Although she soon became friendly with the Érards and liked to spend time with Sébastien Érard's three sisters, she generally had to remain on her own in her hotel room whenever her husband and son were away on tour, so it is no wonder that she grew bored and that her lonely life became more and more of a burden. Perhaps Adam wanted to save money on his wife's accommodation or perhaps he was planning to return to Vienna in the not too distant future. Whatever the answer, she moved in with her sister Therese in Graz in the autumn of 1825, just before her husband and son set off on an extended tour of the French provinces. In the event it was to be the last time that she saw her husband.

Breakdown

Throughout the first six months of 1826 Adam Liszt and his son were almost constantly on the road. Liszt gave recitals in Bordeaux, Toulouse, Montpellier, Nîmes, Marseilles, Lyons and Dijon, appearing no fewer than six times in Marseilles alone and giving a total of twenty-four concerts between early January and the middle of June. At the end of the year he visited Switzerland for the first time, performing in Geneva and Lucerne, with three more concerts in Dijon in between times.[30] Travel at this time was by no means easy, for there were still no trains (not until 1837 was the first line opened in France between Paris and Saint-Germain). A stagecoach or mail coach was the only alternative. The 'Berlin', or 'berline', drawn by four or six horses, was a large covered carriage seating up to six passengers inside, with outside seating for up to ten more on the coach box, on the roof and at the rear. Here the passengers were exposed to the wind and weather and paid much less for that dubious privilege. In total, then, these coaches could carry up to sixteen passengers, together with their luggage. The journey would be broken at various stages, where passengers could alight or clamber aboard, these frequent stops inevitably making the journey much longer. Somewhat quicker was the classic mail coach, but this was far less comfortable.

In any case passengers needed to be patient, for the journey from Paris to Calais – a distance of around 190 miles – took some thirty hours. From Paris to Bordeaux it was either sixty hours via Angoulême or ninety-six hours via Limoges. The journey time from Paris to Geneva was three full days. Not infrequently, journeys were delayed by broken axles and other accidents. It is easy to imagine that during the first six months of 1826 Liszt spent several weeks simply sitting in a mail coach.

His schedule at the start of the following year was no less arduous. In January he gave two concerts in Besançon, and in early April he set off on his third and, for the present, final visit to England, where he and his father remained until the month of June. He again played a piano concerto by Hummel and provoked veritable storms of enthusiasm. But the fifteen-year-old was in a state of inner turmoil. During the three months that he spent in London he kept a kind of diary in French, although the term 'diary' is perhaps misleading for so strange a document. Rather than recording his daily experiences and the impressions left by his visit, Liszt sought to account for his faith and his fear of God, keeping a detailed note of his visits to church and prayers and as if in a book of hours recording his devotional exercises and the number of times he recited the litany. Superficially the diary resembles a collection of pious verse, but it also contains aphorisms that hint at the writer's emotional conflicts. During the sea crossing to Dover on 5 April, for example, he wrote, 'Make sure that all your thoughts, words and deeds satisfy your father and that they are a constant prayer for him.' It seems clear from this that Liszt was not travelling to England voluntarily and that it was his father who had demanded that he should undertake the trip. On his arrival in London he tried to overcome his self-doubts by appealing to his own conscience: 'God orders you to honour your parents; gratitude demands it.'[31]

Time and again he read Thomas à Kempis's *De imitatione Christi*, a best-seller in the nineteenth century that was as much a part of the library of every good Catholic family as its household Bible. The fifteenth-century mystic promoted a 'new piety' notable for its meditative brooding on the life and sufferings of Christ and on God and the individual soul. Particular emphasis was placed on the need for a life of atonement and selflessness on the part of individuals wanting to follow in the footsteps of Christ. Throughout all this, the Saviour appears as a close friend consoling us for life's calamities. For the first time in his life Liszt conceived the desire to become a priest. There were two sides to his piety, which on the one hand was genuine and sincere, and on the other represented a kind of protest against the secularism of his existence as a child prodigy. The more he was repelled by the exertions of his life as an itinerant celebrity, the more he longed for calm and for a life of contemplation. We might almost describe it as a longing for something 'higher'.

Perhaps Adam suspected what his son was going through. 'Your calling is music,' he responded to Liszt's desire to enter the priesthood. 'The fact that you may love something is no guarantee of your calling for it. But you have a calling for music. You belong to art, not to the Church!'[32] In other words, his son would in his eyes have been miscast as a priest. And he knew what he was talking about, for as a young man he himself had thought of entering the service of the Church but had realized his mistake. He now wanted to spare his son the same sense of painful disillusionment. His word was enough, and Liszt averted his gaze from the priesthood, although he was to feel drawn to the Catholic Church for the whole of his life. Decades later, in 1865, he even entered the four minor orders and became an abbé, but in spite of occasional claims to the contrary, he never became a priest. For the present, he had other concerns.

In 1827 a tragic event turned his world upside down. In the middle of August father and son arrived in Boulogne-sur-Mer, where they planned to recover from their exertions, as they had done in 1825. Adam already felt ill when he arrived in the town, and within days his condition had deteriorated markedly. By 24 August he was evidently no longer able to write to his wife in Graz, for we find the fifteen-year-old Franz writing on his behalf: 'Best of women, mother! As I write these lines I am much afraid for my father's health,' he began. 'Father begs you not to lose heart. He is very ill and that's why he wants me to tell you in this letter that you may perhaps have to come to France, but he thinks we should wait a few more days and has said that I can write to you in a few days' time, which I shall certainly not fail to do.'[33]

It is not entirely clear what Adam was suffering from. Some reports suggest that it was typhoid fever, others that it was gastritis. But he knew that he was dying and that his son would now have to carry on the family enterprise himself. Decades later Liszt recalled his father's final words: 'On his deathbed in Boulogne-sur-Mer he told me that

I had a good heart and that I did not lack intelligence, but he was afraid that women might confuse and rule me.'[34] It was to prove a remarkable prediction.

The end came very quickly, and Adam Liszt died on the morning of 28 August 1827. He was only fifty. By the time that Anna Liszt received her son's cry for help, her husband was already dead. He was buried the very next day. Liszt himself appears not to have attended the service. Nor did Anna Liszt ever feel the need to visit her husband's grave even though she returned to Paris in the autumn of 1827 and remained there for the rest of her life.

For the last five years – since the day the family arrived in Vienna in 1822 – father and son had presumably never spent more than a day apart. Adam had accompanied his son to his lessons with Czerny and Salieri. He had watched over his studies, monitored his progress and praised and censured him. Then came the move to Paris and Liszt's early recitals in France, together with his numerous tours of the French provinces and his three visits to England. There had also been the innumerable hours that they had spent together in mail coaches and hotel rooms. Anna Liszt had moved to Graz, but her husband was always with their son.

With his father's death, Liszt's childhood came to an end: to a certain extent it could be said that the man who had invented his life until now had died. Little Franzi was undoubtedly a child prodigy, but Adam had created the myth to go with it. It was he who had founded 'Adam Liszt & Son'.

Franz was only fifteen. And now he had to take control of his life.

REHEARSING AND STUDYING
(1827–35)

Disappointed Hopes

FOR SEVERAL WEEKS AFTER his father's death, Liszt vanishes from sight, but he presumably informed his mother about her husband's death and, having arranged the funeral and dealt with the estate, at some point left Boulogne and returned to Paris. For her part, Anna Liszt turned her back on Graz and travelled to the French capital in order to take care of her son. By October 1827 we find them both in a small apartment in the rue Coquenard (now the rue Lamartine), but only a short time later they moved to another address a few streets away in the rue de Montholon.

How could things continue? All that was certain was that Liszt wanted to stay in Paris. By now he spoke fluent French and was drawn to city life. Above all, friends such as the Érards lived in Paris. But it is no less true that he did not wish to continue with his hounded life as a child prodigy: he now felt only bored by the whole idea of playing bravura pieces, performing in the salons of well-heeled aristocrats and improvising on popular themes. Instead, he wanted to turn his life upside down and start all over again as a 'genuine' artist. Ten years later he recalled that

> when death had carried off my father and I returned alone to Paris, where I began to have an inkling of what art could be and what

an artist should be, I was crushed, as it were, by the insurmountable difficulties that loomed up all along the path my thoughts were taking.

When he realized that his fellow artists were 'slumbering in comfortable indifference,' he was

> overcome by a bitter disgust for art, which had been reduced in my view to a more or less lucrative occupation, a diversion for polite society, and I would sooner have been anything in the world than a musician in the service of the Great Lords, patronized and paid by them on a par with a juggler or the performing dog Munito. May he rest in peace.[1]

Munito was famous in the 1820s – it was said that he could understand French and Italian and bark out the alphabet. It is significant that Liszt ranks musicians alongside circus artists, jugglers and four-legged cabaret turns. He wanted nothing to do with such acts.

Decades later he told one of his pupils that in the 1820s 'there had been bad concerts everywhere in Paris, all of them free'. This, too, was something that Liszt abhorred, and so he withdrew from public life. On the other hand, he still needed to support himself and his mother – 'the capital that Father left me was very small'[2] – and he started to give piano and harmony lessons, thereby falling out of the frying pan into the proverbial fire. If he had previously had his fill of the salons of high society, then he now had to impart the principles of music to the daughters of these same members of high society. Generally he called on his pupils at home but for a time he also taught at a girls' school.

He was evidently in demand as a teacher: 'I taught every day from 8:30 in the morning to 10 at night and barely had time to catch my breath.'[3] He often had to walk miles from one of his pupils' houses to the next, and by the time he returned home late at night, his mother was already asleep. In order not to wake her, he would often spend the night in the stairwell, where he fell asleep from exhaustion and where he would be discovered the following morning. He began to smoke and drink (sometimes more than was good for him), while his eating habits became irregular, and he suffered from lack of sleep. It was during this period that he acquired the unhealthy lifestyle that he never lost.

One of his pupils in Paris was Caroline de Saint-Cricq, the seventeen-year-old daughter of the French minister of commerce. She evidently enjoyed her lessons with her revered teacher and he, in turn, felt drawn towards the attractive young woman, and the two fell in love. Her mother, Jeanne, encouraged the affair, whereas her father did not, and when Jeanne died suddenly on 1 July 1828, Pierre de Saint-Cricq seized the opportunity to put an end to the liaison, giving Liszt to understand that he intended his daughter to marry into her own social class. In other words, a middle-class musician like Liszt was no social match for the de Cricq family. Caroline was obliged to marry Count Bertrand d'Artigaux, and the couple moved to Pau in southern France.

This unromantic ending to Liszt's first romantic attachment plunged both him and Caroline into a state of profound despair, but whereas she tearfully abandoned herself to her fate, he felt that his pride and honour had been insulted. This unwelcome rejection made him painfully aware that while polite society might respect and admire him as a child prodigy, concert pianist and even as a music teacher, it refused to accept him as an equal. Once again he felt that his role was that of an amusing musician and even a fairground entertainer. Although he was permitted to appear in the homes of high society, he had to come and go through the servants' entrance. Whenever it mattered, he simply did not belong there.

His father's death, the brutal ending of his relations with Caroline de Saint-Cricq and the frustrations of his life as a piano teacher triggered another serious crisis, once again causing him to question the whole meaning of his existence. As a result, he often neglected his duties and instead read books on religion and philosophy. Although he still gave the occasional recital, he preferred to go to church every day. It was even rumoured that he had died: on the day after his seventeenth birthday, *Le Corsaire* published a lengthy obituary under the heading 'Death of the Young Liszt'.[4]

Those who met Liszt at this time were puzzled by his religious mania. During the winter of 1828/9, he was visited by the German writer on music, Wilhelm von Lenz, who reports: 'Liszt was at home. That was a very unusual thing, his mother told me – an excellent woman with a German heart, who pleased me extremely. Her Franz was almost always at Church, she said, and – "busied himself no more with music!"' Lenz was ushered into the salon and saw Liszt, 'a pale, haggard young man, with unspeakably attractive features. He was reclining on a broad sofa, smoking a long Turkish pipe, and apparently lost in deep contemplation. Three pianos stood near.'[5]

If Liszt did not let himself go completely, it was his mother he had to thank. 'Madame Liszt's influence lay in the area of the mind,' wrote Liszt's biographer Lina Ramann.[6] Anna Liszt not only provided her son with a comfortable home, she also kept his spirits up and helped him to break out of his melancholy moods. Needing to earn some money, he started to give more concerts and to reappear 'before the public, upon whom my mother and I partially depended for our existence.'[7] But it required a revolution to restore him fully to life.

Ideas and Ideals

On 25 July 1830 King Charles X of France signed his political death sentence. The Bourbon ruler had ascended the throne only six years earlier and from the outset had proved unequal to the task. Whereas his brother, Louis XVIII, had tried to mediate between the demands of the aristocracy and the expectations of a newly self-confident middle class, Charles tried to turn back the clock, refusing to accept a constitutional system of government and claiming that he would rather chop wood than live like an English king. His political views were as reactionary as they were out of touch with reality. It was, he insisted, by God's grace alone that he reigned. The gains of the French Revolution were gradually eroded, and the ghost of the *ancien régime* returned to haunt the country. In turn this meant that the Catholic Church was restored to a position of influence. Such backward-looking policies inevitably provoked the resentment of the middle classes, whose criticisms the king in turn attempted to quell by means of strict press censorship, but the masses continued to seethe, and when the liberals gained a majority in the parliamentary elections in July 1830, Charles and his entourage panicked. On 25 July he signed the three ordinances of Saint-Cloud, dissolving the Chamber of Deputies, further limiting the right to vote (France at this time had a population of thirty million, but of these only some 100,000 were entitled to vote) and curtailing press freedom even more than had previously been the case.

But now the government had gone too far. Workers, members of the middle class, intellectuals and students took to the streets, and in Paris barricades were erected, the Hôtel de Ville was stormed on 28 July 1830 and within a very short space of time the capital was in the hands of the insurgents. Charles abdicated and in the middle of August fled into exile in England. He was succeeded by Louis-Philippe, Duc d'Orléans, who was to go down in history as the 'Citizen King'. He took charge of a parliamentary monarchy that represented a compromise between liberal and conservative tendencies, but he proved more and more of a disappointment. The February Revolution of 1848 was to bring an end to this experiment. But one thing at a time.

Back in the summer of 1830 there was a general atmosphere of jubilation and the sense of a new beginning in society and the arts. Political émigrés from Poland, where a local uprising had been brutally suppressed by the Russians, settled in Paris and included the poet Adam Mickiewicz and the composer Fryderyk Chopin. In the salons in the Faubourg Saint-Honoré and the Faubourg Saint-Germain writers, artists, musicians, philosophers and obscure ameliorists met to exchange ideas. Liszt, too, was seized by revolutionary fervour, the salvos of small-arms fire having wrenched him from his mood of melancholy. 'C'est le canon qui l'a guéri,' his mother used to say in this context.[8] He sketched a 'Revolution Symphony' at this time, but broke off before it was completed.

Liszt now threw himself into the scintillating life of the salons and was regularly seen at tea parties and formal dinners. He spent time with fellow composers, including Meyerbeer, Rossini, Ferdinand Hiller and Mendelssohn, and also cultivated the company of writers such as Heinrich Heine, Charles-Augustin de Sainte-Beuve, Victor Hugo, Eugène Sue, Alfred de Vigny and Alexandre Dumas, all of whose books he devoured. 'He would read a dictionary in the same insatiable way as a book of verse,' Lina Ramann wrote in her 1880 biography. In his own personal copy, Liszt added the word 'True!' at this point in the margin.[9]

There was something dreamy-eyed and questioning about Liszt's life at this time. In his quest for certainty and knowledge he would draw near to various individuals, although not in every case did the contact prove enduring. Like Sainte-Beuve, he was for a time enthusiastic about the Saint-Simonists whose movement had been founded by the writer Claude-Henri de Rouvroy, Comte de Saint-Simon, the scion of an aristocratic family that had fallen on hard times.[10] In his books Saint-Simon laid the foundations for a key position in modern scientific thought: society, he believed, should be guided by science, while politics, too, should be run along precise scientific lines. But although he envisaged a stateless society, he had no time for equality, preferring the concept of an elitist achievement principle according to which the unproductive aristocracy, the clergy and the military were branded as parasites. In his final book, *Le nouveau christianisme* (1825), he preached the moral principle of fraternity as the nucleus of a new religion. When he died in May 1825, two of his pupils, Barthélemy-Prosper Enfantin and Saint-Amand Bazard, took charge and gradually transformed the Saint-Simonist 'school' into a dubious sect, finally anointing themselves its *pères suprêmes* in 1829. Not long afterwards the organization collapsed under the weight of internal arguments and accusations of bizarre rituals. Until then Liszt attended the Saint-Simonists' meetings on a regular basis over a period of several months, even though he was never officially a member. He was particularly fascinated by the idea that in the new and ideal society artists should hold a privileged position and that their 'sacred wisdom' cast them in the role of the missionaries of a new Christianity. In his later years Liszt distanced himself from the Saint-Simonist movement while remaining a convinced believer in its underlying maxim that we should all be treated according to our individual abilities.

Of equally important influence on the young Liszt was the work of the French priest and philosopher Félicité de Lamennais to which he was introduced in the autumn of 1833. Three years earlier, Lamennais had founded the journal *L'Avenir* in which he promulgated his ideas and formulated his demands, including the strict separation of Church and state, freedom of conscience and of the press, and democracy under a republic. This inevitably brought him into direct conflict with the Vatican even though he always acknowledged the authority of the pope in all matters appertaining to faith. His break with Rome came in 1834 with the publication of his pamphlet *Les paroles d'un croyant*, the 'words of a believer' that proved little short of a revelation for Liszt inasmuch as they followed on from ideas that he had already found so inspirational in the writings of the Saint-Simonists, namely, the idea of a just society on the basis of a sympathetic religion. In September 1834 Liszt visited Lamennais on his estates in Brittany, remaining there for three weeks.

But it was not only philosophers and writers who influenced Liszt. Among the key events of this period was his encounter with Hector Berlioz, his senior by eight years. The two men met for the first time on 4 December 1830: 'I spoke of Goethe's *Faust*, which he confessed that he had not read, but which he soon came to love as much as I. We felt an immediate affinity, and from that moment our friendship has grown ever closer and stronger.' The following day Berlioz's *Symphonie fantastique* received its first performance, but there is no concealing the note of venom in the composer's description of Liszt's effortless ability to steal his thunder: 'He came to the concert and was conspicuous for the warmth of his applause and his generally enthusiastic behaviour.'[11]

Liszt was certainly impressed by these 'episodes from an artist's life', to quote the symphony's subtitle. Berlioz had written an autobiographical drama in five movements, describing the love of a young man for a woman who – inevitably – rejects him, an act of murder that the artist imagines in an opium-fuelled dream, his subsequent execution and a final Witches' Sabbath. Music suddenly acquired a subjective programme no longer interested in a naïve description of natural phenomena such as birdsong and storms. Instead, Berlioz had created a highly dramatic and even bizarre detective story in music, which he had additionally succeeded in orchestrating with exceptional brilliance. Liszt was fascinated by all of this. For him, the *Symphonie fantastique* was an adumbration of all that he was later to achieve with his own symphonic poems: a fusion of music and poetry.

Berlioz and Liszt remained close for several decades, and when Liszt became Kapellmeister to the Weimar Court, he organized a series of Berlioz festivals in 1852, 1855 and 1856, when the French composer conducted his own works. Liszt also prepared masterly piano transcriptions of the *Symphonie fantastique* and *Harold en Italie* that helped in no small way to make his colleague's compositions better known. But by the late 1850s their friendship had grown markedly cooler, the egocentric Berlioz being barely able to conceal his envy and grumpy dismay in the face of Liszt's support of another great egomaniac, Richard Wagner. As we shall see, this was bound to end very badly.

But Liszt's relations with Chopin were also fraught with tensions of one kind or another. The Polish composer had settled in Paris in the late summer of 1831, and it was probably towards the end of that year that Fryderyk, now styling himself Frédéric, first got to know Liszt, his junior by around twelve months. When Chopin made his Paris debut in the Salle Pleyel in February 1832, Liszt was in the audience. The two men quickly became friends and spent many happy hours together, sometimes even appearing at joint recitals. Chopin was bowled over by Liszt's piano playing, and in a letter to an acquaintance he admitted that 'I am writing without knowing what my pen is scribbling, because at this moment Liszt is playing my studies and putting honest thoughts out of my head. I wish I could steal from him his way of playing my studies.'[12] When he published his op. 10 Studies the following year, he dedicated them to Liszt.

Chopin was himself a gifted pianist, and we know from numerous eyewitness accounts that he had an extremely delicate touch and that his playing was full of poetry. As a person he was not lacking in a certain eccentricity but on the whole he was retiring by nature, with even a hint of fragility about him. His musicianship was the complete opposite to that of Liszt, who was capable of captivating his audiences, casting a spell on the women in the room and flirting with them, while Chopin shied away from all contact with his public. Referring to Liszt, he once commented that

> I'm not suited to give concerts, the public intimidates me, I feel suffo-
> cated by its breath, paralysed by looks, and am mute before those

anonymous faces. But you, you are destined for it, because when you do not win over the public, you are able to overwhelm it.[13]

There was vitriol behind Chopin's praise and not a little scepticism concerning his friend's character: in Chopin's eyes, Liszt did not convince his audience but simply overwhelmed them through his sheer presence on the platform. All in all, Chopin retained a degree of distrust towards Liszt, and in later years their friendship broke down completely.

One anecdote in particular says much about their difficult relations. When Chopin had to leave Paris for several weeks at the beginning of 1835, Liszt asked a favour of him: Chopin's apartment would be empty during his absence, and so he wondered if he could use it during that time. Guilelessly Chopin agreed, unaware that Liszt would use the apartment for secret trysts with Marie Pleyel, who was not only Berlioz's former fiancée but, to add insult to injury, the wife of Chopin's friend, Camille Pleyel. The affair naturally came to light and Chopin understandably felt that he had been taken in. Pleyel may also have accused him of placing his apartment at Liszt's disposal in order to let him seduce his wife. Whatever the true facts of the matter, Liszt had emphatically gone too far.

But Liszt enjoyed being cast in the role of a Casanova. Years later he bumped into La Pleyel in Vienna and, visibly proud of his earlier feat, he wrote to his current mistress, Marie d'Agoult: 'She asked me if I remembered Chopin's apartment. "Of course, Madame, how could I forget it . . ."'[14]

Paganini, or the Invention of Piano Playing

For years the Italian violinist Niccolò Paganini had terrified his audiences. Known as the 'Devil's violinist', he appeared on the concert platform dressed entirely in black, convincing his more credulous listeners that he was Old Nick incarnate. Born in Genoa in 1782, he had contracted syphilis, which had affected his larynx and destroyed his lower jaw, causing his teeth to fall out and leaving his eyes sunken in their sockets. Marked out by illness, he could move only slowly. In June 1832 Heinrich Heine had attended one of Paganini's concerts in Hamburg and raised a monument to him in his *Florentine Nights*. A reverential silence descended on the hall and

> every eye was directed towards the stage, every ear was strained to hear. My neighbour, a fur broker, took his dirty cotton out of his ears, the better to imbibe the precious sounds that had cost him two thalers' admission. Finally a sombre figure appeared on the stage, having apparently emerged from the underworld. It was Paganini, dressed in his black court uniform.[15]

Paganini's demonic appearance seemed to confirm all the horror stories about him. Although we may smile today, not a few of his contemporaries were convinced that he had originated in hell – how else could he have acquired such virtuosic gifts? The simplest explanation was people's timeless need for gossip and scandal: Paganini was not a person at all but the devil returned to earth in human form. A concertgoer in Vienna even claimed to have seen the devil himself standing beside the violinist. Dressed entirely in red – how could it have been otherwise? – and with horns on his head, he had guided the player's bow. According to another scurrilous rumour, Paganini had murdered his mistress with his own bare hands and spent four years in prison. There he had played his violin every day and in that way acquired a positively diabolical technique. Before being sentenced, he had removed the gut of his lover and used it for his famous G string. It is hard to believe that as recently as 1922 Paganini's German biographer Julius Kapp felt the need to stress that these horror stories were no more than malicious rumours.

It was following Paganini's alleged release from prison – in fact he had been giving concerts in Italy almost continuously since 1810 – that the violinist made his Viennese debut in 1828. Three years later he appeared for the first time in Paris. When he returned to the City of Light the following year, Liszt was in the audience, and the concert on 20 April turned out to be one of the seminal experiences of his life: he was overwhelmed by a level of virtuosity that inspired feelings verging on ecstasy. Here was a musician who effortlessly transcended all the usual technical difficulties, investing his instrument with expressive possibilities hitherto unsuspected and even appearing to reinvent the whole art of playing the violin. Liszt suddenly realized that in spite of his own dazzling technique he was still operating within the confines of the Czerny school of velocity, and he was now determined to leave those limitations behind him. But virtuosity, far from being his goal, was no more than a means to an end, for his aim was to open up the piano to a whole new world of emotions and sensations. He set to work at once: 'For the past fortnight,' he wrote to a friend,

> my mind and fingers have been working away like two lost souls. [...] I am spending four to five hours a day practising exercises (thirds, sixths, octaves, tremolandos, repeated notes, cadenzas, etc.). Ah! provided I don't go mad, you may yet find an artist in me! Yes, an artist such as you desire and such as is needed today![16]

Thanks to the diary kept by Auguste Boissier, whose daughter Valérie had lessons with Liszt in 1832, we know the details of his studies. His starting point was the total emancipation of his fingers: every pianist has at his or her disposal ten fingers, all with equal rights. Anatomical weaknesses must be overcome by training:

> The ring finger, the little finger and the middle finger are the worst and it is these that need attention, although the others, too, must be exercised. And so he instructs the pianist to exercise each finger for a quarter of an hour in turn by raising it very high and then by placing it not on the tip but on the flat of the finger. [...] A further exercise consists in performing trills while the other fingers that are not playing trills are held on the keys.[17]

The fingers must be extremely flexible and supple. To this end Valérie was to 'undertake a whole range of exercises for at least three hours every day – various scales, in octaves and thirds, arpeggios in every shape and form, trills, chords: in short, everything that one can do'.[18] As Liszt was forced to concede, this was often extremely tedious, and so Mademoiselle Boissier was encouraged to read a book while she was practising: 'He does all this for hours on end, while reading to relieve his boredom. It is then that he thinks about his reading matter while exercising his fingers.'[19]

The fact that Liszt had large hands certainly helped him develop his new way of playing, for it enabled him to perform wide leaps and to turn this ability into something approaching a circus trick – an artiste seeming to juggle with the notes. The first product of his interest in Paganini was his *Grande fantaisie de bravoure sur La clochette de Paganini*, a piece based on one of the themes from the final movement of the Italian composer's Second Violin Concerto. It is treated to a pyrotechnical display of pianistic devices featuring trills, breathtaking glissandi, cascading chords, thunderous octaves with both hands, insane leaps and pizzicato effects. For the interpreter, the piece contains nightmarish difficulties, and yet the technical demands it places on the performer are not an end in themselves. In writing this work Liszt had come closer to his ideal of investing the piano with an orchestral dimension. In doing so he had – like Paganini – broken down a barrier. Even so, none of this would have been possible without Sébastien Érard's advances in piano making and his development of double-escapement action. Inventiveness and musical progress went hand in hand.

Liszt did not forget the impression left on him by Paganini in April 1832. Six years later he wrote his *Études d'exécution transcendante d'après Paganini*, which he revised in 1851 and republished in a new and slightly easier version under the title *Grandes études de Paganini*. Common to both works is the desire to translate to the piano the whole capricious sophistication of Paganini's violin playing. His studies were no mere exercises designed to help the performer combat a technical problem but became a new poetic genre all of their own. In all three versions of his twelve *Études d'exécution transcendante* – the first set dates from 1826, its two revisions from 1838 and 1851 – he describes Romantic impressions. The player encounters will-o'-the-wisps in 'Feux follets', embarks on a wild hunt in 'Wilde Jagd', sees a vision ('Vision') and in the final piece ('Chasse-neige') he stumbles into a snowstorm.

But Liszt also prepared transcriptions of all manner of other compositions, including organ works by Bach, Beethoven's symphonies, songs by Chopin, Schubert and Schumann, and countless numbers from the operas and music dramas of his future son-in-law, Wagner. Generally he took his cue from his source, but what he produced were far from mere piano versions. Thanks to his stupendous technique and with the help of sophisticated effects he was able to reinvent each piece for the piano.

A third type of piano piece is the paraphrase. Often Liszt would take memorable tunes from operas that were popular at this time and by means of additional material of his own transform them into dramatic fantasies, 'Variations', 'Réminiscences' and 'Illustrations'. Some of these pieces may now strike us as mannered in the extreme and bombastic to a fault but, as Béla Bartók observed,

> In his youth he imitated the bad habits of the mediocre artists of the period – he corrected and transcribed with brilliant additions masterpieces that not even a Liszt had any right to touch. [...] But side by side with the triviality, he displayed almost everywhere amazing boldness, either in form or in invention. The boldness was really a fanatical striving towards something rare and new. In his works, scattered among many commonplaces, there are more things that are in advance of his time than in those of many other composers whom the average public esteems more.[20]

From Paganini, Liszt learnt not only what music can express when the musician adopts a 'transcendental' approach to his material, but also to appreciate the art of self-representation: the way in which the artist appeared onstage, his way of greeting the audience and of looking down into the auditorium when bowing – Liszt could see that all of this was a part of the magic that drew listeners into the artist's sway. Liszt knew what he looked like and how this affected people. But unlike Paganini, who exuded an aura of the demonic, Liszt successfully embodied the young and prepossessing aristocrat at the piano. The writer Hans Christian Andersen recalled that

> When Liszt entered the saloon, it was as if an electric shock passed through it. Most of the ladies rose; it was as if a ray of sunshine passed

over every face, as if all eyes received a dear, beloved friend. I stood quite near to the artist: he is a slim young man, his long, dark hair hung around his pale face; he bowed to the audience and sat down to the piano. [. . .] When Liszt had ceased playing, flowers showered around him: beautiful young girls, and old ladies who had once been young and beautiful, cast each her bouquet. He had cast a thousand bouquets of tones into their hearts and heads.[21]

Interestingly, Andersen refers almost exclusively to the reaction of the women in the audience, for it was clearly with them that Liszt struck a particular chord, his genius as a musician consorting with his charisma to produce the effect described. The term 'charisma' means more than a mere aura and is not necessarily connected to the person's outward appearance. It is to the sociologist Max Weber that we owe the best definition. Referring to political leaders, Weber writes of

a certain quality of an individual personality by virtue of which he is considered extraordinary and treated as endowed with supernatural, superhuman, or at least specifically exceptional powers or qualities. These are such as are not accessible to the ordinary person, but are regarded as of divine origin or as exemplary, and on the basis of them the individual concerned is treated as a 'leader'.[22]

What matters, therefore, is not whether Liszt actually possessed these qualities, but that his contemporaries perceived them in him. This almost intimate interaction between Liszt and the women in his audience seems to have worked particularly well, but it meant that the music took second place, being effortlessly eclipsed by a pronounced element of eroticism and sex appeal. Like a modern pop star, Liszt was a blank surface on which to project secret desires and fantasies.

Liszt adopted a showman's attitude to all of this, starting with his exclusively black clothing that lent an air of mystery to his slim figure and pallid features. His shoulder-length hair kept falling across his face as he played, causing him to push it back cheekily behind his ears, a gesture that became one of his hallmarks. The boundary between musicianship on the one hand and, on the other, showmanship, affectation, mannered facial expressions and airs and graces is, of course, fluid. Liszt put on an impressive show for his audience which can be summed up in two words: Franz Liszt. 'How powerful, how shattering was his mere physical appearance,' Heinrich Heine noted with caustic scorn:

> How tempestuous was the applause that greeted him! Bouquets of flowers were thrown at his feet. It was a sublime sight to see the triumphant hero standing there serenely calm while these flowers rained down all around him before finally, smiling graciously, drawing a red camellia from one such bouquet and placing it to his bosom.

Heine even claims that some of the ladies in the audience swooned, 'while two Hungarian countesses, seeking to snatch his handkerchief, pulled each other to the ground and fought until they drew blood!'[23]

There were times when Liszt deliberately provoked a scandal by arriving late for a concert or even cancelling an appearance. He loved performing his pirouettes on the social stage, he loved dazzling his audience, flirting with the ladies and playing the part of a vain peacock. As early as the beginning of 1831 he had started an affair with Countess Adèle de la Prunarède – his senior by fifteen years – while at the same time taking up with a certain Charlotte Laborie. Charlotte's mother would have been happy to have Liszt as a son-in-law and understandably saw Adèle de la Prunarède as a threat. When she learnt that the countess had allegedly promised to marry Liszt, she saw an opportunity to put her daughter's rival out of the running by announcing that Adèle was already married. And then there was Mademoiselle Euphémie Didier whose designs on Liszt were encouraged by his mother. Within a short space of time, then, the young Liszt – the cynosure of many a lustful eye – had painted himself into a corner, his only means of escape being to turn down all three women's advances and announce that he would be devoting the rest of his life to music and to his mother. As we know, things turned out rather differently, and many amorous adventures still lay ahead of him.

However anecdotal, these events none the less reveal an underlying pattern. Whenever Liszt's love life threatened to become too complicated

and to throw him off balance, he would seek refuge in flight. Not infrequently he would then lapse into a state of depression when it became
clear to him that he was wasting his time with superficial small talk. 'It's
now more than four months since I've slept or found peace of mind,' he
complained in 1833:

> Aristocracy of birth, aristocracy of talent, aristocracy of fortune,
> elegant coquetry in the boudoir, the heavy and pestilential atmo-
> sphere of the diplomatic salon, the dull-witted tumult of the road,
> the yawns and tense shouts of bravo at literary and artistic soirées,
> the egotistical and offensive delights of the ball, the gossip and fool-
> ishness of tea parties, the shame and remorse of the evening before
> and the morning afterwards, the triumph of the salon, the exagger-
> ated criticism and praise of the newspapers, one's own disappoint-
> ments as an artist, success with the public – I've been through it all!
> I've felt, seen, scorned, cursed and wept.[24]

It says much for Liszt that he was at least able to see through these mechanisms, even though his solutions were not always effective. Soon he
simply donned a new mask and invented another role for himself.

Liszt and women is a subject to which we shall have to return. When
his affair with Caroline de Saint-Cricq came to an end, Anna Liszt had
warned him not to become involved in any more ill-advised adventures.
He should have learnt his lesson, she suggested. But many more lessons
remained to be learnt. And the highest price was exacted by the woman
to whom we must now turn our attention.

The Countess

The rue du Bac in Paris connects the Boulevard Saint-Germain with the
Pont Royal. Here, at the heart of the Faubourg Saint-Germain, Madame
Renée de Maupéou, the Marquise Le Vayer, owned an *hôtel particulier*, a
magnificent private mansion of a kind by no means unusual in the Paris of
this period. An impressive porte cochère giving on to the street led into an
inner courtyard, where visitors were received. The main residential wing

lay on the far side of this inner courtyard and was inhabited for the most part by members of the nobility. Two wings made up the other sides of the courtyard. Buildings like these were often extraordinarily lavishly furnished – money was no object. Sumptuous receptions, formal dinners, concerts and dances were held on the *étage noble*, and no. 42 rue du Bac was no exception. The salon of the Marquise Le Vayer was one of the most famous in the city, a regular meeting place for writers and artists. Since her niece was one of Liszt's pupils, it made sense to invite the pianist to her salon, and it was on one such visit that he was introduced to a woman who was to transform his life in significant ways: the Countess Marie d'Agoult. It is possible that the two of them had seen each other briefly at a Berlioz concert in December 1832, but there was no personal contact between them until they met at the home of the Marquise Le Vayer in January 1833.

'When I entered Madame Le Vayer's salon at 10 o'clock', Marie d'Agoult later recalled, 'everyone was already assembled.' She had been assured that Liszt would be coming.

> Madame Le Vayer was still speaking when the door opened and a strange apparition presented itself to my eyes. I say 'apparition', because I can think of no other word to describe the extraordinary sensation caused by the most extraordinary person I have ever seen.

Even many years later, she could still recall the impression of a man who was

> tall and excessively thin, with a pallid complexion and large sea-green eyes in which the swift flash of light glistened like waves catching the sunlight, a face that expressed both suffering and power, a hesitant step that seemed less to press down on the floor than to glide over it and an air of absent-mindedness and unease, like that of a ghost about to be summoned back into the darkness.

She went on to describe their first conversation:

> When he had been introduced to me and taken his seat beside me, he began to speak familiarly with me with an emboldened grace and as

if he had known me for a long time. I felt beneath the strange exterior that had initially astonished me the force and freedom of a mind that attracted me; and well before the conversation was over, I found his whole way of thinking and speaking – although so unusual in the world in which I had always lived – entirely straightforward.

When she returned home that night, it was a long time before she could get to sleep: 'I was visited by strange dreams.'[25]

Marie d'Agoult's reference to Liszt's whole nature being 'so unusual in the world in which I had always lived' was no accident. Indeed, it is hard to imagine two lives as different as those of the pianist and his admirer. He was a middle-class musician from a poor background, twenty-one years old, a sorcerer at the keyboard who, fond of eccentricity, was the talk of the town, while the twenty-eight-year-old Marie was a member of the aristocracy, distinguished, well-to-do and well educated, the mother of two daughters and for many years stuck in a loveless marriage. When she met Liszt, her life was at a crossroads. In order to understand the situation in which she found herself, we need to take a closer look at her family background.

Marie Cathérine Sophie was born in Frankfurt am Main during the night of 30/31 December 1805. Her mother, Marie-Élisabeth Bethmann, was a member of one of the wealthiest and most influential banking families in Frankfurt. They lived in the palatial half-timbered Baslerhof in the inner city: 'Lady's companions, chambermaids, a reader, a doctor and a chaplain – nothing was missing, and there was even a carriage permanently waiting in the courtyard in case my mother unexpectedly wanted to go out or take one of her visitors home.'[26] Marie-Élisabeth was eighteen when she married Johann Jacob Bussmann, one of her father's business partners, but he died only a short time afterwards. In September 1797, and against her family's wishes, she remarried, her choice being Alexandre Vicomte de Flavigny. The couple had three children: Éduard, Maurice Adolphe and Marie Cathérine Sophie, who was later to become the Countess d'Agoult. When the viscount, in his turn, died in October 1819, Marie, who was barely fourteen, was placed in the care of her maternal grandmother in Frankfurt, a woman notorious for her strictness and for her contempt of her grandchildren: 'Even after twenty years my grand-mother had not forgiven her daughter for her rashness in disobeying her and marrying my father. Her bourgeois pride bridled at the thought of the aristocratic pride that she supposed all three of us shared.'[27] It is no wonder, then, that Marie's upbringing in Frankfurt proved strife-ridden, and in early 1821 it was decided to send her to an 'educational institution' in Paris: 'The one run by the Ladies of the Sacred Heart was felt to be the most refined. I do not believe that there were any other reasons for choosing it.'[28]

In the French capital, Marie was admitted to the salons of all the leading families, and there was no shortage of members of the nobility eager to pay court to the attractive young woman, who was considered an excellent catch:

> A well-born, well-brought-up young woman with a good dowry – my mother was able to give me three hundred thousand francs, a considerable sum of money at that time, [...] not to mention 'solid hopes' of a maternal inheritance amounting to a million francs. As a result, there was nothing that I could not demand.[29]

There is something coldly calculating about such a remark. In general, Marie seems to have been clear in her own mind that she would marry very soon and that it would probably be a marriage of convenience, lacking in any real love.

> In the eyes of the French, marriage is an arrangement, a calculation: two fortunes are joined together in order to create an even larger one, two credits are combined in order to produce an even larger credit. The two biggest fortunes and the two largest credits – that's the ideal![30]

Among Marie's admirers was the forty-five-year-old Auguste Comte de Lagarde. But both parties hesitated, unable to make up their minds. In July 1825 Lagarde left Paris, plunging Marie into a serious crisis, and during the following months countless other men competed for her hand. She was tired, however, of their importunities and told her mother that 'the next time anyone comes a-wooing', Marie-Élisabeth should discuss the matter with her brother 'and say yes or no without speaking to me. I promised to ratify this "yes" on the part of two people whose sound judgement, I admitted, was infinitely better than my own.'[31]

As chance would have it, the next candidate was Charles d'Agoult. Fifteen years older than Marie, he had served in the French army as a cavalry captain and in 1814 had fought alongside Napoleon in the Battle of Nangis, sustaining an injury that left him with a permanent limp. Furthermore, his wealth was not a patch on his future wife's. But Marie seems to have taken no interest in such things. She was as good as her word and married the count on 16 May 1827. Even before that date the count is said to have promised to release her from her vows if she ever regretted the marriage. A year later their first daughter was born, Louise Marie Thérèse, followed two years later, in August 1830, by a second, Claire Christine.

The inevitable happened, as Marie was to recall:

I did not enjoy a single hour of happiness from the day I married my husband. The feeling that I was completely isolated in heart and mind in this new relationship created by conjugal life, coupled with a painful astonishment at what I had done by giving myself to a man who inspired no feelings of love in me, filled all my thoughts with a mortal sadness from the very first day.[32]

Her melancholy fed on the wretched domestic conditions that she had to endure and also on the bouts of depression from which she suffered all her life and which she described as her 'spleen', a feeling that often found expression in psychosomatic ailments. There was evidently a predisposition to brooding introspection and melancholy in her family: her half-sister Auguste tried several times to take her own life, finally throwing herself in the River Main in April 1832 and drowning.

This, then, was the situation in which Marie d'Agoult found herself when she entered Madame Le Vayer's salon in early January 1833. Now twenty-eight years old, she was depressed and disappointed after six years of unhappy marriage. Before her was the twenty-one-year-old, good-looking and charismatic Liszt. Within a short space of time they were secret lovers.

During the early months of their liaison they often played duets together or read the same books and wrote to each other to express their views on what they had read. Throughout, they were painstakingly careful to remain discreet. No one was to know of their secret. Sometimes they even wrote to each other in German or English as they never knew who might break the seal on their letters. In other ways, too, they proved inventive. In August Liszt was offered an opportunity to play the organ in Notre-Dame. Both Marie and the Marquise Catherine de Gabriac were keen to accompany him as unostentatiously as possible, and so they donned men's clothing. But their subterfuge could not be kept a secret and it was not long before all manner of lubricious rumours were circulating in the city's salons. Whether there was any physical contact between the lovers in church we do not know.

The lovers' trysts were increasingly difficult to organize. Although Liszt had visited his mistress at the family's home, the Château de Croissy, to the east of Paris, they were under constant supervision there, especially when the count was in residence. Romantic assignations at Liszt's apartment in Paris were ruled out by the fact that he was still living with his mother, and so during the winter of 1833/4 he rented an apartment where he could meet Marie at any time and that he knowingly called 'The Rat Hole'. But even then they continued to be on their guard, and Marie would arrive for their meetings wearing men's clothing, which, adding additional piquancy to the assignations, she borrowed from her husband's wardrobe.

Their lives together were never free from tension, and a note of shrillness occasionally creeps into their correspondence. Marie was evidently extremely jealous and demanded a detailed account of Liszt's previous life. When she stumbled upon his letters to Euphémie Didier, she made a scene, and Liszt reacted irritably: 'It's 4 o'clock – I've only time to say three times to you, ridiculous, ridiculous and once again ridiculous!'[33] It annoyed him that he had to justify a flirtation dating back to 1831. He assured Marie that since then he had not seen the young lady in question and that he had never for a moment thought of marrying her. Within days Marie was back on the offensive, this time on account of another woman. 'The reproach that you make over the marquise has left me feeling very bitter, he replied. 'I have to say that I find it extremely unjust.'[34]

By the autumn of 1834 their relationship seemed to have run its course, and Liszt was ready to walk away. 'I am ashamed to admit', he wrote to Marie in November, 'that only after a painful period of great hesitation have I decided to reply to your last letter.' He was planning to travel alone to Switzerland at the start of the following year: the end seemed close.

> Yes, there are words that are never spoken in vain, at least at certain moments. The word 'separation' has time and again been uttered by me and by you. [. . .] We must meet, I have to speak to you. Let it be soon. As soon as you can.[35]

Was there another woman in his life? That would be an exaggeration, although it is certainly true that Liszt was showing a certain readiness to embark on a new affair: only a few weeks earlier, in October 1834, he had been introduced to the writer Amantine-Lucile-Aurore Dupin de Francueil, better known as George Sand. Whereas Marie d'Agoult, for all her liberal ideas, remained a product of the French establishment, George Sand – who was born in 1804 – was non-conformist to a fault, a woman who was not in the least concerned about what women in general were supposed or not supposed to do. By preference she wore men's clothes, smoked pipes and cigars, propagated a belief in the passionate love between men and women and declared marriage as an institution to be dead. All of this appeared to fascinate Liszt. The fact that she was involved in a complicated relationship with Alfred de Musset that was on the point of breaking down seems to have provided an additional bond between them, although they were never in fact a couple.

In the middle of October 1834 Marie's six-year-old daughter Louise suddenly fell ill. The symptoms – headaches and a high temperature – were vague, and Marie assumed that the climate in Croissy was to blame, so she took the child with her to Paris. But the child's health showed no sign of improvement: 'Her fever grew worse and the child became delirious, after which she fell into a dead faint.' Louise no longer recognized her parents. 'Her breathing became irregular and ragged. It was heartbreaking. I feared that every moment would be her last.' Days passed. The end came, catastrophically, on 10 December. Marie had briefly left the room, but a feeling of unease drew her back:

> My God! It was appalling! She had sat up in bed. Her eyes were open and were staring wildly. I rushed over to her. She threw her arms round my neck with a gesture of terror as if trying to escape from an unseen hand. I pressed her to me. She uttered a scream, and I felt the dead weight of her weakened body on my breast.[36]

It seems that during Louise's illness there was practically no contact any longer between Liszt and the countess. She remained at her daughter's bedside for days on end, and we may be right in assuming that the child's father was also present during this time. In the circumstances it would have been inappropriate for Liszt to call on his mistress, and so he withdrew. On one occasion he met her chambermaid by chance and was brought up to date, but he learnt of the child's death only from a letter from Marie. Her letter has not survived, but we do have Liszt's touching reply of 15 December 1834:

> You say that you thought about me constantly during these two days – you thought about me at Louise's bedside yesterday and today . . . Forgive me, Marie, if at this time I forget all your anguish and all your troubles and speak to you only about myself and about those words of yours: 'I thought about you constantly.' [. . .] I think I'm going mad – but I love you so much, so greatly and so sublimely.[37]

The lovers met again a few weeks later, on 3 January 1835. The atmosphere was evidently fraught for Marie subsequently accused Liszt of egoism and coldness. He sought to defend himself:

> Your note would easily lend weight to my arguments, but I willingly forgive you. It's too wretched a thing to justify one's suppositions with the sufferings of those whom one loves for me to take any pleasure from giving you a chance to admire my keen intellect.

Once again she tormented him with her jealousy, which on this occasion was directed at George Sand. Liszt was not aware that he had done anything wrong: 'I haven't seen Madame Sand since you left.'[38] But there could be no question of a reconciliation.

What happened next remains cloaked in mystery. In the middle of January 1835 Liszt left Paris for almost two months. Even today we have no idea where he went, whom he met and why he left. He effectively went underground. But by early March we find him back in the French capital, and between 3 and 22 March he met Marie d'Agoult no fewer than seven times, dining with her and on one occasion having breakfast with her and Chopin. It was during this period that Marie conceived their first daughter, Blandine.

Marie must have realized during the spring that she was pregnant, and this will have been the main reason why the couple remained together. They even decided to leave France together. On 26 May, before she left for Basel, Marie wrote to her husband to bid him farewell: 'Your name will never pass my lips, unless it be spoken with respect and the esteem that your person deserves. As for myself, I ask only for your silence in the face of a world that will shower me with insults.'[39] The count kept his word and released his wife from their marriage, continuing to look after their four-year-old daughter Claire Christine and retiring to his château at Croissy.

Marie's decision undoubtedly required great courage. For a grande dame from high society such a step was foolhardy in the extreme. Ignoring her family's social standing, she bade farewell to the world of the French aristocracy. The social scandal was unavoidable, and there was every danger that she would in future be treated as an outcast. Perhaps she recalled the encouraging words of the old Countess Angélique-Élisabeth de Matignon, who once assured a young woman that there was a limit to the hostility of public opinion: 'Take comfort, my dear, from the fact that for women of high society like us our honour grows back like the hair on our head.'[40]

ANNÉES DE PÈLERINAGE
(1835–9)

Doubts

'AGAINST ALL HOPE WE arrived in Basel at 10 o'clock this morning,' Liszt reported to his mother on 4 June 1835. 'My parcels, suitcases, bags and portmanteaus are all present and correct – I didn't give too much to the little beggars we met on the way, so my purse isn't too depleted. [. . .] We're both in fairly good spirits and are not thinking of becoming unhappy.'[1] Marie d'Agoult had left Paris on 28 May, and Liszt had followed her on 1 June. But the journey to Switzerland had not been as straightforward as Liszt had led his mother to believe. Both he and Marie were unsure if they were doing the right thing. The d'Agoult family had turned at the last minute to the abbé Félicité de Lamennais, who had made one final, eloquent attempt to persuade Marie to abandon her plans. The intervention took place with Liszt's express agreement, his action throwing a significant light on his own enthusiasm regarding the decision that he had taken. Marie, too, was in two minds. When her mother suffered a nervous breakdown in the hotel in Basel where she too was staying, Marie promised to return with her to France. Only when Madame de Flavigny had recovered and accepted that her daughter did not want to live in Paris any longer did her scruples seem to vanish.

Liszt and Marie d'Agoult left Basel in the middle of June and spent the next six weeks travelling more or less aimlessly around Switzerland in the company of a chambermaid. It was during this time that Liszt started work on a musical travel diary to which he gave the title *Album d'un voyageur*. Pieces such as 'Le lac de Wallenstedt', 'Vallée d'Obermann' and 'La chapelle de Guillaume Tell' all relate to places visited by the couple. Liszt later reworked the collection, reordering the pieces and publishing them as Part One of his *Années de pèlerinage* (Years of Pilgrimage). Marie recalled that 'no letter reached us on our fantastical walks through the mountains. No one knew our names in the isolated houses and hamlets where we tended by preference to stay.'[2] And so time passed. On 19 July they reached Geneva, where Marie planned to give birth to their first child and where the couple intended to stay until the spring of 1836. It was here, in the rue Tabazan, that they rented a small apartment. 'From my windows I had a splendid view of the sombre mass of the Jura,' she recalled.[3] But Geneva proved to be the worst place for the couple to lead a secluded life, and it became impossible to conceal the arrival of a man as famous as Liszt. Various invitations arrived, which Liszt was delighted to accept – much to Marie's chagrin.

The tensions in the rue Tabazan worsened when Liszt received a letter from his fourteen-year-old pupil Hermann Cohen, also known as 'Puzzi', asking if he could visit his teacher. ' "He has to come," said Liszt, taking the letter from my hands, "I'll write to him." ' Marie was afraid that the young boy would prove a disruptive influence:

> I sensed that as soon as he arrived in Geneva, Puzzi would be unable to keep his distance, as he believed he could. Circumstances were such that they admitted of no reserve in our relations. Inviting Hermann to visit us was tantamount to opening up our house to him and abandoning the intimacy of our hearth. And Franz seemed to find this so self-evident that he did not even ask for my consent.

Liszt had no qualms about giving the boy the occasional lesson, whereas Marie was unable to conceal her jealousy:

> Had I abandoned my own child simply in order to take in another one? This education, these signs of endearment, these bonds of love

between father and son that grew ever closer between Franz and Hermann beneath my very eyes [...] were bound to fill me with bitterness.[4]

Further arguments ensued when Liszt announced his intention of taking part in a benefit concert in early October. And when he additionally offered to teach a class of ten students at the newly opened Basel Conservatory, Marie felt humiliated. The seeds of the subsequent breakdown of their relationship seem to have been sown at this time. To put it bluntly, Marie appears to have wanted Liszt for herself and was unwilling to share him with admirers and pupils, still less with a concert audience. She failed to realize that he needed the amusements of the salon at more or less regular intervals. Right up to the end of his life he would return to the social whirl after periods of withdrawal. It is hard to believe that she really thought she could prevent a thoroughbred musician like Liszt from appearing in public in the longer term.

We know from a letter that Liszt wrote to his mother in the autumn of 1835 how he spent his day at this time:

> I am always fully occupied from 9 in the morning (I rarely get up any earlier) to 11 at night. The conservatory, my practising and my compositions take up the morning, reading, the piano, a few visitors, articles and so on the afternoon. I sometimes spend the evening copying, but at other times I do nothing.[5]

As for Marie, she was heavily pregnant, and we can assume that her condition caused the couple many problems, and yet her imminent accouchement is nowhere mentioned in the letters that have survived from this period. No doubt it was deliberately concealed since no one in faraway Paris was to know of her illegitimate progeny. Their first daughter, Blandine-Rachel, was born on 18 December 1835. The local register of births names Liszt as the child's father, while the mother is given as Catherine Adélaïde Méran, her initials – 'C.Ad.M.' – evidently an anagram of C[omtesse] M[arie] d'A[goult].[6] The secrecy was necessary in order to draw a veil over her adultery, for according to the legal situation at this time the children of a married woman had only one father: the woman's husband. In other words, Liszt's children would have been regarded as the offspring of Charles d'Agoult, since Marie was still married to the count. But the ruse meant only that although Blandine may have had a father, she had no mother, a circumstance that many years later was to play an important role.

The Rival

'There is really no need to worry about the matter about which a number of people have been gossiping in Paris,' Liszt assured his mother. 'Mme d'[A]. was successfully delivered of an altogether delightful and extremely beautiful girl on 18 December 1835. All necessary precautions have been taken in this regard, and so far I can only congratulate myself on the fact that our household is now bigger.'[7] Among the measures mentioned by Liszt were the engagement of a wet nurse to whom the child was entrusted immediately after her birth. In the spring of 1836 she was transferred to the care of a Genevan pastor, Antoine Demellayer. However heartless we may nowadays regard the act of giving away unweaned infants, it was a common practice among well-to-do circles at that time. 'People make a good deal of fuss about maternal love,' Marie wrote in her diary. 'I must admit that I have never shared the sense of general admiration.'[8] Blandine's parents wanted to continue their lives as before.

Liszt now had to support a family of three, together with their nursery maid. Their savings shrank, with no appreciable new income to replenish their funds. Moreover, life in Geneva was expensive, and by the beginning of 1836 Liszt was in financial difficulties. In the course of the preceding months he had written a number of works, including the *Grande valse di bravura*, the *Réminiscences des Puritains* and the *Réminiscences de La Juive*, but the sale of these technically demanding salon pieces could not be expected to bring in enough money to stave off financial disaster. In early April 1836 Liszt organized a concert in Geneva at his own expense, but it was poorly attended and failed to cover its costs. The situation was sufficiently desperate for Liszt to travel to Lyons to give three more concerts, and yet here too he was only moderately successful.

It was at around this time that reports reached Geneva and Lyons from Paris that left Liszt distinctly unsettled. The pianist Sigismond Thalberg had arrived in the French capital and given a private concert there in the middle of November 1835. Even within such an intimate setting, the impact of his playing must have been immense, and when Thalberg – less than a year younger than Liszt – appeared at the Paris Conservatoire before a much larger audience at the end of January 1836, the reviews were ecstatic. In the middle of April he gave another concert at the Théâtre Italien, and again the papers had nothing but praise for him. His flawless technique, his tasteful musicianship and his aristocratic appearance ensured that wherever he went, Thalberg was hailed as an artist of genius. Liszt reacted to these tributes with palpable dismay. 'The works of his that I have seen struck me as very non-descript,' he assured his mother. 'And the praise that has been lavished on him in the newspapers leaves me cold. Is it true that he sent you a ticket for his concert even though he doesn't know you?'[9] It was unimportant whether Anna Liszt had actually received a complimentary ticket. The mere rumour was enough for Liszt to treat it as a declaration of war. Someone was poaching on his territory, an act of presumption he could not endure.

Liszt had known his rival's name before the latter's appearances in Paris but had paid it little attention. Now, however, he needed to know more about the Thalberg phenomenon. First, he asked to be sent some of his rival's works. 'I've played through his fantasy on *La straniera*, it's very mediocre and also makes the mistake of sounding pitifully like its predecessors. I really don't think that this man has anything in him. But we'll see.'[10] These lines to Marie d'Agoult make it sound as if Liszt was whistling in the dark. He must have realized straight away that Thalberg's *Fantaisie sur des motifs de l'opéra La Straniera de Bellini* is a superbly well-crafted work, but he was clearly unwilling to admit as much. He must, however, have sensed that there was something behind all the enthusiasm for Thalberg and that a powerful rival had entered the arena.

Liszt wanted to return to Paris as soon as possible and take up the challenge, but Marie was against the idea: she preferred him to remain in Switzerland, leading a life of seclusion and devoting himself to more serious matters. In her eyes, his rivalry with Thalberg must have seemed a waste of time. She was also afraid that once he was back in Paris he might meet people – women? – of whom she disapproved. 'In the first place I have *absolutely no desire* to go to Paris at present,' he assured his partner. 'The two or three people with whom it might have given me some pleasure to renew contact have become profoundly antipathetic and alien to me.' In any case, Thalberg had already left the capital.

> Oh! since this temptation has now passed for good, I freely admit that for two or three days I was tormented beyond measure by an unbridled desire to go to Paris and attend Thalberg's concert with the orchestra of the Théâtre Italien on the day of my arrival. I felt and knew that the spectator would attract more attention than the principal actor. It would have been a kind of return to Elba – I might have wanted to applaud him and shout 'Bravo' at him in a contemptuous tone of voice, for now I feel something loftier and more powerful beating in my breast.

At this point Liszt could have ended his letter, which he wrote from Lyons on 28 or 29 April 1836. But what he had written so far was no more than a friendly skirmish, for he was determined to go to Paris and so he proceeded to list some of the reasons why such a journey was necessary. In the process he hoped to reconcile Marie to the idea. He had to meet the piano maker Sébastien Érard, he needed to look for certain scores in his music library, he had to deal with publishing matters, and so on. Hypocritically, he even offered to run various errands for Marie:

> Be that as it may, there are two things that are definite:
>
> 1) *I shan't leave unless you formally order me to do so* (and you know what I mean by that); in other words, you must be convinced that I need to leave.
>
> 2) *I shan't in any case spend more than four or five days at most there* [. . .]. As for appearing in public or in private, I have absolutely no wish to do so. As long as Thalberg was there, it was fine; but now it would be more than puerile.[11]

Liszt's long-winded request for permission to travel to Paris met with no response – Marie was unwilling to grant him such a favour. Unsure how to react, he went from one extreme to the other: 'I shall not be going to Paris,' he announced on 1 May. 'This is *final* and *irrevocable*. [. . .] Now not even the archangel Michael and Satan could make me go there.'[12] But Liszt was merely playing with words, for his brain was seething, the business with Thalberg having robbed him of his peace of mind. By the following day he was writing that 'at his final concert, with its programme unworthily thrown together, Thalberg is said to have made far less of an impression'.[13] A breakthrough in this absurd dilly-dallying came only when Marie arrived in Lyons to spend a week with Liszt and he was evidently able to convince her that his trip to Paris made sense.

Liszt arrived back in the capital on 13 May 1836. Five days later he appeared before a select audience in the Salons Érard. Both then and at a further concert on 28 May he played mainly the works that he had written in Geneva and that he now wanted the world to know about. Earlier writers claimed that he also played Beethoven's 'Hammerklavier' Sonata op. 106 in an attempt to put his rival in his place, but this is merely a tenacious legend with no discernible truth to it.[14] Even so, Liszt was able to celebrate a veritable comeback: his recitals were greeted with enthusiasm, and his latest works impressed their listeners. As a virtuoso he was again in vogue. But his showdown with Thalberg was still to come.

The Duel

Liszt had successfully marked out the terrain, and yet his financial problems remained obstinately unresolved. His concerts in Lyons had netted between 500 and 600 francs each, whereas Thalberg is said to have received around 10,000 francs for a single appearance at the Théâtre Italien. This inequality gnawed at Liszt's self-esteem. He contemplated concerts in England and the Netherlands and a visit to Leipzig, a city famous for its musical life. All told, he planned to be away for six months and to spend the rest of the year living a life of seclusion with Marie. In the event his plans came to nothing, not least out of regard for Marie, who was unenthusiastic about a lengthy concert tour. But it was clear that there was no future for the couple in Geneva: the town was too small, its musical life too provincial, and its upper classes incapable of satisfying Liszt's need for adulation. They decided to return to Paris for a while. Liszt hoped to build on the success of his concerts in the spring, and Marie, too, harboured certain hopes: she reckoned that if society were willing to take her back after more than a year, she would be socially rehabilitated. Before they returned to Paris in the middle of October 1836, Liszt gave a series of concerts in Lausanne and Dijon, then the couple spent the month of September in Chamonix in the company of George Sand, to whom they had in the meantime drawn much closer. A walking tour of the Swiss mountains rounded off their late summer vacation.

In Paris Liszt and the countess lived at the Hôtel de France, where they were soon joined by George Sand. For a time Marie even shared a salon with her. Among the composers who graced their salon were Rossini, Meyerbeer, Berlioz and Chopin, while writers included Balzac and Victor Hugo. Together with George Sand, the couple attended the opera and frequented the city's other salons. Their companionable existence ended only when George Sand returned to Nohant in early January 1827. Here, in the *département* of Indre, she owned a late seventeenth-century country house that she had inherited from her grandmother. A month later she was followed by Marie, who spent four weeks there before returning to Paris in the middle of March.

At the beginning of 1837 Liszt made an error of judgement that was to have far-reaching consequences. On 8 January an article appeared in the *Revue et Gazette Musicale* that he was said to have written. On a superficial level it discussed Thalberg's *Grande fantaisie* op. 22 but it was in fact a malicious attack on Liszt's rival. Although Paris was one of the leading centres of music in Europe, the writer argued, this did not allow one to draw conclusions about the critical faculties of the French. The gallantries of the French language and the French propensity for charlatanism and hot air meant that certain artistic achievements were depicted in a wholly false light. As evidence of this crude theory, the author held up the figure of Thalberg. The local newspapers, he went on, had treated Thalberg's Paris debut as if it were an important event, whereas it was in reality nothing of the kind. Thalberg's compositions were humbug and not capable of satisfying an audience's need for entertainment. The anonymous writer did not even shy away from personal insults, referring to Thalberg – pianist to the Austrian court – in the same breath as the court jesters of a bygone age. All in all, the article was in the worst possible taste, and badly written to boot. Anyone reading between the lines would have had no difficulty in detecting immoderate envy coupled with wounded pride.

The reviewers of the other music journals recognized this. 'If only someone other than Herr Liszt had said this!' complained the *Allgemeine musikalische Zeitung*, hitting the nail on the head, for Liszt was criticizing the very thing to which he owed his own success. The hypocritical nature of his argument was plain for all to see. He poured scorn on the *savoir-vivre* of the French even though he himself was a product of that whole attitude. He expressed himself in dubious commonplaces about the French language, and yet this was his language of choice. He took exception to the hyperbole surrounding Thalberg, while himself remaining unsurpassed in the art of manipulating such techniques. 'I should have preferred it if – for his own sake – Herr L. had said nothing,' the critic concluded.[15] Liszt had made himself look foolish.

Readers could not know that the article in the *Revue et Gazette musicale* had in fact been written jointly by Liszt and Marie d'Agoult – in a letter to her, he speaks specifically of 'our article'.[16] This circumstance places a rather different gloss on Liszt's reasons for wanting to get even with his rival, for quite apart from his understandable envy of Thalberg, he was evidently trying to prove himself in the eyes of his lover: in short, he was anxious to please her. Marie, as we know, had no time for the mere display of his virtuosity but wanted him to champion what she regarded as serious artistic objectives, rather than performing superficial operatic paraphrases in the city's salons. Her vicious attack on Thalberg was an example of her projecting on to the latter her feelings about her own lover. At the time, Liszt himself was presumably unaware of the fact that he was doing himself no favours with this article.

Thalberg returned to Paris in the spring of 1837, and within weeks he and Liszt were limbering up for a confrontation. Liszt took part in four *séances musicales*, while Thalberg appeared once again in the Salons Zimmermann, where Liszt finally had a chance to hear him. There were also plans for a major concert at the Conservatoire, but problems arose over the date, clearly leaving Liszt very angry: 'People are saying that Thalberg's concert has been postponed. My God, how stupid! This imbecile is really starting to annoy me. But his game will soon be up!'[17] Thalberg finally performed on 12 March, and a week later Liszt responded with a brief appearance at an opera performance conducted by Berlioz, who made time during the interval for his friend's recital. There followed other performances by both pianists. Liszt is even said to have offered to appear together with Thalberg, performing duets on two pianos, an offer that Thalberg allegedly turned down with a complacent sideswipe: 'I'm not keen on being accompanied.'

The showdown finally came on 31 March at a benefit concert held in the salon of Princess Cristina Belgiojoso and featuring other artists besides Thalberg and Liszt, who remained, however, the main draw. The two pianists were the talk of the town, and so tickets were at a premium, changing hands for forty francs each. The two rivals launched their respective bids with operatic paraphrases – Liszt played his *Divertimento sur une cavatine de Pacini*, a bravura display piece based on a melody from Pacini's opera *Niobe*, while Thalberg chose his own *Fantaisie sur des thèmes de l'opéra Moïse de Rossini* op. 33. In the event, the contest – inevitably – remained indecisive: the performers were equally acclaimed, and the press reported a stalemate, their accounts differing only on points of minor detail. Princess Belgiojoso declared both men winners, and the contest was said to be over. It was as simple as that.

From then on Liszt refrained from attacking his rival in public, although for a long time afterwards he remained piqued at the outcome. 'We're on the best of terms with Thalberg,' he lied, after meeting the latter in Vienna in the spring of 1838. 'He said to me yesterday, naïvely and good-naturedly, "In comparison to you I've only ever enjoyed the occasional *succès d'estime* in Vienna." What a delightful thing to say! And so true!'[18]

Bella Italia?

Liszt gave his final recital of the season in the Salons Érard on 9 April 1837, then, in early May, he and Marie travelled to Nohant, where they spent the next three months with George Sand, who had acquired a grand piano for the duration. It was during this period that Liszt prepared piano transcriptions of Beethoven's Fifth, Sixth and Seventh Symphonies and of a number of Schubert's songs. Among other visitors were friends and acquaintances such as the writer and journalist Charles Didier and George Sand's current lover, Michel de Bourges:

> We spent the night on the terrace, sitting round a table at which we were all preoccupied according to our tastes and abilities. In the silence of nature, the sound of our disjointed conversations, the concentrated light of our lamps, the bluish reflections of the spirit lamp on George's scarlet dress created a fantastical scene in which the witches of Macbeth or the Blocksberg would not have been out of place.[19]

The couple left Nohant at the end of July and travelled via Lyons and Geneva to Italy. In Étrembières, a village just outside Geneva, they were reunited with Blandine, who was still living with Pastor Antoine Demellayer: 'I found her very beautiful. The wondrous development of her forehead, and her serious and intelligent air suggest a child very much out of the ordinary,' Marie noted in her diary. 'She is both quick to show anger and sensitive. While I was there, she pinched her wet nurse, but in the very next instant, and in a spontaneous expression of her feelings, she embraced her with touching concern.'[20] Although Marie was again pregnant, she does not mention this fact in her diary. After her flying visit, she left the child with the seventy-two-year-old pastor, and the couple continued their journey.

It was the middle of August by the time they reached Lake Como. 'A long road lined with plane trees, acacias, linden trees and chestnut trees leads to Como,' Marie wrote in her diary. 'The lake is incredibly beautiful.' They spent the following weeks exploring the whole of the lake's southern and eastern shores. 'It is framed by mountains which, coming closer and retreating again, form a series of little lakes of infinitely varied aspect.' In Blevio they visited the sixteenth-century Villa Pliniana and in Bellagio the gardens of the Villa Melzi. But they also undertook longer excursions to Milan, some thirty miles to the south, where they were handsomely entertained by Tito and Giovanni Ricordi, who ran the famous publishing house: 'Carriage, box at the opera and country house were all placed at the disposal of the Paganini of the pianoforte.'[21]

The couple finally found a secluded property at Bellagio and settled there in early September. 'What is there in the world apart from work, contemplation and love?'[22] Liszt generally spent the afternoons at the piano, composing or arranging other composers' works, while Marie kept her diary up to date or read, including a book on architecture. 'I am living in the most beautiful country on earth,' Liszt told his mother. 'I am the happiest man alive.'[23] He regularly wrote to her, asking her to run errands for him and Marie. On one occasion she was to buy several dozen gloves in various colours and several pairs of shoes in black English leather and send them to Italy. The financial worries that had plagued him only a few months earlier had evidently been resolved. 'It is a great luxury to have 100,000 francs in your desk and not know what to do with them!'[24]

At this date Liszt was also providing for other members of his family, including Eduard Liszt, the stepbrother of Liszt's father and, therefore, his uncle. The fact that the nephew was five and a half years older than his uncle was evidently felt by both parties to be so odd that they treated each other as cousins. In later years the men became close, Eduard acting as Liszt's confidant, but in the 1830s Liszt preferred to avoid his kinsfolk. 'Try to persuade people to write as few letters as possible, especially to *me*,' Liszt begged his mother. 'I'm sick to death of letters.' But apart from requests like these, Liszt rarely wrote to his mother, understandably causing her annoyance. 'Your reproaches have struck home,' he apologized half-heartedly.

> From now on you'll hear from me frequently and directly. I don't know why I imagined that it was enough for you to learn from my friends that I am contented and in good health. Your advice for saving money is excellent, even if all too familiar.[25]

Liszt celebrated his twenty-sixth birthday on 22 October. 'At 9 in the morning we set off into the mountains,' Marie noted in her diary. 'Mounted on a "sommarello", the term of affection used hereabouts for a donkey, I made my way across gently rolling expanses covered in chestnut and scattered olive trees.'[26] Such an expedition into the mountains must have been fairly tiring for the thirty-one-year-old countess, not least because she was seven months pregnant. As the date of her confinement drew closer, the couple moved from Bellagio to Como, and it was here, on 24 December 1837, at the Albergo dell'Angelo, that their second daughter, Gaetana Cosima, first saw the light of the world. As had been the case two years previously, the documents relating to the birth were discreetly edited: although Liszt was named as the child's father, the mother was recorded as an imaginary Caterina de Flavigny. The child was baptized two days later in Como Cathedral. Marie d'Agoult did not attend the ceremony as she was still recovering from what had been a difficult birth.

By the end of January 1838 she was feeling sufficiently well to join Liszt in Milan, where they spent some weeks before finally settling in Venice, Cosima having been handed over to a wet nurse. Liszt immediately fell in love with La Serenissima, whereas Marie felt only disgust and loathing. The sense of harmony and happiness that had marked her stay on Lake Como had vanished. 'I have made the acquaintance of the Countess Polcastro,' she complained shortly after her arrival in the city. 'She's ugly and seems not to have the wit that normally comes with ugliness.' She hated everything about Venice: sometimes it was the local shops that allegedly had only 'cast-offs from Paris', while at other times it was the bookshops that excited her contempt for stocking only books 'good for chambermaids'. 'I asked Countess Polcastro if she has any books, but she hasn't.'[27] And so it went on. She complained incessantly: nothing was to her liking. 'During the night a bunch of flowers that had been left on a table made me ill.' She grew depressed.

> I sometimes think that I'm going mad. My mind is weary. I have wept too much. [. . .] My heart and mind are desiccated. It is an ill that I brought into the world with me. Passion raised me aloft for a moment, but I sense that I am lacking the life principle.[28]

She was once again feeling splenetic.

Marie was increasingly dissatisfied with her life at Liszt's side. She felt that she was being badly treated, minor arguments escalated, and time and again there were emotional scenes that concealed a conflict of roles: Marie regarded herself as Liszt's muse but was eventually forced to admit that that was precisely what she was not. 'You are not the woman I need,' he had once told her. 'You are the woman I desire.'[29] The relationship had reached an impasse – and Liszt again sought refuge in flight.

Decision Time in Vienna

'One day, ignoring his usual practice, Liszt came storming into my room, waving a German newspaper. He had just been reading a report on terrible flooding on the Danube; there was no end to the hardship that it had caused.' The natural disaster had struck Hungary in March 1838, when dams had been breached and entire towns had disappeared beneath the brown floodwaters. Tens of thousands were homeless, and more than 150 had died. In the Franzenstadt district of Pest only nineteen out of a total of over 500 buildings had withstood the onslaught. The rest had collapsed or had to be torn down. A native of Hungary, Liszt was suddenly seized by a sense of patriotism that he had never felt before: his immediate thought was to travel to Vienna and raise money for the flood victims with a series of benefit concerts. 'It will take eight days at most. What do you think?' he asked Marie. ' "It's a generous notion," I answered, but to myself I was thinking: "Others could help these people, but who will come to my aid when I am alone and sick?" '[30]

Liszt left Venice on 7 April, and it was not eight days but eight weeks before he saw Marie again. Vienna was a good choice as a city in which to launch his relief action, for it was the capital of the kingdom of Austria and, as such, the seat of government. Above all, it was home to an art-loving aristocracy and a plentiful source of financial assistance for the suffering citizens of the multiracial empire. For Liszt, it was also the city in which he had studied with Czerny and Salieri and the scene of his early triumphs. Fifteen years earlier he had still been a child prodigy when he had left what for him was a mythical place, and now he was returning as a European celebrity. It was a comeback in the most literal sense.

As chance would have it, Liszt was staying at the same hotel as the pianist Friedrich Wieck and his eighteen-year-old daughter Clara – later Frau Schumann. It is clear from her diary what a tremendous stir Liszt's arrival caused in the city. 'We've heard Liszt,' Clara noted, following a private concert in the workshops of the famous piano maker Conrad Graf. 'You can't compare him to any other player – he stands alone. He inspires terror and amazement but he's a most delightful person. His appearance at the piano is incredible – he's an original – he's completely subsumed by the instrument.' In Weber's *Concertstück* Liszt broke three strings but was not in the least inconvenienced – 'he must be used to it'. Time and again the strings would break when Liszt was playing, a problem bound up with the weak construction of many of the instruments at this period. In spite of this, Liszt could count on creating a great impression each time he destroyed an instrument in this way: it was all part of the myth that was Liszt. At his first official concert on 18 April there were no fewer than three grand pianos on the stage. 'All three were pummelled to pieces. But it was inspired – the applause was incredible – the artist quite at his ease and most affable – everything he played was new and unheard – but only pieces by Liszt.'[31]

From every point of view, Liszt's weeks in Vienna were a triumph. He appeared at the Musikverein, played for the Austrian court and at the Redoutensaal and dazzled his audiences in the city's salons. He met Czerny, Prince Metternich and numerous representatives of the court, including the Archduchess Sophie. In addition to his charity concerts, he also gave seven recitals whose takings he was able to pocket himself. In total he earned some 20,000 francs. The city went wild with excitement, and the erstwhile prodigy was welcomed back like a pop star. 'Just two words,' he wrote to Marie, ecstatic with enthusiasm, following his first recital. 'Tremendous success. Cheering. Between fifteen and eighteen curtain calls. Full hall. Universal delight.'[32] A few days later Marie received an update: 'I'm now the height of fashion. Within 24 hours 50 copies of my portrait have been sold. I hope you won't insult me by thinking that this has left the least impression on me.'[33]

But Marie was in no mood for joking, and in an autobiographical fragment she later reproached Liszt in no uncertain terms: while he was leading the life of Riley in Vienna, she had fallen ill and for a time had been close to death. An acquaintance who was looking after her had summoned Liszt back to Venice, but he had refused to come. It is difficult to know how much truth there is to these accusations. Nor do we know the nature of Marie's illness and if it was really life-threatening or if the whole episode was an elaborate and overdramatic hoax. Whatever the reality, Marie was convinced that Liszt 'was abandoning me for the most trivial reasons. It wasn't for any great enterprise or out of devotion or for reasons of patriotism but was simply for a few salon successes, for fame in the newspapers and for invitations from princesses.' In Vienna women had thrown themselves at him and he had been unfaithful to Marie:

> He was no longer embarrassed at his own failings. He explained them away as a philosopher might. He spoke of necessity and on every point was determined to place me in the wrong; he was elegant in his dress, he spoke only of princes, he was secretly in love with his life as a Don Juan. One day I said something very wounding to him and called him a 'Don Juan parvenu'. I summoned up all my pride as a woman, as a grande dame and as a republican in order to judge him from a position of superiority.[34]

Marie did not believe Liszt but dismissed his charity work as a self-serving waste of time. Instead of collecting money for flood victims, she expected him to remain with her in Venice and then she would not have fallen ill. It was not only jealousy that she was expressing here but, as her autobiographical note makes clear, a profound ignorance of Liszt's true character. She reproached him for his elegant clothes and for his love of social ostentation, incapable, as she was, of understanding that such peacock-like vanity was an integral part of his personality.

In Vienna Liszt was seized by the desire to travel, and to that extent his visit to the city proved a turning point in his career. Among the plans that he formed at this time was the idea of touring for eighteen months in order to raise the capital needed to settle with Marie in Italy. In the event, of course, things worked out rather differently, for his relationship was already starting to unravel. The long and painful ending had begun.

On the Run

The couple spent most of the second half of 1838 on the road, although not necessarily together. Among the places they visited were Genoa, Milan, Como, Lugano, Florence, Padua, Bologna, Ferrara and Ravenna. The month of August found them both in Ravenna. 'Utter solitude,' Marie noted in her diary. 'The lake is sad. The town is a filthy hole.'[35] At this point the couple's third child, Daniel, was conceived. In September they again went their separate ways, and while Liszt travelled on to Milan, Marie returned to Como on her own. One has the impression of two people on the run from one another.

In early January 1839 Marie and Blandine met again in Milan: 'I feel that I shall be tremendously fond of this child, [. . .] and that my life is changing and improving. I don't know if this feeling will last, but when I think of her I feel a great inner peace.' But within two days she was taking back what she had written:

> I've already broken my promise and caused him [Liszt] pain: I've wounded him. His travel plans, the idea of my settling in Florence have made me very sad. I was ill. I reproached him for the unfeeling way in which he spoke of our separation.[36]

The couple moved to Rome, where their son Daniel was born on 9 May 1839. He too was entrusted to the care of a wet nurse, and it was not until the winter of 1841/2 that his parents saw him again. Their flight continued. During the months that followed the birth of their son, the couple remained in Italy, leading a life of inconstancy. Liszt gave concerts in Rome and Florence, and together the couple visited Lucca, San Rossore and Pisa. By mid-October they were back in Florence, where they again went their separate ways. After spending a few more days in

Italy, Liszt set off for a further round of concerts in Vienna, while Marie returned to Paris with her two daughters. 'How could I abandon this dear land of Italy without bidding you a final farewell?' she wrote to Liszt from Genoa, where she had broken her journey. 'How could I stand by and not express a sense of regret as two such beautiful and eventful years fade out of my life?'

Marie's two daughters provided her with consolation for her separation from Liszt. It was the first time in months that she had been able to spend any time with them. Blandine ('Mouche') looked liked Marie, whereas Cosima had her father's features, especially his strikingly large nose. Although Cosima was said 'to resemble the enchanting Mouche, feature for feature,' Marie assured Liszt, 'she is far less beautiful and above all less distinguished. Their *education* is the same. The wet nurse says that I must *immediately* give her *everything* she asks for or she will die! I shall try to teach her to live differently.'[37]

The previous day Liszt had celebrated his twenty-eighth birthday.

LIVING LIKE A LORD
(1839–47)

Preconditions

THE YEARS BETWEEN 1839 and 1847 are generally described as Liszt's 'virtuoso years'. Older biographers referred to this period as his *Glanzzeit*, a time of unprecedented brilliance, though Liszt spoke rather more prosaically of 'living like a lord'. This was the period in his life when he was almost permanently on the road, undertaking major recital tours. Even by the standards of today's jet-setting artists, his achievements border on the incredible, for in only eight years he gave more than one thousand concerts, an average of 125 a year or one concert every third day. This involved vast distances, from Lisbon to Moscow and from Glasgow to Naples. He undertook countless tours of France and Germany, travelled the length and breadth of Great Britain and Ireland and visited Madrid, Gibraltar, Riga, Königsberg (modern Kaliningrad), Copenhagen, Odessa, Bucharest and Hermannstadt (modern Sibiu), to name only some of the more far-flung ports of call. Crowned heads received him and paid court to him – he played before kings, princes and counts, including the queen of England, the sultan of Constantinople and the tsar of Russia.

Liszt not only revolutionized piano playing, he also simplified the way in which a concert programme was presented. Until then a pianist had mostly had to share a platform with other artists and accompany singers and other instrumentalists, whereas Liszt performed alone and may be said to have invented the piano recital. The piano had previously been positioned lengthways to the audience, but Liszt placed it in the position familiar to us today, at an angle to the auditorium. This position, as well as being preferable from an acoustic point of view, also had the advantage that the performer was no longer lost behind the instrument. Now that Liszt was completely visible, the audience could focus on his profile, his facial expressions, his gestures and his body language. In short, he was the first modern concert pianist. As he himself put it: 'Le concert c'est moi.'[1]

This enormous workload in terms of travel and concert-giving could be mastered only by dint of an impressive degree of organization. The railways were still in their infancy, and so Liszt was largely dependent on the stagecoach as a means of land transport. In February 1840 he spent 2,000 francs on his own carriage, an investment that quickly paid for itself as he was no longer dependent on company timetables and standard routes. Travel became far more comfortable, although he still had to cover thousands of miles and must have spent many months of his life in his coach. In 1841 Liszt also engaged a private secretary who accompanied him on his long journeys. Gaëtano Belloni assumed the role of a tour manager, negotiating contracts, dealing with travel arrangements, including all written communications, keeping an eye on the concert receipts and over the years becoming a close friend to whom his employer could also confide troublesome family matters.

Liszt enjoyed playing the part of a snob when he arrived at a concert venue with his secretary in a private carriage. Belloni would open the carriage door and Liszt would alight with an air of seigneurial grandeur. It was 'indispensable' if he was to make any impression, he assured Marie d'Agoult.[2] Here we see an aspect of his character that was generally denied by his earliest biographers, who were keen that Liszt should appear as a model of spotless brilliance. But such vanity and a tendency to give himself airs and graces were undoubtedly parts of his personality. He was a brilliant pianist, but one with a love of ostentation. For him, it was never just about the music but also involved an element of showmanship. He offered his audiences a great spectacle that revolved around a single actor: himself.

Meanwhile, Marie had settled in Paris with her daughters, Blandine and Cosima. In December 1839 she rented a spacious apartment in the rue Neuve-des-Mathurins. 'I had no fixed plans when I returned to Paris,' she later recalled. During her early months in the city she often felt alone. Old friends had turned their backs on her many years earlier, and relations with her family remained strained.

> I did not know what to do. To be honest, I had no idea how my life would turn out. The desire to make up for the harm I had inflicted on others and to the best of my abilities assuage the suffering that I had caused was very powerful.

She wanted to take control of her life, not least because she clearly could not count on Liszt's imminent return to the domestic fold.

> I was appalled at the whirlwind of the artist's life into which Liszt had allowed himself to be drawn in what for me was the most incomprehensible and unexpected way, and I felt with painful clarity that to follow him was neither possible nor permissible.[3]

This already sounds like a formal separation, even if the definitive breach was not to come until May 1844.

In deciding to leave Charles d'Agoult in order to follow Liszt, Marie had set the cat among the aristocratic pigeons, and so caution was of the essence if she was to renew contact with her family. Above all, she would have to take account of the aristocratic customs and sensitivities of the Flavignys, a rapprochement made more difficult by the presence of her three children by Liszt. Her mother, Madame de Flavigny, was not only not at all proud of her grandchildren, but wanted nothing to do with them. In her eyes, Blandine, Cosima and Daniel were simply bastards. 'Don't mention Blandine in my mother's presence,' Marie begged the writer Georg Herwegh. 'Her obstinate silence is a perpetual protest against the very existence of these children, and she gets terribly worked up whenever they are mentioned.'[4] It was clear that her attempts at reconciliation with her family and a new start in Paris would succeed only without her offspring. Legally speaking, they had only a father – on their birth certificates they had all been given imaginary mothers – and so Marie had in any case no right to call them her own.

But what was to become of the children? For a time Liszt toyed with the idea of settling in Paris with his mother and the three children, but soon abandoned the notion as his foreign tours would keep him away from the city for most of the time. The situation was complicated, but it may be summed up very simply: neither father nor mother was able or entitled to take the children. And so Liszt decided that Blandine and Cosima would move in with his mother, while Daniel would remain with his wet nurse in Rome. Marie was far from happy with this solution: 'Tomorrow they [the children] will sleep with your mother,' she wrote to Liszt in the middle of November 1839. 'Mouche is delighted, whereas I am extremely saddened.'[5] Liszt remained steadfast: 'As I have already said, I am entirely of the opinion that the two Mouches should be brought up by my mother. On this point there can be no hesitation.'[6] Marie gritted her teeth and agreed, albeit while pouring out her venom in her letters to Liszt and making often spiteful remarks about his mother, whom she described as common and uneducated. As a *femme du monde*, Marie found it beneath her dignity to deal with a woman like Anna Liszt. It was, she went on, an absurd *idée fixe* on Liszt's part that 'two women like us should have to live together'.[7] This was unjust, for although Anna Liszt may not have enjoyed the exquisite education lavished on the countess, she was generous and kind-hearted to a fault. She loved her grandchildren, and it was she who for the first time in their lives gave them anything approaching a mother's love and who was able to offer them a proper home, first in the rue Pigalle and later the rue Louis-le-Grand. The years between 1839 and the end of 1850, when the two girls were taken from their grandmother, were arguably the happiest of their childhood. While it is true that Liszt really had no idea what to do with his dependants, it is no less true that he alone was responsible for their education and support: Marie d'Agoult maintained an aristocratic reserve on this point.

This, then, was the situation by the winter of 1839/40: Marie was trying to find her way back into Paris society, the girls were living with

Anna Liszt against Marie's wishes, and Liszt himself was on the point of conquering Europe.

Sabre Dance

In October 1839 Liszt left Marie d'Agoult in Paris, returning via Venice and Trieste to Vienna, where he arrived on 15 November. Over the course of the next four weeks, he gave six major concerts and took part in several smaller events. Even the first of his concerts was attended by members of the imperial court, including Archduchess Sophie. But within days of his arrival in the city, Liszt fell ill and for a week he took to his bed. His recovery was slow, in part because of a constant stream of visitors: 'However firmly I close my door and leave a large note signed by my doctor at the foot of the stairs,' he complained, 'it makes no difference – my room is always packed, it's insufferable.'[8] But Liszt himself refused to take things easy, and when the conductor Heinrich Eduard von Lannoy asked him at short notice to take part in a concert in the Redoutensaal, Liszt spontaneously agreed. On the programme was Beethoven's Third Piano Concerto, a piece he had never played before. But in spite of the fact that he was ill, he learnt the work in twenty-four hours and performed it 'with the most unprecedented success.'[9] Few could compete with Liszt in such matters.

While in Vienna, Liszt received an invitation to return to his native Hungary. The invitation, which was extended by a group of Hungarian dignitaries, had a number of different aims. In part, it was to thank Liszt for his charitable work on behalf of the Hungarian flood victims, but there was also a political dimension to it. Hungary had been a part of Austria for over 150 years, and Vienna had repeatedly ridden roughshod over Hungarian national sentiment, sidelining the Magyar language and suppressing Hungary's sense of a cultural identity. Liszt's international triumphs awoke a feeling of national pride in Hungarians, and sixteen years after he had left the country, his return amounted to a political demonstration. 'In Pressburg and Pest acts of sheer madness are expected,' he told Marie.[10] He was to be proved right.

His first concert in Pressburg (modern Bratislava) took place on 19 December and for the audience was tantamount to a demonstration of national pride. 'My concert has just finished,' Liszt wrote to Marie. 'Enthusiasm impossible to describe.'[11] He played his own *Divertimento sur une cavatine de Pacini*, two transcriptions of Schubert songs and his *Grand galop chromatique* of 1838, an insanely difficult piece in which the hands never stop scurrying over the keyboard. After every piece the audience chanted 'Éljen! Éljen!' – 'A long life to you!' The next day Liszt gave a benefit concert for the poor. Here, too, the enthusiasm knew no bounds, and when Liszt finally launched into his highly effective arrangement of the Rákóczy March, Hungary's unofficial national anthem, the mood became positively frenzied.

Liszt's next concert was in Pest and here, too, there were ecstatic scenes. He performed at the city's National Theatre on 4 January 1840 and had just finished his arrangement of the Rákóczy March when a group of high-ranking Hungarians wearing their country's national costume appeared onstage. After delivering a brief speech, one of their number, Count Leo Festetics, presented a visibly shaken Liszt with a jewel-encrusted sabre bearing the inscription: 'To the great artist Ferenc Liszt, for his artistic merit and for his patriotism, from his admiring compatriots.' Liszt was deeply moved and, addressing the audience in French (he did not speak Hungarian), he thanked his 'dear compatriots':

> This sabre, which has been so vigorously brandished in former times in our country's defence, is placed at this moment in weak and pacific hands. Is that not a symbol? [. . .] Does it not say, gentlemen, that men of intelligence and industry have also a noble task, a lofty mission to fulfil among you?

Liszt was evidently so overcome by his own patriotic outburst that at the end he struck an emphatically strident note:

> And if ever anyone dares unjustly, and with violence, disturb us in the accomplishment of this task, well! gentlemen, if it must be, let our swords be drawn again from the scabbard (they are not tarnished, and their strokes will still be terrible as in former times), and let our blood be shed to the last drop for freedom, king, and country![12]

Liszt's martial address soon made the rounds, and it was not long before it had reached Paris and the ears of contemporaries who, less sympathetic to the Hungarian cause, shook their heads in disbelief. Others thought that Liszt's sabre-rattling was merely another example of his eccentric attempts at self-promotion. But whatever the interpretation that is placed upon it, Liszt's action had disastrous consequences, for non-Hungarians laughed at him and produced all manner of malicious caricatures centred on him and his ominous sword. The newspaper *Le Miroir Drolatique*, for example, joked about the 'Chevalier Liszt' in a lampoon of venomous virulence:

Entre tous les guerriers, Litz [*sic*] est seul sans reproche,
Car malgré son grand sabre, on sait que ce héros
N'a vaincu que des doubles croches
Et tué que des pianos.[13]

[Of all warriors Liszt alone is blameless, for in spite of his sabre we know that this hero has vanquished only semiquavers and slain only pianos.]

But let us return to that memorable day in January 1840. Among the audience was the writer Franz von Schober, and it is to him that we owe a detailed account of what happened next:

When Liszt left the stage and came outside, the square was packed with thousands of people, and a mass of torches surrounded his carriage, their numbers constantly swelling to the point where they could no longer be counted. At the same time, the crowd itself increased in size, and one might have thought that the entire population of Pesth and Ofen [i.e. Buda] had assembled here, so tremendous was the throng that surged all over the large square and filled the adjoining streets. A few young people wanted to unharness the horses and pull the carriage themselves, but they were voted down. [. . .] The procession now moved off. It was so long, and the shouts of 'éljen' and 'long live Liszt' so tempestuous and uninterrupted that

two full-size military bands that were marching at the front and back
of the procession and playing Janissary music were simply unable to
hear each other.[14]

Liszt himself summed up the scene in a letter to Marie d'Agoult: 'It was
the kind of victory parade known only to Lafayette and to some of the
men who fought in the French Revolution.'[15]

Liszt returned to Vienna in early February 1840 and gave a further
series of acclaimed recitals. He also took the opportunity to visit his
birthplace at Raiding, where he was received like some feudal lord. 'The
entire population (around a thousand people) had turned out,' Liszt told
Marie. 'The children – boys and girls – knelt down as I walked past
them, and it was all I could do to persuade them to get to their feet.
Some of the farmers came over to kiss my hand, but most of them maintained a respectful distance.'[16]

Liszt had been used to applause from his earliest childhood. He knew
what it was like to be the centre of attention and to be worshipped and
acclaimed. But what he experienced in Hungary was on an altogether
different scale. Here simple enthusiasm was transformed into a cult with
an element of quasi-religious ecstasy. We may assume that it was not
always easy for him to deal with his popularity, and it is no wonder that
he sent Marie such detailed accounts of his journey. In doing so, he was
not so much boasting as questioning the whole point of his actions. 'I'm
completely exhausted with my outer life, which literally does not leave
me with a quarter of an hour of free time,' he wrote from Vienna in the
middle of February 1840.[17]

Meanwhile Marie was establishing herself as a *salonnière* whose apartment in the rue Neuve-des-Mathurins was frequented by writers of the
eminence of Victor Hugo, Eugène Sue, Alphonse de Lamartine, Charles-
Augustin de Sainte-Beuve and Georg Herwegh. Among other frequent
visitors was the English diplomat and writer Henry Lytton Earle Bulwer,
Baron Dalling and Bulwer, whose amorous attentions were by no means
unwelcome to Marie. Liszt, too, was not above flirting at this time. 'I must
tell you about a kind of passion to which I succumbed for forty-eight hours,'
he wrote to Marie in February. 'Don't be jealous. It's the woman [...] in

Ödenburg [modern Sopron] – *very beautiful* and [...] *the only one for whom I've felt any real attraction* for three months.'[18] Unfortunately, a corner has been cut from the letter, removing any incriminating evidence that would allow us to identify the woman in question.

The couple had evidently agreed that neither would raise any objections if the other engaged in the occasional affair – today we would speak of an open relationship – but there is something odd about the way in which Marie asked Liszt for his advice on such matters. She admitted that several men were hopelessly in love with her. Count Bernard Potocki had even offered to marry her, but she was unsure whether to accept, for there was also Henry Bulwer. As Marie explained, 'Yesterday evening Monsieur Bulwer. Again Monsieur Bulwer! Always Monsieur Bulwer. He seems to find me very amusing.'[19] On one occasion she even asked Liszt for 'une petite permission d'infidélité'. Liszt was unmoved:

You're asking me for my permission to be unfaithful? My dear Marie, you haven't mentioned a name, but I assume it's Bulwer. But it really doesn't matter. [...] I want you to retain your freedom, and I like it that it is so, for I'm convinced that you will always use that freedom nobly and discreetly, at least until the day when you tell me that this or that man has felt more energetically and understood more intimately than you what I *am* and what I can *be* – until that day there will be no infidelity, and nothing, *absolutely nothing* will change between us![20]

Elsewhere there was a note of bittersweet mockery to his words: 'Unless you're completely deluded about him [i.e. Bulwer], he seems almost worthy of your affection.'[21]

Were Liszt and Marie merely playing a whimsical game with each other? Or did she want to make him jealous? Shortly afterwards she turned the knife in the wound: 'Yesterday Bulwer asked me in all seriousness if he could adopt the little one [i.e. Blandine],' she wrote at the end of February 1840.[22] The idea was clearly absurd, and Liszt wasted no time in dismissing it, but Marie persisted. She was convinced, she explained, that Bulwer 'loves me with all the selflessness that is possible'.[23] Elsewhere she described the other men who were visiting her in her salon: 'All these men are more or less in love with me. [. . .] Will that grieve you very much?'[24]

Marie's flirtations with Bulwer, Potocki and others like them were essentially a cry for help, a desperate attempt to draw attention to her own unfortunate situation. For, as she openly conceded, she was in a state of turmoil:

> This long absence will have been good for me by making me clearly aware of my needs, of my tastes and of the way of life best suited to me and, as a result, of the reasons – hitherto only dimly suspected – for a certain unease and a certain constraint that has sometimes oppressed me in our lives together and above all in our lives *when accompanied by others*. We shall discuss all this and much else besides, for your arrival will be a time of crisis [. . .] for me *probably* and for you.[25]

This sounded worrying. Two more months were to pass before Liszt and Marie were to meet again, a period that he spent giving concerts in Leipzig and Dresden. In Leipzig he met Mendelssohn and – for the first time – Schumann, who the previous year had dedicated to him his great Fantasy in C major op. 17. The two men spent a good deal of time together, playing the piano and evidently allowing their friendship to deepen, so that it was not long before Liszt felt that he had known his colleague for a good twenty years. Schumann, his elder by a year, was initially rather more distant: 'Schumann is extraordinarily reserved,' Liszt wrote to Marie. 'He scarcely ever speaks, except occasionally with me, but I think he will become very attached to me.'[26]

There were good reasons for Schumann's shyness, for Liszt carried on in Leipzig as if he were the cock of the walk. Schumann wrote to his fiancée, Clara Wieck,

> Liszt arrived here with his head quite turned by the aristocracy and did nothing but complain of the absence of fine dresses and of

countesses and princesses, until I was so vexed that I told him that we too have our aristocracy, namely, 150 bookshops, 50 printing works and 30 newspapers, so he'd better behave himself.[27]

Liszt laughed at Leipzig's aristocracy of the mind: the printing houses were of no interest to him. Instead, he succeeded in the shortest possible time in transforming the social life of the city into a dizzying whirl, leaving Schumann aghast at his capers: 'Throughout the whole of the last few days', he wrote to Clara,

> there have been nothing but dinners and suppers, music and champagne, counts and beautiful women: in short, he has turned all our lives upside down. We are all wildly in love with him, and yesterday he again played like a god at his concert – the furore was indescribable.[28]

But however enthusiastic Liszt's audiences may have been, the papers were not: clearly they were taking revenge for the fact that Liszt had treated the Leipzig establishment with such a degree of condescension. 'Perhaps this made him think of what I had said about our aristocracy,' Schumann sneered, 'for he has never been so amiable as during the last two days, since he was hauled over the coals.'[29] Business is business.

When Liszt arrived back in Paris in early April, six months had passed since he had last seen Marie d'Agoult. If she hoped that she might now spend some time with her partner, she was to be disappointed, for Liszt had decided to conquer England.

Four Visits to Great Britain

Between May 1840 and May 1841 Liszt paid no fewer than four visits to the British Isles. Thirteen years earlier he had been acclaimed there as a child prodigy and had retained fond memories of the country, but much had changed in the meantime. Liszt arrived in London for the first of his visits on 6 May 1840 and within two days he had already given his first concert at the Hanover Square Rooms. The audience was enthusiastic, and Liszt was accorded an exceptionally friendly welcome by the English aristocracy, with the result that he was invited to numerous receptions and formal dinners held in his honour. Even Queen Victoria and her consort, Prince Albert, received him at Buckingham Palace, where he performed for them.

But then something completely unexpected happened – the press tore into his recitals with extraordinary savagery. The articles that appeared were in stark contrast to the hymns of praise that he normally received. This dismissal by the London press was a singular event in his life; nowhere else was he accorded such annihilating reviews. We can only speculate about the reasons, although it seems that the English journalists did not regard Liszt as a serious artist. His exuberant way of playing the piano and his tendency to self-promotion were no doubt felt by the press to be the result of charlatanry and of bombastic, empty showmanship. His effrontery in breaking with the tradition of mixed programmes and in announcing 'Recitals on the pianoforte' may have been a further reason for this reaction.

Liszt said nothing to Marie as he had no wish to upset her, not least because she had announced that she would be joining him in England. Back in Paris, hypocritically solicitous acquaintances had been all too eager to report on Liszt's alleged adventures in Vienna. He 'broke women's hearts', insinuated Honoré de Balzac, who for his part never missed an opportunity to indulge in an affair. Marie had had enough. By the time she arrived in London on 9 June, their relationship was at a low ebb, and it is hardly surprising that the four weeks the couple spent in the capital, before returning together to the continent, were underpinned by tension. While they were still in London, Liszt wrote to Marie, beginning by quoting a sentence from her letter to him of only a few hours earlier:

'There is nothing else I can do at this moment – and probably for ever – except live absolutely alone!'

That is what you had to tell me!

Six years of utter devotion have produced only this outcome.

And so it is with so much of what you say! Yesterday (to remind you of only a single occasion), on the whole way from Ascot to Richmond you didn't say a single word that wasn't wounding or insulting.[30]

Liszt left for his second tour of England in the middle of August. The impresario Louis Henry Lavenu had made him an offer that he felt unable to refuse: Liszt would be the star attraction of a motley group of artists that would tour the English provinces. The first such tour lasted from the middle of August until the end of September and concentrated on the south and west of England, while the second began on 24 November 1841 and ended on 29 January 1841, taking in the north of England, as well as Scotland and Ireland. In return Liszt was offered the sensationally high sum of 37,000 francs. He agreed. He needed the fee not only to support his three children and his mother but also because his elegant lifestyle was consuming vast sums of money. Liszt had in any case a poor grasp of finances: time and again he spent huge amounts on luxurious trifles while also donating generously to charitable causes. As soon as he had spent all he had – which in spite of his sizeable income was often the case – he would simply organize another round of concerts. From that point of view, Lavenu's offer seemed like a gift from heaven.

Liszt had to work hard for his fee, for Lavenu had put together a programme that demanded a lot from all involved. There was little respite between concerts, and no time at all to relax. 'Just imagine what my week looked like,' Liszt wrote to Marie in January 1841:

At 7 in the morning the day before yesterday we arrived in Edinburgh from Glasgow. Concert in the evening. Set off back to Glasgow at 11 o'clock yesterday morning (the journey normally takes 5 hours, but we took 6½). Concert in the evening. Returned from Glasgow today at 5. Concert shortly. Tomorrow morning we return to Glasgow: concert in the evening – and after a night spent in the coach, *Morning Concert* in Edinburgh on Saturday![31]

All in all, the musicians gave more than eighty concerts in the course of the two tours and covered around 3,500 miles. Moreover, the tours proved far less successful than hoped. Although a number of Liszt's concerts were well attended – in Dublin, for example, on 18 December 1840 he performed before an audience of around 1,200 – most drew no more than 200.

The tour was almost over when the bombshell exploded: Lavenu was bankrupt and the enterprise at an end. Liszt was initially reluctant to believe the report:

> The end of Lavenu's tour went fairly well – but with outgoings of more than 120,000 francs, it's impossible that he won't have made a loss. Moreover, his arrangements were not especially good, rather the opposite. But for my own part I've come out of it fairly well. Now I just have to pocket my money. But I believe him to be honest.[32]

In the event, the two tours of England turned out to be a financial disaster. Not only did Liszt fail to earn even a penny but he ended up making a huge loss. By his own reckoning he lost a total of 15,000 florins, or 43,000 francs,[33] a vast amount of money.

In spite of this, Liszt returned to England for a fourth time in early May 1841 – perhaps he needed to prove something to himself or to Marie d'Agoult. And yet even this two-month visit turned out to be a disappointment, at least from a financial standpoint. 'It's clear', he admitted to Marie,

> that I shall earn no money in London this season. This really is the strangest situation that one can imagine. I lack a theatre or a salon in which to appear on a regular basis. But no one is doing anything about it or, indeed, can do anything about it.[34]

In the light of all these experiences, Liszt had had enough of England for a considerable time to come, and another forty-five years were to pass before he returned to the British Isles in 1886, the year of his death.

Lisztomania

The small island of Nonnenwerth lies in the Rhine near Bad Honnef. A Benedictine monastery was founded there as early as 1126 but fell victim to secularization in 1802 and was finally abandoned nineteen years later, when it was converted into a guesthouse. Among its famous visitors were the writers Ernst Moritz Arndt, Ferdinand Freiligrath and James Fenimore Cooper. Liszt had discovered the place during one of his tours of the Rhineland and immediately fell in love with it. Here he and Marie d'Agoult spent the summer and autumn of 1841 and 1843. For a long time it was believed that they also returned here for the summer of 1842, but it is now clear that they spent this period in Paris.

In 1841 the couple remained on the island almost continuously from early August to early November, the main exceptions being the concerts that Liszt gave in nearby towns such as Bonn, Cologne, Koblenz, Wiesbaden and Mainz, during which time Marie was left on her own. 'Every day I look out of my window and see ten or twelve ships passing up and down the river,' she wrote to Charles-Augustin de Sainte-Beuve:

> Their smoke dies away in the branches of the larches and poplars; none of the ships ever stops; Nonnenwerth and the inhabitants of this island seem not to engage in trade with the rest of the world! Like everywhere that I enjoy visiting, I say to myself: I'll come back. But of course one never comes back, and one is right not to do so.[35]

Whenever Liszt returned to the island, there were often violent scenes between the couple; there was no longer any question of a harmonious coexistence. The marriage plans that they had repeatedly discussed only a few years earlier no longer played any part in their acrimonious altercations, nor did their idea of one day settling in Italy together. It was during this time that Marie wrote an unfinished autobiographical piece under the dramatic title of 'Nonnenwerth Suicide':

> I arrived in the month of August and installed myself there on my own. He then offered me his friendship, his devotion. I rejected them. Whether out of rashness or folly, I broke off this relationship. That day witnessed the start of a life whose ordeals and temptations and feelings of bitterness I cannot recall without a shudder.
>
> When people saw that I wasn't taking the veil, when they thought me happy and when they guessed my thoughts – 'outbursts of fury'.[36]

It is not entirely clear what the couple argued about, although Marie was evidently once again suffering from her 'spleen' – the violently fluctuating emotional states that she herself regarded as a congenital disease. She was certainly prone to depression. Nothing that people did was right, and Liszt suffered most of all in this regard. When she left Nonnenwerth for a few days in the middle of August, she wrote him a parting letter:

> My dear Franz, *madness* having again seized possession of my brain, I cannot take any more. I feel incapable of living in this state of perpetual agitation.
>
> You cannot understand this, and so let us cease our sad deliberations, and let me withdraw from these touching tokens of your affection, which spring up beneath your feet in such numbers. I am leaving for Paris. I shall make a better *friend* than I ever was a *lover*. I know very well that I have nothing for which to reproach you, but I also know . . . I know only that I am suffering and that I shall always make you suffer if I remain. Farewell then. As our excuse we can both tell people about a sick child, and the world will ask no further details.
>
> Farewell, Franz, this is not a *break* but an *adjournment*. In five or six years from now we shall both laugh at the torments that I am suffering today. Adieu.[37]

Although Marie later returned to Nonnenwerth, the couple were increasingly uncertain whether things could continue as they were.

At the beginning of November 1841 the countess returned to Paris, and Liszt set off for another tour of Germany. He arrived in Berlin just before Christmas and in the course of the next two months gave more than twenty concerts, all of them frenetically acclaimed. Even his very first concert at the Singakademie was attended by King Friedrich Wilhelm IV and an assortment of Prussian princes and princesses. Fellow musicians honouring Liszt with their presence included Mendelssohn, Spontini and Meyerbeer. 'Not since Paganini have I heard such a magisterial musician,' Karl August Varnhagen von Ense noted afterwards in his diary.

'He ended with a Chromatic Galop that finished me off: he had total control of my pulse, and his playing caused it to race so much that I grew quite faint.'[38]

The news of Liszt's sensational debut spread like wildfire, generating a momentum of its own that surprised even Liszt, accustomed though he was to success. 'While it is true that Berlin did not go mad,' recalled the physician Adalbert Cohnfeld,

> it certainly made itself look very foolish. Liszt was fêted, serenades were performed in his honour, a woman knelt before him and begged to be allowed to kiss his fingertips, while another embraced him in public at one of his recitals, and a third poured the dregs from his tea cup into her scent bottle. Hundreds of women wore gloves bearing his likeness. Many were robbed of their senses by him. Indeed, everyone wanted to lose their wits over him. An art dealer prepared glass-paste brooches bearing his likeness and sold them as items of jewellery, thousands sought to beg or borrow his favours and his money. [. . .] Folly celebrated its greatest ever triumph.[39]

Liszt was a superstar, a hero and an idol. This no longer had anything to do with piano music or with Bach, Beethoven, Chopin or Schubert. Central to it all was a social spectacle that the crème de la crème of Berlin society was determined not to miss. Such collective behaviour is familiar from experiments in mass psychology: in the anonymity of a large crowd such as a concert audience an infectious momentum builds up, inducing all those who are present to behave irrationally and even insanely. Certainly, much that happened in Berlin during these weeks can only be described as mad. There were women who forgot everything, including their family's good name and their refined upbringing, to be close to their god. One eyewitness recalled that 'on one occasion a woman snatched up a half-smoked cigar that Liszt had cast aside and in spite of repeatedly retching she continued to smoke it with feigned delight'.[40] Baronesses and countesses tore at each other's hair in trying to lay hands on a glass or handkerchief that Liszt had used. Incredible though it seems, all of this actually happened.

The writer and satirist Adolf Glaßbrenner devoted a whole issue of his popular *Berlin as It Is and as It Drinks* to Liszt. His comedy *Franz Liszt in Berlin* introduces us to the character of Baroness von Sinnen – the name implies that she was out of her mind. We accompany her to her elegant salon:

> BARONESS VON SINNEN (*lying on her divan, resting her head on a cushion on which Liszt's features have been embroidered, while holding his portrait in her hand. She gazes at it rapturously, speaking slowly and quietly*): Sweet and higher being in a human shell, gaze down on your maidservant with friendly grace! (*She kisses the portrait.*) O most refined blossom of soulful, divinely wild Romanticism, how I worship you! [. . .] How manly and noble is your whole expression, as is everything about you – your dress-coat, your waistcoat, your shirt, its buttons: everything about you is physiognomy! Ah, I am exhausted by such high regard! (*She rings.*)
>
> SERVANT: You rang, madam?
>
> BARONESS VON SINNEN: A glass of water. But the polished glass engraved with Liszt's portrait. (*Exit Servant.*) Ah! (*Sighing deeply.*) You yourself are never unpolished. (*Sighing even more deeply.*)
>
> SERVANT (*with the glass*): Here, madam!
>
> BARONESS VON SINNEN: Go over to the sideboard with my trinkets and pour some eau de Liszt on my handkerchief.
>
> SERVANT (*in some surprise*): Eau? (*Does as he is told, while clenching his fist and muttering to himself.*) Oh![41]

When Heinrich Heine heard what was going on in Berlin, he shrugged his shoulders in disbelief, initially assuming that the population was simply delirious:

> When I asked a doctor who specialized in women's ailments about the spell that Liszt had cast on his public, he smiled in an extremely odd way and said all manner of things about magnetism, galvanism, electricity, contagion in a stuffy room lit by countless wax candles

and packed with several hundred perfumed and perspiring men and women, of hysterical epilepsy, of the phenomenon of titillation, of musical cantharides and other scabrous things that I believe relate to the mysteries of the bona dea.

But Heine eventually found this diagnosis too ludicrous to take seriously. 'I sometimes think', he mused, 'that this whole ensorcellment can be explained by the fact that there is no one in the entire world better able than our Franz Liszt to organize his successes or, rather, their *mise en scène*.' In short, the audience's enthusiasm was the result of an immaculately organized piece of showmanship. In turn, this led Heine to criticize Liszt and his secretary Gaëtano Belloni, whom he described as the 'general administrator of his notoriety'. The two men were said to 'hire fans' who, 'admirably trained', guaranteed the necessary euphoria inside the concert hall – even the flowers and laurel wreaths that the ecstatic women threw on to the stage had all been ordered in advance. Heine's reference to the 'cost of these ovations' was nothing if not malicious. Audiences should not trust their senses, he concluded: Lisztomania was nothing but fraud.[42]

Certain details of Heine's criticisms may have been unjustified, but they pointed in the right direction. We do not know if Liszt or Belloni ever hired a claque, but the truth of the matter is that Liszt did not need to do so, for it is clear from countless reports that the enthusiasm triggered by his playing was spontaneous, immediate and genuine. But Heine was right to speak of Liszt's gift for self-promotion. His facial expression and gestures, his clothes and the way he moved onstage, the glances he cast at the audience – it was all part of a great spectacle. Liszt was fully conscious of his impact on listeners, and he controlled these mechanisms to perfection.

His departure from Berlin on 3 March 1842 resembled a royal progress, as one eyewitness recalled:

A carriage drawn by six white horses pulled up outside his hotel, and to the cheering of the crowd Liszt was almost carried down the steps and lifted into the carriage, where he took his seat between senior members of the University. Thirty smaller carriages, each of them drawn by four horses and filled with students, accompanied him, as did a number of individual riders dressed in academic regalia. Countless other carriages followed, and a crowd of several thousand seethed all around the departing travellers.[43]

Don Juan Parvenu

Turning his back on his turbulent time in Berlin, Liszt set off for St Petersburg, travelling via East Prussia and Riga and giving concerts along the way. His incessant appearances and the rigours of the journey took their toll. 'I am terribly highly strung – ill – exhausted,' he wrote to Marie even while still in Berlin:

Four days ago I simply fell over and was delirious for more than two hours. At the time of writing I have withdrawn to another room in my hotel, leaving my suite to Belloni and Lefèvre and asking *all* my friends not to come to see me for at least four days. I feel an all-consuming need for rest.

Eight consecutive concerts and four matinees for the Princess of Prussia at which I alone did the honours, absolutely and exclusively, playing seven or eight pieces on each occasion. Dinners, soirées, balls, smoking parties, incessant conversations, correcting proofs, secretarial tasks, instrumentation – all of this provides a *physical* explanation of my corporeal state.

You will understand this better when I tell you that I need you and feel how much I miss you in the midst of so much extreme agitation.[44]

Liszt failed to mention that these weeks had also witnessed a number of amorous encounters that did not remain undetected. Berlin's society newspapers joked about his far from unworldly activities, albeit without naming names. Not infrequently women were already waiting for him when he returned to his rooms at the Hôtel de Russie, a number of his admirers even disguising themselves as men in order to avoid detection. One particularly infatuated admirer wanted to mark out her territory and stood naked on the balcony of Liszt's room in order to show the world what had apparently just taken place.[45] The actress Charlotte von Hagn seems to have been particularly smitten, starting an affair with Liszt that lasted until the winter of 1842/3. When Liszt left Berlin in early March 1842, Charlotte followed him as far as Müncheberg, some thirty-five miles to the east of the capital, where the couple spent two days together, incognito. Marie was not allowed to find out, of course. Liszt and Charlotte continued to exchange letters using a go-between and arranged to meet again in the autumn in either Koblenz or Cologne. Inevitably, the deception was uncovered.

When Marie d'Agoult learnt about the liaison, she confronted Liszt, but he evaded the issue and trivialized the affair. By now she had had enough and in early November 1842 wrote to Liszt, breaking off their relationship once and for all. Only now did Liszt seem to realize that he had been playing with fire, with the result that in his reply he asked to be given another chance, promising to give Charlotte von Hagn her marching orders and at the same time agreeing to one of Marie's principal demands: he would end his career as an itinerant virtuoso at the end of 1844 and then settle down with her and live a life of almost total seclusion. Marie agreed. In April and May 1843 Liszt returned to Russia for a further series of concerts in St Petersburg and Moscow, and by mid-July he and Marie were together again for their second visit to Nonnenwerth. A few years later Marie recalled that 'when I arrived there with Liszt for the last time, he said to me: "Nonnenwerth will be either the temple of our love or its grave." He had a gift for seeing things very clearly at certain moments in his life.'[46]

It seems almost as if Liszt and Marie were afraid of each other's company, with the result that the two and a half months that they spent on the island witnessed visits from a whole series of friends and acquaintances, leaving them with barely a minute to call their own. In the circumstances, there could be no question of any real attempt to bring things out into the open. Instead, the situation grew worse, and if their visit to Nonnenwerth had been intended to bring about a reconciliation between them, it ended, rather, with the certainty that their relationship was doomed. On 3 October 1843 Liszt left for a tour of southern Germany, and a few days later Marie returned to Paris via Cologne. Within months of her arrival in the capital she had begun to plan her revenge, a point to which we shall shortly return.

During the second half of February 1844 Liszt gave several recitals in Dresden, and it was here that he chanced to meet a woman whom he would have done better to avoid: Maria de los Dolores Porrys (or Porry) y Montez, better known as Lola Montez. The twenty-three-year-old dancer claimed to have been born in Seville but, like so much else in her life, this was invention on her part. Her real name was Elizabeth Rosanna Gilbert, and she had been born in Ireland. Two years earlier, in 1842, she had learnt the odd word in Spanish, but the deception was soon discovered, and she was obliged to flee London in June 1843. Dresden proved more credulous. An accomplished swindler, Montez would not be worth any further attention if she had not ensnared a considerable number of eminent and highly respectable men, even including King Ludwig I of Bavaria, who raised her to the nobility, making himself a laughing stock in the process. His abdication in March 1848 was not unconnected to these events.

Back in the spring of 1844, Lola Montez would have heard of the world-famous pianist, whose presence in Dresden was the subject of almost daily gossip in the local newspapers. And so she set her sights on Liszt, no doubt hoping that her acquaintance with him might help to further her career. It remains unclear what in fact took place between the two of them, although it seems unlikely that it was more than a passing encounter. But Liszt made the mistake of appearing in public with the dancer when the two of them attended a performance of Wagner's *Rienzi* on 29 February. A German newspaper reported the detail in passing, and this was picked up by a journalist working on the *Revue et Gazette musicale de Paris*. His French colleagues gratefully followed up the story and published two short pieces on the encounter. A scandal was born.

From now on titillating rumours circulated in Paris's salons, where it was claimed – inaccurately – that La Montez was Liszt's mistress and that she was accompanying him on a concert tour. He was also reported to have put in a good word for her at the Paris Opéra, a claim that may or may not have been true. When these reports came to Marie d'Agoult's attention, her patience finally snapped: by now she had had enough of Liszt's notorious infidelities. For her, his alleged affair with Lola Montez was the last in a long series of humiliations. For all her liberal views, she remained a product of the French aristocracy where her honour as a *femme du monde* was sacrosanct. It was this sense of honour that Liszt had repeatedly violated with his various affairs. He was, she felt, trampling on her feelings and humiliating her in the eyes of the world. As early as 1839 Balzac had already published a *roman-à-clef, Béatrix*, in which Liszt and Marie d'Agoult appeared in the guise of Gennaro Conti and Béatrix de Rochefide. Marie was beside herself with fury and demanded that Liszt demand satisfaction from Balzac, but Liszt refused, pointing out that Marie's name was nowhere mentioned in the book and that he regarded the matter as over. But Marie continued to brood on Liszt's affairs – imagined or real – and to reproach him for his flirtation with Charlotte von Hagn and his disgusting involvement with a disreputable Spanish dancer who was no better than a whore.

Liszt and Marie d'Agoult met again in Paris on 8 and 9 April 1844, while the Montez scandal was on everyone's lips. An argument was inevitable, and the next day Marie, who had had all she could take, penned yet another of her parting shots:

My dear Franz, if I were not convinced that I am, and can only be, a source of pain and importunate suffering in your life, you may well believe that I would not be taking the decision that I have taken, a decision that has cost me the deepest mental anguish. You have strength, youth and genius on your side, and many things will grow again on the tomb in which our love and friendship will find their final resting place. If you have any desire to spare me in this final crisis, which I would not have delayed for so long if only I had had a little more foresight and pride, then you will not react with anger and irritation to the few requests that I make of you. [. . .]

I would also ask you and beg of you not to confide in anyone except Ronchaud, who has been kept up to date with most of the things that have happened since Nonnenwerth, and I would also ask you to avoid adopting a jocular or mocking tone when referring to something that for both of us is perhaps an act of folly or at least the result of such an act, albeit an act of folly that should be respected and taken seriously.[47]

Liszt appears not to have reckoned that Marie would show such resolve. Perhaps he had imagined she would calm down again. But the situation had now changed. Liszt was shocked:

> I am extremely sad and profoundly affected.
>
> I am counting each and every sorrow that I have inflicted on your heart. And nothing and no one will ever be able to save me from myself.
>
> I no longer want to speak to you or see you, still less do I want to write to you.
>
> Did you not tell me that I was an actor? Yes, like those actors who play the dying athlete after having drunk hemlock.
>
> No matter.
>
> Silence must seal all the torments of my heart.[48]

Georg Herwegh was acquainted with both Liszt and Marie and tried to mediate between them, advising the countess to attempt a rapprochement and not abandon Liszt. But she refused, arguing that a definitive break was unavoidable. 'It would really be too naïve to retain even the vestige of a hope,' she told Herwegh. 'What do I have in common with an amiable good-for-nothing, a Don Juan parvenu, half fairground entertainer, half conjuror, who makes thoughts and feelings vanish up his sleeve and complacently observes the dumbfounded audience that claps its hands at him?'[49] This hardly sounds like a willingness to be reconciled. But she was still brooding on her revenge.

Nélida, or The Art of Hating a Person

In the summer of 1844, only a few months after she had finally broken with Liszt, Marie d'Agoult completed a novel with the remarkable title of

Nélida. The fact that she had turned to literature at all was in part the result of an acquaintance she had made in her salon only a few years earlier.

Among the many high-ranking men and women who frequented Marie's salon in the rue Neuve-des-Mathurins were the influential publisher Émile de Girardin and his wife, Delphine Gay. Girardin was much taken by Marie and there is even a suggestion that they briefly had an affair. 'He seemed to enjoy his visits to my place,' Marie recalled, striking a somewhat evasive note, 'for he returned and it was not long before we were discussing my concerns – my strange situation and my plans. "My plans? I don't have any," I told him.' Girardin had an idea and suggested that she might like to publish something in his paper, *La Presse*. He asked her to provide an example of her writing, and when she produced a review of an exhibition at the École des Beaux-Arts, he responded enthusiastically. Although he claimed to have no inkling of the fine arts and had no idea whether Marie's account was accurate, he was none the less convinced that she was talented. Marie was flattered but initially declined the publisher's offer to reproduce the piece in the pages of his newspaper as she did not want to cause herself and her family any further difficulties. 'If I am criticized in the papers,' she explained to Girardin, 'I don't want anyone to have to come to my defence as a matter of personal honour.'[50] But Girardin refused to be discouraged and suggested that if Marie was reluctant to publish her article under her real name, she should use a pseudonym. This was not a problem, and a suitable nom de plume was soon decided on. The transmogrification of Marie d'Agoult into Daniel Stern in December 1841 marked the start of an impressive career as a writer. Further reviews followed, as well as two novellas, *Hervé* and *Julien*.

Marie began work on *Nélida* in early November 1843, only a few weeks after she had returned to Paris from the second of her two disenchanting visits to the island of Nonnenwerth, and an initial draft was finished by the summer of 1844. A thorough revision was made in the spring of 1845, before the novel appeared in a series of instalments in the *Revue indépendante* in early 1846, with a complete publication in book form following shortly afterwards. Friends and acquaintances had advised Marie against publication, notably the writer Pierre-Jean de Béranger: 'It's not a bad novel,' he argued,

> but it's not as good as those of Balzac and Madame Sand. [. . .] Some readers will think that they recognize themselves and will say that you have painted their portraits; they will hold this against you and will denigrate both you and your talent. You'll have endless annoyance.

Béranger's objections went unheard: 'I felt a blind and almost irresistible need to break free from my emotional and spiritual isolation, for my mind had already driven me repeatedly to the point where I thought of suicide. I needed to escape from myself and find some new meaning to my life.'[51] This new meaning was in fact the desire to be avenged on Liszt.

The plot of *Nélida* – an anagram of Daniel – is clearly autobiographical: the beautiful and well-to-do Nélida de la Thieullaye abandons her former existence in order to start a new life with Guermann Régnier, a young painter from a poor background. It is not difficult to guess the models for Nélida and Guermann, but other characters, too, have real-life precedents, including the Marquise Le Vayer and the abbé de Lamennais. Marie also included events from her years with Liszt, such as their flight to Switzerland, their visits to Italy, Liszt's duel with Thalberg and Marie's serious illness in Venice: all of these incidents find encoded expression in her narrative. In a key episode in the novel, Guermann is appointed to the seat of a minor German grand duchy, where he is expected to produce a colossal painting, but he proves unequal to the task and stands as if paralysed before the white walls, unable to make even a single brushstroke. He then falls gravely ill. On realizing that he is artistically impotent, he begs Nélida for forgiveness for all that he has done to her and finally dies in her arms. Guermann was bound to fail as an artist because he had spurned her inspiration.

The reader may be left to decide whether this sentimental tale has any merit as a work of literature, but what is beyond doubt is that it lays bare Marie's complexes and frustrations: she could never forgive Liszt for refusing to regard her as his muse and for the fact that he was obviously not dependent on her for his artistic inspiration.

When Liszt read the first instalment of *Nélida* in the *Revue indépendante* in early February 1846, he reacted with astonishing calm, claiming that he did not recognize himself in Guermann and that the artist in question was his friend, the painter Henri Lehmann. The letter to Marie in which he recounted his impressions on reading her novel is a masterpiece of mocking contempt:

> Charm and aristocracy of style. Here and there a certain mannerism in terms of the posturing of the characters (especially in the Introduction) ... a little like Thomas Lawrence as translated by Lehmann. A lack of breadth and of simplicity in the way the action unfolds ... but grace and extreme elegance in the phrasing – even in the slight tenseness that you've always found hard to lose.[52]

In fact, Liszt was only pretending to be calm, and it is clear from his later letters that he was deeply hurt by Marie's very public attempt to humiliate him. Although she declared that she had not written the novel as an attack on Liszt and had had no desire to harm him, her apology was half-hearted at best and marked the start of a long-running battle between the former lovers.

The Invisible Father

Following their decision to go their separate ways in the spring of 1844, Liszt and Marie d'Agoult had initially agreed that their three children, Blandine, Cosima and Daniel, would live with their mother. For the sake of his children, Liszt was willing to accept all manner of compromises and even to renounce his legal right to bring them up, assuring his own mother, Anna, that his principal aim was 'to avoid all friction on this side. Sooner or later things will move in the direction that they must: as for the present, we need to be patient.'[53] But within a few weeks rumours were circulating that 'Mme d'A. wants to return to her husband'. This lifted a load off Liszt's mind: 'This arrangement suits me down to the

ground – it couldn't be better and strikes me as the only sensible solution. Sooner or later it was bound to happen – and it would radically
simplify the question regarding my children.'[54] As the result of her
reconciliation with Charles d'Agoult, Marie would of course have had to
renounce her illegitimate children, but in the event things were to work
out rather differently.

Before long any talk of an agreement between the parents concerning
their progeny was out of the question. Quite the opposite, in fact, for the
tensions between the couple continued to worsen: 'Our children's
upbringing seems to have become a source of inextricable difficulty for
you,' Liszt reproached his former lover. 'From the moment when you set
yourself up as my enemy, I could not possibly allow them to return to
your safekeeping.'[55] By now Liszt had other plans. The eight-year-old
Blandine was to receive a proper schooling at the genteel girls' boarding
school run by Louise Bernard and her daughter Laure in the rue
Montparnasse, while her younger sister and brother would for the time
being remain with Anna Liszt. Being solely responsible for his children,
Liszt was acting within the terms of the French legal system of the time,
with the result that there was no mention in all this of the children's
birth mother. For her part, Marie reacted with emotional reproaches,
culminating in the charge that Liszt was seeking to rob her of the fruits
of her womb: 'From now on, Monsieur, your daughters no longer have a
mother – that is what you want. [. . .] One day your daughters will
perhaps ask you where their mother is. And you will answer that you did
not want them to have one.'[56]

Liszt began an extended concert tour in the summer of 1844 that
took him through southern France to Spain and Portugal and lasted
until the following April. Afterwards he toured Switzerland, the
Rhineland and the French provinces. Throughout his long absences he
continued to write to his mother, but for the day-to-day running of his
children's lives, Anna Liszt was thrown back on her own resources. She
turned sixty in May 1848, and we may assume that it was not always
easy for her to bring up three small children. Worst of all were the
constant quarrels with Marie d'Agoult, which affected Anna Liszt deeply.
She was often worried that Marie might simply turn up and take the

children away. 'Blandine and Cosima shall both remain where they are,' Liszt sought to reassure his mother, 'one of them with Mme Bernard, the other one with you.' If, in spite of this, Marie were to try to take the children,

> I shall answer force with force and come to Paris and take all three of them away with me, either to Cologne or somewhere else. But I hope that she will not force me to fall back on such an extreme measure and that a scintilla of sound common sense will come to her aid.

His mother should not be afraid of thunderbolts from the rue Neuve-des-Mathurins – 'they are by no means fatal'.[57] Marie withdrew from her children's lives, and it was not until early 1850 that she finally saw them again.

In the middle of 1846 Liszt decided that it was time for Cosima too to enter Madame Bernard's institute. But for Daniel he had other ideas – his son was to prepare for entry to the prestigious Lycée Bonaparte with the help of a private tutor. All three children continued to spend their weekends and school holidays with Anna Liszt. Superficially, they lacked nothing and were brought up in the style of the age, receiving lessons in music and deportment, learning several languages and acquiring a knowledge of history and religion. But the money that Liszt earned on his concert tours and sent to Paris on a regular basis could hardly compensate his children for the fact that their father had become invisible. Decades later Cosima complained that she had 'come into the world strangely disinherited',[58] a polite way of saying that her parents were never there when she wanted them. On another occasion she recalled that 'from childhood onwards, the impression that he left on me whenever he flew past was that of some fantastically legendary phenomenon'.[59] This says it all: Liszt seemed to his children to be some impressive natural event, crossing the night sky like a comet that disappeared as quickly as it came.

Between the beginning of 1846 and the end of 1853, Liszt gave Paris a very wide berth, forcing his daughters to resort to all manner of ruses in an attempt to lure him to the city. They promised they would practise the piano harder than ever if he visited them, and there were times when they even prayed for his return. Throughout this period he repeatedly announced his visits but in the event he did not even attend their First Communion. It was with a mixture of pride and sadness that Cosima wrote to him at the time: 'This visit would have made us so happy, but you've postponed it too often, although I'm sure that this isn't your fault and that you, too, want to see us again.'[60]

Not infrequently, three or four months would pass before Liszt made any further contact. During the intervening period his children would cut out articles from newspapers and collect everything they could lay their hands on about their famous father. When he finally sent news of his activities, all three children would celebrate. 'Blandin [sic] and Cosima were beside themselves with joy on receiving a little letter from you,' Anna Liszt assured her son. 'Daniel too takes a lot more interest whenever I receive a letter from you, and when you write again you should include a few lines specially for him.'[61]

When Liszt received this admonitory note from his mother at the end of 1846, he was on a tour of eastern Europe. By February 1847 he had met a woman who was to change his life completely. Nothing was to be the same again.

WEIMAR
(1847–61)

A Turning Point

'**D**O YOU WANT TO know the latest news?' Liszt asked Marie d'Agoult in a letter to her in February 1847:

> Quite by chance I recently met an exceptional woman in Kiev, really exceptional and distinguished – so much so that I decided to undertake a detour of twenty leagues in order to spend a few hours chatting to her. And I was delighted to do so. Her husband's name is Prince Nicholas Sayn-Wittgenstein, and her family name is Iwanowska. It's from their house that I'm writing to you now.[1]

In this passing reference Liszt was describing one of the central events in his life. The story is well known: it was during the winter of 1846/7 that the thirty-five-year-old Liszt first met Princess Carolyne von Sayn-Wittgenstein, who was soon to become his companion in life. And, as if that were not enough, Europe's most famous pianist bade farewell to the stage at the peak of his international career and settled down in the little town of Weimar.

Liszt had held the honorary title of 'Kapellmeister in Extraordinary' at the Weimar court since November 1842, an appointment he owed to the initiative of Crown Prince Carl Alexander of Saxe-Weimar-Eisenach. Born in 1818, Carl Alexander was the son of Grand Duke Karl Friedrich and his wife Maria Pawlowna. Karl Friedrich had no real interest in the arts, whereas his son proved to be a man of vision, keen to revive memories of the golden age of his grandfather, Karl August, who had been a friend of Goethe, and in particular to support the arts and sciences.[2] Liszt's appointment must be seen as a part of this wider context. At the end of 1842 Carl Alexander had been eager to forge long-term ties with Liszt, and in 1848 his plan finally paid off when Liszt made a number of decisions that affected his life in fundamental ways. But one thing at a time.

When Liszt arrived in Vienna at the end of February 1846, it was the start of an eighteen-month tour de force. His third European tour began in the Austrian capital and took him through Hungary, Transylvania and Russia as far as Constantinople (modern Istanbul). Between March 1846 and September 1847 he gave more than ninety concerts. In March and April 1846 alone he appeared nine times in the Musikverein in Vienna, while also taking part in two concerts at the court and sharing the stage with other artists in eight other mixed programmes. During this period he also made flying visits to Brno some eighty miles away and gave three recitals there. Within the first five weeks of his tour, then, he made more than twenty appearances. But this was only the beginning, for between then and late September 1847 he also appeared in Prague, Olmütz (modern Olomouc), Pest, Grätz (Hradec nad Moravici), Troppau (Opava), Ratibor (Racibórz), Teschen (Cieszyn and Český Těšín), Rodaun, Graz, Marburg an der Drau (Maribor), Rohitsch-Sauerbrunn (Rogaňška Slatina), Agram (Zagreb), Ödenburg (Sopron), Güns (Kőszeg), Dáka, Szekszárd, Fünfkirchen (Pécs), Gran (Esztergom), Mohács, Bánlak, Temesvár, Arad, Lugos, Hermannstadt (Sibiu), Klausenburg (Cluj Napoca), Nagyenyed, Bucharest, Jassy, Kiev, Woronince, Krzemieniec, Lemberg (Lviv), Czernowitz (Czernovtsy), Galatz (Galaţi), Constantinople, Odessa, Elisavetgrad and finally back to Vienna. He also revisited Raiding.

At each recital Liszt performed between five and seven works, tailoring their individual order to the needs of the occasion and rounding off the performance with various encores that the audience always expected of him. Included in his programmes were works by Schubert, Chopin, Beethoven, Handel, Weber and others, but it was his own compositions that predominated, notably his *Réminiscences de Don Juan*, his barn-storming *Réminiscences de Robert le diable* (performed under the title 'Valse infernale'), the *Harmonies poétiques et religieuses* and the *Mélodies hongroises*. And he also obliged, of course, with popular favourites such as the *Grand galop chromatique* and knuckle-breaking transcriptions such as Schubert's *Erlkönig* that could be counted on to impress their listeners. Everywhere he went, Liszt was frenetically acclaimed, and in Vienna he could even afford to give concerts that began only after the theatres closed at around ten in the evening. Like all his other appearances, these were sold out. Liszt had reached the very pinnacle of his career: he was the most famous pianist in the world and regarded by many as the uncrowned king of piano playing.

And yet there was a sense that a new age was dawning. According to the music critic Eduard Hanslick,

> the year 1846 may be regarded as the culmination of the golden age of virtuosity. This was the year in which Liszt returned to Vienna for a series of recitals and repeated his former successes. [. . .] The delight of his audiences and the delirium of the newspapers showed no sign of abating. It seems likely that Liszt's enthralling artistic personality would have been the only one to extend beyond 1848 with its virtu- osic victories: the fact that Liszt himself abdicated at the very peak of his artistry and never again played in public is perhaps the best possible proof that the whole movement was on the point of dying out, a point clearly recognized by its greatest representative.[3]

How long could Liszt have led such a hectic life? Surely he had long been tired of constant travel and the inconstancy of life in hotel rooms. In early October 1846 he had written to Carl Alexander to announce that the time had come when he would no longer

> hide behind my virtuosity but give free rein to my ideas – without straying too far in the process! If it weren't for the fact that I have to wrestle so often with these wretched financial problems and if it weren't for these more or less infectious fantasies of my youth, I might already be four or five years further down the road than I am now.[4]

At first sight, it must seem strange that Liszt repeatedly found himself in financial difficulties. After all, one would think that an artist like him would be a top earner. In fact there were periods when he did indeed earn a lot, but we should not forget that he also had to support his three children and his mother in faraway Paris, while his own often luxurious lifestyle added appreciably to his outgoings, not least because he often forwent his fee, which he donated instead to charitable causes. There were occasions, therefore, when the fêted pianist was short of money and was unable to pay his hotel bills. This situation arose in Vienna in April 1846 when Liszt was staying at the Hotel Zur Stadt Frankfurt, where he had repeatedly entertained friends and acquaintances to supper. 'Within the short space of two weeks,' recalled an eyewitness,

> he had run up a bill of more than a thousand florins – a not inconsiderable sum. As he was leaving, he called the landlord over: 'I'm now leaving for Prague in order to give several concerts there and shall be back in six weeks. Can you give me credit till then?'

But the landlord refused and insisted on being paid at once, leaving Liszt with no choice but to borrow the money. This was deeply embarrassing, but Liszt then summoned all the hotel employees and settled his bill in their presence, before turning to the staff: 'I'm very pleased with you all! Here are two hundred florins for you all! Have my carriage brought round! Farewell! Farewell!'[5] It was incidents like these that confirmed Liszt in his conviction that he had to do something about the life he was leading. As yet no solution was in sight. But it needed only a slight shove to thrust the barriers aside.

The Princess

Liszt was already approaching the end of his recital tour when he arrived in Kiev in late January 1847. At that date in its history, the city on the Dnieper was still part of Russia, with a population of around 200,000 that made it an important cultural and religious centre. The cityscape was dominated by around thirty churches belonging to different

denominations, as well as ten monasteries and a number of syna-
gogues. Its university was founded in 1834, and it also boasted scientific
societies, libraries, museums and galleries. Depending on the standpoint of the observer, Kiev was described as either the 'Paris of the East'
or the 'Jerusalem of the North'. But it was also an important trading post,
and every year in early February it held a major fair attended by land-
owners, farmers, cattle breeders and manufacturers, who flocked to
Kiev from neighbouring districts to sell their wares and sign deals that
were sometimes worth millions of roubles. The Kiev Contract Fair was
the high point of the city's economic and social calendar, and so it is
unsurprising that Liszt organized three concerts while the fair was
taking place. The second of them was given in the Great Hall of the
University on 14 February 1847 (New Style) and was attended by the
woman who was to change his life in a not uncertain way: Jeanne
Élisabeth Carolyne von Sayn-Wittgenstein. Liszt was told that she had
donated 100 roubles at his charity concert, information that understandably piqued his curiosity and made him want to thank his benefac-
tress in person. Their first meeting evidently took place later that same
day, for by the next day – a Monday – the princess had already issued an
invitation to Liszt to visit her on her estates. Liszt set out at once and
remained there for around ten days, although we do not know what
happened there. None the less it is clear from Anna Liszt's letters that
her son suddenly abandoned his fastidious habit of writing to her regularly, for she repeatedly complained about his silence. Had he fallen in
love, with the result that he had no thought for anyone else? And who
was this portentous princess?

Carolyne Iwanowska, to use her maiden name, had been born on
8 February 1819 in the village of Monasterzyska some ninety miles
to the south-east of Lviv. She was the only daughter of a fabulously
wealthy landowner, Peter Iwanowsky, and his wife, Pauline Podowska.
Their fortune must have been enormous as they were said to need more
than 30,000 serfs to maintain the family estates.[6] They lived in a part of
Russia known as Podolia. Now situated in the south-west corner of the
Ukraine, this country has witnessed a long and vicissitudinous history:
in the fourteenth century it was overrun by Tartars and Lithuanians, in

the fifteenth and sixteenth centuries it fell under Polish influence, and in the seventeenth century it was for a time under Ottoman rule, before most of the country passed into Russian hands in 1793. In Woronince, an isolated backwater around 150 miles south-west of Kiev, the Iwanowskys owned lands that Carolyne later received as her dowry. It was here and in Monasterzyska that she spent her childhood. At Woronince, with the exception of the Iwanowskys, the local population was reduced to living in mere wooden huts, enduring an inhospitable climate of extremely hot summers and permanent frosts in winter. The Iwanowskys were, however, cut off from all this suffering and misery, for they lived in a kind of parallel universe, lacking nothing in the way of creature comforts and residing in a vast villa with numerous rooms designed to impress visitors, including a large library, a music room and a billiard room. (The property was destroyed in the Second World War.)

Carolyne's parents separated when she was eleven. She remained with her father and was brought up by a French governess, although she remained in contact with her mother, with whom she undertook long trips to the capitals of Europe. In March and April 1832, for example, we find the thirteen-year-old in Geneva, after which she travelled to Berlin and Frankfurt. Regular visits to Paris, Vienna and St Petersburg were also a part of her annual round of activities.

Unsurprisingly, the Iwanowskys aped the customs of international high society. As Catholics of Polish extraction they belonged to the religious minority in Orthodox Podolia and preferred to take their cue from Paris rather than Kiev. Although Carolyne learnt to speak Russian and Polish, she generally conversed with her parents in French, just as she did with her friends and acquaintances. Her German, conversely, was always very stilted, so that it was almost always in the language of diplomacy that she communicated with Liszt.

Carolyne was very much her father's child. If her relations with her capricious and cosmopolitan mother were strained, her dealings with her father – a man notorious for his strictness – were sincere if somewhat eccentric. Peter Iwanowsky was a bookworm who would sit up all night reading, in his library, where Carolyne often kept him company. He thought nothing of it if she smoked the occasional cigar. From a financial point of view she was undoubtedly a good catch, and had she been physically more prepossessing she is likely to have been assailed by suitors. Rumour has it that her homely appearance was a source of much sorrow to her mother, 'who sought to comfort her by telling her that she should simply wait because after the resurrection she would be a miracle of loveliness.'[7]

In 1836 Peter Iwanowsky decided that it was time for his seventeen-year-old daughter to marry, and his choice fell on Prince Nicholas von Sayn-Wittgenstein, the youngest son of Field Marshal Ludwig Adolph Peter von Sayn-Wittgenstein, who was a legend in his own lifetime. He had successfully defended St Petersburg against Napoleon's army in 1812 and, although his later career was less distinguished, his fame remained undiminished. In 1834 King Friedrich Wilhelm III of Prussia raised him to the nobility and invested him with the title of the Prince of Sayn-Wittgenstein-Ludwigsburg. In turn this meant that his son Nicholas, who was born in 1812, became a prince of Prussia. Carolyne – or so her father reckoned – would become a princess. From the outset this was a marriage of convenience: the Sayn-Wittgensteins were looking for a wealthy daughter-in-law, while the Iwanowskys coveted the aristocratic title of their future kinsfolk.

For Peter Iwanowsky, the whole affair was already settled when he wrote to his daughter on 20 January 1836:

> The day after I arrived in Kiev – in other words, the 19th – I received a visit from Prince Nicholas Wittgenstein, who asked for your hand in marriage and at the same time gave me a letter from his father, a copy of which I am enclosing herewith. With your consent, I accepted his offer and gave him a letter for his father, which he wanted to pass on in person. I am enclosing a copy of this letter, too. Inasmuch as I regard this agreement as binding, it remains only for me to ask for Heaven to grant its holy blessing both to you and to the man to whom you are binding yourself for ever in life.

As a good Catholic, Iwanowsky went on:

> Such is my concern for you that before I agreed to the marriage I made a point of asking Prince Wittgenstein if he would promise to

agree to your daughters' being brought up in the religion of their mother. He agreed to this without a moment's hesitation.[8]

This horse-trading must strike the modern reader as calculating and even shameful, but at the time such provisions were by no means unusual. And yet what happened next was something that no one had predicted: Carolyne put a spanner in her father's works by turning Nicholas down – and not just once. Three times he asked for her hand in marriage, and three times she sent him packing, leaving him humiliated. Her father, who regarded his word as binding, tried to make his recalcitrant daughter see reason, and witnesses later claimed that he even beat her in an attempt to break her will.[9] In the end a tearful Carolyne bowed to her fate, and the Catholic wedding took place at the end of April 1836. Iwanowsky remained at his daughter's side throughout the ceremony, so afraid was he that she might take refuge in flight. Finally he boxed her ears in the presence of the assembled congregation, an act which – strange though it must seem – ultimately worked to her advantage, for the public rebuke demonstrated that Carolyne was marrying against her will. The Codex Iuris Canonici, or canon of Catholic Church law, included a provision for declaring null and void any marriage contracted on the basis of fear or constraint.[10] In any later divorce proceedings Carolyne would be able to cite her father's blow to her face as valid grounds for annulment.

Immediately after the marriage the couple moved to Kiev, but Carolyne felt unhappy there, and it was not long before they returned to Woronince, where their only daughter, Marie Pauline Antonia, was born the following February. Yet their marriage remained an unhappy one, and within four years they had decided to go their separate ways. It was an amicable separation, and the two of them remained in contact, while easily adapting to their new situation. A bon vivant, Nicholas frequented the salons of Europe, while Carolyne and Marie remained behind in Woronince. Carolyne occasionally met men who were interested in marrying her, and the Marquis de la Tigrière even wrote her a series of touching love letters: 'Your poor Marquis de la Tigrière is here and loves you so much that words fail him.'[11] But nothing came of the approach. Carolyne preferred to bury herself in her library: 'She loved to turn her nights into days,' Marie recalled much later. 'She would spend all night studying and often did not go to bed until the morning, just as I was getting up. Her life was never run along regular lines. One day we would have lunch at one time, the next day at another. She was indifferent to life's practicalities.'[12]

The situation changed when Peter Iwanowsky died in early October 1844. He is said to have suffered a stroke and died in church. Whatever the truth of the matter, Carolyne inherited a vast fortune and became one of the wealthiest women in Russia. As long as Carolyne and Nicholas were officially man and wife, the Sayn-Wittgensteins had a certain claim on Carolyne's millions and were therefore not interested in a divorce or in the annulment of the marriage. To that extent they were keen to keep a close eye on the burgeoning relationship between Carolyne and her famous visitor.

This brings us back to 1847. After his ten-day visit to Woronince, Liszt set off once again on his recital tour, reaching Lviv in the middle of April and remaining there for over a month, during which time he gave four concerts. After that he travelled to Czernovsty, Jassy and, finally, Constantinople, where he twice performed for Sultan Abdul-Medjid Khan, a man known for his love of art who rewarded Liszt with a large sum of money, a valuable snuff box and a diamond-encrusted order. While in the city, Liszt also gave several recitals at the Russian Embassy, in every case performing on an Érard grand piano that had been sent to him specially from Paris. Only Liszt could have got away with such a logistically complex demand.

By the end of July Liszt was in Odessa, where he remained until the middle of September, giving a total of ten concerts. Here, too, he was visited by Carolyne von Sayn-Wittgenstein, and it seems likely that they agreed to meet again very soon in Woronince. By the time he arrived in late October in order to spend the autumn on her estates, he had completed his recital tour in Elisavetgrad some 220 miles away, where he had given four recitals – the last he ever gave during his years as a virtuoso.

Decisions

'I shall soon be taking a series of decisions that will affect my entire future – an event as decisive as it has been unexpected seems to have shifted the balance to the side of happiness, affluence and a definitive goal that is worthy of me,' Liszt wrote to his mother in September 1847. 'It would require a particularly disagreeable and unpredictable set of random circumstances to ruin things.' As if his hints were not already broad enough, he went on a few lines later: 'You do know, don't you, that it's not impossible that I shall end up concluding an excellent deal? But I don't yet dare speak about it, for fear of being laughed out of court.'[13] It seems clear that Liszt had a plan involving a lot of money. Did the words 'une très bonne affaire' refer to his liaison with Carolyne von Sayn-Wittgenstein? But when Anna Liszt, her maternal curiosity piqued by rumours of marriage that had started to circulate in Paris, confronted her son on the subject, he turned on the charm and avoided the issue: 'But what makes you think that I'm getting married? I've not said anything about being in love. You're really getting ahead of yourself, dear mother, while I'm advancing with all the speed of a tortoise.'[14] But these lines were scarcely calculated to calm Anna Liszt. Instead, she continued to worry about her son. 'Madame la Princesse', she told him, was an 'admirable woman', but he should avoid becoming involved with 'noblewomen' – 'you've already paid for this lesson.'[15] The 'noblewoman' in question was Marie d'Agoult, who had famously brought him no happiness. But Anna Liszt's maternal advice came too late, for in Woronince the couple had long since decided to remain together. Carolyne and her daughter Marie would leave Russia and settle in Weimar with Liszt.

Not a few of the couple's contemporaries expressed surprise at this remarkable alliance, for even on a purely physical level Liszt's new companion in life hardly conformed to his image of the ideal woman: until now he had consorted only with beautiful women such as Marie d'Agoult. Carolyne von Sayn-Wittgenstein could not have been more different: not only was she Marie's complete antithesis, she was also the very opposite of beautiful – short and unattractive, with raven-black hair. Yet she, too, must have felt something for Liszt, otherwise she would scarcely have turned her back on Russia and bade farewell to her former life in order to embrace a far from certain future.

The love between two people is notoriously hard to fathom, so the attraction felt by Liszt and the princess will ultimately remain their secret. And yet we can at least attempt an explanation, starting with Carolyne. When Liszt entered her life, he encountered a woman who was feeling frustrated by ten years of unhappy marriage. Her union with Prince Nicholas had turned out to be a huge disappointment, and the couple were now living apart, having next to nothing to say to one another. Although Carolyne was immensely successful as a business-woman, capable of profitably managing her vast estates, she found it intellectually and artistically unchallenging. Liszt's artistry, his genius as a musician, his charisma as a person and, not least, his virile attractive-ness all had an immediate effect on her. Meeting the thirty-six-year-old pianist marked the end of a long search and convinced her that at his side she had finally found her true place in life.

Conversely, the quality that Liszt most admired in Carolyne was the overwhelming power of her intellect. Throughout his life he remained fascinated by her universal education, her literary interests, her perspica-cious judgement and her compelling eloquence. To quote his own assess-ment of her: 'She is undoubtedly a quite exceptional and "complete" de luxe example of soul, wit and intellect.'[16] Liszt found in her a companion who took a profound interest in his own ideas and plans, including his compositions, a point on which she differed from Marie d'Agoult, who had really had little time for Liszt's work as a composer. Here, instead, was a woman who was prepared to abandon everything for Liszt and make a new start in life. He must have been deeply impressed by this radical attitude on her part. And the fact that she was also a member of the European aristocracy and well-to-do will certainly not have discour-aged Liszt, who had a weakness for titles and social etiquette.

Suddenly everything moved very quickly. Liszt left Woronince for Weimar in January 1848, while Carolyne waited a few days before setting off for Kiev, where she said goodbye to her mother, who had been living in the city since her separation. The two women were never to see each other again, for Pauline Iwanowska died only two years later. But Carolyne also wanted to sell some of her estates in order to raise enough capital to start a new life in Germany. All her negotiations had to be kept a close secret as no one could be allowed to know that she was planning to leave the country with her eleven-year-old daughter. And she needed to be particularly careful where Prince Nicholas and his family were concerned as she was understandably afraid that they would do everything in their power to thwart her designs. In the event, all went well, and Carolyne managed to obtain the best possible prices. Since, however, she was unable to take such large sums of money out of the country by any legal means, she was obliged to smuggle most of it across the Russian frontier, which she crossed in the company of Marie, the latter's governess Janet Anderson, and a maidservant known only as Alexandra. At the end of their nerve-wracking flight, Carolyne could look forward to starting a new life with Liszt in Weimar.

Liszt was completely surprised by Carolyne's resolve and tenacity. Decades later, he told his granddaughter Daniela that he had never expected her to make good her promise, but he received a letter asking him to collect Carolyne and her daughter at the border. According to Daniela, Liszt had replied, 'Mais je ne vous aime pas', prompting Carolyne to retort: 'Cela ne fait rien, j'ai une mission.'[17] Daniela was very fond of her grandfather and is unlikely to have invented this story. Perhaps there was a certain coquettishness to his claim, 'I don't love you', but Carolyne's reply certainly sums up the whole nature of her relationship with Liszt: 'That doesn't matter, for I have a mission.'

The Altenburg

For the four travellers from Russia, their flight was finally over on 18 April 1848. A friend of Liszt's, Felix von Lichnowsky, had placed at the composer's disposal his castle at Racibórz in Upper Silesia, and it was here, at Schloß Krzyzanowitz, that the reunion took place. Liszt was evidently happy to be able to welcome Carolyne and her daughter with open arms, while Janet Anderson and Alexandra, too, had apparently survived the rigours of their journey unscathed. The party then spent several weeks in Vienna, before settling in Weimar in July. The travelling piano virtuoso now became the local court Kapellmeister.

For the present, the couple lived apart, or at least they gave the impression of doing so. There were good reasons for their dissimulation. Before leaving Russia, Carolyne had asked the archbishop of St Petersburg to annul her marriage to Prince Nicholas of Sayn-Wittgenstein, and in order not to jeopardize a process that was as complicated as it was delicate, she had to take account of social and aristocratic conventions, not least because the Grand Duchess Maria Pawlowna was a sister of Tsar Nicholas I. On no account was Carolyne to be seen as an adulteress, so gossip had to be avoided at all costs. Officially the couple lived under separate roofs, Liszt taking rooms at the Erbprinz Hotel, while Carolyne and Marie moved into the Altenburg. Only when it became clear in the autumn of 1848 that Carolyne's marriage would not be annulled in the foreseeable future did Liszt abandon all pretence and move in with her.

These were the years of the Altenburg's heyday, a time when the building acquired an almost legendary status. It not only provided Liszt and Carolyne with a comfortable home, but it was also a melting pot of new ideas and a laboratory of the mind. Its inhabitants composed and wrote poetry, performed music and taught, argued over philosophy and politics and led lives of sybaritic pleasure. It was here, too, that Liszt's pupils lived, quickly coming to regard the villa as their home. Visitors came from all over the world and valued the house's creative, open atmosphere. The list of contemporaries who called on Liszt and Carolyne is long and reads like a who's who of the nineteenth century, including, as it did, the composers Berlioz, Brahms, Hiller, Smetana, Vieuxtemps and Wagner; the pianists Hans von Bülow, Anton Rubinstein, Clara Schumann and Carl Tausig; the violinist Joseph Joachim; the singers Joseph Tichatschek and Pauline Viardot-García; the writers Bettina von Arnim, George Eliot, Friedrich Hebbel, Hoffmann von Fallersleben, Fanny Lewald and Alfred Meißner; the architect Gottfried Semper; the painters Wilhelm von Kaulbach and Friedrich Preller; the sculptor Ernst Rietschel; and the scientist Alexander von Humboldt. There is no doubt that during the twelve years that Liszt lived there, the Altenburg was a centre of European culture.

This shrine to nineteenth-century culture lay on a small hill just outside the inner town. The three-storey structure had been built in 1811 – the year of Liszt's birth – for the court equerry Friedrich von Seebach and it remains one of Weimar's most important neoclassical residences, its name recalling an early medieval refuge whose foundations were once part of the property. Shortly before Liszt and the princess arrived in the town, Seebach's daughter sold it to an estate agent, who leased it to Carolyne. But recurrent problems with the landlord, who in all seriousness wanted to open a beer garden in front of the house, prompted Maria Pawlowna to intervene in May 1851 and buy the Altenburg outright. She then placed it at Liszt's disposal free of charge.[18] Its inhabitants lived the high life, Carolyne being happy to leave others to work in the kitchen and keep the building clean. The chambermaid Alexandra and a housekeeper by the name of Antoinette Kostenecka saw to the running of the household, while Liszt himself had two servants at his beck and call. Finally, there was Janet Anderson, who saw to Marie's education.

Their new home provided more than enough room for its three permanent residents. The main reception rooms were at the front of the building and included a dining room, a large library said to be the largest private library in Germany at this period[19] and a music room, together with the private apartments of the princess and her daughter. All were furnished with choice fabrics and accessories commensurate with their inhabitants' status. Money was no object. One eyewitness recalled that 'the dining room was pale yellow and reddish brown, while the furniture, curtains and portières were red velvet. Magnificent silverware – enormous tureens and salvers – was placed on the wide cornices above the doors. The small salon is dark blue, extremely tasteful and comfortable.'[20]

Liszt's private rooms were in a side wing looking out on to the garden. Here, in his 'chambre bleue', with its view of the greenery outside, he could find the peace and concentration he needed for his work. Throughout the house were musical instruments, including a grand piano once owned by Beethoven and a spinet that had belonged to Mozart. Over the years this collection grew to prodigious proportions. By the end of his life, Liszt owned seven grand pianos, Mozart's spinet and a 'piano-organ', a combination of the two instruments that he had had specially designed by a firm in Paris.

A number of guest rooms were available for visitors as well as for Liszt's private pupils. One such pupil was Hans von Bülow, who arrived in Weimar in June 1851 at a time when Liszt himself was out of town. The twenty-one-year-old was instructed by letter to move into a room in the Altenburg, where everything was ready for him. This was typical of Liszt's generosity, although it also reflected his high opinion of himself as a teacher: his 'apprentice' was to profit in every way from daily contact with his 'master'. Liszt's idea of piano lessons could hardly be further removed from the standard practice of drumming fingering into a pupil. What mattered most to him was an intense intellectual exchange that included not only the study of music and evening concerts but also reading books together. As a rule Liszt taught every pupil for two hours a week, demanding no fee in return. But the pupil was expected to undertake various tasks, including the copying of scores, a task that Liszt knew could be highly instructive.

Liszt, Carolyne, the young Princess Marie and Liszt's pupils lived together like one big family. When the head of the household was away on tour, Carolyne would take care of his charges. 'Yesterday', she informed her partner in September 1856, 'Tausig lunched with us and played the two studies "Eroica" and "Mazeppa". We all demanded an encore. He's not yet in complete command of "Mazeppa" but he brings very real fervour to the wonderful "Eroica".'[21]

By the time that Liszt left Weimar in 1861, his pupils in the town had included not only Tausig and Bülow but also such famous musicians as Joachim Raff, Peter Cornelius, Karl Klindworth and Julius Reubke. 'Liszt seems literally to have set up a factory for keyboard virtuosos,' the composer Pius Richter mocked. 'One is for ever reading about pupils of Liszt being sent out by the Weimar firm and making it big in the keyboard industry. The man certainly understands how to set up a party.'[22]

Disillusionment

Carolyne had managed to escape from Russia and the lovers of Woronince had found a beautiful and imposing new home in Weimar. All seemed well with the world, and yet it was not long before a sense of disillusionment made itself felt on various fronts. The artistic conditions that obtained in Weimar when Liszt took up his appointment in the town were sobering, to put it mildly. In 1851 the court orchestra was made up of only thirty-five players, the chorus of twenty-nine singers, the ballet of two male and four female dancers.[23] By the time Liszt resigned his post eight years later, the situation had barely changed: there were now thirty-nine orchestral musicians and a chorus of twenty-seven. The ballet meanwhile had shrunk to three female dancers.[24] When compared to companies elsewhere in Germany, this was frustratingly meagre. The Meiningen orchestra, for example, had fifty permanent members at this period. Today the Berlin Philharmonic has 129 permanent positions – three times more than Liszt had at his disposal in Weimar. Many nineteenth-century composers wrote for elaborate orchestral resources, with the result that whenever Liszt wanted to perform large-scale works by Wagner or Berlioz, he was obliged to employ a large number of extra players.

Financially, too, the court orchestra had its wings clipped, for it emerges from surviving files that in the mid-1850s the players' incomes had remained unchanged for four decades and that no attempt had been made to align them with the rise in the cost of living or inflation. Their annual salary ranged from 100 to 350 thalers, depending on their instrument. The principal cellist received 350, the leader 400. Only the famous virtuoso violinist Joseph Joachim was accorded 500 thalers for each of the two years when he was leader. One and a half centuries later, it is almost impossible to recalculate these figures in pounds or euros, but various comparisons make it clear that musicians' incomes at this period were pitiful in the extreme.

At the time that Liszt took up his post in Weimar, the right to vote in Weimar and Eisenach presupposed an annual income of at least 500 thalers, although elsewhere in the grand duchy the amount was only 300. The fact that as a rule orchestral musicians did not earn enough to be entitled to vote says much about their social and economic status. The court officials regarded orchestral musicians not as artists for whose welfare they were responsible but as subordinate lackeys. Many of them barely earned a living wage. In mid-December 1851, for example, the tuba player Friedrich Randeckart realized that he had insufficient money to see him, his wife and his six children through to the end of the month, and so he appealed to the lord chamberlain's office that was responsible for his employment. The reaction was one of annoyance, and after a certain amount of procrastination he was granted 10 thalers with clear instructions 'not to trouble the Grand Duke's Lord Chamberlain's office any further'. Before he received the handout he was required to sign a declaration: 'Herr Randeckart expressly promises not to seek any further support in future.'[25]

Liszt's own finances rested on much sounder foundations. His annual salary in 1848 was 1,500 thalers, and although this fell to around 1,300 thalers in the three subsequent years, it rose in 1852 to 1,660 thalers and remained at that level until 1858. If he performed additional duties for members of the grand duke's family – he occasionally gave music lessons to one of the princesses, for example – then his income was further supplemented, an increase that the pianist, who was said to spend between 800 and 1,000 thalers a year on feeding his nicotine habit, described mockingly as his 'cigar money'.[26]

These payments came not from the court coffers but from the privy purse of the Grand Duchess Maria Pawlowna. In short, Weimar's court Kapellmeister had no contractual claim to a particular salary but was entirely dependent on the grace and favour of the court. And yet he does not seem to have been troubled by the fact that his whole existence in Weimar was dependent on his superiors' goodwill. Instead, he pressed ahead with his plans to improve his players' lot, repeatedly plying his employer's family with submissions and memoranda. They responded in classic fashion by arbitrarily granting some of his requests and summarily dismissing others.

In such difficult and undignified circumstances, it amounts to little short of a miracle that Liszt was able to achieve so much in Weimar. As a composer, he completed no fewer than thirteen symphonic poems between 1849 and 1882. And – a complete novelty at this time – he combined music with poetry. In the world at large this enterprise was greeted with a shake of the head and described dismissively as 'the music of the future', before the term New German School gained greater currency after 1859. Under Liszt's leadership, the followers of this trend pleaded for a new ideal in music based on the conviction that the symphony as an expression of Viennese classicism had now outlived its usefulness and should be replaced by a new form of music with both symphonic and poetic pretensions. It was to include non-musical ideas derived from nature, literature and painting and draw on music to develop these ideas a stage further. The result was to become known as 'programme music'.

Liszt's symphonic poems are single-movement orchestral works, the very titles of which indicate their poetic or artistic programmes. *Orpheus, Prometheus, Tasso* and *Hamlet* draw their inspiration from mythological or historical characters, while *Les préludes* and *Die Ideale* were based on poems by Lamartine and Schiller respectively. Dating from 1856–7, *Hunnenschlacht* takes as its starting point a painting by Wilhelm von Kaulbach. Liszt additionally wrote two multi-sectional programme symphonies that are among his most important works.

The *Faust* Symphony is a three-movement work made up of three 'character sketches', each of which is devoted to one of the three main characters in Goethe's play: Faust, Gretchen and Mephistopheles. Lasting some seventy-five minutes in performance, the work was written in a matter of only a few weeks between August and October 1854 but revised three years later, when Liszt added a setting of the closing words from *Faust* Part II: a male-voice chorus conjures up the Eternal Feminine and the power of forgiveness in a radiant C major apotheosis.

Liszt completed his *Dante* Symphony in 1856. Its opening 'Inferno' paints a picture of hellish torment, whereas the following 'Purgatorio' describes the process of purification, the soul of the departed being prepared for acceptance into Heaven. As in Dante's *Divina commedia*, Liszt planned to add a third movement, 'Paradiso', but Wagner advised against it, and so Liszt brought the work to an end with a *Magnificat* for women's voices that fades away in weightless ethereality.

In the early 1850s Liszt published fifteen Hungarian Rhapsodies that are now among his best-known works. In each case a slow and richly ornamented introduction, or *lassú*, is followed by a quick section, or *friss*, in which rapidly repeated notes, glissandos and virtuoso leaps are used to imitate the tempestuous playing of groups of gypsies familiar to the composer from his childhood days in Hungary.

In addition to his work as a composer, Liszt also rewrote the history of music as a conductor. Prior to his resignation from his Weimar post in 1858, he conducted more than forty different operas that included not only well-known classics by Gluck, Mozart and Beethoven and older Italian operas but also world premières such as Schubert's *Alfonso und Estrella*, which he staged in June 1854, more than twenty-six years after its composer's death. More significantly, his total of forty operas included twenty-five works by contemporary composers. In September 1852, for example, he gave the local première of Verdi's *Ernani* and two months later conducted the German première of Berlioz's *opéra semi-seria, Benvenuto Cellini*.

But no production caused such a sensation as the world première of Wagner's Romantic opera *Lohengrin*, which Liszt unveiled on 28 August 1850 – Goethe's birthday. Liszt and Wagner had got to know each other in Paris in 1840, but it was not until 1848 that the contacts between them became any closer. In 1849 Liszt conducted the Weimar première of Wagner's *Tannhäuser* on the occasion of the birthday celebrations of the Grand Duchess Maria Pawlowna. But then the May Uprising broke out in Dresden, an insurrection in which Wagner himself, then Kapellmeister at the Royal Court Opera, played an active part, hoping to topple King Friedrich August II and establish a republic in his place. When the revolution failed, Wagner fled to Weimar, where Liszt sheltered him in the Altenburg. On 16 May 1849 a warrant was issued for Wagner's arrest. Since the warrant bore a lithographic likeness of the composer, it became necessary to conceal him outside the town. On 24 May he finally fled to Switzerland on a false passport that Liszt himself had obtained.

For Liszt to stage *Lohengrin* only a little over a year after this failed *coup d'état* amounted to a revolutionary act in itself. But Liszt revealed great courage not only from a political standpoint, for *Lohengrin* stretched the company's resources almost to breaking point. The Weimar Court Orchestra normally boasted eleven violins, whereas eighteen were needed. Other instruments such as the bass clarinet were missing completely and had to be hired for the occasion. A generous grant of 2,000 thalers made it all possible. Liszt placed almost inhuman demands on himself and his company, holding the unprecedented number of forty-six rehearsals. 'Our first performance passed off relatively well,' he wrote to the composer after the first night. 'The court and the few people in Weimar who understand such matters have nothing but admiration for your work. As for the bulk of the general public, there is no doubt that they will stake their honour on applauding what they do not understand and on finding it beautiful.'[27]

The world première of *Lohengrin* was a milestone in more ways than one, for it not only cemented the lifelong friendship between Liszt and Wagner, it also laid the foundations for Wagner's definitive breakthrough as a composer. Liszt's enthusiasm for Wagner – his junior by only two years – survived the passage of time. Between August 1850 and May 1851 *Lohengrin* was performed five times in Weimar, and in the spring of 1853 Liszt even mounted a regular Wagner Festival, with performances of *Der fliegende Holländer, Tannhäuser* and *Lohengrin* all within the space of three weeks.

As an itinerant piano virtuoso, Liszt had been his own master, but with his Weimar appointment he found himself caught up in an unyielding administrative machine. Every member of the ruling house had his or her own household, the extent of its bureaucracy apparent from the number and variety of its titles: equerry, grand marshal, lord high cupbearer, senior chamberlain, grand master of the hunt, grand master of the forest, chamberlains, ladies-in-waiting, gentlemen of the bedchamber, maids of honour, court hairdressers, personal physicians, court surgeons, a court dentist, a court apothecary and so on.

The court Kapellmeister's immediate superior was the marshal of the grand duke's household, whose sphere of authority extended from the grand duke's wardrobe to the court kitchen, the cellar and confectionary and from the silver room to supervision of the royal bedlinen, laundry, gardens and stables as well as the court theatre and court orchestra. Although Liszt could generally count on the goodwill of the grand duke's family, he had few friends among the marshal's staff, which was made up of officials whose only desire was to see everything working smoothly. Special requests were regarded as disruptive, and the famous conductor's friendly dealings with the members of Carl Alexander's family were eyed with suspicion. Some contemporaries felt that Liszt was taking on too much, while others again described his activities as unnecessary. As early as November 1851 Wagner had put his finger on the basic problem when he wrote to Liszt and asked: 'What do you still hope for from Weimar? It is with sad sincerity that I tell you I am bound to regard your efforts in Weimar as fruitless. [. . .] Indeed, I can look on only in sadness! Beside you I see only stupidity, narrow-mindedness, baseness – and the empty conceit of jealous courtiers who are envious – with such lamentable justification – of genius's every success!'[28]

Wagner was merely stating what Liszt was presumably unwilling to admit to himself, namely, that the majority of Weimar's residents failed to understand what Liszt was trying to achieve or dismissed his activities as meaningless. Generally Liszt kept his feelings under control and avoided showing how much he was hurt by professional intrigues and malicious gossip, but there were times when the situation became intolerable. Wagner witnessed one such incident in May 1849, when Liszt was overcome with fury at the hypocritical mendaciousness of the people all around him:

> He normally gave the impression of a man at peace with himself and the world, but on this occasion he was so provoked as to be reduced to a truly alarming state in which, almost gnashing his teeth with rage, he inveighed against the world, a world that had reduced me too to feelings of total indignation.[29]

Liszt must have been beside himself, for Wagner refers to comments so 'frightening' that Liszt suffered a 'violent attack of nerves' in consequence.

When Liszt was angry, he often found himself in conflict with the authorities. It was 'scandalous', he complained in January 1849, 'that people hereabouts are haled before the criminal courts for trifles'. He had, he went on, been repeatedly

> punished for the most petty misdemeanours that would have been a matter of the utmost indifference in any other town or city, but the authorities here – each and every one of them – are quite dreadful. This is very much the home of narrow-mindedness and philistinism, the people of Weimar are all dolts.

Liszt's intemperate tub-thumping certainly had an effect, not least with the clerk of the Weimar Criminal Court, Constantin von Uslar, who happened to overhear the remark and, feeling that his own honour had been impugned, accused Liszt of insulting him. The case was discussed by the regional government, which at that date in its history still doubled as a court of law. The prosecutor announced smugly that 'Dr Lißt [*sic*] is known to us only as a European figure notable for his piano playing but otherwise is totally unknown, so that we are unable to understand how it could ever occur to him to comment on the criminal court.'[30] Liszt was finally fined 10 thalers, which he refused to pay. The court of appeal in Jena later quashed the sentence, arguing that it had been impossible to prove the alleged offence.

Although this particular incident ended in Liszt's favour, he had numerous other opportunities to find himself in difficult situations. Berlioz recalls one such episode in Prague, when Liszt drank 'whole rivers of champagne' at a gala dinner in the city, before setting off back to his hotel at two in the morning. Berlioz and his secretary Gaëtano Belloni had their hands full trying to persuade him not to engage in a duel with a passing stranger 'at two yards' range':

> When daylight came we felt somewhat anxious for Liszt, who was giving a concert at noon. At half-past eleven he was still asleep. They finally woke him; he climbed into a carriage, arrived at the hall, entered to a triple-barrelled broadside of applause, sat down, and played as I do not believe he has ever played in his life. Verily, there is a God for pianists.[31]

Role Playing

From the outset the most poisonous thorn in the relationship between Liszt and Carolyne von Sayn-Wittgenstein proved to be its unresolved legal dimension. Unable to marry (we shall later have occasion to recount the history of their attempts to do so), they had no alternative but to live in sin, and although this state of affairs may be completely normal today, it was regarded by the couple's contemporaries as an affront to society. Carolyne, after all, belonged to the European aristocracy, while Liszt's post as Kapellmeister in Extraordinary to the Weimar court thrust him into the public spotlight. In a small town with a population of some 12,000 inhabitants, nothing could go unnoticed, and the couple's cohabitation in the Altenburg high above the town was deemed immoral by a good number of Weimar's residents.

As if this were not already bad enough, Liszt was forever having to justify his liaison. Many observers could simply not get it into their heads that he had made a deliberate choice in the matter, and even in faraway Paris society tongues wagged about the alleged misalliance. When Anna Liszt reported that Parisians were making fun of Carolyne's unattractive appearance, Liszt defended the princess in words both affectionate and touching:

> I don't know why Princess G[agarin] told you that Princess W[ittgenstein] isn't beautiful. If the occasion arises, you should tell your friends and acquaintances that I believe myself to be a connoisseur in such matters and that Princess W[ittgenstein] is beautiful, indeed I would even say that she is very beautiful in terms of that significant and indestructible beauty that the rays of the soul are alone capable of giving to the physiognomy and to every other detail of a living organism.[32]

Liszt's honest declaration of his love may have impressed his mother, but it did nothing to reassure Weimar's self-styled guardians of morality. Whenever conversation turned to the princess, the reaction in the town was one of scandalized offence. Her poor grasp of German, her foreign accent, her chain-smoking – in Weimar she was always regarded as an outcast and as the 'princesse russe', even her physical appearance making her suspect in the eyes of the locals. 'Dark hair and eyes, together with her sallow complexion, made her look somehow foreign,' recalled Adelheid von Schorn, a friend of both Liszt and Carolyne. 'After all, she was of pure Polish stock. A fairly large nose gave her face a curious importance, around her mouth lay an indescribably friendly expression.'[33] And then there were her clothes! Carolyne was fond of wearing unusual dresses and gaudy hats, making her resemble nothing so much as a magnificent exotic bird and testing the tolerance of the narrow-minded townspeople to its very limits.

Her high-handed manner and tendency to sound overexcited when speaking also antagonized the locals. Nor was it easy to keep up with her in conversation, as Hans von Bülow reported:

> The next day I lunched with Liszt and had an opportunity to get to know the princess a little better, especially to hear her speaking, for she talks for hours on end and scarcely allows her interlocutor half a minute to reply. [. . .] Liszt was not present at this conversation, which the princess conducted with admirable perspicacity, constantly making new assertions that were never superficial and all the while smoking the strongest imaginable cigars that produced a terrible, noxious cloud of smoke.

Once she got into her stride, there was no stopping her:

> Alchemy and the French actress Rachel, painting and German nationality – in short, the entire macrocosm and microcosm were passed in review, and the princess was once again the centre of every conversation. [. . .] It was all so interesting that I was unable to tear myself away; but I finally did so, and not a moment too soon, for I had a violent headache all evening, so much had the princess's conversation affected me.[34]

Carolyne was more than capable of talking the hind leg off the proverbial donkey, leaving even Wagner amazed at his friend's ability to put up with it. The 'Frau Kapellmeister', as he mockingly referred to her, frequently got on his nerves, and when Liszt and his lover spent several weeks staying with Wagner in Zurich in 1856, he unburdened himself on Bülow:

> We did a lot together, but the time that we spent in each other's company would have been even more productive if illness on the one hand and the princess's appallingly professorial manner on the other hadn't disrupted us to such an appreciable extent. But inasmuch as the woman is as she is, namely, a *monstrum per excessum* in terms of both mind and heart, it's impossible to be angry with her for long, only it takes Liszt's incomparable temperament to endure all this vivacity; a poor devil like me often felt ill in consequence – I really can't abide this constant excitement.[35]

From today's point of view, Carolyne's professorial manner seems as amusing as it is curious, saying much about her eccentric character, while also revealing certain aspects of her life with Liszt at the Altenburg. 'Liszt does not have much ambition of his own,' recalled the diplomat Theodor von Bernhardi.

> He seems to be weak by nature, someone who simply goes with the flow; an indulgent enjoyment of life and having his vanity flattered would probably always have been enough for him, or at least they would have sufficed for a very long time. But Carolyne has enough ambition for the two of them, she wants to make something of him – and no doubt she is planning to play a role in all this herself.[36]

It is not hard to guess that Bernhardi thought little of the court Kapellmeister and his companion, and it is entirely possible that his assessment is unduly gloomy, but in general he was not wrong, for Carolyne was indeed obsessed with the idea of saving Liszt and of saving him, moreover, from himself. She believed he was indolent by nature, on which point she was by no means wide of the mark, and she was convinced that he himself suffered more than anyone from his occasional tendency to become bogged down in routine. In short, she felt called upon to organize Liszt's life for him and to give that life a new sense of meaning, hence her intemperate ambition.

It was but one small step from seeking to inspire her partner to controlling his life and clipping his wings. She began by refusing to let Liszt out of her sight when he was composing. Her own reading of the situation was as follows:

> I always worked in the same room as him, otherwise he would never have composed any of the works that date from his Weimar period. He wasn't lacking in genius, he just lacked the ability to sit still for any length of time, a virtue no less important than hard work and perseverance. If there's no one around to help him, he can't work – and if he feels that he can't work, he resorts to stimulants.[37]

By 'stimulants' Carolyne meant alcohol. She regarded herself as Liszt's adviser, activator and enabler and ultimately as his muse, in which regard she inspired him not by her beauty or charm but by forcing him to sit at his desk by sheer willpower. Berlioz saw for himself what this involved. When he admitted to her in a letter that he lacked the courage to start work on his planned opera *Les Troyens*, she demanded that he should come to a decision: 'Listen, if you shrink from the difficulties this work can and must bring you, if you are so feeble as to be afraid to face everything for Dido and Cassandra, then never come back here – I refuse to see you again.' Berlioz's laconic comment was that 'Milder words than these would have been enough to decide me.'[38] *Les Troyens* ultimately became his masterpiece.

To a certain extent, Liszt was happy to be forced to work in this way. Indeed, he even sought out the princess's help, especially for his literary endeavours. When in 1855 he set about writing a 100-page article on Berlioz and his symphony *Harold en Italie*, Carolyne protested. Their discussion centred on its title, which Liszt felt should contain the term 'programme music'. 'I can't tell you how strong is my aversion to having these words in the title,' she wrote back:

> At all events, it seems unnecessary and possibly even harmful and presumptuous. I don't suppose I need tell you that what is at stake here is not foolish obstinacy or some literary standpoint but that I

would regard it as a kind of presumption that ill assorts with the calm and relaxed nature in which you treat these themes. It sounds as if what you are saying is this: 'Although I am speaking about Berlioz, B. is just an excuse to speak about myself. Pay close attention.' [. . .] The term 'programme music' strikes me as too direct, something I find profoundly repugnant. That's what I wanted to tell you. But let me know if you plan to keep it or whether you'll do me the kindness of sticking to the initial heading.[39]

Liszt gave way and the article was published under the harmless heading of 'Berlioz and his *Harold* Symphony'.

A second example shows Carolyne dispensing sensible, well-considered advice. On this occasion the object of discussion was Liszt's assistant Joachim Raff, who was born in 1822 and came to Weimar in early 1850 in order to help Liszt by copying scores, dealing with his correspondence and generally running errands for him. As a composer in his own right, Raff had experience of orchestration, a field in which Liszt himself was still untried in his early years in Weimar, and so Liszt entrusted his assistant with this task between 1850 and the end of 1853. Decades later this state of affairs resulted in the misguided claim that Raff was the creative brains behind Liszt's orchestral music, a claim that is in fact absurd. The composition sketches that Liszt gave his assistant to orchestrate were already covered in instructions, and as soon as he received them back, he would work through Raff's version bar by bar, undertaking countless retouchings, corrections and revisions. Moreover, Liszt repeatedly revised his early orchestral compositions in the course of his time in Weimar, with the result that there is ultimately no doubt that every printed note was his and his alone.

Liszt evidently thought nothing of all this, whereas Carolyne clearly felt otherwise, regarding his approach as unthinking and even dangerous. As if anticipating the problems that were later to arise, she wrote to him in July 1853:

But why ever are you leaving the orchestration to Raff? Which painter would be content to draw the outlines and leave the colouring to his pupils? 'Raff isn't the pupil of a painter,' you will reply. But nor is he you. Orchestration is part and parcel of an individual style, and his style is ponderous. [. . .] Perhaps I'm talking nonsense, but it seems to me that the style – the way in which the idea is covered and clothed to which you rightly attach such importance – invariably suffers if this style is initially applied, prescribed and effectively determined by someone other than the work's inspired creator. Although I myself have little patience in this regard, if I had this creative talent, I would prefer the other person to hone, smooth, tighten up and polish the work rather than defining the outlines and the conception of my draft. It would be impossible for me to develop the sketches of anyone else and to lend them any fervour even if I had drafted and inspired them myself.[40]

In spite of her reservations in the case of Raff, Carolyne had no hesitation, conversely, in meddling herself in Liszt's activities as a writer, so much so, indeed, that we are left wondering who really wrote the books and articles that appeared under his name. Around two-thirds of these texts date from Liszt's years in Weimar, when the Altenburg resembled nothing so much as a medieval scriptorium, with Liszt dictating and Carolyne noting down what he said. In some passages he insisted on a literal transcription, but other sections he merely outlined and left Carolyne to work them up. He would then ask his scribe to read through the whole text and if necessary make corrections, adding new material or altering the existing wording. Carolyne then prepared a fair copy which she would entrust to one of his secretaries to translate into German (Liszt himself preferred to work in French). Peter Cornelius translated many of Liszt's writings into German, including an article on Wagner's *Das Rheingold* that appeared at the beginning of 1855, shortly after Cornelius had submitted his work to Liszt and the princess for their approval. Liszt himself expressed his satisfaction. Cornelius reports what happened next:

As soon as he [i.e. Liszt] left the room, she started on a third round of changes, turning everything upside down so that I grew positively alarmed. Every word was criticized and argued over. But when we'd finished and she started all over again on a fourth round of changes, trying to tease even more subtle nuances from the text, I felt as if I'd go mad. She wanted to find an alternative to 'Vergangnes' ('past') and having exhausted 'Durchlebtes' ('experienced') and 'Dagewesenes' ('erstwhile') and so on, I said: 'Just write "Passiertes" ("happened")' – and she did, but later she said to me with the sweetest of smiles: 'Perhaps you'll find a better term – it does sound a little prosaic.' I was very annoyed at this whole afternoon. If it had been something important! But it's all just clichés, it's just an exercise in the art of concealing one's thoughts.[41]

Liszt himself was guilty of adopting an unduly florid style, but the princess's additions make his writings unreadable, their phraseology risibly inflated and teeming with elaborate archaisms. This was certainly true of his monograph on Chopin, which was published in 1852. 'I very much doubt if the subject could be treated in a more appropriate or poetic way by anyone other than Liszt,' Hans von Bülow wrote to his mother, 'but there is a lot that I find unattractive, not least because I suspect that it is a collaboration with the princess.'[42] Years later, when a new edition was being planned, Carolyne assumed complete control, and the *Chopin* that appeared on the market under Liszt's name in 1879 had little in common with the original version and was entirely Carolyne's handiwork.

The princess was undoubtedly motivated by good intentions when she encouraged Liszt to work and discouraged him from using 'stimulants', and from that point of view it is questionable whether the Weimar years would have been as productive without her. But it is also true that Liszt allowed himself to be humiliated by her in ways that now seem simply embarrassing. His letters to her – and he always used the formal 'Sie', rather than the more intimate 'Du' as a form of address – were often signed 'Fainéant' (Lazybones), suggesting at least a note of self-irony. But Carolyne continued to demand more and more evidence of his love and affection, demands he met with typical generosity:

You ask me in today's letter: 'What is your first thought when you wake up, what is your first concern of the day?' Well, do you not hear

it, do you not feel it, do you not sense it with the same infallible
certainty that you would feel if you could touch it with your own
fingers? – You and again you and unceasingly you! I speak to you and
weep for you – I praise you, bless you, worship you and love you!⁴³

Elsewhere he struck a similar note: 'How small and weak I feel beside you,
and above all how wretched I am when I am not near you! I don't even
dare speak to you about my love – but you understand me, you feel my
heart beating in yours, don't you? And the dear Lord will take pity on us!'⁴⁴

Carolyne generally replied with adoring epistles whose wearisome
length is surpassed only by their stilted style. The letter she wrote from
Carlsbad on 11 July 1853 assumed epic proportions, three pages of
personal information being followed by more than ten pages of religious
observations on Moses and King Solomon and by four pages of altogether bizarre protestations of love. The following day she continued in
the same vein: 'I lie at your small and beloved feet – I kiss them, I slip
beneath their soles and place them on the back of my neck – with my
hair I sweep the path that you must take and lie down in your footsteps.'
Liszt, she went on, was 'the handiwork of God [. . .] made to be cherished, venerated and loved, yea, verily unto death and madness.'⁴⁵ On
another occasion, she wrote:

Adieu, idolized angel! I kiss your beautiful little feet and cling to your
lips, so that my gaze and my soul may lose themselves in the infinity
of your own gaze, from which two rivers of honey flow, drowning me
in sweetness and infinite pleasure. Oh, my beloved, how good you
are to the woman who is so in love with you! – and who in all that she
is is yours alone.⁴⁶

Carolyne often signed her messages 'ton Sclavichon', 'your little slave',
although it is not always apparent who was the slave of whom. Whatever
the answer, it is clear that with the passage of time Liszt found it ever
more difficult to respond in kind and confess to his feelings of love for
Carolyne in the way she demanded. On 22 June 1852, for example, we
find him writing to her that

If I cannot tell you how much I love you at all times and in all things,
you must forgive me and put it down to my nerves. Otherwise you
risk not only being unjust to me but mean towards yourself – the
only form of meanness of which you are capable and which you must
rectify without delay, because it pains me.[47]

Was this merely linguistic acrobatics or, rather, the voice of a man who
increasingly found himself lacking the words to express his true feelings? Presumably both aspects are true. Liszt wanted to gratify the princess and sought refuge in artifice and the formulaic. On one occasion,
when Theodor von Bernhardi became embroiled in an argument with
Carolyne over her inordinate enthusiasm for the Catholic Church, Liszt
leapt to her defence: 'He *must*, it seems, take on this defence; at least, he
tries, while speaking, to read in Carolyne's eyes how far he may, or
should, go. His arguments, however, are again merely superficial, rather
like those of a police officer.'[48]

Bernhardi was a diplomat with a good understanding of people
and immediately noticed that Liszt merely reflected the views of
his mistress, whereas his own opinions remained nebulous: 'It is a
definite system with him never to express an opinion on anything, even
the most trifling matters, so as not to compromise himself or give
offence.'[49]

Liszt was a man of many faces or, to put it another way, a man with
many masks, a man whose ability to present a façade to the world many
of his contemporaries found bewildering and even annoying, not least
his propensity for bombast, affectation and play-acting. But under
Carolyne von Sayn-Wittgenstein's influence he now revealed a different
aspect of his personality to his three children, Cosima, Blandine and
Daniel. To this new aspect we now turn our attention.

Short Shrift

If Daniel uses his good qualities and gradually becomes a man of
distinction, generous of spirit, hard-working and intelligent, honest
and steadfast in character, I shall help him, I shall serve him and I

shall guide him, but he should not expect to find in me a weak father
who is easy to take in.

Liszt was furious, and in a letter to his mother of 21 September 1848, he
threatened to give 'short shrift' of his son, 'for I can hardly not give a
damn when I see people drawn into stupidity and idleness'.[50] Liszt's
words were extreme, since his son had done no wrong, but the letter is
interesting in that it marks the beginning of a chapter in his life when his
relations with his three children were to undergo a significant change.
Until then he had been a father typical of many artists, invariably absent
but good-natured in his own way. Suddenly, however, he appears as the
strict head of his family, issuing warnings and dispensing punishments.

It is worth recalling at this point that Blandine and Cosima were
attending the Institut des Demoiselles run by Louise and Laure Bernard
in the rue Montparnasse in Paris, while Daniel was being privately
taught and preparing to sit for his entrance examination at the city's
prestigious Lycée Bonaparte. All three children spent their weekends
and holidays with their grandmother, of whom they were extremely
fond. For the present, conversely, they had no contact with their mother,
Marie d'Agoult. And so the years passed by.

In early January 1850, however, a change took place, when Blandine
and Cosima, out for a walk, decided to call on their mother. It was five
years since they had last seen each other, and suddenly Marie was
standing face to face with her daughters. Both sides were happy to be
reunited, but the girls said nothing to their grandmother about the
encounter. On 8 January 1850, Anna Liszt left for Weimar to visit her
son and his partner, leaving the children on their own in Paris for the
first time. Further meetings with the countess were arranged. In mid-
February, a month after their first spontaneous encounter, Blandine
mentioned their contact in passing in a letter to her father: 'We've seen
Mama again, and so great was our joy that it made us forget the pain of
such a long separation.' In all innocence, she added: 'Mama longs to see
us more often.'[51]

If Blandine had imagined the fury she would unleash, she would
presumably have kept silent. Liszt was beside himself. For five years

Marie d'Agoult had not shown any interest in her children, he fulminated, although she could have visited them at any time – after making
prior arrangements with Mme Bernard. He felt that his former partner
had gone behind his back. Then it was Blandine's turn to receive a
dressing down. 'You were wrong, and you wronged me by assuming that
there were not compelling reasons for my refusal to allow you to have
any contact with your mother, contact that in the natural order of things
would, of course, have existed.' Liszt did not shy away from emotional
blackmail, claiming that Anna Liszt in particular had wept 'bitter tears'
at her grandchildren's inconsiderate behaviour. As a punishment
Blandine and Cosima were to leave the Institut. 'You have behaved
badly,' he ranted,

> but what's done is done, and so you must make every effort to make
> good your mistake, and this will be possible only if you refrain from
> corresponding with your mother and from having any other contact
> with her until such time as I order otherwise.[52]

Prayers and entreaties were in vain. Liszt remained implacable, and the
sisters had to take their leave of their much-loved teacher, Laure Bernard.

But what was to be done? Should Liszt invite his children to the
Altenburg? Such a course of action was impossible, for the Weimar
court would never have allowed it. But Liszt himself had no interest in
surrounding himself with his 'fillettes', as he called his daughters. For the
present, the children returned to live with their grandmother, at least as
a short-term solution. But then Carolyne proposed a way out of the
dilemma.

The Visit of the Old Lady

It was only with great difficulty and in considerable pain that Louise
Adélaïde Patersi de Fossombroni was able to alight from the train in
Weimar after she had spent the entire journey from St Petersburg to the
Thuringian provinces sitting bolt upright in her compartment. The
seventy-two-year-old was a woman of principle, and since she knew

very well what was seemly, she had deliberately refused to lean back into the upholstery. By the end of her journey her muscles and joints were so stiff that she was barely able to move. Two months were to pass before she had recovered from her ordeal.

Her visit was undertaken at Carolyne's suggestion. She had been living in retirement for some time, having previously worked as a governess in leading households in Paris and elsewhere and assumed responsibility for the education of the children of prominent aristocrats. Among her charges had been the Comtesse Isaure de Foudras and Ludemille de Thermes, as well as Zénaïde Françoise Clary, who in 1835 married Napoléon Berthier, Prince de Wagram. But, at least from our own point of view, her most famous pupil was none other than Carolyne Iwanowska, otherwise known as Carolyne von Sayn-Wittgenstein. Mme Patersi was eagerly awaited at the Altenburg, for Carolyne had great plans for her former governess, who was to travel to Paris and take charge of Liszt's recalcitrant daughters.

As chance would have it, Madame Patersi's elder sister, Jeanne Claire de Saint-Mars, was already living in Paris in the rue Casimir-Périer. Events now moved swiftly. Even before Mme Patersi had arrived in the French capital, Liszt had already written to his mother to ask her to hand over Cosima and Blandine to Mme de Saint-Mars. He would brook no objections:

> I have asked Mme Patersi never to let my daughters go out without her and to visit you often. I am convinced that you will soon get to know her so well that you will come to value and love her for the good that her guidance will bring to my children. She will decide what they should fittingly be permitted to do and what should be forbidden them; she is thoroughly familiar with my ideas on the subject of their upbringing and of their future, ideas that coincide in every way with her own.[53]

This decision had far-reaching consequences for the sixty-two-year-old Anna Liszt, who had to give up the grandchildren she loved, and since her apartment was now too big and too expensive, she had to move into a smaller one in the rue Penthièvre. Her household was broken up, and part of its contents, including Liszt's library, was handed over to the children's new governess.

Why was Liszt's reaction to his children and their mother so extreme? It seems, after all, to have been completely disproportionate to any offence they may have caused. And it has to be said that he had no real interest in his family. His children had to ensure merely that they did not annoy him. But by visiting Marie d'Agoult they had brought a degree of disquiet to his life that he thought he could resolve by engaging the services of the elderly Mme Patersi and her sister. His tactics were undoubtedly inspired by the princess, who for her part had an ulterior motive in behaving as she did. Since the two governesses were devoted to Carolyne, the latter was effectively installing her own plenipotentiaries in the French capital, their most important task being to keep Marie d'Agoult from seeing her children. Carolyne felt nothing but contempt for the countess, despite the fact that the two women had never met. Marie was to be stigmatized as a bad mother, while Carolyne was the children's new mother and, above all, a better mother than her predecessor.

This could be achieved only by rigorous means. What began at the end of 1850 with Mme Patersi's arrival in Paris and lasted until August 1855 amounted to an authoritarian regime not dissimilar to that used for breaking in horses. Her charges were to learn and inwardly digest the norms of social behaviour as defined by Mme Patersi, whose view of society belonged to the *ancien régime*. She was born in the Brittany village of Saint-Hilaire-de-Chaléons in 1778 and, the product of a bygone age, had taken little interest in social and political developments in Europe since 1789. Daily life in the rue Casimir-Périer was characterized by a contempt for modern life and for all things 'bourgeois'. The two governesses demanded total subordination from their charges and were anything but old-maidish in achieving this aim. Childish defiance, protests and disobedience were severely punished. 'Tears are just water', the two old women mocked when Cosima and her sister were reduced to weeping.

As the years went by, the two young sisters learnt ways of repressing their emotions. They wrote letters to their father in distant Weimar, expressing only what they believed he wanted to hear. They censored their own words and behaviour and, superficially at least, they came to terms with their situation in order to prevent it from becoming any worse than it already was. The line between hypocrisy and fawning obsequiousness was necessarily fluid. On one occasion we find Blandine writing to her father to report that Mme Patersi was implacable in her attempts to teach the young sisters to be good wives: 'She assures us that our husbands will no longer allow us to get away with all the things for which she now reproaches us.' And she went on: 'We have little experience in these matters but we understand very well that she is perfectly right.'[54] In another letter Blandine assured her father: 'Mme Patersi is excellent for us, she gives us really motherly advice, and every day I grow increasingly fond of her. Sometimes we argue, but that certainly doesn't alter our feelings of affection for her.'[55] Cosima was forced to add her voice to this chorus of approval and promised her father that

> We would give anything to make you happy, you who feel such great love for us and who are so kind to us. We are surrounded by the maternal care and genuine interest on the part of these ladies and shall proceed along the lines that you desire.[56]

Carolyne, too, could be satisfied with Mme Patersi's work. In a letter written jointly, Blandine and Cosima assured her:

> Madame or, rather, dear mother, for how else could we address you since you yourself call us your daughters, and the tenderness that you express in your letters is that of a mother. Yes, Madame, please be our mother, for you have long been so in our eyes.

The young sisters had clearly been brainwashed, praising their stepmother to the skies:

> All the lessons that your letter contains, dear mother, were taught us long ago by Mme Patersi. We are keenly aware of Mme Patersi's merits. She certainly does not spoil us, and yet we are grateful to you for

having entrusted us to her care. She often tells us about your afflictions, and, believe us, dear mother, when we say that our hearts go out to you and that the day that brings an end to those sufferings will be blessed a thousand times in our sight, as it will be by all who love you.[57]

What the two young sisters actually felt was very different. Although they were aware of the atmosphere of hypocrisy, repression and false etiquette in which they were brought up, there was no one in whom they could confide, least of all their father and their stepmother, and so they turned to a private diary. Blandine's unpublished papers, now in the Bibliothèque nationale in Paris, include the following 'Scène de la vie intime'. Amusing though it may seem at first sight, it is almost certainly based on a true event, so that any laughter it might induce must surely die on our lips.

It is 10 o'clock in the morning of 28 February 1855. All upper-class houses at this period still had a concierge who generally lived on the ground floor, where a porter's lodge was situated next to the main entrance. Here letters would be left and visitors had to report. The concierge – Dandy – and his friend, the coachman, are alone on this particular Wednesday morning and whiling away their time together:

CONCIERGE: It's my name day today. I'd rather be enjoying a drink than having to sweep these stupid stairs.

MME *** (*entering*): Mme de Saint-Mars?

CONCIERGE: She has just left, Madame, I don't know where to, but I think she'll be away for at least two hours as she was carrying a number of parcels. She may have gone to the market, which is some distance away, but she may also be visiting Monsieur Barbe. There's a letter for her there. I don't know how urgent it is.

MME *** (*exiting*): What a disrespectful and garrulous concierge. His chatter was the last straw.

COACHMAN: Didn't you say you wanted a drink?

CONCIERGE: Yes, I did. And I do. I've no desire to go on stitching this jacket. It's as much fun as cleaning out the cellar. Come on, let's be off.

COACHMAN: Yes, gladly. But do you have any money on you?

CONCIERGE: No, damn it. I recently took fifty francs too much for an article of clothing, but I've already spent it. And I don't suppose you've got any either, you idiot?

COACHMAN: No, I recently had to pay a fine because I'd forgotten to return to the square. It really wasn't worth it. I wasn't thinking straight.

CONCIERGE: Yes, I can see that. You've something on your mind. I can see it from that crafty look in your eyes.

COACHMAN: Really? I can't tell you how happy that makes me. You're the only person, my only friend, who thinks of me as crafty.

CONCIERGE: Yes, but that's not the point. The point is that we need to find some money. Up there on the fourth floor there are two elderly ladies and two girls . . . but someone's coming: I'll tell you later. Come back in five minutes. We don't have much time. Old Mme Saint-Mars won't be gone for much longer. And once she returns, everything will go wrong. (*Someone approaches the porter's lodge. The Coachman leaves.*)

The scene changes to a cheerful and friendly living room with old red furniture and a large mahogany grand piano, two windows, two doors and a hearth fire. On the mantelpiece are a clock, two vases, two candelabra and two ear pieces. Mme Patersi is writing at a desk in the middle of the room, Cosima is at the piano, Blandine is reading near the window.

MME PATERSI: I've written to dear Caroline. I tell her everything. She thinks that crafty people are just stupid people.

COSIMA (*exchanging a conspiratorial glance with Blandine and whispering to her across the room*): I'd give anything for something to happen to prove that crafty people aren't so stupid.

BLANDINE: Shush! Opportunities like that arise all the time – today, tomorrow, the day after tomorrow, perhaps even as we're speaking.

MME PATERSI: My dear children, wasn't it made clear to you at your boarding school what reason is, what purpose it serves and how it helps us to avoid all the minor inconveniences of practical life?

COSIMA (*animatedly*): No, Madame, they weren't as stupid as that.

Mme Patersi: You disrespectful child! Go to your room this instant! (*Cosima laughs and leaves.*)

Blandine (*very seriously*): We weren't told, Madame, but if you'd be so kind as to explain it to me, I promise to listen carefully.

(*She laughs because Cosima has returned and sat down beside her without Mme Patersi noticing.*)

Mme Patersi: Well, my dear child, reason or judgement or the noble art of understanding all of the things that cannot be perceived by crafty individuals who are merely stupid leads to something both admirable and at the same time practical . . .

Cosima (*aside to Blandine*): I can't wait to hear the end!

Mme Patersi (*continuing*): . . . it is this that stops you from becoming caught up in a moral predicament that is worse than poverty: misery!!!

Blandine (*very cheekily*): Thank you, Madame, this definition is perfectly clear in my mind.

Mme Patersi: Wait, I haven't finished!

Cosima (*aside to Blandine*): Damn it, that was already too long.

Mme Patersi: People are taken in by cunning not only in ethical matters but in private affairs as well. But you must decide whether we should hold reason in high regard . . . (*laughs*) . . . My dear Blandine, I don't know how we shall end this quarter. Decide whether we should show cunning the door and take care to retain its enemy, noble judgement.

(*There is a ring at the door.*)

Cosima: A timely visit! A thousand thanks!

Blandine (*bored*): Oh, it's the washerwoman.

Mme Patersi: It's my shoemaker.

Cosima: It's a man, I can tell from his gait.

Maidservant (*entering*): Madame, there's someone here to see you.

Mme Patersi: Who is it, my dear Madeleine?

Maidservant: A gentleman demanding the price of a coach ride.

Mme Patersi: What, pray? What? I'm coming.

(*The Coachman enters.*)

Blandine (*to Cosima*): I'd far rather this took place here.

COSIMA: In this way we have a daily drama.

COACHMAN (*talking loudly and with exaggerated friendliness*): Madame, er, Madame, I'm here because I wanted to ask you about the money for a coach ride that you took with these young ladies (*bowing*). I recall it very clearly, Madame.

MME PATERSI (*puzzled*): Which day, my dear man?

COACHMAN: Shrove Tuesday.

BLANDINE: But we didn't go out on Shrove Tuesday.

MME PATERSI: Be quiet, child! Let me sort out the matter with this good man.

COSIMA (*aside to Blandine*): There you have an apology for noble judgement. This is sheer deception.

COACHMAN: Well, Madame, Madame didn't pay me. You gave me a tip and told me that you'd come to the office to pay the rest.

MME PATERSI: Well, my dear man, what do you want? I don't recall the matter. Normally I pay at once as I don't like to run up debts. That's not in my nature as it casts a shadow on the good name of an honest woman.

BLANDINE (*to Cosima*): Instead of throwing him out as a thief, which is what he is, she lectures him on morality and explains her principles to him.

MME PATERSI: So how much do I owe you, my dear man? My sister will be back soon and she would rebuke me if she knew I was paying for coach rides.

COSIMA (*to Blandine*): Oh, how nice!

COACHMAN: Seven francs, Madame, for two and a half hours. You see what a good memory I have. I also remember seeing these young ladies.

COSIMA (*animatedly*): That's not true! You're lying!

MME PATERSI: My God! Is that how I've brought you up, my dear child? Well, my good man, I'll give you four more francs for the impertinence that this badly brought-up girl has shown you. I'll fetch the money.

COACHMAN (*bowing*): Thank you, Madame, I knew that Madame's memory would soon return.

(*The same, except for Mme Patersi.*)

COSIMA (*animatedly to the Coachman*): You're a thief. You're abusing her credulity. Kindly give us your number.

COACHMAN: Forgive me, Mademoiselle!

COSIMA: That won't help you. You need taking to the police station.

MME PATERSI (*entering*): What have you been saying to this good man, my dear? (*She gives him fifteen francs.*) Come! Give us your number and we'll use your carriage when we next go out. That will help to make things up to you.

THE COACHMAN (*disappearing with the words*): Long live life and Dandy!

BLANDINE AND COSIMA: Human misery!

MME PATERSI: The man was right. It showed true judgement to pay him and not give in to the vanity that misleads us into never admitting our mistakes.

COSIMA: One should allow oneself to be led by the nose.[58]

This scene says much about the narrow-mindedness of an old governess, but it tells us even more about the spiritual and intellectual confines of the world in which the two young women grew up. And none of this sheds a good light on Liszt. Why did he do nothing to save his daughters from being subjected to such bigotry and iron discipline? The answer is hardly flattering to him. Presumably he was simply unaware of his daughters' suffering. Although he noted that Blandine and Cosima had 'a tendency to burst into tears and make scenes', he evidently gave no further thought to the matter. For him, this was simply one of those characteristics 'that are among the most annoying in women and especially in yourselves, for I find such a quality supremely unsympathetic'. And that was the end of the matter: 'Tears are attractive only on festive occasions, which, thank God, are infrequent enough. This blubbering is a parody of those beautiful tears, and as such I abhor it.'[59]

Basically, Liszt just wanted to be left in peace, although it may be said in his defence that during the five years of Mme Patersi's reign of terror he and Carolyne were having a particularly difficult time themselves.

Although this is no excuse for his behaviour, it may at least help to explain it.

The 'Wittgenstein Affair'

This is the title of a substantial set of documents now lodged in the Thuringian State Archives in Weimar. It contains a total of 387 documents bound in fifteen individual volumes and running to over 1,000 pages. Those who wrote and received these letters, memoranda and notes were all members of the Weimar court. The civil servants who worked in the grand duke's archives were undoubtedly highly efficient and gathered together everything relating to the 'Wittgenstein Affair' that came to their attention. In addition to jottings made by Grand Duke Karl Friedrich, his wife Maria Pawlowna and their son Carl Alexander, there are also papers prepared by various ministers, ambassadors, clerks, lawyers and, last but not least, members of the Sayn-Wittgenstein family. Countless letters from Carolyne and her husband Prince Nicholas, their daughter Marie, Nicholas's siblings and Liszt himself are all of invaluable interest to the biographer, making it all the more remarkable that this collection of documents has been largely ignored in writings on Liszt.

The first document dates from July 1848, the last from the summer of 1860 – Carolyne had left Weimar for good only a few weeks earlier, on 17 May 1860. In short, the files cover the twelve years that Liszt and the princess spent together in Weimar. Of course, there are many other sources for this period granting much important information about life in Weimar in general and at the Altenburg in particular. We can trace in detail Liszt's work as a composer during this period, we are familiar with his pupils, and we know about his recitals and his concert tours. But these recently discovered documents allow us to see the story of Liszt and the princess in a new light reflected through the lens of diplomats and politicians. At first sight these documents deal with Carolyne's attempts to annul her marriage so that she could marry Liszt. As we know, both of these endeavours failed. But this is only one of the themes that run through these fifteen volumes, albeit the principal one. The

'Wittgenstein Affair' – the very title of the file speaks volumes – was a political matter that exercised the diplomatic corps in Rome, Weimar and St Petersburg. The result is a veritable detective story whose cast includes the Russian tsar, the Roman Catholic pope, a number of ambitious cardinals, various scheming family members and in the leading roles Liszt and Carolyne themselves.

We should begin our trawl through these documents by noting that in the Catholic Church divorce is not permitted and that only in certain circumstances can a marriage be declared null and void. In short, there was only one way in which Carolyne could marry Liszt during her first husband's lifetime: she had to persuade the authorities in Rome to annul her marriage to Prince Nicholas. She made an initial application to this effect in May 1848, when she wrote to the Consistory Court in Mohilow, justifying her request by arguing that she had been forced into the marriage by her father, who had literally beaten her into submission. The judges questioned the Iwanowskys' domestic servants at the time, who confirmed that force had been used. But there were clearly doubts about the reliability of the evidence provided by these witnesses, with the result that the matter was referred to the Consistory Court in Zhitomir.

From the outset Carolyne acted in full agreement with her husband, who knew all too well that his marriage was over and that his wife would never return to him. For him, there was only one reason for him to undermine the process, and that was the Iwanowskys' money. As long as the two were married, Nicholas had a claim on a part of the princess's vast fortune, and so he would agree to an annulment only if he could derive some pecuniary advantage from it. Carolyne was aware of this and, making a virtue of a necessity, she agreed to a deal under whose terms Nicholas would receive Carolyne's estates at Belany, while she herself would be content with a mere 200,000 roubles. All other landed estates would pass to their daughter Marie. This agreement was reached by the couple's negotiators in 1850.

Although Nicholas agreed to the arrangement, it was reached without the knowledge of the Consistory Court in Zhitomir, whose judges declared the marriage valid in 1851 and referred the matter back to their colleagues in Mohilow. Things looked bad for Carolyne. 'It is to be supposed and feared', wrote the distinguished lawyer Moritz Henzschel in a report dated 14 May 1852, 'that notwithstanding the proof that has been adduced the annulment will not be granted and may never be granted since the complaint was raised only years after the marriage was entered into'.[60] To make matters worse, Henzschel also observed that the agreement reached in 1850 violated Russian law since promises bound to a court decision were invalid. His only advice to the appellants was to reach some other agreement.

By the autumn of 1852 the case had ground to a halt, the use of lawyers and intermediaries merely having served to prolong the matter yet further. In order to get things moving again, Nicholas declared his willingness to visit Carolyne in Germany and to speak to her in person. Arrangements for the visit were placed in the hands of Apollonius von Maltitz, a diplomat who had been born in 1795 and who worked as chargé d'affaires at the Russian Embassy in Weimar. He was one of the central figures in the unfolding drama.

Prince Nicholas arrived in Weimar on 12 September 1852, a few days after the Prussian diplomat Theodor von Bernhardi, who had learnt the details of the visit from his fellow diplomat, Baron von Maltitz. Maltitz reported being drawn into the affair against his will, and declared it had caused him nothing but trouble. There was no prospect of a successful outcome since Catholic canon law was very strict. According to Bernhardi,

> Caroline [sic] Wittgenstein claims to know better, she invariably thinks she knows better than anyone else – Maltitz says she is characterized by 'low cunning', that she effortlessly and by preference errs from the straight and narrow and that as a true Pole [sic] she believes that there is nothing that money cannot buy – anywhere.[61]

She had even offered Maltitz money. It is not hard to imagine that the two diplomats did not have a good word to say about the princess.

On the day of his arrival, Prince Nicholas was invited to dine with the grand duke at Schloss Belvedere just outside Weimar. The invitation was a clear snub to Carolyne, who had never been accorded such an honour. The following day Maltitz accompanied Nicholas to the Altenburg.

When he announced Prince Nicholas, Caroline [sic] Wittgenstein again referred him to Liszt, whose behaviour can only be described as impertinent: the prince must not be admitted, he declared, he must not be allowed to see his daughter (by what right?) – he would box the prince's ears (what a poltroon!). Finally, Maltitz asked the furious couple whether they really thought that they would improve their case by using violence.

Once tempers had cooled, the visitors were invited in, but the reunion between Carolyne and Nicholas proved a frosty occasion. 'Their daughter had been well schooled, for she was very cold towards her father and reproached him for the pain that he had caused her mother.' When Bernhardi found Liszt alone a few hours later, he was forced to listen to 'further attacks on the prince, whom he simply referred to as "Nicolas".'[62]

Nicholas von Sayn-Wittgenstein remained in Weimar for a week. On 17 September he and Carolyne signed an agreement in the presence of Marie and Liszt that gave legally binding form to the one reached in 1850. The other arrangements, conversely, were fraught with difficulties. Nicholas, who was a Protestant and who had recently formed a new liaison with a widow living in Berlin, was to obtain a Protestant divorce, while Carolyne was to pursue an annulment through the Catholic Church. Nicholas would then be able to remarry, allowing Carolyne to inform the Catholic judges that her former husband had taken this step. As Bernhardi observed in his diary,

This is highly problematic since it is a basic principle of the Catholic Church that it pays absolutely no heed to what happens outside its own circle. It seems as if Prince Nicholas wants to safeguard his fortune and get married, after which Caroline [sic] will be left to wait and see if she can achieve her aims.[63]

A few days later Bernhardi bumped into Nicholas in Berlin and learnt that everything had worked out to his satisfaction. But Liszt would do better to keep out of his way in future 'in order to avoid an encounter that might be more unfortunate for him than for me'.[64] A proud aristocrat like Nicholas was bound to feel that his honour had been threatened by Liszt's attitude and especially by the threat to box his ears. He could have challenged Liszt to a duel, but presumably he felt that as a middle-class musician Liszt was incapable of offering him satisfaction. In any case, Nicholas wanted only his wife's money, and there were other ways of wreaking vengeance on her and Liszt.

But Nicholas suddenly demanded that Marie should no longer live with her mother and her partner. The atmosphere at the Altenburg had something narcotic about it and was unworthy of an honourable young lady. Maria Pawlowna should invite the fifteen-year-old child to live with her in Weimar and give her an education appropriate to her rank. This demand was a blow for Liszt and Carolyne. And Nicholas's plan was a sophisticated one. After all, he was well within his rights as Marie's father to concern himself with her welfare. And what possible objections could there be to Marie – a Russian citizen – being cared for by the sister of the Russian tsar? Carolyne, who was herself dependent on Maria Pawlowna's protection, refused to admit defeat and repeatedly delayed Marie's move to the grand duke's palace. But the affair took a new and unexpected turn at the end of 1852, a development that was to Carolyne's advantage.

'I've received a letter from Baronne de Talleyrand and another one from the Duchesse de Sagan,' she informed the grand duchess.

> Both of them request my daughter's hand in marriage in the name of the Baron de Talleyrand. In the course of the many occasions on which we have met him, my daughter has come to the conclusion that he is worthy of her choice, and I consider her decision to be a wise one since it seems to me that they are a perfect match in terms of their characters and their whole nature.[65]

The husband-to-be was the thirty-two-year-old Charles-Angélique Baron de Talleyrand-Périgord, a diplomat attached to the French consulate in Weimar. Liszt and Carolyne undoubtedly knew him well as he often attended the matinées at the Altenburg and was a frequent guest of the composer and his household. Even so, it remains uncertain whether the fifteen-year-old Marie had really chosen a Frenchman more than twice her age as her future husband. But his courtship opened up entirely new perspectives in the battle over Marie, for if the two were to marry, Carolyne reckoned that Marie would acquire French nationality and, with it, diplomatic immunity.

Nicholas immediately saw through the ruse. 'This offer of marriage is undoubtedly very honourable,' he wrote to Maria Pawlowna,

> and I would be extremely happy to see my daughter married to a man like the baron. But in view of her age – she has not yet reached her sixteenth birthday – and in consideration of her frail constitution and impaired health, I am very keen to see this wedding postponed.

He ended by striking a maudlin note:

> I hope that your Imperial Highness will grant this exceptional favour to a father who has been sorely afflicted by family misfortunes and who, having long been obliged to forgo domestic happiness of his own, wishes only to ensure that his beloved child may enjoy that happiness herself.[66]

Going even further, the prince then wrote to Tsar Nicholas I, asking him to intervene and to summon Carolyne back to Russia. In the middle of February he wrote to Maltitz:

> You know the questionable character of my wife and the unfortunate situation that exists between us. In order to be able to accommodate His Majesty's [i.e. the tsar's] instructions and give him an unequivocal answer, I see myself obliged to ask Your Excellency for your kind support to persuade my wife to give an official yes or no. Any attempt to prevaricate on her part would be tantamount to a rejection and I should be obliged to inform His Majesty of this.[67]

By now the 'Wittgenstein Affair' had assumed a dimension that went far beyond a mere family dispute, for the appeal to the tsar turned a marital drama into an affair of state. Maria Pawlowna was caught between two stools, for on the one hand she was fond of her Kapellmeister and undoubtedly wanted to help him and his partner, whereas on the other hand she could not ignore her brother's wishes and orders. Torn this way and that, she repeatedly sought the advice of her minister of state, Christian Bernhard von Watzdorf, whose own position was by now unequivocally clear.

In Watzdorf's view, it had to be made absolutely plain to Carolyne that the grand duchess was not in a position 'to do anything more for her and that it must be left to her to decide whether or not to pursue the matter and place her own future and that of her daughter at risk but that in no circumstances can Your Majesty offer her your protection'. If the Russian government were to demand Marie's extradition, their request could not be turned down. Watzdorf urged the grand duchess to

> stick to the answer given even if Dr Liszt threatens to leave and even if he actually does so. No one knows more than I the significance of the loss that this would cause to Weimar. But no one feels as griev- ously as I do the fact that Dr Liszt's presence is being bought at a very high price and that the Grand Duke's court cannot take any further steps to protect this relationship without causing irreparable damage to far more valuable possessions.[68]

In short, Watzdorf regarded the welfare of the state as more important than Liszt's presence in the town. Even so, he tried to exert an influence on Carolyne by appealing to Liszt. Liszt, however, turned down his approach. 'He claimed that it is simply the Wittgenstein family's intrigues that have rendered impossible a Catholic divorce,' Watzdorf noted, following his meeting with Liszt. 'He seemed, therefore, to approve of the princess's decision to reject her husband's latest demand and repeatedly assured me that in no circumstances would she change her mind.'[69] At the Altenburg they were preparing for the worst. If Marie were to be deported, then Liszt hoped that Watzdorf might at least alert him in advance so that he and Carolyne could leave the country in good time.

Liszt now took a risk by informing Maltitz that he could

no longer alter Princess Wittgenstein's resolve. Unless she is to gamble with her honour and with the dignity of her entire life, she can say only no to an ultimatum issued in conditions like those that have been stipulated by Prince Nicholas. [. . .] But the regrettable consequences that are to be feared in the light of such a reply cannot be laid at the princess's door, since she has, after all, showed great honesty and a great willingness for reconciliation and self-sacrifice. It would be like robbing a traveller of his clothes and then blaming him for the chill that he caught as a result of this incident.[70]

By the spring of 1853 a resolution to the affair seemed further away than ever: the grand duchess's attempts to act as go-between had failed to produce any results, the Russian government was still demanding Carolyne's return and Baron Talleyrand was still awaiting a response to his request for Marie's hand in marriage. Nicholas on the one hand and Carolyne and Liszt on the other had risked such high stakes that it was all but impossible for either side to back down without losing face.

To make matters worse, Watzdorf was finally beginning to lose patience with the inhabitants of the Altenburg and had started to plead openly for an end to the *union libre* that was being publicly flaunted high above the town. In a letter to Maria Pawlowna, we find him sinking to new depths of subversion:

I cannot simply sit back and say nothing, for even at the risk that Liszt would leave us for good, it is my duty to inform you that I would see it as a source of genuine good fortune for the town and especially for the Grand Duke's household if the princess were to leave the town as soon as possible. On the last occasion that I saw her, her waistline struck me as highly suspicious and all manner of fears rose up inside me, the realization of which would be truly sad. Even if, as I hope, I am mistaken, this hardly helps the situation. The fact that a married woman who has not yet been divorced keeps house publicly with her lover and lives with him without the least vestige of shame is a violation of morality of a kind rarely found even in large cities but which cannot be allowed to unfold in smaller towns without sooner or later having extremely unfortunate consequences and is in any case little conducive to the good name of our society.

For all he cared, Princess Marie could marry Baron Talleyrand, but if so, Marie's mother must be told quite clearly that 'as long as she continues to live with Dr Liszt as she has done hitherto, then her departure from Weimar would be highly desirable'.[71]

A 'suspicious' waistline? Since ministers do not normally take an interest in the weight issues of prominent members of society, there must have been a more important reason for Watzdorf's concern. In short, he believed – or wanted the grand duchess to believe – that Carolyne was pregnant. Of some relevance in this context is the fact that in the summer of 1853 Carolyne again left Weimar for several weeks: between the middle of July and the middle of August she was at the spa of Carlsbad (Karlovy Vary), some 160 miles away. Officially, she was taking the waters, but there is also the possibility that she was having a child.

Liszt's biographers, especially those of an earlier generation, have always sought to portray the relationship between the composer and the princess as one based purely on friendship, and even the distinguished Liszt scholar Alan Walker does not believe that his protagonist fathered any unplanned children during his years in Weimar. But why should the princess not have conceived a child by Liszt? She was born in 1819, while Liszt was her senior by eight years. In the early 1850s both were in the prime of life and still capable of reproduction. Moreover, Liszt and Carolyne lived together as man and wife – why should they not have slept together? And in an age when there were no reliable methods of contraception, why should the princess not have become pregnant?

Carl Maria Cornelius raised this possibility as long ago as 1925: 'Three children sprang from this union – they were born away from Weimar and housed in Brussels'.[72] One would suppose that he would know what he was talking about since he was the son of Liszt's pupil and secretary, Peter Cornelius, but we need to remember that he was only six when his father died in 1874, meaning he could have gleaned this information only at second or third hand. His comments are certainly not incontrovertible proof of anything. Indeed, we shall probably never know for certain how many children Liszt and the princess may have had, especially since all trace of them would inevitably have been lost once they were taken abroad. If the liaison between Liszt and Carolyne produced any offspring, then their parents' attempts to conceal the truth were undoubtedly successful.

But why should Liszt and Carolyne not have acknowledged their progeny? The social status of the Kapellmeister and the princess was in any case precarious in Weimar, and the birth of an illegitimate child would have been politically explosive, making it impossible for Liszt to have continued his association with the town and with its court. Indeed, there is no doubt that he would have had to leave at once. Moreover, any illegitimate progeny would have meant that Carolyne's attempts to annul her marriage to Prince Nicholas stood no further chance of success. For Liszt and the princess, too much was at stake. Children would again have got in their way.

The Spy in Lace Petticoats

'I have just been brought your dear letter from Badenweiler,' Carolyne wrote to Liszt in mid-July 1853:

> Oh, my angel, do you really think that I think that it is easy for you to be far away from me? Do you not know that I have only one desire in this world, one wish, one longing, one hope, which is to become an indispensable habit for you, just like tobacco and your slippers? That you should need me for your personal wellbeing just as you need your cigars?

While Carolyne was taking the waters in Carlsbad, Liszt had been meeting Wagner in Zurich and was now on his way home to Weimar:

How tired you must be. Ah, I hope that you can at least sleep properly not only at night but also during the daytime – a little after
breakfast, a little after lunch and, finally, a lot after your evening
meal. My beautiful angel, sleep, sleep a lot. You know very well how
envious I am of all those people who see you and speak to you whenever I am not there and how much I prefer to think of you asleep
rather than sacrificing yourself and indulging your love of worldly
pleasures. Do you really not have better things that you could be
doing in Weimar?[73]

It is entirely possible that the princess was mistaken about Liszt's state of
mind, for it was at precisely this time – the middle of 1853 – that a young
woman entered Liszt's circle and left him emotionally shaken. The
woman in question was Agnes Street-Klindworth. Practically everything about her was, until relatively recently, a mystery: her background,
her family and even her date of birth were for a long time obscure.
Although a number of facts about her have emerged over the years, the
mere mention of her name continues even today to raise more questions
than it provides answers. Secretiveness was in fact a part of her makeup,
for she came from a family who preferred not to leave behind any written
evidence. Hers was a life of spying and deception, of secret machinations and treason, of bribery and pimping.

Agnes Street-Klindworth was born in Bremen in October 1825.[74]
Her father, Georg Klindworth, is one of the great unknowns of the nineteenth century. He worked variously as a lawyer, a theatre manager and
a journalist but was in fact one of the most influential spies of his age.[75]
Between the Congress of Vienna in 1814–15 and the 1870s he provided
entire generations of politicians with secret information. The Austrian
diplomat Johann Bernhard von Rechberg described him as

a man of great ability, but venal and willing to serve anyone as a spy,
providing only that that person was prepared to pay him. He invariably served several countries at once and betrayed to those who paid
him the highest price the secrets that had been entrusted to him by
others.[76]

In the course of his career, Klindworth worked for Austria, Prussia, Württemberg, Russia, France, England and Spain, while at the same time establishing a complex network of contacts that he used to virtuoso effect. It helped that he was entirely devoid of moral scruples. Contemporary commentators portray him as a highly intelligent and yet ruthless power-seeker who would stop at nothing to achieve his aims.

Starting in around 1842, his then seventeen-year-old daughter Agnes began to develop a taste for her father's work as a spy, accompanying him on his travels, conducting discreet background talks and delivering secret messages. Various police reports relating to Klindworth explicitly describe Agnes as his accomplice. She is said to have been married to an army captain by the name of Ernest Denis-Street, but there is no evidence to support this claim and it is entirely likely that the marriage never took place and that it was merely another false lead. After all, secrecy was a point of principle in the Klindworth household.

Agnes is portrayed as a cosmopolitan woman with an all-round education. She spoke German, Italian, French and Spanish fluently, was entirely at home in the world of diplomacy and evidently played the piano extremely well. This was her entrée to the Altenburg. Cosima Wagner later recalled that in 1853 Agnes 'wrote to my father, asking if she could have lessons with him and signing herself D. Street. My father said he was expecting a young man and was extremely surprised to see a highly attractive and intelligent woman arrive.'[77] Did Agnes really want no more than piano lessons from Liszt? This seems to have been nothing but a pretext, for the truth of the matter is that her father had sent her to Weimar to act as his spy. The town was in a state of upheaval: Grand Duke Karl Friedrich had died on 8 July 1853 and the throne had passed to his son Carl Alexander, whose political orientation needed to be established. The small grand duchy seemed to Klindworth to be a suitable base from which to keep an eye and ear on Russia. After all, Carl Alexander's mother, Maria Pawlowna, was the sister of the tsar, while the Russian ambassador, Apollonius von Maltitz, was said to be extremely well connected. As a piano pupil of Liszt, who was in the service of the court, Agnes had the perfect cover.

But it is possible that Agnes had another reason for coming to Weimar, for it has been suggested that not only was she there to provide local reports on Weimar's relations with Russia but that she was also a double agent working for the Russians. To this day rumours continue to circulate to the effect that she had been engaged by the Sayn-Wittgensteins as part of their struggle to retain Carolyne's millions. The beautiful spy was intended to seduce Liszt and provoke an embarrassing scandal that would lead to the separation of Liszt and his lover. Carolyne would then have been spirited away to Russia, and who knows what might have happened to her there? It must be admitted that there is no written evidence that Prince Nicholas's family had sent Agnes Street-Klindworth to Weimar as an agent provocateur, but the fact that such evidence does not exist does not necessarily mean the assumption is misplaced. After all, we are dealing with a world of espionage where every attempt was made to ensure that no incriminating evidence survived. And since Agnes was her father's best pupil, it would be a minor miracle if any relevant papers were ever to turn up. In short, we are dependent on speculation.

One of the many uncertainties in this whole matter is the exact date of Agnes's arrival in the town, although it seems likely that it was during the second half of 1853. On the other hand, we know exactly when she left Weimar: it was on 5 April 1855. At some point during this period Liszt and his piano pupil must have felt a mutual attraction. In the course of his long life, Liszt had many amorous affairs, and yet his relations with Agnes Street-Klindworth had something special about them. Of course, he felt attracted by her wide-ranging education and by her artistic gifts in general. Her French upbringing and cosmopolitan life-style certainly struck a chord with him. And yet these were really super-ficialities. There were many deeper reasons why Liszt fell hopelessly in love with his pupil, for whereas Marie d'Agoult and Carolyne often tormented him with their emotional reproaches, he could meet Agnes as an equal. And whereas the countess and the princess tried to mould Liszt in their own image, Agnes accepted him as he was. Their liaison seems to have been more uninhibited and more natural, a point that also finds expression in their correspondence. Since Liszt destroyed all of

Agnes's letters to him, we can consult only his side of the correspondence. The 160 letters that he wrote to her between December 1854 and the beginning of July 1886 are strikingly free from the formulaic protestations of love that make his missives to Carolyne so unbearable. For a time, Liszt seems to have regarded his affair with Agnes as a salutary counterpart to his life with Carolyne, and while the latter fought increasingly doggedly to annul her marriage to Prince Nicholas, Liszt sought refuge in a kind of parallel universe that seemed to him all the more carefree in consequence. Despite the fact that he needed to keep their relationship a secret – or perhaps precisely because of that fact – he was able to forget many of his problems in Agnes's presence.

In early October 1853 Liszt travelled via Karlsruhe to Basel, where he met Carolyne, Marie and Wagner. The group then continued their journey to Paris, where Liszt was planning to be reunited with his children, whom he had last seen in 1846. Throughout the previous seven-year period, Cosima, Blandine and Daniel had repeatedly prayed for their father's visit, and their prayers had finally been answered. Blandine, who was now seventeen, and Cosima fifteen, were already regarded as *demoiselles*, whereas the fourteen-year-old Daniel was still a *garçonnet*. But if they hoped that after their long separation their father would spend some time with them, they were bitterly disappointed, for Liszt and his entourage preferred to spend time at the Opéra or with Berlioz and the journalist Jules Janin and to attend lavish banquets. Meanwhile the three children remained at home with Madame Patersi. Recalling these events many years later, Cosima noted that they were 'never taken anywhere but thought it entirely natural that he should go out with Caroline [*sic*] and Marie'.[78] It is no wonder, then, that the mood of their reunion was so formal. Wagner recalled an evening in the rue Casimir-Périer:

> It was a new experience for me to observe my friend in the company
> of these girls, who were already growing up, and his son, who was
> just entering adolescence. He himself seemed a little bemused by his
> role as a father, from which over the years he had derived only the
> cares and none of the satisfactions.[79]

Within a week the visit was over, and the visitors disappeared as swiftly as they had arrived.

Following his return to Weimar, Liszt's affair with Agnes Street-Klindworth took a surprising turn, for in December she left the town for Hamburg, where on 21 January 1854 she gave birth to a son, Ernst August Georg Klindworth. Evidently she wanted to avoid awkward questions, preferring to bring the child into the world away from parochial Weimar, which was a notorious hotbed of gossip. The identity of the child's father is unknown. It is certainly surprising that if Captain Ernest Denis-Street really *was* her husband, she did not name him in the register of births. Georges Street, as he later called himself, became a musician and a composer. His colleague André Messager, who was exactly the same age and who worked with him for a time, reports that Georges's father was Liszt but gives no source for the rumour, and the child's paternity, like so much about this episode, remains obscure. Agnes and her infant son returned to Weimar in the autumn of 1854.

Meanwhile, the Altenburg was in a state of turmoil. Nicholas von Sayn-Wittgenstein had discovered that his daughter Marie had spent the entire summer in Carlsbad with her mother, in spite of the agreement he had reached with Carolyne whereby Marie would live with the Grand Duchess Maria Pawlowna. When Nicholas learnt that he himself was said to have asked the grand duchess to leave his daughter with her mother, his fury knew no bounds. He suspected the Altenburg of plotting against him and even believed that Carolyne might have forged a letter to the grand duchess. 'There is no doubt that Princess Caroline's actions have always been marked by a certain frivolity,' he wrote to Baron von Maltitz, 'but I would never have thought her capable of such an action.'[80] Carolyne, he went on, must abide by the agreements that she had reached and leave Marie as Maria Pawlowna's ward of court until her eighteenth birthday. 'How and by what right is it that she is already being described as Baron de Talleyrand's fiancée?' Nicholas fulminated, adding that he had given no such permission.

Is it not possible to see in all this the dangerous influence of a mother who has poisoned her own life and who is now persuading her own daughter to begin her life by committing the greatest transgression that a daughter can commit towards her father?

He ended by stating darkly that 'everything to do with this unhappy affair is being observed by the government', a remark that can only be interpreted as a threat directed at Liszt and at Carolyne.[81]

Not even Grand Duchess Maria Pawlowna knew how to extricate herself from this dilemma. Should she have Marie brought to her palace, if necessary by force? 'Her mother will not allow herself to be separated from her daughter,' Watzdorf informed the grand duchess.

> I would have thought that the most suitable solution would be for the daughter to be taken to her father without delay. I must beg you not to ask me to speak to Kapellmeister Liszt on this matter. I shall undoubtedly be required to act in this sad affair in my ministerial capacity, which is why I must beg that in the interests of my office I be relieved of all private contacts, which I have carefully avoided for many years for this very reason.[82]

The noose was slowly tightening, and as it did so, Liszt and the princess found that they had few friends left in Weimar.

As the pressure on her increased, Carolyne handed over her daughter to Maria Pawlowna in the middle of March 1854. A short time later Marie's governess, Janet Anderson, joined her at the palace. But Carolyne's change of heart had come too late and she was unable to prevent the affair from escalating. After she had ignored a further deadline for her return to Russia, the Russian authorities, headed by the Imperial Council, began proceedings against her. The St Petersburg lawyer Nikolai Tomau explained to Maltitz what would happen next:

> Once the trial starts, the accused will lose all possibility of disposing freely of her possessions and also forfeit her family rights. She will, however, retain her title until the court's sentence is ratified by His Majesty. This must be published in the Empire's official newspapers, and until then Princess W. retains the right to use her title and remains a Russian citizen but is deemed to be a criminal.

In the event of her deciding to return home in the meantime, 'the Russian authorities must treat her in accordance with the preventive laws aimed at criminals'. In other words, she would be arrested and held in prison. 'Her intelligence notwithstanding, Princess W. has unfortunately followed bad advice,' Tomau concluded. In particular, her hostile actions towards her husband represented 'a great provocation for all concerned and have destroyed all possibility of a reconciliation or of an agreement between them, even though such a solution would have reflected the imperial will'.[83]

Whereas Carolyne had previously enjoyed the protection of Grand Duchess Maria Pawlowna, the latter's patronage was now at an end. According to one observer, 'the princess was no longer invited to court and was completely ostracized'.[84] She was branded an outsider and barred from the aristocratic establishment. Passers-by would cross to the other side of the street and look away, offended, whenever they saw her approaching. Adelheid von Schorn describes another painful incident: 'There was a group of well-known people in the apartments, mostly women. When they saw the princess, they ostentatiously withdrew, leaving her alone there.'[85]

This social fall from grace affected Carolyne deeply: a woman who until then had set such store by etiquette was now treated like a leper. She reacted to her stigmatization with a degree of non-conformism that assumed an almost comic quality designed to give the impression that her social isolation was a matter of indifference to her:

> She sometimes tried to shock philistines, notably by her uninhibited behaviour, smoking cigarettes in inappropriate places or placing her feet on the balustrade of her box in the theatre, which the usher would then draw to her attention by tapping her disrespectfully on the shoulder and saying 'You're not allowed to do that, Frau Kapellmeisterin!' The man's form of address was symptomatic of the voice of the people, for the princess was generally regarded as the illegitimate wife of Weimar's Kapellmeister 'in Extraordinary'.[86]

'So test, therefore, who join forever'

Any biographer seeking to reconstruct the course of a subject's life will encounter periods when important events come thick and fast. In Liszt's case the year 1847 was of central importance thanks to his first meeting with Carolyne von Sayn-Wittgenstein, for it persuaded him to abandon his career as a virtuoso and settle in Weimar with her. A further year that witnessed a whole series of major decisions was 1855, for during this twelve-month period life in the Altenburg took a decisive turn in more ways than one.

First there was the planned wedding between Marie and Baron de Talleyrand. Nicholas and Carolyne had by now been fighting over their daughter for three years. Whereas Carolyne was in favour of her daughter's marriage to the French diplomat, her husband tried to delay it by all manner of subterfuges, the latest of which was Nicholas's demand that his daughter should be placed in Maria Pawlowna's guardianship until her eighteenth birthday on 18 February 1855. After much hesitation, Marie had finally agreed to her father's demands, albeit with a bad grace, only to return to the Altenburg in November 1854. According to the local medical officer of health, Heinrich le Goullon, her health was so delicate that it would be better for her to stay with her mother.[87] Although Maria Pawlowna sent word to Nicholas that his father's rights would be respected in Weimar, her hands were ultimately tied. Should she have used force to tear an allegedly sick child from her mother's arms and send her back to Russia? Such a course of action was unthinkable. Nicholas had played his last card, and by the beginning of 1855 there no longer seemed to be any way of further delaying the wedding.

Nicholas's elder brother Ludwig now set to work negotiating a marriage contract with Talleyrand. Suddenly, however, events in St Petersburg took a dramatic turn, when Tsar Nicholas I died on 2 March 1855 and was succeeded by his eldest son, Alexander I, who was keen to settle the tiresome 'Wittgenstein Affair' as quickly as possible. By July he had drawn a line under the affair, which had been before the courts since March 1854, by declaring the princess guilty. Carolyne was stripped of her Russian citizenship and condemned to a life of exile. 'I do not believe that it is possible to overturn this verdict or to influence the princess's position in any way,' Peter von Oldenburg wrote to his aunt, Maria Pawlowna. There followed the all-important remark: 'As for her possessions, these pass to her heirs, which in this case means her daughter, who must, however, sell them, since she is marrying a foreigner.'[88]

Clearly, Carolyne had not thought through the implications of her actions: since she and her daughter could not travel to Russia in person, they would have to sell their vast estates through intermediaries in the event of Marie's marrying Talleyrand. We may assume from all that we know that the Russian authorities would have done everything in their power to prevent such a sale, with the result that Marie, although the legitimate seller, would have received no more than a pittance. But Carolyne and Marie needed all the money they could find for their luxurious lifestyle at the Altenburg as well as for their visits to expensive spas. To make matters worse, Weimar's mayor now added his twopenn'orth: he had read an official communication in which the Russian Embassy had announced that Carolyne had been stripped of her Russian citizenship and so he demanded financial securities, a demand she indignantly rejected. Meanwhile the grand duchess's entourage could only shake their heads in disbelief when confronted by her whimsical behaviour. 'I can understand that the princess is sorely moved,' wrote Watzdorf to Maria Pawlowna, 'but I do not understand why she couldn't have foreseen what has happened and why she didn't avert it by acting in a more sensible and intelligent way.'[89]

The wedding of Marie and Charles-Angélique Baron de Talleyrand-Périgord now seemed to be a distinctly bad idea, and it is easy to imagine the subsequent course of the affair: Marie withdrew her consent to the marriage in November 1855 and broke off her engagement. She wrote to her father:

The delays that have come about were fatal to my marriage, just as I had suspected they would be. After everything had initially seemed so clear and so straightforward, the matter has suddenly become impossible as a result of the changes that have come about through the passage of time. I can feel only great respect and sympathy for Monsieur de Talleyrand, sentiments which, he assures me, he likewise feels for me.[90]

Nicholas felt his paternal pride offended by his daughter's cold and evasive explanation. 'Such a letter can only have been dictated to her by the woman who was once my wife,' he wrote indignantly to Maltitz, 'and who continues to use this poor young girl to achieve her own ends without regard for the wrong that she is doing her own daughter. One day both women will see this for themselves, but by then it will be too late.'[91]

Negotiations and arguments had been taking place on the highest level for three years. The grand duchess and the tsar were involved, as were ministers and diplomats. Lawyers had drawn up contracts, and hundreds of telegrams had passed to and fro between Weimar and St Petersburg. Was it all to have been in vain? If Nicholas had initially wanted only to delay his daughter's wedding, he finally saw a chance to get even with his wife. It must have left him feeling deeply frustrated that his plans had been thwarted after such wearisome toing and froing. He now lost all interest in reaching any agreement with Carolyne.

In early April 1856 he petitioned the Consistorial Court of the Evangelical Church in St Petersburg, asking it to 'annul the marriage between him and his wife, which no longer exists in fact, and which should be annulled by the Church, too, quoad vinculum, granting him the rights of the innocent party'. He justified his demand by claiming that 'the former Princess Caroline Wittgenstein née Iwanowska has been declared dead under civil law'.[92] The language is significant: Carolyne had ceased to exist for Nicholas and had died before her time. The Evangelical Church finally agreed to his request and his marriage was annulled. Within a year the Protestant Nicholas von Sayn-Wittgenstein had remarried. Curious though it must seem, his divorce and remarriage had no influence on Carolyne's attempts to have her marriage annulled by the Catholic Church. Reality was one thing, the Catholic Church's canon law another. Ultimately, then, Carolyne was thrown back on her own devices and could no longer expect any support from her husband.

It is extraordinary that in spite of the emotional burden that these events implied, Liszt was still able to shoulder a tremendous workload. Early in 1855 he organized a series of gala events devoted to his friend and colleague Hector Berlioz, who came in person to Weimar and conducted a concert in the grand duke's palace on 17 February in the course of which Liszt himself gave the first performance of his Piano Concerto no. 1 in E flat major. Four days later Berlioz conducted a performance of his oratorio *L'enfance du Christ*, during which Liszt played the bass drum. The rest of the spring months proved no less fruitful. In early April he conducted the local première of Schumann's opera *Genoveva* and in May he attended the music festival in Düsseldorf. In early June he conducted a further performance of Wagner's *Tannhäuser* in Weimar – he had introduced it to the town as early as May 1849 – and at the end of the month he gave the local première of Otto Nicolai's comic opera *Die lustigen Weiber von Windsor*. As if that were not enough, he completed his 'Gran' Mass on 1 May, a task that had taken three months.

Liszt had been invited to write a solemn Mass for the consecration of the gigantic basilica at Gran (Esztergom) in northern Hungary. It is a work whose vast dimensions reflect those of the church where it was first performed, a building covering 60,000 square feet. Liszt demanded soloists, a chorus and a large orchestra that included not only an extensive wind and percussion department but also a harp and an organ. Its musical language is flamboyant, heroic and overtly dramatic, creating the impression of a mixture of opera and church music. Until 1855 he had written little sacred music, but on completing his 'Gran' Mass he returned on many occasions to the medium, continuing to explore the genre right up to his final years.

Certain sections of the press – especially those from Catholic circles – shrugged off the work. 'I was interested in the often highly ingenious instrumentation and the affectionate elaboration of individual elements in the text,' noted the composer Pius Richter, 'but at no point did I warm to the work, which failed to elevate me or instil a feeling of reverence.' A bon vivant like Liszt was the last person he expected to be singing God's praises:

The 'Gran' Mass does not create this mood but merely proclaims its author's blasé attitude and a sense of inner turmoil. Good old Liszt has enjoyed most of the pleasures of this world and means to enjoy the joys of Heaven while still here with us on earth. He eyes the ascetic and at the same time seeks to regenerate music in spite of his three or four illegitimate children.[93]

But the event that arguably affected Liszt the most in 1855 was non-musical: the departure of Agnes Street-Klindworth, which he learnt about only a few days before she left. The reasons for her hasty departure are unclear. Was her mission in Weimar over? If she really was in the pay of the Russians, then the death of Tsar Nicholas I on 2 March 1855 would have robbed her of her raison d'être. Perhaps her Russian employers stood her down when it became clear that Nicholas's successor was pursuing a different policy in the 'Wittgenstein Affair'. This is possible. But there was also another reason. When Agnes packed her bags, she was already six months pregnant, and we may suppose that as with her earlier pregnancy she wanted to avoid any social unpleasantness. Her son, Ernest Auguste Georges ('Charles') Street was born in Brussels on 18 July 1855. His father was named in the register of births as Captain Ernest Denis-Street. Alan Walker believes that Agnes and her ostensible husband met briefly in the autumn of 1854, otherwise she could not have conceived his child.[94] On the other hand, there is no evidence to support this claim. While Denis-Street may indeed have been the father, we could equally well assume it was Liszt. We simply do not know from whose loins the infant sprang.

Agnes's departure left Liszt in a state of shock, and when he passed her house for the first time afterwards, his feelings overwhelmed him: 'What affliction and gloom greet me now at those two windows where I used to see you so often!'[95] A few days later he admitted: 'I still cannot pass by those windows without trembling.'[96] Liszt was obsessed by the idea of seeing Agnes again as soon as possible, and at the end of May he lured her to Cologne and Düsseldorf, where he attended a music festival and where the couple spent a few days together which Liszt could still recall long afterwards: 'Keep the memory of our *cabin* alive; tell me it remains sweet and radiant in your heart.'[97] When Carolyne left Weimar for several weeks in August and September, Liszt issued a series of unambiguous invitations to Agnes, all of which she ignored. It was also during this period that he stopped addressing her as 'tu' and switched to the formal 'vous', perhaps a reflection of his realization that his love for Agnes had no future.

Throughout the summer of 1855 Liszt was torn between two women. While Carolyne was struggling – doggedly and intractably – to have her marriage dissolved, Liszt's relationship with her was slowly beginning to change, love and devotion gradually giving way to respect. And yet it was no more possible for him to abandon the princess than it was to admit publicly that he was in love with Agnes Street-Klindworth. He was on the horns of a dilemma. At the end of August he wrote to Agnes, 'The illness from which you know I suffer has not improved since your departure – and there is every indication that I shall never get over it.'[98] To make matters worse, new problems were already looming.

Anguish

The news from Paris gave cause for concern: Mme Patersi was said to be seriously ill, Cosima and Blandine were misbehaving, and Marie d'Agoult was dictating events. It was reports such as these that set the alarm bells ringing in the Altenburg. Suddenly Liszt and Carolyne had to pay the price for their lack of interest in what had been going on in the rue Casimir-Périer over the course of recent months. When Baron Talleyrand was called to Paris on business in May 1855, Carolyne asked him to sort out the situation there.

'The news that he has brought concerning Mme Patersi is sad,' Carolyne reported to Liszt. Now seventy-seven, the children's governess had an abscess on her head, leading Talleyrand to conclude that she had little chance of surviving. The lives of Liszt's children had been ruled by Mme Patersi and her sister for the last five years, but it appeared that they were no longer in a position to maintain their grip on their charges' lives. Now nineteen and seventeen respectively, Blandine and Cosima were already young women and refused to submit any longer to their elderly governesses' attempts to tell them what to think. Cosima in particular was the object of Carolyne's suspicions:

> Cosimette appears to be extremely grown up and has started to make highly suggestive remarks. Saucy glances, risqué remarks, and according to Talleyrand she seems to take entirely after her mother. In general the two of them have left a not very positive impression on him. There is a sense of seething unrest and inner turmoil. They have lost their gentleness of manner and appear to be suffocated by their surroundings. Mme Patersi is at her wits' end. She complains at how shameless they are and says that she is completely incapable of imposing her will on them.[99]

Who could take on the two young women? Their father refused. 'These little girls play such a minor role in my present way of life as it shapes itself ever clearer,' he told Agnes Street-Klindworth, 'that I do not have much place for them in it, and to me it seems simpler to love each other from afar.'[100] It would, of course, have been possible to return the two girls to their mother, but both Liszt and Carolyne considered this out of the question, especially since Carolyne felt only profound contempt for the Comtesse d'Agoult. Liszt's mother was herself in poor health and by now too old to take on the responsibility, quite apart from which Carolyne suspected that Anna would be far too indulgent towards her two granddaughters. As in 1850, it was the ever-inventive Carolyne who came up with a solution to the problem.

Her plan was for Franziska von Bülow, the mother of Liszt's favourite pupil, to invite the two girls to Berlin. Franziska was now fifty-five and after two failed marriages was living with her son in the German capital, where Hans had been working as a piano teacher at the Stern Conservatory for the last few months. Neither Blandine nor Cosima was to know about their imminent move. Marie d'Agoult, too, had to be kept in the dark, for otherwise it was feared that she might thwart the plans and even abduct the children. Liszt was guilty of failing to put his cards on the table when he wrote to his mother and told her that he wanted to spend a few carefree days with his daughters: 'Mme de Bülow is being kind enough to collect them from Paris and bring them to Weimar, where I plan to house them in a style that they will always be pleased to recall.'[101] Blandine and Cosima were certainly looking forward to spending some time with their father. At this point there was no mention at all of Berlin. Only Anna Liszt was sceptical and seems to have been unwilling to believe her son's hypocritical assurances: 'I was extremely surprised,' she told her son, 'because when I was in Weimar I heard you say more than once that I couldn't bring Cosima and Blandine to the town.'[102] Her suspicions were to prove only too well founded.

Liszt and Carolyne had planned their coup in detail. While Blandine and Cosima were sitting in a train on their way to Weimar, safe from their mother's interference, Carolyne set off for Paris in order to initiate Anna Liszt into her callous plan. 'The princess told me this with complete indifference,' Anna complained to her son.

> There was practically nothing I could say, except that the children are now too big for yet another upheaval. The princess replied that Mme d'Agoult will never stop writing and that for some time she has adopted a highly impertinent tone in her letters to you.[103]

Anna Liszt's objections were ignored, and Blandine and Cosima had no choice but to submit to their fate. Only Daniel was allowed to remain in Paris and complete his schooling there.

Before their move to Berlin, the sisters were able to spend a few days with their father in Weimar. 'My daughters are taking up two-thirds of my day,' Liszt wrote to Agnes.

> They are pleasant young people, intelligent, vivacious, and even a little sniffish. They take after both papa and mamma, – but almost too much after mamma for my liking. [. . .] They are not overjoyed either about the move to Berlin, although it is the most sensible and favourable choice for them.[104]

Liszt was flattering himself, for the truth of the matter is that he simply did not know what to do with his daughters, driving them from the pillar of Mme Patersi to the post of Franziska von Bülow.

From all that we know about her, Franziska von Bülow was a strict and loveless woman and, as such, could be described as Mme Patersi's natural successor. While she assumed the task of bringing up Liszt's daughters, her twenty-five-year-old son took charge of their aesthetic education. 'As for my girls,' Liszt informed him in September 1855, 'you must allow me to tell you the great importance that I attach to your making them work very hard, for I believe that they are sufficiently advanced in their musical studies to be able to profit from your lessons.' But Bülow should also be very strict with them: 'They already respect you, and so it won't be hard for you to drum things into them.'[105]

But in October 1855 something happened that no one in the Altenburg had anticipated: Cosima Liszt and Hans von Bülow fell in love. Liszt was initially reluctant to take their dalliance seriously, writing to an outraged Franziska von Bülow that it would not be hard for her son 'to find a far more advantageous match than either of my two daughters'.[106] His remark was hardly flattering. Worse, he had completely failed to grasp the situation. In April 1856 the inevitable happened and Bülow asked for Cosima's hand in marriage: 'It is more than love that I feel for her,' he explained to his future father-in-law:

Rather, the idea of drawing even closer to you, whom I regard as the man who, more than any other, has helped to establish and motivate my present and future existence, sums up all the happiness that I can expect to feel here on earth. In my eyes Cosima Liszt towers above all other women not only because she bears your name but also because she resembles you so much and because so many of her qualities make her a faithful reflection of your own person.[107]

Bülow's request placed Liszt in a difficult position, for although the latter was keen to see his daughter married in keeping with her social standing – and Bülow was what was known as a 'good match' in the middle-class circles of the time, being on the threshold of a great career – Liszt was also fully aware of the fact that Bülow, whom he loved and treated as a son, had his demons, beginning with his delicate health. All his life Bülow suffered from recurrent migraines, hyper-nervousness and a whole series of other malaises. His eccentricities were also hard to take. From an early age Bülow had developed a caustic and sarcastic attitude designed to demonstrate a strength and virility that his enfeebled body lacked. He was a cynic who raised intelligent irony and venomously wounding mockery to the level of a point of principle. The elaborate wordplay of his correspondence may still be a source of pleasure to readers today, but for Bülow's contemporaries, his keenly cutting witticisms were a source of fear. Liszt was aware of all this, and he no doubt suspected that Cosima's life at the side of so eccentric a genius would not be simple. But did Liszt have any choice in the matter? Could he have refused his favourite pupil his daughter's hand in marriage?

Liszt reacted to the difficult situation in which he found himself by showing a tactical sensitivity that we might not have expected of a father who was otherwise so unfeeling. He played for time, arguing that Cosima was still too young to commit herself to a lifetime of marriage and that it would be better to wait a year. Perhaps he hoped that in the meantime the couple would rethink their relationship and the problem would resolve itself. But his calculations proved wrong, for after a year Cosima and Bülow were still as resolved on marriage as ever and Liszt had no choice but to give his consent. The Catholic wedding ceremony took place on the morning of Tuesday 18 August 1857 in St Hedwig's Church in Berlin in the presence of only a handful of family members.[108] The bride's father, who was also one of the witnesses, travelled on his own from Weimar to Berlin. Her mother, Marie d'Agoult, had vigorously opposed the match from the outset and demonstratively stayed away, as did Carolyne von Sayn-Wittgenstein, who clearly did not want to be cast in the role of wicked stepmother. Other absentees were Anna Liszt, Blandine and Daniel.

As we shall see, the wedding of Hans von Bülow and Cosima Liszt proved to be a terrible mistake. Cosima's own analysis of the situation, which she recorded in her diary twelve years later, is significant in this regard:

> It was a great misunderstanding that bound us together in marriage; my feelings toward him are today still the same as 12 years ago: great

sympathy with his destiny, pleasure in the qualities of his mind and heart, genuine respect for his character, however completely different our temperaments.[109]

There was no question of love – both partners confused true love with self-sacrificial friendship. On the eve of his wedding, Bülow had assured his colleague Richard Pohl: 'My wife is such a perfect friend to me, it is almost impossible to imagine a more ideal situation.'[110] It is hard to imagine a clearer explanation of the reasons why the marriage was doomed to fail.

Hindsight is a wonderful thing. 'Herr von Bülow should never have married,' the elderly Cosima confided in her daughter-in-law Winifred towards the end of her life.[111] It would have been more accurate to say: 'Herr von Bülow should never have married me.'

Descent

The year 1857 began with a musical surprise, when Bülow gave the first performance of Liszt's B minor Piano Sonata in Berlin, a work that stands out like an erratic block from the rest of the piano repertory of the nineteenth century and is, indeed, one of the most important works ever written for the instrument. Its title is misleading, for although the sonata's traditional multi-movement form may be dimly discernible behind the masterly single-movement structure, the work, which lasts some thirty minutes in performance, is astonishingly dense. Liszt had completed the piece on 2 February 1853 and published it a year later with a dedication to Robert Schumann – a late homage to a colleague and friend who had dedicated his own C major Fantasy to Liszt in 1839. But Schumann remained oblivious of the dedication: in February 1854, suffering from a serious nervous disorder, he had tried to take his own life and subsequently had himself admitted to a private asylum and clinic at Endenich near Bonn. Liszt sent the sonata and a number of other pieces to Schumann's wife, Clara, whose reaction was less than enthusiastic: 'The compositions are dreadful,' she confided in her diary. 'Nothing but noise – there is not a wholesome thought in them, everything is confused; there is no sign of any clear harmonic progression. And to crown it all I must write and thank him – it really is dreadful.'[112]

That four years elapsed between the completion of the sonata and its first performance was also due to its formidable technical demands, and even an exceptional pianist like Bülow needed two years to prepare so extraordinary and novel a piece before he felt ready to perform it in public. Critical responses to the performance were mixed, the press dismissing it as unmusical and even absurd, while the audience acclaimed both the work and its interpreter.

Liszt's activities in Weimar took a decisive new turn in the autumn of 1857, for until then he had been working with general administrators at the town's theatre who lent him their support. The theatre had originally been used for both spoken drama and works of musical theatre, but thanks to Liszt's charismatic personality and the success with which his labours were generally crowned, the balance had shifted, with the result that the spoken drama was now overshadowed by his grandiose operatic and symphonic projects. With the appointment of Franz von Dingelstedt as the theatre's new administrator on 1 October 1857, Liszt found himself working alongside a man determined to redress that balance and give priority to the spoken drama. It is one of the ironies of music history that it was Liszt himself who had championed Dingelstedt's appointment, for he had allowed himself to be taken in by his new colleague's diplomatically shrewd and obliging nature. By the time he became aware of Dingelstedt's true aims, it was too late. The latter, his junior by three years, is reported to have said to his face: 'Theatres are a necessary evil, concerts completely unnecessary.'[113]

The story of Liszt's descent from Weimar's Mount Olympus is inextricably linked to the name of one particular opera: *Der Barbier von Bagdad*. Written by his friend and assistant Peter Cornelius, it was not completed until the spring of 1858. Liszt played through the first two acts, sight-reading them at the piano, and was sufficiently enthusiastic to suggest that the opera be staged in Weimar. His reaction was entirely typical: even though the subject matter, based on one of the tales from the Arabian Nights, was not really after his heart, he recognized Cornelius's talent, which he hoped to promote by giving the opera's world première. Dingelstedt gave his backing to the idea, and a suitable date was finally found: 15 December. Cornelius himself must have suspected that the general administrator's office was only lukewarm in its support, for we find him writing to his brother in late November: 'It's remarkable how Dingelstedt manages to rub everyone up the wrong way. It's as if he needs hostility as much as his daily bread.'[114]

The theatre was packed to the rafters that Wednesday evening in mid-December. Even Grand Duke Carl Alexander was present. But as soon as Liszt took his place on the conductor's podium, a murmur spread throughout the auditorium and for the first time in his career the applause was accompanied by hissing that was clearly designed to unsettle the performers. In the event the performance passed off without mishap and all in all was excellent. But during the final curtain the situation became worse. According to Cornelius's own account, 'Right from the outset a faction unique in the annals of the Weimar theatre opposed the applause with persistent hissing, which was well organized by individuals who were dotted around the house to create the maximum impact.' Dingelstedt should have intervened to stop such rowdy behaviour, but he did nothing. 'At the end a battle broke out that lasted ten minutes. The grand duke had applauded throughout, but the hecklers continued in spite of this.'[115] Liszt was white with anger. He was convinced that Dingelstedt was behind the whole intrigue and that he had enlisted the services of a claque. Dingelstedt had clearly not counted on Liszt getting to the end of the performance. According to Cornelius, he was said to have told Carl Alexander: ' "Your Majesty! I had prepared a comedy in case the thing was booed off the stage after the first act." At this the grand duke is reported to have made a dismissive gesture.'[116]

In spite of this, the coup proved successful. The intrigue had been aimed not at Cornelius and his harmless opera, but at Liszt, who was to be publicly disavowed. Dingelstedt's minions did all that was asked of them and more, with the result that Liszt is said to have shouted at his colleague immediately after the performance: 'After all that has happened this evening, I'll never again set foot in your showman's booth.'[117]

If there was a chance of persuading Liszt to change his mind, then Carl Alexander missed it. While showing a degree of human decency by receiving Cornelius at a private audience after the first-night fiasco, he failed to offer his unequivocal support but preferred to prevaricate, not wanting to lose his Kapellmeister but at the same time shying away from putting Dingelstedt in his place.

'The whole court was unmusical,' was how Carolyne's daughter Marie summed up the situation many decades later. Carl Alexander was said to have been 'flighty' and never really to have understood Liszt. 'No one had any inkling about the significance of the New German School and they were all bored to tears by Wagner's long operas.' Liszt was seen as 'an old crone who was none the less treated indulgently in order not to lose the intelligent and reliable friend whose international reputation still imparted a reflected glory'.[118] Two months after the first night of *Der Barbier von Bagdad* Liszt was still waiting for a word of clarification, at which point his patience finally snapped, and on 14 February 1859 he wrote to Carl Alexander, asking to be released from his contract and bringing to an end a significant chapter in the history of European music.

Ill Fate

With Liszt's resignation, life became almost intolerable for the inhabitants of the Altenburg. The princess had already been treated like a leper for some considerable time, but now her partner, too, was regarded as a pariah. The couple could no longer bear to remain in Weimar. Liszt spent the spring months of 1859 visiting Berlin, Löwenberg and Breslau, while Carolyne spent a number of weeks in Munich. At the end of May we find them both in Leipzig, where an international gathering of musicians opened on 1 June. The editor in chief of the *Neue Zeitschrift für Musik*, Franz Brendel, marked the twenty-fifth anniversary of the first issue of the periodical in 1834 by inviting more than 300 musicians and journalists from half of Europe to gather in the city. Liszt's family was well represented not only by Liszt and Carolyne but also by Hans and Cosima von Bülow and by Blandine and her husband, the French politician Émile Ollivier, whom she had married in 1857. The meeting opened with a gala concert at which Liszt conducted his own symphonic poem

Torquato Tasso and the local première of the prelude to Act One of Wagner's *Tristan und Isolde*. (Wagner himself was prevented from doing the honours as he was still persona non grata in Germany.) The following day Liszt led a performance of his 'Gran' Mass in St Thomas's Church, which was filled to overflowing by an audience of some 3,000. Both concerts proved sensationally successful, and Liszt was universally acclaimed. In the course of the meeting it was decided to found an Allgemeiner Deutscher Musikverein, or Universal German Music Society, that would be launched at the organization's next meeting in Weimar in August 1861.

It was at around this time – the summer of 1859 – that Carolyne received an unexpected visit from one Władisław Okraszewski, whom she already knew from the Ukraine, where he had been one of her tenants. Her attempts to have her marriage annulled had stalled, but with the sudden arrival of Okraszewski entirely new prospects opened up, promising an end to a process that had dragged on for over ten years. Carolyne was galvanized into action, and Liszt was moved to write to Carl Alexander:

> Herr Okraszewski, of whom Your Royal Highness may already have heard, brought Princess Wittgenstein a decision reached by the Metropolitan Archbishop of St Petersburg with regard to her divorce, which states that Herr O. must travel to Rome to ask that orders be given to take up this case again in Russia and to have it reviewed by His Excellency the Metropolitan Archbishop. Since this does not fall under the jurisdiction of the Court of Rome, it is to be hoped that there will be no difficulty in issuing these instructions.[119]

Liszt failed to mention in his letter to Carl Alexander that in the event of his intervention proving successful, Okraszewski was demanding 70,000 silver roubles for his services. It is not entirely clear whether he wanted this vast sum for himself or whether he intended to use some of it to bribe clerics with an interest in the affair. When Maltitz learnt about the approach, he turned it down, regarding the whole business as an attempt at extortion and insisting that it would be wrong to do business with dubious characters such as Okraszewski. Objections such as these left Carolyne unmoved: she was determined to use every available means to pursue her case. Since she had transferred the bulk of her fortune to her daughter, Marie had to confirm the arrangement and, as it were, vouch for her mother. Maltitz continued to advise against such a course of action, but Marie was a dutiful daughter and so we find her penning the following lines to Maltitz:

> In keeping with your wishes and in response to your objections, I am writing to inform you of my firm and irreversible decision to sign a contract with Herr Okraszewski, under the terms of which I agree to pay him 70,000 silver roubles if he achieves the divorce of my mother, Princess Carolyne von Sayn-Wittgenstein, under canon law. In this way I am obeying my duties as a daughter and at the same time making use of the rights that the law affords me.[120]

Okraszewski set off on his journey in September 1859.

Marie von Sayn-Wittgenstein had celebrated her twenty-second birthday only a few months earlier. She was still living at the Altenburg, where there was no shortage of admirers. Liszt's pupils and the many visitors were enchanted by her beauty, but after her abortive engagement to Baron de Talleyrand she had had her fill of wedding plans. Then, while spending a few weeks in Munich in April 1859, she had met Prince Konstantin Victor Ernst Emil Karl Alexander Friedrich Prince zu Hohenlohe-Schillingsfürst, a member of a Franconian family of aristocrats first documented in 1153. Two of his brothers had gone into politics: Victor as leader of the Prussian House of Lords, Chlodwig as prime minister of Bavaria and later German chancellor. A fourth brother, Gustav Adolf, who was born in 1823, entered the priesthood and later became a member of the College of Cardinals. We shall meet him again on more than one occasion in the course of our subsequent narrative.

On leaving school, Konstantin had entered the service of the Austrian crown, and by the time he met Marie he was already an aide-de-camp to the emperor Franz Joseph. He began to court her in Munich. The driving force behind his eagerness to marry was his brother Chlodwig, who had married a daughter of Nicholas von Sayn-Wittgenstein's eldest brother Ludwig in 1847. Chlodwig's wife, who, confusingly enough, was also called Marie, was therefore Carolyne's niece. Thanks to these ties, the Hohenlohes were fully apprised of the family situation. They knew about Carolyne's personal problems but also had a clear idea about her daughter's immense wealth: Marie struck them as a good match who would free Konstantin from a life of financial worries. The result was a kind of business deal, to which Carolyne was happy to put her name. She knew that she could not keep her daughter for herself for ever and regarded the marriage to Prince Konstantin as an entirely worthy union. On this occasion nothing could be allowed to go wrong as she wanted no further scandals after the humiliating episode with Talleyrand. Perhaps she also hoped that if her daughter became the sister-in-law of Gustav Adolf zu Hohenlohe, this might help Okraszewski in his negotiations in Rome. It could do her cause no harm, she would have reckoned, to be related by marriage to one of the leading figures in the Vatican. As so often with arranged marriages in the nineteenth century, Marie's thoughts and feelings were of only secondary importance. Indeed, Marie was evidently less than wholly enthusiastic about Prince Konstantin, who was her elder by nine years, since she is known to have had feelings for the writer Friedrich Hebbel, feelings that Hebbel returned. When the writer discovered that Marie and Konstantin were to be married, he broke off all contact with her.

After only a brief engagement the couple were married in St John's Chapel in Weimar on 15 October 1859. The wedding breakfast was held at the Altenburg, after which the couple began their everyday lives, Marie moving to Vienna, where her husband was already living. Carolyne, who had sobbed all through the ceremony, initially missed her daughter very much and sought refuge from her loneliness in Paris, leaving Liszt on his own in Weimar, where he celebrated his forty-eighth birthday on 22 October. At one o'clock the doorbell rang. It was Cosima. She had come from Berlin to offer her birthday greetings in person. But she also brought word of her brother Daniel. And the news was not good.

Daniel had turned eighteen in May 1857 and shortly afterwards had moved to Vienna to study jurisprudence. He had enjoyed university life

and spent much of his time with his father's former pupils, Peter
Cornelius and Carl Tausig, while also enjoying long country walks,
attending concerts and visiting the theatre. At the end of the summer
term in 1859, he made his way to Berlin in order to spend some time
relaxing with his sister and brother-in-law. But within days of his arrival
he had fallen seriously ill. The doctors initially assumed that it was no
more than an ordinary fever until Daniel started to cough blood. Anna
Liszt, too, was worried. 'How is Daniel?' she wrote to her son in the
middle of September. 'Cosima hasn't mentioned him for the past twelve
days. I only hope he's on the road to a full recovery.'[121] Five weeks later
she returned to the subject: 'Cosima has said nothing about him in her
recent letters and has never said anything at all even though I asked her
some time ago what illness he's suffering from. She only told me it
doesn't have a name.'[122]

Cosima undoubtedly wanted to spare the feelings of her seventy-
one-year-old grandmother, but it is also true that the doctor who was
summoned to Daniel's bedside had no idea what the problem was and
was groping around in the dark. Daniel continued to grow weaker and
to waste away before the eyes of his despairing hosts. 'It's sad in the
house, too,' Bülow complained to a friend in early October; 'poor Daniel
still refuses to get any better – he's been in bed for almost two months!'[123]
Throughout these weeks Cosima showed almost superhuman strength,
sitting by her brother's bedside day and night, reading to him or simply
holding his hand. By early December the situation appeared hopeless
and Cosima cabled to her father in Weimar, asking him to come to
Berlin at once.

Liszt arrived in the capital late on the evening of 11 December and
the next morning made his way to the Bülows' home, where he barely
recognized his emaciated son, who was already close to death and
speaking feverishly, his words making no sense at all. But then he recovered sufficiently to recognize his father and express his delight at his
being there. In a moment of lucidity he announced: 'Je vais préparer vos
places!'[124] Liszt and Cosima remained at his side throughout the rest of
the day. The following morning – 13 December 1859 – Bülow collected
his father-in-law from his hotel and, tears in his eyes, told Liszt that

Daniel's final death agony had begun. It lasted several hours, and it was not until twenty past eleven that evening that his suffering was finally over. Cosima was kneeling beside her dead brother's bed. A few minutes elapsed before Liszt announced that he could no longer hear any breathing. Cosima 'laid her hand on his heart. It was no longer beating. Before that there had been barely a sigh – he had passed away.'[125] The burial took place two days later – 15 December – at St Hedwig's Catholic Cemetery on the Liesenstraße.

The whole family was badly affected by Daniel's death. 'Liszt is calm but is suffering greatly,' Bülow reported to Raff. 'His illness did not have a name: he wasted away, his life gradually extinguished – his life force had been enough for a mere twenty years.'[126] Blandine and Cosima, too, were inconsolable and numb with grief. For years they and their brother had formed a secret society directed against the princess and her hench-woman, Mme Patersi, their experiences having forged a close bond between them. With Daniel, a part of their childhood had died. 'I shall always regret not being with him during his final moments,' Blandine wrote to Cosima.

> Why didn't you summon me to his bedside? Why didn't you tell me the truth about his condition? [...] There is no comfort for me because unlike you and my father I was unable to lighten his final hours. My dear Cosima, look after yourself, take care of yourself and keep yourself well for the sake of those who love you, including your Blandine, who worships you and who would like to be with you in order to speak to you, to embrace you and to overwhelm you with my love.[127]

In the eyes of both Cosima and Blandine, Carolyne von Sayn-Wittgenstein was in part to blame for their brother's premature death: 'His loss may have been due to my father's having sent him to Vienna on the advice of Princess Wittgenstein,' she noted in her diary many years later, an entry that attests to her abiding despair.[128] The climate in the Austrian capital, she argued, had harmed his delicate constitution and undermined his already poor health, a point that the princess should have known. And when Cosima visited her brother's grave in 1871, she was overcome by emotion: 'Sombre mood; he was the victim of my father's and my mother's thoughtlessness and the cruel indifference of Princess Wittgenstein; at the time I was too young and inexperienced to oppose them effectively and take firm measures. Much soreness of heart standing at this grave.'[129] Elsewhere she complained that 'Princess W[ittgenstein] described us to my father as having been born under a curse, and the preservation of our lives thus of no special account.'[130]

Daniel's death came at the end of what had been a terrible year for Liszt, a year that had begun with the painful aftermath of the scandal surrounding *Der Barbier von Bagdad*, leaving him in no doubt that the situation could not be allowed to continue as it was. His life had to take a new course. 'Liszt is leaving Weimar early next year,' Cornelius informed a female correspondent in December 1859. 'Once he has left Weimar, the people there will say "Yes, there was someone special." And once he is no longer alive, the whole world will say the same. Until then Liszt's dictum remains as true as ever: "Mundus vult Schundus" [The world wants rubbish].'[131]

1 Liszt's father, Adam (1776–1827). Anonymous gouache, 1819. 'Unfortunately, his father wanted to derive great pecuniary advantage from him,' recalled Carl Czerny.

2 Carl Czerny (1791–1857), Liszt's music teacher in Vienna. Anonymous oil painting, 1857. Czerny later recalled that his pupil was 'a pale, sickly looking child who, while playing, swayed about on the stool as if drunk, so that I kept thinking he would fall off'.

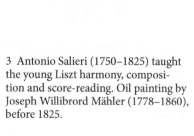

3 Antonio Salieri (1750–1825) taught the young Liszt harmony, composition and score-reading. Oil painting by Joseph Willibrord Mähler (1778–1860), before 1825.

4 Beethoven's famous kiss of consecration. Detail from a lithograph published in 1873 to mark the fiftieth anniversary of Liszt's Viennese debut. The scene depicted here is almost certainly apocryphal.

5 and 6 Franz Liszt and Marie d'Agoult (1805–76). Oil paintings by Henri Lehmann (1814–82) dating from 1839. 'You are not the woman I need,' Liszt once told her. 'You are the woman I desire.'

'I say "apparition" because I can think of no other word to describe the extraordinary sensation caused by the most extraordinary person I have ever seen,' Marie d'Agoult recalled her first meeting with Liszt.

7 Among the many women who fell under Liszt's spell in the salons of Paris was the cigar-smoking George Sand, the pen name of Aurore Dupin, Baroness Dudevant (1804–76), depicted here in a caricature by her son, Maurice (1823–89), probably dating from 1837. The caption reads, 'Maman bien étonnée d'entendre Liszt' (Mummy very surprised to hear Liszt).

8 The young seducer. Pencil drawing by Jean-Auguste-Dominique Ingres (1780–1867), dating from 1839.

9 Liszt at thirty. Daguerreotype from around 1841.

10 An icon of the Romantic movement. Liszt improvising at the piano. Oil painting by Josef Danhauser (1805–45), 1840. Seated (from left to right) are Alexandre Dumas (1802–70), George Sand (1804–76) and Marie d'Agoult (1805–76); standing (from left to right) are Victor Hugo (1802–85), Nicolò Paganini (1782–1840) and Gioachino Rossini (1792–1868). On the piano is a bust of Ludwig van Beethoven (1770–1827) sculpted in 1821 by Anton Dietrich (1799–1872), and on the wall is a portrait of Lord Byron (1788–1824).

11 Caricature by Jean Ignace Isidore Gérard Grandville (1803–47) depicting the Paris salon of Delphine Gay de Girardin (1804–55), where members of the city's high society would meet to plan their intrigues. Here, too, Marie d'Agoult assumed the nom de plume of Daniel Stern. Seen here (from left to right) are Honoré de Balzac (1799–1850), Frédéric Soulié (1800–47), Alexandre Dumas, Delphine Gay de Girardin, Liszt at the piano, Jules Janin (1804–74) and Victor Hugo.

12 Court Kapellmeister in Weimar. Photograph by Franz Hanfstaengl (1804–77), 1858.

13 Princess Carolyne von Sayn-Wittgenstein (1819–87), Liszt's new partner in life. Daguerreotype taken in Odessa in 1847. 'I don't know why Princess G[agarin] told you that Princess W[ittgenstein] isn't beautiful.'

14 Between 1848 and 1861, Liszt and Carolyne von Sayn-Wittgenstein lived at the Altenburg in Weimar. Throughout this period, the house was an intellectual melting pot where new ideas were forged. From a lost watercolour by Carl Hoffmann, painted for the American organist and educator James M. Tracy, December 1859.

15 'Tears are just water': Daniel (1839–59), Cosima (standing) (1837–1930) and Blandine (1835–62) lived with their grandmother, Anna Liszt (1788–1866), in Paris until 1850, when at their father's bidding they were sent to live with a new and strict governess, Madame Patersi de Fossombroni (*c*.1778–*c*.1862), seen here on the right of the picture. Photograph taken in Paris in 1855 by Carol Szathmari (1812–87).

16 The pianist and secret agent Agnes Street-Klindworth (1825–1906) was one of the most important women in Liszt's life. The two had an intense affair. 'The illness from which you know I suffer has not improved since your departure,' Liszt wrote to her on 29 May 1867, 'and there is every indication that I shall never get over it.'

17 Abbé Liszt in Pest in August 1865.

18 A double life: Cosima von Bülow (1837–1930), Count Leo Festetics (1800–84), Franz Liszt and Hans von Bülow (1830–94). By the time this photograph was taken in Pest in 1865, Cosima was already Wagner's mistress.

19 Paris, March 1886. Photograph taken by Paul Nadar (1856–1939) in his studio.

20 According to Lajos Haynald (1816–91), 'Formerly Liszt came to the nations, but now it is the nations that come to him.' The festival committee set up to organize the celebrations marking the fiftieth anniversary of Liszt's concert debut (from left to right): Cardinal Lajos Haynald, Imre von Huszár (1838–1916), Franz Liszt, Count Imre Széchenyi (1858–1905), Ödön von Mihalovich (1842–1929), Baron Antal Augusz (1807–78), Count Albert Apponyi (1846–1933), Hans Richter (1843–1916), Count Guido Karácsonyi (1817–85) and János Nepomuk Dunkl (1832–1910). Photograph by Ferenc Kozmata (1846–1902), Budapest, November 1873.

21 Liszt on his seventy-third birthday
in Weimar in 1884. Front row (from left
to right): Saul Liebling, Alexander Siloti
(1863–1945), Arthur Friedheim (1859–
1932), Emil Sauer (1862–1942), Alfred
Reisenauer (1863–1907) and one of Liszt's
friends, Alexander Wilhelm Gottschalg
(1827–1908); back row (from left to right):
Moriz Rosenthal (1862–1946), Viktoria
Drewing, Mele Paraninoff, Annette
Hempel-Friedheim and Hugo Leonhardt
Mansfeldt (1844–1932). Photograph by
Louis Held (1851–1927).

22 In the spring of 1886, Liszt returned
to London, where he was fêted repeatedly
and received at Windsor Castle by Queen
Victoria (1819–1901). Caricature by
'Spy' (i.e. Leslie Ward [1851–1922]), first
published in *Vanity Fair* on 15 May 1886.

ROME
(1861–8)

All Roads Lead to Rome

'YOU MAY WELL IMAGINE that for the past three weeks all we've done is wait for Okra's arrival,' Liszt wrote to Marie in Vienna on 7 April 1860. 'Minette [Carolyne] can neither eat nor drink nor sleep – As for me, I continue to hope and hope and hope.'[1] Władisław Okraszewski had begun his diplomatic mission the previous September, and now, six months later, expectations were running high, not least in the Altenburg, where the tension was palpable. The news, when it came, had a liberating effect on all concerned, for Wenceslaus Zylinski, the archbishop of Mohilow, had declared Carolyne's marriage null and void. But the jubilation was short-lived, for the bishop of Fulda, in whose diocese Weimar was situated, issued a decree rescinding the earlier decision. The bishop was acting on the instructions of Antonino Saverio de Luca, the papal nuncio in Vienna from 1856. Yet not even de Luca was a free agent, for the real villains were the Hohenlohe brothers. Monsignor Gustav Adolf zu Hohenlohe had provided de Luca with secret information purporting to demonstrate that Okraszewski was a knave and that the 70,000 roubles that he had demanded for his dubious services were no more than a bribe. Above all, there could be no question of a forced marriage between Nicholas and Carolyne, with the result that there were no legal grounds for an annulment. The papal nuncio was alarmed at this turn of events. Why were the Hohenlohes so hostile?

Konstantin had no interest in seeing his mother-in-law remarry. Liszt's position in all of this was less important to him, for what mattered in his view was more basic: if Carolyne were to be successful in her attempts to have her marriage annulled, then her daughter Marie would be declared illegitimate, which would mean that she would presumably lose the vast fortune that Carolyne had made over to her. Moreover, Carolyne could still bear children, with the result that if she were to marry Liszt and if the couple had a legitimate child, then Konstantin was afraid that the question of Carolyne's inheritance would be resolved at the expense of his wife. Such an idea was unthinkable. In short, the Hohenlohes' concerns were entirely worldly.

Marie's marriage into the Hohenlohe family suddenly seemed to be a terrible mistake. But Carolyne could not yet be aware of her son-in-law's machinations. Or perhaps she thought the Fulda decree a misunderstanding, an interpretation that is certainly possible. Be that as it may, she believed that she was close to achieving her goal. And in order to ensure that her efforts were crowned with success, she decided to travel to Rome in person, leaving Weimar on Thursday, 17 May 1860 in the company of Władisław Okraszewski and her chambermaid, Augusta. Little can she have suspected that it would be sixteen months before she saw Liszt again and that she would never return to Weimar.

Within days of Carolyne's departure, Liszt grew tired of his own company. 'I had been planning to come to Brussels for a couple of days this spring,' he wrote to Agnes Street-Klindworth at the end of May,

> but various commitments have prevented me from moving from here. [...] Perhaps you will break your journey in some region not too far from Weimar where I could join you and tell you how much I am still very truly fond, grateful, and devoted to you.[2]

Agnes accepted his invitation to a romantic assignation, and they agreed on a discreet meeting in Gotha or even Weimar during the month of July. Liszt described Carolyne's attempt to obtain an annulment as the 'grande affaire' of the princess's life. Yet in spite of this he put himself first, an attitude that sheds a significant light on his eagerness – or otherwise – to marry. Peter Cornelius seems to have had a vague idea of the way in which things would develop when he wrote to a female friend: 'I believe that the princess will end her days where she is. Hence Liszt's entire nature and behaviour after her departure. Heed well what I have said, Marie: it was a separation. Would to God that I may be wrong.'[3]

On her arrival in Rome, Carolyne immediately sought out Gustav Adolf zu Hohenlohe. Together they visited the city's churches, dined out at his invitation and even undertook excursions into the surrounding countryside. Simultaneously he was keeping a note of everything that Carolyne told him and passing it on to Vienna. Not until three months had passed did she finally see through him and in a letter to Liszt referred to his 'unbelievable act of betrayal'. He had, she went on, made her look foolish in the eyes of all and sundry, including the pope, and portrayed her as a hysterical and ridiculous old woman.[4] De Luca even denounced her as a bigamist, which in Rome was tantamount to a death sentence. In spite of this, she was able to obtain an audience with Pope Pius IX, sinking to her knees before him on 9 September. The Holy Father is said to have assured her that he would not forget her. And he kept his word by asking a College of Cardinals to re-examine the case. By 22 September 1860 the committee had agreed to dissolve the marriage, a judgement confirmed by Pius. But Carolyne had reckoned without her new family, and the Hohenlohes continued to stake everything on blocking the annulment. Liszt, too, was aware of their machinations and at the end of October discovered that his in-laws in Vienna were planning to approach the tsar. He cabled to Carl Alexander, who was visiting Warsaw and intending to meet the tsar: 'Vienna trying to instigate new measures against princess with Tsar Alexander in Warsaw. I entreat Monseigneur to prevent this.'[5] But the tsar posed no threat as he had no wish to become involved in the 'Wittgenstein Affair'.

In the meantime, Liszt had been travelling extensively and visiting Zwickau, Magdeburg, Vienna and Leipzig. By the end of November he was in Berlin for the baptism of the Bülows' first daughter, who had been born on 12 October and named Daniela in memory of Liszt's dead son. He then returned to Weimar to await the decisions that were expected in Rome. The war of nerves came to a provisional end on 7 January 1861, when the pope confirmed that the marriage of Nicholas and Carolyne was null and void. 'A triumph, a complete triumph,' Carolyne crowed in a letter to Liszt.[6] Nothing stood in the way of their marriage any longer and she could have packed her bags and returned to Weimar at once. At that time the journey from Rome to Weimar took seven days, which is to say that by the middle of January she and Liszt could have been married in Weimar's St John's Chapel. 'And now events took a tragic turn,' Marie later recalled. 'Rome now seemed indispensable to my mother in her quest for happiness in her life.'[7]

Carolyne had taken it into her head that she wanted to get married in Rome and had even settled on 22 October 1861 – Liszt's fiftieth birthday – as the date in question. Although it still lay some distance ahead, she was willing to wait another nine months. What could go wrong in the meantime? After all, she had the pope's decree. Indeed, she was so certain of herself that she signed her letters to Liszt 'ta fiancée'. Her decision to postpone the wedding was to prove a fatal mistake, because her enemies were able to use the intervening period to prepare for their final assault on the couple.

The Thwarted Wedding

Prior to his arrival in Rome on 20 October 1861, Liszt had travelled extensively, including a visit to Paris, his first return in eight years to the scene of his early triumphs. His four-week stay in May and early June had resembled nothing so much as one long bachelor party. As if wanting to prove that he could still dazzle Parisian society, he plunged back into the life of the capital, visiting numerous old friends and acquaintances such as Berlioz, Jules Janin and Alphonse de Lamartine, lunching at the home of the Austrian ambassador, dining with fellow musicians including Gounod, Rossini, Halévy and Wagner, and being received by Emperor Napoléon III on two occasions. He was appointed a Commander of the Legion of Honour on 29 May.

Particularly significant were his three meetings with Marie d'Agoult. Following their reunion on 27 May she noted in her diary: 'He has aged a lot but has remained very handsome. His face is sun-burnt, his eyes no longer as fiery, but in his whole bearing he is still young. His beautiful hair falls in long strands down both sides of his noble and much-saddened face.' The next sentence suggests that the atmosphere was emotionally charged: 'He chatters away, wittily enough, but without any naturalness, in a way that is designed to be cutting and sententious.'[8] Four days later the couple met again: 'He gives the impression of a man who is content to be rich, to lead an elegant life, to be à la mode in Paris and to be well connected. But sad, profoundly sad at bottom. And he has certainly not reached his goal.'[9] Liszt saw the countess one last time on 8 June, the day of his departure: 'While saying goodbye, I spontaneously got to my feet and hugged him, deeply moved. [. . .] Undying charm. He is still the man that he was, and he alone is capable of letting me feel the divine mystery of life.'[10]

Following his return to Weimar, Liszt found himself at the centre of the town's musical life – the last time that he was to do so. The Allgemeiner Deutscher Musikverein was founded on 7 August, a project that he had championed using all the charisma of his personality, and the organization's statutes clearly bore his imprint. In addition to cultivating and supporting music, he was especially keen to preserve and foster the professional interests not only of musicians but also of their dependants. These principles pointed far into the future: from now on musicians were not just to be dependent on the goodwill of their employers but also to have their own professional representation.

Many of Liszt's friends descended on Weimar for the occasion, among them Wagner, Carl Tausig, Peter Cornelius, Hans von Bülow, Eduard Liszt and Blandine and Émile Ollivier. Liszt locked up the Altenburg on 12 August, then spent a few days in a hotel before leaving Weimar on the 17th. In the course of the next few months he visited his friend Prince Konstantin zu Hohenzollern-Hechingen in Löwenberg and the Bülows in Berlin. After that he travelled to Marseilles, where he boarded a ship to Italy on 17 October.

By the time Liszt arrived in Rome on the 20th, he had not seen Carolyne in over sixteen months. Nor did they have much time, because

Carolyne had made all the necessary preparations for their wedding, preparations that were meticulously conscientious and even conspiratorial. Within hours of his arrival the couple had gone to the Vatican to deal with the last remaining formalities. The actual ceremony was due to take place in the Church of San Carlo al Corso on the morning of 22 October. There, on the evening of the 21st, they met Francesco Morelli, the priest who was to conduct the service. The altar was already decorated with flowers and candles when Carolyne and Franz received Communion. Both then returned to their separate lodgings. Only a few hours remained until the event for which both had been waiting for so long. Then, at eleven o'clock at night, Carolyne received a message from Morelli: the pope had withdrawn his consent, and the wedding had to be postponed. As yet, Carolyne and Liszt were unaware that only a few days earlier a cousin of the princess had managed to obtain an audience with Cardinal Prospero Caterini, accompanied by two other members of the Wittgenstein family. It was none other than Gustav Adolf zu Hohenlohe who on 18 October had written to his colleague to ask him to agree to the audience, insinuating that a major scandal threatened the Church if the wedding were to go ahead as planned.[11] Caterini received the emissaries, listened to their complaints and finally persuaded the pope to intervene.

After a fourteen-year struggle, the family won. Initially, it had been only the Wittgensteins who had undermined Carolyne's attempts to have her marriage annulled, but by joining forces with the Hohenlohes, they had formed a powerful alliance. Over the years Carolyne had had to contend with a whole series of defeats, and even now she could have resumed the struggle by asking for an audience with the pope, especially in view of the fact that his intervention had merely postponed the wedding. In short, the last word had yet to be spoken. And yet Carolyne declined to pursue the matter, simply lacking the strength to go on. 'J'ai entièrement échoué,'[12] she wrote to an acquaintance: she had failed completely.

As for Liszt, we do not know how he reacted to the fiasco of 21 October, for he failed to record his thoughts on the matter. It will presumably also remain a mystery what he and Carolyne discussed with each other following the news that their wedding would have to be delayed. Adelheid von Schorn speculated that

> During the time when he was separated from her, Liszt had become more indifferent, and the idea of a legal union with her was no longer something he thought necessary. She noticed this when he arrived in Rome on 21 October, and he himself confirmed it by never again asking whether or not it was still possible for the wedding to go ahead.[13]

Presumably it was this circumstance that persuaded Carolyne to lay down her arms: the couple had grown apart.

Liszt was initially uncertain what to do next. A return to Weimar was out of the question, and so he remained in Rome. Carolyne, too, wanted to settle in the city, but neither of them was interested in continuing the sort of lives that they had led at the Altenburg. They would, of course, still see each other in the future, attending concerts, visiting museums, listening to each other's conversation and sharing in each other's lives. But the days of their *union libre* were over. Their cohabitation in Weimar gave way to an orderly and formal friendship in Rome. Marie zu Hohenlohe recalled that 'these events marked the start of the tormented martyrdom of these two human beings, who had been everything to each other and who continued to search blindly for one another without ever finding what they were looking for'.[14]

Liszt moved into a small apartment in the Via Felice (now the Via Sistina), while Carolyne found rooms in the vicinity of the Via del Babuino, an 'appartamento mobiliato' where she increasingly hid herself away. Visitors who climbed the three flights of steps to her rooms were often shocked at its primitive appearance, which was completely at odds with their expectations of an apartment inhabited by a wealthy aristocrat. According to the writer Richard Voß,

> Her rooms were authentically Roman, being furnished in the most tasteless and garishly colourful manner imaginable, the furniture itself almost meagre. She lived in the same rooms for more than

twenty years without ever feeling the need to introduce any beauty or charm to her surroundings. Of course, she herself was lacking in both of these qualities.[15]

The apartment consisted of several connecting rooms. The first contained only a large table on which several busts of Liszt were displayed. Another was clearly the owner's library, books being piled as high as the ceiling, covering even the tables and chairs as well as littering the floor. The main room was the adjoining salon, where Carolyne lived and worked and even took her meals, in spite of the existence of a dining room. Heavy curtains in front of the windows meant that the rooms were permanently dark, an array of candles merely adding to the gloomy effect. Worse, the windows were never opened, since Carolyne lived in constant fear of draughts and a resultant chill. The air was correspondingly damp and stuffy, and one can well imagine how it smelled thanks to Carolyne's continuing love of strong cigars.

Some visitors were left standing in breathless amazement when they entered this cave-like apartment, unable to believe their watering eyes. Sitting in the middle of the room was Carolyne, like an exotic spider in her web, creating a sight that was both beautiful and eerie. 'She lay permanently stretched out on an ottoman,' recalled Richard Voß. 'Her clothes were old-fashioned, an enormous, disfiguring bonnet on her strikingly large head, the ribbons of which were tied beneath her chin. By framing her head in this way it seemed to accentuate yet further her already sharp features.' Voß was bemused when Carolyne announced that she was a spiritualist, continuing to commune with a whole series of ghosts regardless of his presence: 'It was no agreeable sensation when with ecstatic cheerfulness she reported the names of the deceased men and women who were currently standing beside her.'[16]

Carolyne buried herself in her work as a writer, and in the course of the next twenty-six years she published a total of forty-five works that included a study of the Sistine Chapel, a 254-page disquisition on Buddhism and Christianity, books about angels, church music and a guide to 'Practical Conversations for the Use of Society Ladies'.[17] But her principal work was her *Causes intérieures de la faiblesse extérieure de l'Église en 1870*, which by the date of her death in 1887 had grown to no fewer than twenty-four volumes. Since all were published privately in small print-runs at the author's expense, few examples have survived. Many potential readers will simply have failed to find copies of Carolyne's magnum opus. Nor has there ever been a scholarly examination of her literary output. In conversation with Adelheid von Schorn, the theologian Ignaz von Döllinger expressed the view after reading the early volumes that they contained such erudition 'that only someone who had studied church history in detail would be able to understand them'.[18]

One thing is certain: the Vatican's moral guardians obtained copies of the work and clearly read them very carefully, placing several volumes on their *Index Librorum Prohibitorum* in July 1877 and again in February 1879.[19] Catholics were banned from reading these volumes on pain of excommunication. Curious though this circumstance must seem at first sight, it becomes clear on a closer reading that although Carolyne was a devout Catholic, she was also an independent thinker whose claims that the 'external weakness of the Church' was caused by imperfect humans were a blatant provocation in the eyes of the Curia. Carolyne was warned on several occasions not to overstep the mark, but she refused to heed such advice. In Alan Walker's felicitous phrase, writing was a form of 'therapy' for her.[20] In this way she dealt with the emotional conflicts caused by her thwarted wedding.

During his early months in Rome, Liszt socialized a good deal, clearly enjoying the city's *savoir-vivre*. Writing to Richard Pohl, he assured his correspondent that 'There is no lack of interesting and agreeable acquaintances here.' It was, he went on, a matter of indifference to him that Rome's musical scene could not hold a candle to that in Paris or Weimar. 'I may add in passing that I feel very well (uncalled for!). Several of my former acquaintances tell me that I look even better than I did a few years ago. The local climate suits me admirably.'[21]

Liszt's new circle of friends included the historian Ferdinand Gregorovius, whose own description of the composer contradicts the latter's assessment: 'I have got to know Liszt,' he noted in his diary in the middle of April 1862, 'a striking, demonic appearance; tall, thin, long grey hair. Frau von S. thought he was burnt out and that only the walls were still standing, with a little ghostlike flame flickering inside them.'[22]

Death in Paradise

The town of Saint-Tropez is situated in the south of France in the *département* of Var. When Liszt's daughter, Blandine, and his son-in-law, Émile Ollivier, arrived there in January 1860 in their search for a country estate, the place had yet to be discovered by the international moneyed classes. Only fishing boats were anchored in the tiny harbour, and there were no expensive cafés or bijou boutiques. In the 1860s Saint-Tropez was still an insignificant fishing village, albeit one that was exceptionally beautiful. Some two miles away from the centre of the village the Martin family from Roquebrune a little further to the east owned property that was now on sale. Blandine and her husband were delighted by it: the Château des Salins was to be their new home. The sale was quickly agreed, and by the autumn of 1860 the Olliviers had already moved in.

The little château is situated less than 300 yards from the beach in a park covering fourteen acres of land. Visitors arriving at the house drive past a grove of palm trees and along an avenue of laurel and mimosa. Émile and his father, Démosthène Ollivier, laid out the garden themselves, creating an Eden of magnolia, camellia, cypress, yucca and wisteria, the air being scented with jasmine. The house itself lies at the end of the avenue. On its ground floor were a library housing over 4,000 volumes, an architecturally impressive dining room, Émile's study and two smaller salons, while the first floor was given over to bedrooms, nurseries and a number of other rooms. Over the years Ollivier had numerous extensions added, culminating in 1883 in the addition of a wing known as 'La Toscane'. Renamed the Château de la Moutte by the Olliviers, the house retains its late nineteenth-century appearance, giving present-day visitors the impression that its owners have left only briefly and that they may return at any moment.

It is hard to imagine that a terrible tragedy unfolded in this idyllic setting only two years after the Olliviers had moved in. In January 1862

Blandine wrote to inform her father that she was expecting her first child. The whole family was delighted and looked forward with excitement and anticipation to the child's birth that summer. Émile was tied up in Paris and so he asked his younger sister, Josephine, and her husband, Dr Charles Isnard, to keep an eye on his wife. She went to stay with them at Gémenos, less than twenty miles to the east of Marseilles, in the middle of May 1862. Josephine had two small children of her own, and since Isnard was a doctor, Blandine seemed to be in the best possible hands. Her pregnancy was straightforward, and on 3 July 1862 she gave birth to a son – Liszt's second grandchild. In memory of her dead brother she named him Daniel. The young mother quickly recovered her strength. But in early August Isnard noticed a swelling on her left breast, which he feared might impede the flow of milk. In order to prevent this, he summoned a number of infants from the village whom Blandine was also required to suckle. In addition he used a kind of milk pump that caused her further distress. All in all, his treatment proved fatal: the breast became inflamed and the swelling finally started to suppurate. In the middle of August, Isnard, by now at his wits' end, attempted an operation but failed to use an effective anaesthetic or a proper antiseptic – it was the height of summer and the operation was conducted in a room in Isnard's home. The result was septicaemia.

Isnard ordered arsenic and laudanum (a mixture of alcohol and opium), but Blandine's temperature remained obstinately high. At the end of August Blandine asked her husband to take her home to Saint-Tropez, a good sixty miles away. Somehow she survived the strenuous journey, but it proved the beginning of the end. Back in the Château de la Moutte she was unable to eat and grew increasingly weak, fading away before the eyes of her helpless husband and even more helpless doctor. Her sufferings finally came to an end in the early hours of 11 September 1862. She was only twenty-six years old.

Less than three years had passed since Liszt's son Daniel had died in Berlin, and now the family had to deal with a second blow of fate. A widower at thirty-seven, Émile Ollivier was inconsolable and in his grief blamed himself for his wife's death and for the credulous trust that he had placed in his brother-in-law's abilities. 'Presumably there was a lack of expert medical help,' Bülow ventured – a cautious, if tactless, reproach. Above all, it had been criminally irresponsible to carry out such an operation in less than professional conditions. Anna Liszt was particularly affected by her granddaughter's death: in Bülow's words, she was 'forced at the end of her life to watch one after another of her grandchildren die, grandchildren to whose childhood she had devoted the true cares of a mother.'[23]

As for Liszt, 'Blandine has her place in my heart alongside Daniel,' he wrote to his 'oncle-cousin': 'Both remain to me as expiation, purification and intercessor with the cry "Sursum corda!"'[24] However much Liszt may have struggled to retain his composure and to comfort his mother and son-in-law, there is no doubt that Blandine's death came as a terrible blow. He had last seen his eldest daughter in August 1861 and had been due to visit them in Saint-Tropez the following October. The guest room was already prepared when he called off his visit at the very last moment. 'The shock was so great that I needed some time to recover,' a disappointed Blandine had written to her father on that occasion. 'While I was getting your room ready, I was already communing with you. I could already see myself in your arms and had for a moment left behind me this cold planet of ours. Now I have to return to it.'[25] Perhaps Liszt read through this letter again and was reminded of the opportunity he had missed. Now it was too late.

It was under the impression left by this tragedy that Liszt completed a piano piece in November 1862 that clearly contains autobiographical features: his Variations on Johann Sebastian Bach's *Weinen, Klagen, Sorgen, Zagen*. The piece is based on a brief falling motif from Bach's Cantata 12 that is subjected to all manner of variations. There are times when the music explores depths of sadness almost unique in the history of music, while at other times it rears up in a paroxysm of anger, only to fall back into anguished tenderness. The father's despair is palpable when chords build up and seem to ask: why? Liszt created a fifteen-minute masterpiece that encapsulates a world of grief while ending on a note of reconciliation. Like Bach, Liszt concludes by appending a chorale to his set of variations, at which point the key of F minor that is traditionally associated with sadness modulates to a radiant F major and we hear the theme associated with the words 'Was Gott tut, das ist wohl-getan' (What God doth, that is rightly done). The melody that Bach set to the words 'es wird mich Gott ganz väterlich in seinen Armen halten' (e'en so will God, / All fatherhood, / Within his arms enfold me) is marked 'dolcissimo' (very tender), making it sound as if Blandine is already with her maker.

Minor Orders and Higher Instincts

'The day after tomorrow I shall be leaving my apartment in the Via Felice and moving to the Monte Mario (an hour away from the city),' Liszt informed Franz Brendel in the middle of June 1863. In the months following Blandine's death he had come to see Rome with different eyes. If, until then, the city's bustling social life had appealed to him, he now found it merely tedious, with the result that an invitation from an acquaintance could not have been better timed: Father Agostino Theiner suggested Liszt move into rooms at the monastery of the Madonna del Rosario on the Monte Mario. According to Theiner, the site, which covered a large area, had long been neglected, and only two monks still lived there. Liszt was enthusiastic, as he explained to Brendel:

> The view is indescribably magnificent. I shall try to settle in there in keeping with my nature and hope that I shall be able to come closer to my monastic-artistic ideal. [...] In the meantime you may continue to laugh at me to your heart's content.[26]

Not a few of Liszt's contemporaries expressed their surprise at his remarkable move: 'Some people are claiming that he is preparing to enter the monastery formally,' the diplomat Kurd von Schlözer reported, while voicing his disbelief at the rumour. 'For the present this way of life is probably no more than one of his usual bizarre forms of behaviour intended to ensure that the world takes note of him; but precisely for that reason he could be preparing to surprise the world.'[27] Even the German newspapers felt that it was worth reporting on Liszt's new domicile, as Agnes Street-Klindworth discovered from an Augsburg daily. After an interval of nearly two years, she picked up her pen again, evidently concerned for her friend's wellbeing. In his reply, Liszt assured her that he was 'leading a simpler sort of life' and that 'the Catholic piety of my childhood has become a regular and regulating feeling'.[28]

The seclusion of his new home and the institution's monastic regime evidently appealed to Liszt and offered him support and a sense of direction. Even so, he occupied three rooms on the first floor of the building, which dated from 1628, and had no need to forgo any of the creature comforts to which he had grown accustomed since his manservant Fortunato Salvagni had been allowed to follow his master on the spiritual road he had chosen. Liszt specifically mentions the monastery's excellent food, so that we may assume that at least from a culinary standpoint his stay on the Monte Mario was agreeable. All in all, he was a comic saint who attended Mass each morning. According to Kurd von Schlözer, 'He sits like a prince in a box provided with a window partition which is only a few paces from his cell – like Charles V at the monastery of Yuste, although Charles was also able to hear Mass from his bed.'[29] Liszt at least stopped short of this particular expedient.

Another visitor, Vilmos von Csapó, recalled that Liszt had

> three rooms, the first of which was a salon divided from his study and bedroom by a corridor. His valet escorted me into the salon and after a few minutes the Master appeared, bidding me a warm welcome; a fire was lit in the hearth (with vines!), after which he offered me cigars and a liqueur prepared by the Benedictines, an agreeably smelling drink.[30]

On the other hand, Liszt did not have a grand piano at his disposal and had to make do with an old, out-of-tune upright missing the low D, causing visitors to rub their eyes in disbelief: 'This is the instrument now used by that same Franz Liszt before whom the most massive pianos in Europe once trembled, and who for half a generation ruled the entire world of art like a *Jupiter tonans*.'[31]

Twice a week Liszt left the monastery, descending the countless steps and making his way to the home of his Italian pupil Giovanni Sgambati on the Piazza di Spagna, where he taught a motley band of musicians that included not only Sgambati himself but also the English musician Walter Bache. Another member of his entourage in Rome was his pupil Nadine Helbig who, according to Richard Voß's malicious account, was

> famous not only for the goodness of her heart but also for her enor-
> mous size, with the result that she was feared by every coachman in
> the city. As soon as she heaved into sight, all the coachmen fled as if
> seized by a panic attack.[32]

No doubt Liszt, too, was impressed when she sat down at the piano, seized both corners of the heavy instrument with her hands and pulled it towards her. Her husband, Wolfgang, worked as a secretary at the German Archaeological Institute in Rome. The couple's service flat on the Capitol was much frequented by Liszt, who also gave piano lessons there. In general, he took an active part in the musical life of the city, performing at charity concerts and occasionally playing in private settings. He also visited Carolyne, of course, dining with her and appearing with her in society.

From time to time he received visitors in his rooms at the monastery. Kurd von Schlözer happened to be present when the English vice-consul in Naples, a Mr Douglas, paid his respects:

> Douglas suddenly went over to Liszt with the words: 'May I ask a
> favour?' – 'With pleasure.' – 'May I play *one* chord on your piano?' –
> 'As many as you like.' – Whereupon Douglas strode majestically to
> the piano, played a chord, took out his notebook and wrote therein
> that at four o'clock in the afternoon of Monday, 30 May 1864, he had
> been in Franz Liszt's room at the monastery and played a chord on
> his piano.[33]

But undoubtedly the most famous visitor to Liszt's rooms on the Monte Mario was Pope Pius IX, who called to see him on 11 July 1863. Well known for his love of music, the pope asked Liszt for a demonstration of his abilities, whereupon Liszt finally sat down at his ill-tuned piano with its missing D in the bass and played *St François d'Assise: La prédication aux oiseaux*, a piece he had completed only a short time earlier. When he then started to play 'Casta diva' from Bellini's opera *Norma*, Pius is said to have sprung to his feet, gone over to the piano and sung the aria from memory in his commanding baritone voice. A few days later Liszt was received at a private audience in the Vatican and in July 1865 he visited Pius at his summer residence at Castel Gandolfo. These meetings did not pass unnoticed, eliciting all manner of questions. One Budapest newspaper, for example, noted that 'The Viennese newspapers are reporting that he is completely wrapped up in his religious reveries in Rome and intends to don the penitential shirt of the Dominicans in order to end his days in penance.'[34] Liszt himself added to the rumour mill, striking a markedly mysterious note when telling Franz Brendel in the middle of July 1863 that His Holiness had uttered 'some highly significant words' and admonished him 'to strive after heavenly matters in earthly ones and use his temporal harmonies as a means of preparing himself for the timeless ones'.[35] A good two months later he wrote to his friend Carl Gille: 'My stay in Rome is not a temporary one for me; it marks the third (and presumably final) section of my often troubled but none the less industrious life as that life seeks to raise itself up.'[36]

Was this merely a sentimental outburst on the part of a man in his early fifties? Or did it perhaps conceal something else? Did Liszt feel drawn to higher things or even to the priesthood? There were several considerations that motivated him during the following twenty-four months and that led to the events of July 1865. But first we need to remind ourselves of his state of mind when he arrived in Rome. The 'Wittgenstein Affair' that had dragged on for more than a decade, the frustrating end of his activities in Weimar, the dramatic failure of his plans to marry Carolyne and Blandine's tragic death – all of these had left their mark on Liszt. He was burnt out, and the former socialite longed for a life of greater interiority and contemplation. Since his earliest childhood he had felt close to the Catholic Church, and now Roman Catholicism and the Vatican promised him something akin to a new home. He also had an ulterior motive, as a letter that he wrote in

November 1862 makes clear: 'Now that I have largely completed the symphonic task that was set me in Germany and done so, moreover, to the best of my abilities, I want to meet a similar challenge in the field of the oratorio.'[37] His friendly contacts with the pope and with high-ranking Vatican clerics flattered him and confirmed him in his idea of exploring the world of religious music. His place, he believed, was the Vatican. He seems to have been thinking of the post of director of music of the Holy See.

Liszt may well have reckoned that it was only natural, therefore, to enter the hierarchy of the Church. In this he had the support of Carolyne von Sayn-Wittgenstein, who regarded him as a latter-day Palestrina. The Italian composer Giovanni Pierluigi da Palestrina had breathed new life into church music in the sixteenth century, and now, three centuries later, it was Liszt's duty to continue this task. 'From now on he was to write music only for the greater glory of God' was how one contemporary witness summed up the princess's plans. 'He was to become director of the Papal Chapel and regenerate their institution, to which end he had to become an abbé.'[38] Behind these plans lay a further calculation: if Carolyne was prevented from possessing Liszt herself, no other woman would have him either. According to Kurd von Schlözer: 'So concerned was she that Franz might marry another woman, she activated the Vatican in order to have Liszt appointed a canon at St Peter's.'[39]

Liszt began by undertaking a detailed study of theology. While reading devotional works such as the *Catechism of Steadfastness* in Italian, he also wrote concert paraphrases of two numbers from Meyerbeer's grand opera *L'Africaine*, which had just been posthumously premièred in Paris. These *Illustrations de L'Africaine*, as the two pieces were jointly titled, are typical of Liszt's bravura style. Clearly he had no difficulty leaping back and forth between works written for the edification of Catholic readers and Meyerbeer's operatic exoticism, a circumstance that raises questions about the credibility of his religious conversion. The spiritual atmosphere of the Eternal City undoubtedly appealed to the Catholic believer. But did Liszt's ostentatious spirituality reflect an emotional need? Or was his valet-serviced stay in the monastery not another example of his eccentric desire for self-promotion?

Presumably all these factors played a part. Observers such as Ferdinand Gregorovius certainly harboured doubts about Liszt's allegiance to the Church. 'Liszt is demonstrating a quite fanatical Catholicism,' the German professor noted in March 1864.[40] There is, of course, a subtle distinction between *being* a fanatical Catholic and *demonstrating* that quality, for it implies that there was something of a façade to Liszt's demonstrative devotion. Once again it was Hans von Bülow who hit the nail on the head when he wrote many years later that 'My father-in-law strikes me as being outwardly too much of an abbé and inwardly too little of one.'[41]

In the spring of 1864 an event occurred that was to have a considerable impact on Liszt's future plans: Prince Nicholas von Sayn-Wittgenstein died on 10 March, leaving the way open for Liszt to marry. Friends such as Grand Duke Carl Alexander expected him to marry Nicholas's widow in Rome without any further delay, and when there was still no sign of any wedding bells ringing in the Eternal City by March of the following year, Carl Alexander demanded an explanation:

> I should like you to send me a clear report at once. How are things with you? Since Prince Wittgenstein died a year ago, there are no longer any human reasons or earthly powers standing in the way of your union. If you none the less do not consummate that union, then the reason must be sought in you yourself or in her. Please send me an answer to this question.[42]

Liszt let several weeks pass by before he put pen to paper. His reply was evasive:

> It is indeed the case that I have not had anything going on for more than three years and that since I have settled in Rome, there is nothing whatsoever that I have expected, demanded or sought – nothing that could in any way be said to resemble something going on. The duration and development of exceptional feelings do not depend on external circumstances. 'The heart has its reasons that

reason does not know.' It is these reasons of the heart that have always been crucial for me, and thus they will always remain.[43]

The vagueness of Liszt's reply can hardly have convinced the grand duke. But Carl Alexander cannot have known that at the time he wrote these lines the composer had long since decided on a step of which no one would have thought him capable. The fifty-three-year-old was preparing to enter the minor orders and take the cloth. The minor orders date from a time when the Catholic Church still had a special order for every liturgical function, be it acolyte, exorcist, lector or porter. The rite was abolished in 1972, and since then only members of the laity have been invested with these offices.

This move represented another radical change for Liszt, and as if he wanted to lend additional weight to it, he took part in a charity concert in the Palazzo Barberini on 20 April 1865. It was intended as a kind of farewell performance and included – significantly enough – his highly virtuoso transcriptions of Schubert's *Erlkönig* and Weber's *Invitation to the Dance*. 'A curious farewell to the world,' Ferdinand Gregorovius opined. 'I'm glad that I heard Liszt again; he and the instrument seem to be one, as it were, a piano-centaur.'[44] According to Kurd von Schlözer, 'It is said to be the last time that he will be heard in public. Soon he will be a monsignor and then perhaps pursue very different interests.'[45] But this was not to be the case, for Liszt did not become a monsignor. Nor did he bid farewell to the concert platform. Liszt's 'farewell concert' was just one more example of his penchant for self-publicity.

Five days later Liszt entered the ecclesiastical state when he received the tonsure. Significantly, it was the two-faced Monsignor Gustav Adolf zu Hohenlohe who removed a coin-sized area of hair as a symbolic preparation for the act of ordination. Liszt was now a member of the lower clergy. That same day he left the Monte Mario and moved into Hohenlohe's private apartments in the Vatican, where he was to remain for fourteen months. 'What has occurred here today will undoubtedly cause a sensation,' Schlözer rightly supposed. 'Well, now that the bombshell has exploded, people will rub their eyes in utter amazement.'[46] Rumours abounded, and it was even said that Pius himself had heard

Liszt's confession, which had allegedly gone on for five hours. 'Basta, caro Liszt!' the pope is said to have cried out in exasperation. 'Go and tell the rest of your sins to the piano!'[47] But this whole account is a myth.

Liszt entered the four minor orders of the priesthood on 30 July 1865 in Tivoli, some twenty miles from Rome. Once again it was Hohenlohe who officiated at the ceremony. Liszt was not a priest as he had not entered the major orders and was unable, therefore, to say Mass or hear confession. But he *was* allowed to call himself abbé and to assist the priest during church services. As a cleric he was committed to leading a life of piety and to dressing in a manner suited to his position, which generally meant wearing a cassock. But he was not obliged to remain celibate and, as the canon lawyer Raphael Molitor has explained, he could change his mind at any time: 'Even today the tonsure does not oblige the individual to maintain the ecclesiastical state either then or ever after. Still less was he committed to a life of celibacy.'[48]

Liszt's elderly mother was shocked to learn the news: 'It was only yesterday that I received your letter of 27 April, and it left me profoundly shaken, so much so that I burst into tears. Forgive me, but I was really not expecting to receive such news from you.'[49] Liszt's friends reacted with incomprehension. 'To me this Catholic rubbish is repugnant to the very depths of my soul,' Wagner noted in the diary that he kept for Cosima's benefit. 'Anyone who takes refuge in that must have a great deal to atone for.'[50] Grand Duke Carl Alexander was informed by letter of the news from Rome. 'I read it with a feeling of deep personal anguish,' he wrote to Liszt.[51] The general public was mystified: how was it possible that a womanizer like Liszt was now parading around Rome in a cassock? The city's salons were rife with rumour, Kurd von Schlözer recalled, but in all of them the Princess Wittgenstein 'plays the chief role. Some maintain that fear that the unpredictable Franz might yet marry some young woman agitated her so much that that she set the whole Vatican in motion to see that influential clerics gently propelled the good Franz into the clergy.'[52]

It is entirely possible that Liszt was hoping to embark on a career in the Vatican, believing that in this way he might impress the Church authorities, and yet genuine religious motives may also have played a role here. Moreover, any attempt to explain the situation needs to take into account that, as we know, Liszt had drifted apart from Carolyne during his final years in Weimar, with the result that she was now his friend rather than his partner. To that extent he will long since have welcomed the Church's rigorous attitude towards Carolyne's divorce, while the enforced abandonment of his marriage plans had finally relieved him of the need to take a step that he could no longer have undertaken with a clear conscience. Now, in the wake of Prince Nicholas's death, Liszt must surely have been afraid that Carolyne's eagerness to marry him would once again be rekindled. Curious though it must sound, his decision to enter the lower orders of the priesthood represented a public sacrifice offered up to his former companion in life. After Carolyne had spent so many years fighting a losing battle, he wanted to renounce life at least outwardly and by entering the ecclesiastical state he was keen to ensure that marriage was out of the question once and for all – and not just marriage to Carolyne.

But is this really what he did? What had changed for him? Kurd von Schlözer was fascinated by the idea of 'seeing the good Liszt again in his new costume'.[53] A costume? The abbé's black cassock was undoubtedly a form of disguise, yet another of the many masquerades that Liszt organized in the course of his life. It is no surprise, then, that sceptical observers refused to see Liszt as a God-fearing cleric. 'It is said that he already regrets his metamorphosis', sneered Ferdinand Gregorovius in November 1865.[54] Nor did Liszt show any signs of abandoning the piano: 'At the piano he looked like a Mephisto, triumphantly hurling those demoniacal glances of his to left and right', Schlözer noted after a private concert on 26 May 1865.[55]

But the abbé's black cassock evidently made Liszt even more desirable in the eyes of many women – perhaps it was this life of piety that made him all the more attractive. Just as had been the case two decades earlier, he was again able to trigger an outbreak of Lisztomania, a point attested by Ferdinand Gregorovius: 'Countess Tolstoy told me yesterday that an American lady living here had caused the covering of a chair, on which Liszt had sat, to be framed and hung on the wall.'[56] At the end of February 1866, when Liszt took part in the local première of his *Dante Symphony* in Rome, the ecstasy he instilled knew no bounds. As abbé,

he 'reaped an Indian summer of homage. The ladies of the gallery overwhelmed him with flowers from above – Frau L. almost slaying him
with a laurel wreath.'[57]

At the end of November 1866, Liszt moved to the Monastery of Santa
Francesca Romana on the Roman Forum. His new apartment was on
the first floor of the building and consisted of five rooms furnished in
only the most Spartan manner: an antechamber, a dining room, a study,
a salon and a bedchamber. Here, too, Liszt was rarely left in peace, at
least if we may believe the account of his pupil Olga Janina, who was
later to cause him a good deal of trouble:

> The foreigners who invade Rome in November all knocked at the
> door of Santa Francesca Romana. They went to see X [i.e. Liszt] just
> as one goes to see the giraffe at the zoo: and they took advantage of
> the cordiality of his welcome to purloin everything possible from
> him, even the bits of paper on which he wiped his pens. Others asked
> for photographs with a personal dedication, and the boldest asked
> him to play the *Erlkönig* and the *Invitation to the Dance*. It was then
> that one had to see the English at work. While he was playing they
> queued up behind him, gravely removing hairs with tweezers, their
> preference being for those that had already turned silver. When one
> person had collected enough, he would put them in a paper bag and
> yield his place to the next. Absorbed in his music, X either felt
> nothing or was disinclined to make a fuss about so small a matter.[58]

Synchronicities

There are times when the biographer stumbles upon remarkable
synchronicities: while the hero or heroine of his narrative is busy
committing a sin of omission or commission, elemental events are
taking place in the life of another person. I am referring, of course, to
Liszt, his daughter Cosima, son-in-law Hans von Bülow and colleague
Richard Wagner. While Liszt's own marriage plans were foundering
and he found himself heading for a monastery, arguably the most

famous act of adultery in the recent history of music was being committed. For the most part, these events are already well known, so that we do not need to rehearse them in detail. But a brief account of their prehistory may not go amiss.

By early May 1864 Wagner was so heavily in debt that he was on the run from his creditors. At the very last minute he received news that King Ludwig II of Bavaria had decided to see to the welfare of a composer whom he had long admired and to liberate him from the life of quotidian calamity that he had been leading until then. The handsome but misanthropic king had just turned eighteen and had ascended the Wittelsbach throne two months earlier. He loved Wagner's operas and music dramas and was besotted with their composer. Ludwig not only paid off Wagner's debts and extricated him from a confused and difficult situation but also – unwittingly – triggered a terrible marital tragedy. The story began on Lake Starnberg, where Wagner settled in the middle of May 1864, bringing with him his Swiss servants Franz and Anna Mrazek, who had also served him in Vienna. King Ludwig had provided a luxury villa for his hero in the sleepy village of Kempfenhausen on the north-east shore of the lake. The Villa Pellet, as the property was known, was entirely to Wagner's taste, its twenty-two rooms and large park gratifying the now fifty-one-year-old composer's feelings of self-esteem. But within weeks of his arrival, he realized he needed company.

'I am inviting you, your wife, your child and your maid to spend as long as you like with me this summer,' he wrote to Bülow on 9 June:

> Come and populate my house, at least for a time! This is at the very heart of my entreaty! Don't forget that this is the most significant thing that has ever happened to me; a great epoch, an extremely important section of my life! Let us collect our thoughts and together see what significance all of this has for us and what significance it may yet have for us! [. . .] For heaven's sake, children! Children! No is not an option. I simply couldn't bear it.[59]

Wagner told Cosima that Bülow should give up his post in Berlin and settle in Munich as the king's pianist in residence. It sounded tempting, not least because Bülow had for some time been disenchanted with his work at the Stern Conservatory, while the Munich court was willing to guarantee a salary of at least 1,500 florins a year. Bülow agreed to travel to Munich to examine the matter in situ, leaving fate to take whatever course it might choose.

Events unfolded with surprising speed. Bülow was detained in Berlin on business, and so Cosima turned up without him at Lake Starnberg on 29 June 1864, bringing with her her two daughters Daniela and Blandine, the second of whom had been born in March 1863. Fifty years later Wagner's servant Anna Mrazek told a court that she was

> convinced that Frau Cosima gave herself to Richard Wagner on that occasion. In general, it was easy to tell in Starnberg at that time that there was something going on between Frau Cosima and Richard Wagner. The two of them were always together and were always walking in the grounds, arm in arm.

They slept together that week. Nine months later their first daughter, Isolde, was born. By the time Bülow finally arrived at Kempfenhausen on 7 July, his wife and his friend were already a couple. He had no idea what was going on. As Anna Mrazek told the court: 'To the extent that he noticed anything at all, Bülow seemed not to make much of it. At the time I thought that he regarded the relationship as one between friends, although even at that time I myself already viewed it as one between lovers.'

Anna Mrazek's husband witnessed an incident that summed up the whole drama of the situation. Franz Mrazek told his wife that he had seen

> Bülow trying to enter Wagner's bedroom, but the door was locked as Frau Bülow was in there with Wagner. (My husband knew that Frau Bülow was in the room with Wagner.) My husband went on to say that Bülow returned to the living room and threw himself on the ground, shouting and screaming and beating the floor with his hands and feet like a madman.[60]

But Bülow accepted the situation and said nothing, demanding no explanation either from his wife or from his rival.

And so the situation remained until 19 August 1864, when Bülow moved into rooms at the Bayerischer Hof Hotel in Munich to be treated for a 'nervous disorder' – the psychosomatic dimension of his illness is not hard to guess. Cosima, meanwhile, travelled to Karlsruhe to see her father, who had left Rome for the first time in three years in order to attend the third annual meeting of the Tonkünstlerverein, which was held there between 22 and 26 August. On the programme were Liszt's setting of Psalm XIII, his First Mephisto Waltz, his symphonic poem *Festklänge* and his B minor Piano Sonata, all of them important pieces. Bülow was due to run the festival and play the sonata but he had to be replaced at the last minute, a circumstance that Liszt did not discover until he arrived in the city. 'Personally and artistically his absence affected me deeply,' he wrote to Eduard Liszt a few weeks later, 'and yet I cannot complain about the performances, while the audience response, especially to my Psalm, was gratifying in the extreme.'[61]

Cosima had travelled to Karlsruhe on her own initiative, evidently wanting to inform her father in person that her marriage to Bülow was over and that she was in love with Wagner. We do not know at first hand how Liszt reacted to this revelation, but we may assume that he showered her with reproaches and that he sided with Bülow. He could not be indifferent to the fate of his daughter and of his favourite pupil, quite apart from the pain caused by the threatened failure of their marriage. Many years later Carolyne von Sayn-Wittgenstein recalled that 'I was with him during the deaths of his son, his daughter Blandine and his mother, but nothing compared to his despair over this.'[62] Religious scruples, too, may have played a part here since Liszt was already thinking about entering the minor orders at this date.

None the less, the principal reason for Liszt's 'despair' was of a different order, for he mistrusted Wagner and considered him a morally reprobate knave and a dangerous and egocentric demagogue who used his fellow men and women for his own self-centred ends. Wagner's affairs were well known: he had separated from his wife of twenty-five years' standing at the end of 1862 and had had affairs with a whole series of women, including Mathilde Maier, the daughter of a notary in Mainz; the actress Friederike Meyer; and the daughter of a Viennese butcher and her sister; and so on. Liszt must have heard about them all. The idea that Cosima should take her place in a long line of Wagner's conquests must have been unsettling, to say the least.

In Liszt's eyes, Wagner was a charismatic opportunist with a deficient set of moral values. As early as 1859 he had asked Hans von Bülow: 'Don't you think that he should be treated like a great sovereign – a little sick and therefore not really responsible for his actions?'[63] In spite of his misgivings about Wagner as a person, he continued to respect and admire him as a colleague, with the result that even in 1867, when their relations were at rock bottom, he paid him a musical homage with arguably his most famous piano transcription, 'Isolde's Love-Death' from Wagner's music drama *Tristan und Isolde*.

On hearing Cosima's admission, Liszt was determined to persuade his daughter to examine her conscience and salvage her marriage. After six days in Karlsruhe, they travelled together to Lake Starnberg. Wagner was shocked to see Cosima, as he recalled in his diary a year later: 'Restless, faint, frail, miserable, lacerated! It was dreadful! I felt an anguish beyond all compare!'[64] Liszt and Wagner had not seen each other for three years, but the atmosphere in which their reunion took place could hardly have been more strained. Initially they sought to maintain appearances and even made music together, but on the afternoon of 30 August a violent argument broke out, in the course of which Liszt heaped reproaches on Wagner's head. 'There were also numerous other reasons to be agitated', Wagner hinted mysteriously in a letter to Mathilde Maier, 'Liszt's visit – against such a background etc.'[65]

Liszt spent several hours at his son-in-law's sickbed. It is difficult to know if they discussed what already seemed obvious, namely, that Cosima already belonged to Wagner. All we can say for certain is that Liszt and Bülow talked about King Ludwig's offer: 'Many considerations kept me from immediately accepting the king's offer', Bülow explained to Joachim Raff. 'But after mature reflection and in the light of my father-in-law's advice I have now definitely decided to see if a new era may dawn for me elsewhere.'[66] In other words, it was Liszt who advised

Bülow to accept the Munich appointment, bringing Cosima permanently into Wagner's orbit. He evidently believed that her infatuation with Wagner was a passing fancy and that his remonstrations were already bearing fruit. He clearly did not know that his daughter was pregnant, quite apart from which Wagner had revealed his most accommodating side and apologized for his actions. Liszt appears to have believed him and had even praised his 'common sense'.[67] This was to prove a tremendous mistake.

Throughout this period Liszt was almost permanently on the move. In early September, when the Bülows returned to Berlin from Munich, he travelled to Löwenberg to visit his friend Prince Konstantin zu Hohenzollern-Hechingen and at the end of the month he saw the Bülows again in Berlin, where it was agreed that Cosima would accompany her father on a journey that was planned to last some weeks, a plan evidently designed to distract his daughter and keep her away from Wagner. Prior to leaving for France, Liszt called on Grand Duke Carl Alexander at his hunting lodge at Wilhelmsthal near Eisenach, his five-day visit taking place in a friendly atmosphere. After meals, which Liszt took with the grand duke's family, he would entertain his hosts on the piano. Carl Alexander was profoundly moved and even described Liszt's playing as 'divine'.[68] The two men also held a number of private conversations, in the course of which Carl Alexander made an interesting offer: 'Spent a long time with Liszt, with whom I discussed the necessity of his coming back,' he noted in his diary. 'He more or less promised to do so.' In the event, five years were to pass before Liszt kept his word, but Carl Alexander had evidently struck the right note. Liszt bared his soul to his host in a way that was by no means typical of him, and when asked about his present situation, he poured out his feelings. Carl Alexander's diary captures his dilemma in a particularly focused manner:

It is impossible not to be affected by the fatalistic side of his destiny. The affection that he felt for the princess, her passion for him, the fetters that this created, his departure for Rome, his wedding that was thwarted at the last minute by the pope just as he was on the point of celebrating it, two years of waiting, then the death of the prince, the princess's husband . . . this is one of the most curiously affecting psychological dramas that life could produce.[69]

When Liszt left Schloss Wilhelmsthal in early October, he seemed more thoughtful than usual. Carl Alexander accompanied him as far as the Rennsteig, a few miles away, 'where I said goodbye to him with great sadness'.[70]

Liszt then travelled to Eisenach, where he met Cosima and the two of them continued their journey to France, arriving in Paris on the morning of 4 October. Liszt was particularly keen to see his mother, who had been feeling increasingly lonely and whose health had suffered following a bad fall. For some years she had been staying with Liszt's son-in-law Émile Ollivier. It was the last time he saw her: she died in early February 1866.

During their week together in Paris, Liszt and his daughter visited many of their old friends and acquaintances, meeting Berlioz, Rossini, Jules Janin and Camille Érard, the widow of the piano manufacturer Pierre Érard, as well as Marie d'Agoult, whom neither Liszt nor Cosima had seen for the last three years. Unfortunately, we know very little about this meeting, although from Liszt's point of view it was evidently marked by sadness and nostalgia. Afterwards Marie noted in her diary:

> He said: I've always loved you. For three years I have loved you in a way that is a little less unworthy of you. I live alone etc. He says he is poor and that some of the deprivations that he suffers are hard to endure. Not even in Paris is he controversial. He works six hours . . . He speaks the language of Catholics. Seems to obey a strict morality and to continue to have a great deal to do with the aristocracy. He has aged during the last two years. Far less good-looking, but calmer and more affectionate. Great tenderness for Cosima.[71]

After a week in Paris, Liszt and Cosima continued their journey via Toulon to Saint-Tropez, where they saw Émile Ollivier again. All three of them visited Blandine's grave at the Maritime Cemetery. But the sight of his daughter's last resting place left Liszt profoundly shaken. By the next day he and Cosima were already on their way to Marseilles, where they went their separate ways, Cosima returning to Germany and to a marriage that was filled with uncertainty, while Liszt boarded a ship that took him back home – to Rome.

Hans and Isolde

If Liszt had been hoping that Cosima's visit to France would help to save her marriage and persuade her to forget her lover, then he was to be bitterly disappointed. Wagner had left the Villa Pellet on Lake Starnberg in October 1864 and settled in Munich, where he took over an entire villa in the Brienner Straße in the city's most fashionable quarter. An architecturally impressive building, it was placed at his disposal by King Ludwig II. The Bülows arrived in the Bavarian capital in late November and moved into rooms in the nearby Luitpoldstraße, marking the beginning of a *ménage à trois* whose tensions were immediately apparent to Liszt's former pupil and secretary, Peter Cornelius, when he called on the Bülows on New Year's Day 1865: 'Hans was ill,' he noted afterwards in his diary, 'his condition is giving cause for concern. They are both noble, fine-feeling people, but heaven only knows what may happen, given the way they live together – in time I expect that this will become clear to me.'[72] Cornelius sensed that something was not right. Cosima was leading 'a sad life between her husband, who is slowly fading away, and her eccentric fatherly friend', we read a good two weeks later.[73] For all that he may have been 'fading away', Cosima's husband was only thirty-five years old at this time.

Cosima was leading a double life, performing routine chores in the Luitpoldstraße before making her way to the Brienner Straße and spending the rest of the day with her 'eccentric fatherly friend', organizing his daily round, running his household and even dealing with his correspondence. By now her relations with her husband had reached a new low, leaving him to throw himself into his work at the theatre in Munich or on tour – clearly he could no longer bear to be cooped up within the confines of his own home. When he returned to Munich on 2 April after an extended recital tour, his wife was about to give birth.

Liszt's fourth grandchild was born at 8:40 on 10 April 1865. Isolde Josepha Ludovika was her third daughter – and Wagner's first.

Even Cosima's midwife was in no doubt about the child's true parentage and found it hard to believe that Bülow ever regarded himself as the father. Years later, Anna Mrazek testified that 'whenever she went to see Frau Cosima during her lying-in period, the midwife told me that she always found Richard Wagner sitting by her bedside'.[74] Bülow remained ostentatiously calm. A few days after the child's birth, he joked that 'for the third time' he had 'become "a mother"', as they say in Berlin whenever a daughter puts in an appearance'.[75] Perhaps Bülow was merely trying to put a brave face on an impossible situation. Or perhaps Cosima had been intimate with both men at the time the child was conceived, allowing Hans to believe that he could indeed have been the father. Be that as it may, Isolde was described in the baptismal register of St Boniface's Parish Church in Munich as the 'legitimate daughter of Hans and Cosima von Bülow'. In order to complete the deception, the child's natural father – Wagner – was listed as one of the godparents.[76]

Within days of Isolde's birth, Bülow had left for The Hague, where on 15 April he gave the world première of Liszt's *Totentanz* for piano and orchestra, a work that conjures up a veritable portrait of hell by presenting a set of six variations on the Gregorian *Dies irae* depicting the Last Judgement. Death stalks the score in the form of strident trills and brutal chords. The percussive use of the piano, the bold harmonies and the work's implacable momentum make the *Totentanz* an extraordinarily modern piece, the piano writing confronting the soloist with uniquely challenging difficulties. It is little less than a miracle that Bülow was able to find the strength to master so demanding a composition at such an emotionally testing time. But perhaps his work on it was also a form of therapy that allowed him to endure his problems at home. On his return to Munich he achieved an even greater feat by finding the necessary calm and concentration to rehearse the world première of Wagner's latest musical drama, *Tristan und Isolde*. In spite of all the emotional and psychological wounds that Wagner had dealt him, he was simply incapable of breaking free from the composer's gravitational pull, continuing to feel mysteriously drawn into its sway. After countless individual music calls and no fewer than twenty-one orchestral rehearsals the work received its first performance on 10 June 1865 in the presence of King Ludwig II. *Tristan und Isolde* was a great artistic triumph that was acclaimed by the first-night audience. At the end Wagner and Bülow stood together onstage, overwhelmed and touched by the response. Liszt sent his apologies, attending neither of these two world premières, since he was otherwise occupied in Rome, preparing to enter the minor orders.

By the summer of 1865 Liszt was obliged to admit that nothing had changed in the relationship between his daughter and Wagner – it was presumably Peter Cornelius who had kept him informed. And so he tried once again to intervene. In early August he travelled to Pest for the first performance of his great oratorio *The Legend of Saint Elizabeth* and peremptorily invited the Bülows to accompany him. Officially he wanted them to attend an event of considerable musical significance, but the truth of the matter is that he wanted to keep Cosima away from Wagner and evidently hoped that the time that she spent with Bülow in Hungary would amount to a second honeymoon. The first performance of *The Legend of Saint Elizabeth* took place in Pest's recently opened Redoutensaal on 15 August 1865 and was conducted by Liszt wearing a Franciscan habit that he had had made while in the city. Five hundred singers and orchestral players were gathered on the stage, and there were more than 2,000 people in the audience. The performance was a great success. 'He is in excellent health, and his entourage, his nation and his family are all extremely happy,' Bülow reported from Pest. 'Repeat performance tomorrow. Will go even better and presumably elicit as much enthusiasm as last time.'[77]

Liszt managed to prolong his visit to Hungary by means of various ruses, taking the Bülows to the nearby town of Fót to visit a friend and later accompanying them to Gran some thirty miles away. On 29 August, again in the Redoutensaal, he gave the world premières of his two Franciscan *Legends*. Afterwards he claimed to be so exhausted that he needed a few days to recover before sailing down the Danube – still with the Bülows – to Szekszárd. Throughout this whole period – Cosima was

away for more than five weeks – Wagner remained behind, seething
with fury and venting his rage in the pages of his diary, a gift from
Cosima and intended for her eyes alone: 'Cosima! Cosima!--And once
more – Cosima! – Shall I now be angry with your begetter, – that won't
do? But that's what he is aiming at, the devil! – Adieu!'[78] The previous
month he had written that he would

> finally come to hate my Friend completely! I do not believe in his
> love. He has never loved. [. . .] Your father is repugnant to me. – and
> when I was able to endure him, there was more Christianity in my
> blind indulgence than in all his holier-than-thou piety.[79]

Even trivia now annoyed him: 'Your father seems to enjoy making you
look old: his favourite way of arranging your hair makes you ugly and
quite alien to me: it doesn't suit you. – God knows why he likes it.'[80]
Cosima, too, was subjected to Wagner's reproaches, culminating in the
accusation that she was neglecting their child, now four months old, in
order to go gadding across Europe: 'And you've spent the last five weeks
running away from little Isolde –: This is how you deserve such a sweet
child! If you go off in search of adventure again, I shall take charge of the
child myself.'[81]

The Bülows returned to Munich in the middle of September. A
month later the situation took a dramatic turn for the worst – Wagner
himself dated the decisive event to 11 October 1865. Power and money
were involved. He had meddled in Bavarian politics and incurred the
enmity of the powerful court secretariat. When he continued to make
shameless financial demands on his benefactor ('Be open-handed as
only a king can be, and leave it to my conscience to decide how I may
one day reciprocate this royal trust!'),[82] influential circles associated
with the prime minister, Ludwig von der Pfordten, and with the cabinet
secretary, Franz Seraph von Pfistermeister, had finally had enough. On
1 December Pfordten gave the king an ultimatum: 'Your Majesty is at a
fateful crossroads and you need to choose between the love and reverence of your beloved people and your friendship for Richard Wagner.'[83]
Ludwig chose to abandon Wagner, who on 6 December was instructed

by an intermediary to leave Munich. Four days later, accompanied by his servant Franz and his dog Pohl, he arrived in exile in Switzerland. For the present Cosima remained with her husband in Munich.

The news that Wagner had been told to leave Munich filled Liszt with considerable concern, prompting him to write at once to his daughter:

> How are things? And, above all, where are you? Will you remain in Munich? What is Hans's view of the situation? What are W[agner's] thoughts on the matter? – Where will he go, what will he do? – Tell me at once as clearly as you can so that I can help you.

He would travel to Paris in early March in order to attend a performance of his 'Gran' Mass at Saint-Eustache:

> Perhaps Hans would agree to come too. I don't mean my suggestion to sound like an excursion. Rather, it seems to me that if his post in Munich must be regarded as lost (which in the absence of more detailed information I cannot say is the case or not) and if a decision has to be made, then Paris would offer many advantages that cannot be found in Germany.[84]

Liszt clearly believed that Cosima could still be persuaded to stay with Bülow and that she might even be prepared to leave Munich with him. However caring Liszt's suggestion that the Bülows should move to Paris may have been, it reflected a profound misunderstanding of Cosima's feelings. For her, Bülow belonged to the past: she had long since decided to throw in her lot with Wagner. Cornelius summed up the situation far more aptly when he wrote that

> Wagner and Cosima are in a real relationship. It may even be supposed that she will follow him with the children. Once we had said goodbye to Wagner, she returned not to her own house but to Wagner's. [...] How will this affect Bülow? Has he abandoned his wife to Wagner as part of some ultra-romantic deal?[85]

Cornelius was to be proved right. As a result, Liszt travelled to Paris on his own, arriving in the city in early March 1866. His mother had died there over a month earlier. Émile Ollivier, who had looked after her at great personal cost right up to the end, had left her apartment exactly as it had been during her lifetime. Overcome by a feeling of melancholy, Liszt now stood before her few worldly possessions. 'We have just opened my mother's desk and her cupboards,' he wrote to Carolyne von Sayn-Wittgenstein in Rome. 'She left very few things of any value – a bracelet, two clocks, a few rings, a shawl, a little lace – that's all!'[86]

Liszt's presence in Paris sparked the usual displays of adulation, and the habitués of the city's salons looked forward with eager anticipation to a visit by the gallant abbé in his clerical collar and black soutane, not least because various rumours were circulating about him – he had lost none of his diabolical charisma, he was as fond of women as ever and much more besides. In short, Liszt was the most sought-after man in the capital. Four days after his arrival he gave a recital at the Palais Metternich, the home of the Austrian ambassador and the focal point of Parisian society. Liszt played his Franciscan *Legends*. 'Never again shall we see or hear anything like it,' Camille Saint-Saëns recalled many years later.[87] Another eyewitness described Liszt as a

> priestly lion, taking his success as a matter of course. There are a succession of dinners in his honor, where he does ample honor to the food, and is in no way bashful about his appetite. He does a great deal of beaming, he has (as some one said) 'so much countenance'.

He had 'a very seductive way of looking at you while playing, as if he was only playing for you, and when he smiles you simply go to pieces. I don't wonder he is such a lady-killer, and that no woman can resist him.'[88]

But the mass hysteria was deceptive, for the local press was highly sceptical, many of Liszt's contemporaries refusing to take seriously his newfound religious beliefs and, even worse, dismissing the whole affair as an eccentric affectation. The performance of his 'Gran' Mass at Saint-Eustache on 15 March was so badly prepared that it was a fiasco, with chorus and orchestra often going their separate ways. The audience in the vast church behaved inappropriately, gossiping throughout the performance, which was frequently interrupted by a military band that also happened to be present. In short, it was a caricature of the piece that the audience had heard that Thursday, providing the press with the ammunition that it had been looking for and allowing reviewers to write spiteful squibs ridiculing the work and its composer. Liszt was particularly hurt by the fact that Berlioz failed to defend him in public: the two men were never to meet again. Liszt himself was so mortified by all these attacks that he avoided Paris for the next twelve years.

Liszt saw Marie d'Agoult three times during his 1866 visit. At their last encounter, she informed him that she was planning to publish her memoirs, an announcement that abruptly ended their attempts at a rapprochement between 1861 and 1864. 'Nélida told me that she intends to publish her confessions,' he wrote to Carolyne von Sayn-Wittgenstein. 'I told her that I did not think it possible that she could write a confession of this kind, because anything that she might describe as "confessions" would ultimately be nothing more than lies and calumnies.' Liszt was afraid that Marie would again use the occasion to get even with him in print. He undoubtedly knew his former partner only too well, and *Nélida* had provided painful proof of the way in which love could turn to hate.

> For the first time I spoke to her directly about the question of right and wrong! These are big words, but I had to use them in order to do my duty towards her. Any continuation of the exchange of ideas that has been going on between us would have been immoral – and so I had no choice but to appeal to her conscience.[89]

Although Liszt's worst fears were not to be realized, Marie's description of herself certainly played fast and loose with the truth. Her book teems with blatant attempts to retouch and rewrite her life – but that is another story.

Liszt left Paris at the end of April and travelled to Amsterdam, where two concerts were planned in his honour. He was looking forward to seeing Bülow, who had agreed to appear as a soloist, as the news that he had in the meantime received from Munich had been less than heartening. In early March – at the very time that the Bülows should have been making a new start in Paris – Cosima had travelled to Switzerland with her daughter Daniela in order to be with Wagner. It was during this visit that Wagner and Cosima had crossed Lake Lucerne and on a spit of land on the opposite shore saw the whitewashed Villa Tribschen that Wagner had immediately leased using money made available to him by Ludwig, moving into the property in the middle of April, while Cosima and Daniela returned to Germany. Liszt was annoyed by his daughter's visit, regarding it as a signal demonstration of her lack of tact. On learning of her father's anger, she decided to accompany Bülow to Amsterdam. 'Cosima is making the journey in order to patch things up with her father,' Cornelius informed his fiancée: Liszt had been furious with her 'for travelling to Geneva to see Wagner'.[90]

Liszt's attempts to mediate proved unsuccessful, for only days after her return to Munich, Cosima joined Wagner in Switzerland, this time taking all her children with her. 'I almost felt I'd never see her again,' Cornelius told his fiancée, 'but that would be perfectly acceptable! I no longer have any dealings with her, my entire nature is completely alien to her.' On 12 May – the day after Cosima left – Cornelius and Bülow discussed the matter in confidence: 'He's so nice when she's not there, he's an entirely different person.' Bülow admitted that 'he would perhaps bid farewell to Munich and go to Italy. Everything is bound up with the departure of the whole family'.[91]

The situation became even worse when the Bavarian newspapers reported on Cosima's regular visits to Switzerland, their reports taking the form of venomous articles attacking Bülow's honour. He responded by resigning his position on 6 June, before travelling to Zurich, while Cosima returned to Munich. On 10 June they met at Tribschen – according to Cornelius, 'an anxiously awaited day of decision': 'I know how it will turn out. Cosima will remain with Wagner, for this must happen if Cosima's destiny is to be fulfilled. And Wagner's too.'[92]

For the present a final decision was delayed, the Bülows remaining at Tribschen until early September 1866 and attempting to put on a brave face. The two rivals would occasionally look daggers at one another but otherwise did what they could to conceal their true emotions. It seems clear that Bülow called neither of the lovers to account, even though – as he told Raff – he had 'been in absolutely no doubt since February 1865 about the nature of a situation that is rotten to the core. But never in my wildest dreams did I imagine that this situation would become public, still less did I have nightmares about it.'[93] Bülow was an inordinately proud man, and his honour was sacrosanct, with the result that he preferred to say nothing while being inwardly consumed by his anguish. As Cornelius aptly put it, he became 'the martyr of his circumstances'.[94] Only once did he hint at his true feelings in his letter to Raff: 'You have no idea of what has been taking place: even in person I would find it difficult to make you understand the horror and frightfulness of all that has befallen me, I could certainly not tell you about it in a letter.'[95]

The drama that unfolded that summer in Lucerne was greeted with complete incomprehension on the part of both Liszt and the princess, neither of whom could accept it. Carolyne wrote to Eduard Liszt – and we may assume that she was speaking for Liszt as well – that

> I fear, alas, between ourselves, that Cosima has no more brains than sense, a great misfortune for a woman. They would have been able to keep their position in Munich [. . .] if, without *repudiating* Wagner, who had brought them there, they had very gradually parted from him.

And she went on:

> The Bülows, by identifying themselves with Wagner after his departure, have acted with unrealistic sentimentality, because that particular patron does not deserve it, and I greatly fear that they have made their stay in Munich impossible too. I am deeply saddened by that. Seeing Liszt's own children sacrifice the fine position they could have had in relation to him, to Art, for a rogue of Genius like that Wagner, is really hard![96]

The Force of Destiny

In early 1867 a new act began in the drama of love, jealousy and betrayal, when Wagner's second daughter, Eva Maria, was born at Tribschen on 17 February. Bülow had settled in Basel six months earlier but arrived at Tribschen on the day of the birth, sitting down beside his wife and saying, 'Je pardonne', to which Cosima apparently replied: 'Il ne faut pas pardonner, il faut comprendre' (It's not a question of forgiving, but of understanding). With Eva's birth, the situation became intolerable. Together with her four daughters, Cosima was now living with her lover, while Bülow was leading the life of a bachelor lacking all creature comforts. As so often, he sought refuge in cynicism:

> A pretty situation in which I find myself – six months on my own as a bachelor, without a family and without hearth and home – all my possessions still in Munich, where I'm paying for the apartment until the end of April, etc. Long live King Ludwig II of Bavaria, who is to blame for all of this wretchedness![97]

Ludwig did indeed play a key role in these developments, for Wagner and Cosima continued to enjoy his protection in spite of the rumours and salacious jokes that were circulating in Munich about the *ménage à trois* that Ludwig was not yet prepared to believe. Not until some months later was his faith in what had seemed to him to be the harmless Tribschen idyll finally shattered. As if the situation in Munich was not already difficult enough, Bülow was appointed Court Kapellmeister in March, an appointment made at Wagner's instigation but one that represented more of a trap than a way out of his present predicament. While Bülow may have been credulous enough to see in it his social rehabilitation, Wagner was acting for entirely selfish reasons. His aim was to ensure that the first performances of his new opera, *Die Meistersinger von Nürnberg*, were conducted by the brilliant Bülow, who duly fell into the trap and moved back to Munich in the middle of April 1867. But Wagner, too, paid a high price for his coup, as Cosima, for better or worse, was obliged to return to her husband: with Bülow holding such a prominent position at court, she could not possibly have remained living in sin with her lover.

Liszt was delighted at this turn of events and in a letter to Agnes Street-Klindworth he hailed Bülow's return to Munich as an 'excellent thing'.[98] He evidently hoped that their enforced reunion would salvage the Bülows' marriage, a hope that once again was to prove misplaced when the couple went their separate ways, remaining together only in Bavaria. While Bülow sought to regain his health in Sankt Moritz, Cosima went back to Tribschen, not returning to Munich until mid-September when Liszt announced his visit to the city.

Although the Bülows had a sizeable apartment at their disposal, Liszt preferred to put up at a hotel, attending early morning Mass before calling on his family in the Arcostraße. In the evening he met a number of old and new acquaintances such as the Bavarian prime minister, Chlodwig zu Hohenlohe-Schillingsfürst, the French ambassador the Duc de Cadore and the painter Wilhelm Kaulbach. He spent a total of four weeks in the Bavarian capital.

During this time he paid a flying visit to Wagner at Tribschen, a trip organized with all the secrecy of a commando raid. Knowing that any visit to his famous colleague by the no less celebrated abbé Liszt could hardly pass unnoticed, he decided to travel incognito. Claiming that he was planning to inspect a college of music, he left in the first instance for Stuttgart, where he met his former pupil Richard Pohl and asked the latter to accompany him on a visit to a female friend in Basel. Only when they reached Switzerland did Liszt announce to a surprised Pohl that he was planning to call in on Wagner on his way back to Germany. Pohl was puzzled at such secretiveness: 'I finally realized that the journey to Basel was merely a pretext and that the real aim of the trip was the visit to Triebschen.'[99] We know from Pohl's account that the two composers spent around six hours in conversation together. 'Liszt's visit: dreaded but pleasant,' Wagner noted afterwards.[100] A few days later he wrote to King Ludwig: 'Liszt visited me here, and we rediscovered the good old days that we had formerly spent together. He is a kind, great, unique man!'[101] Liszt, too, was equally taciturn and kept his meeting with Wagner a secret, 'not even allowing the fact that it had taken place at all to become public knowledge'.[102] Only once did he hint at the occasion in a mysterious comment to Cosima: 'I was with Wagner – it was the best thing that I could have done. I feel as if I've just seen Napoleon on St Helena.'[103]

There seems little doubt that Liszt was inwardly torn. Within the family tragedy he naturally sided with his son-in-law, Hans von Bülow, regarding Wagner as a roué and his liaison with Cosima as a particularly heinous sin. At the same time, however, Liszt was reluctant to abandon Wagner, more especially after the latter had successfully ensnared and delighted him that October evening in Tribschen by introducing him to the score of Die Meistersinger von Nürnberg. Pohl came into the room while Liszt was examining the work: 'It was astonishing, not to say unique, to see how Liszt was able to sight-read this difficult score – one of the most difficult that there is – while Wagner sang: I have never heard a finer performance of the work.'[104] Liszt and Wagner continued to play the piano together until shortly before midnight, at which point they retired for the night. The visitors left Tribschen at first light the following day, and it was not until September 1872 that Liszt and Wagner were to see each other again. On his return to Munich, Liszt was forced to accept that there was nothing he could do other than look on as a passive observer: he could help neither the Bülows nor Wagner to extricate themselves from their complicated situation. By early November 1867 he was back in Rome.

In Munich the first six months of 1868 were given over to preparations for the world première of Die Meistersinger von Nürnberg. As had been the case with Tristan und Isolde in 1865, the conductor was Hans von Bülow, who was once again obliged to work with his rival. To make matters worse, Wagner again stayed with the Bülows in their apartment in the Arcostraße, carrying on as if his presence under their roof were the most natural thing in the world. It is hardly surprising that the rehearsal period was marked by tensions and sudden outbursts: 'Heavy, dull sense of Hans's profound hostility & alienation,'[105] Wagner noted at the time, striking a note of hypocrisy. In spite of the emotional challenges, the first night on 21 June 1868 proved a triumphant success. Within days Wagner had returned to Tribschen, whither Cosima followed him at the end of July. Over the course of the following months it became increasingly clear to Wagner and Cosima that the situation could not be allowed to continue: the Bülows would have to separate. Cosima wrote the decisive letter to Bülow on 3 October 1868, presumably – the letter has not survived – declaring her intention of leaving him and of moving in with Wagner. On 14 October she travelled to Munich with her four daughters and asked her husband for a divorce. 'Anxious expectations,' Wagner noted in his diary. His confusion was understandably great, not least because he could make no sense of Cosima's telegrams. And when she cabled to him at Tribschen, informing him of her resolve to go to Rome, evidently to speak to her father, Wagner lost his nerve, afraid, as he was, that Liszt, who was on Bülow's side, would try to talk his daughter out of a divorce. For his part Wagner asked Cosima's half-sister, Claire de Charnacé (the second child of Marie and Charles d'Agoult), to go to Munich to make Cosima see reason, a request that infuriated Cosima. A laconic entry in Wagner's diary reflects his own feelings at this time: 'To Rome? – Confusion & desperate concern: to Cl. Charnacé – to Munich. C. beside herself. Great dejection: decide on journey, with visit to Arcostraße. C. more forgiving. To Munich on 1 Nov.'[106]

Wagner's visit to Munich could hardly have been less well timed, since the Bülows' eleven-year marriage was now drawing to an end. His presence was a distraction. By the following day he had left for Leipzig, after which he returned to Tribschen. By now Cosima was either unable or unwilling to travel to Rome, and so she wrote to her father, informing him that her marriage had failed. Her letter has not survived, but we can gain some idea of its contents from another source, a letter she wrote to Marie von Schleinitz in late May 1871:

It was my wish that he [Liszt] should initially spend some time with Herr von Bülow and tell the world what Herr von Bülow was unable and unwilling to do, namely, that our divorce was imminent, and that he was therefore providing Herr von Bülow with physical and emotional support. I did not believe that I was asking him to do anything that ran counter to his new spiritual calling by expecting him to offer comfort to a man who was lacking that comfort.

Although written nearly three years after the events in question, Cosima's
lines reflect her sense of mortification at her father's behaviour in 1868:
'Instead of coming, he wrote me a letter in which he described the wrong
that I had done, together with its consequences, while he wrote to Hans
to tell him to use force to prevent me from taking the step that I was
intending to take.'[107]

Liszt's answer is, indeed, a remarkable document. Striking a harsh tone,
he appealed to his daughter's conscience and even attacked her directly:

> Where are you going? What are you telling me? What! Everything is
> dead for you except a single person to whom you think you are
> necessary, because he says he cannot do without you? Alas! I can
> foresee that this *necessity* will soon be an encumbrance, and by
> possessing you in this fashion, you will necessarily become inconve-
> nient, annoying, contrary to him. Although you might well only
> want to live for him, that would not be enough at all, and would
> hardly be feasible because fatal poisons would begin to seep from the
> rock on which you aim to rest yourself.
>
> God save me from judging you wrongly. I know that 'nothing
> infamous, nothing low, nothing futile is subjugating you' but you
> have become giddy and are dissipating the vital and holy forces of
> your soul by sealing an evil deed with approval. This perversion, this
> adulteration of God's gifts breaks my heart!
>
> You speak of living alone and raising your children. How will you
> manage that? W.'s notoriety and his extremely dependent position
> from a material point of view will work against your best plans. After
> such a scandal, I doubt whether convention will allow you to live in
> Switzerland or Germany. Probably you will be forced to seek some
> refuge as far away as America. The hand of your royal friend and
> benefactor might slacken its grip, if not withdraw, as a consequence;
> embarrassment and shameful financial difficulties would dog your
> footsteps. Even if you were to bear them bravely, would the *other one*
> put up with them because of this?
>
> And what about your children? What are you teaching them?
> Does not the model contain the precepts? Will they understand

that one should call Evil Good, call night day, call bitter things sweet?

Yes, my daughter, what you are planning to do is bad in God's eyes and man's. Indeed, my convictions and experience protest about it to you, and I beg you by your maternal feelings to renounce this fatal plan, drive away the subtleties of sophisms, stop sacrificing [yourself] to the implacable idol. Instead of abjuring your God, fall on your knees before him; he is truth and mercy in one; invoke him with all your soul and the healing light of repentance will enter your conscience.

It is Hans to whom you are *necessary*; it is him you must not fail. You married him of your own free will, with love – and his behaviour towards you has always been so noble that on your side it calls for another 'gegenseitige Übereinstimmung' [German in the original: mutual agreement] than the one pleaded before the courts. What madness to ask him now to subscribe legally to your dishonour!

You are also *necessary* to your four children, and deserve their respect, [which] must be for you the first priority. Now the more than precarious future the yoke of your passion would bestow on them exposes you to their most cruel reproaches, which your conscience will ratify. I will not speak to you about public opinion, [about] which nonetheless one should not exaggerate one's contempt to the point of absolving everything it condemns, and Jean-Jacques [Rousseau] himself warns of the danger of this contempt when it 'pushes us to the other extreme, and even makes us brave the sacred laws of decency and honesty'.

By falsely crushing the sublime, one does not change the immutable nature of duty. You must not leave the noblest of husbands; you must not mislead your children; you must not bear witness against me and plunge madly into an abyss of moral and material misery; and finally you must not deny your God.

Passion consumes itself when it is not enlivened by the sense of superior duties. It withers away or becomes poisoned in wealth, dies in poverty, and passes with frightful rapidity; but remorse remains.

Not only do I rightly condemn what you are proposing, but I am telling you this while begging you to take hold of yourself and not allow yourself to be removed from my blessing.

May God grant my prayers, and may the memory of your father make you become again the child of God our Father and our All in Eternity.

F. Liszt

2 November 1868, Rome[108]

After writing these lines and seeking to interfere yet again in his daughter's life, Liszt can hardly have imagined that she would reconsider the matter. Wounding in the harshness of its tone, his dressing down merely had the opposite effect to the one intended: Cosima's decision was now unshakeable. She left Munich on the afternoon of 16 November 1868 and said goodbye for ever to her husband. For the present she left Daniela and Blandine with him out of her concern for the feelings of a man who was by now in a state of total despair.

'The first Frau von Bülow was far too big for me, also in terms of her height.' Bülow struck a note of sarcasm when reflecting on his failed marriage.[109] His life lay in ruins. His colleague Ludwig von Hartmann summed up the domestic tragedy in a letter to an unidentified correspondent:

Frau von Bülow, whose monomaniacal infatuation with Wagner was tolerated by her husband, finally went to Lucerne in order to live full-time with Wagner, while her husband, who had on several occasions sacrificed his whole existence to Wagner and who took inspiration to almost excessive lengths, now discovers that the great Jew-eater has seduced his own wife. Divorce proceedings have unfortunately been initiated. You know my veneration for Wagner's works. How shaming to have such an embarrassing character. Frau Tausig, too, ran away from her husband 2½ months ago. But whoever finds her and hands her in at the nearest police station will not receive a reward. Bowed low by fate, Bülow wrote to Bechstein, ending on a laconic note: 'It is Wagner who is most to be pitied'![110]

The rest of the story can be briefly summarized. Cosima brought her fifth and final child into the world on 6 June 1869, her only son, Siegfried. Liszt was unaware of the boy's birth. But on 22 May 1870, Wagner's fifty-seventh birthday, he sent a telegram to his former friend: 'In rain and shine for ever with you.'[111] His brief greeting was a tentative attempt to renew contact, his words carefully chosen and intended as more than just a sign of life: in spite of all the unpleasantness, Liszt wanted Wagner to know that he was thinking of him and that they might one day renew their friendship. Cosima, at least, was delighted and relieved at her father's démarche: 'A telegram from my father pleased and moved me greatly,' she noted in her diary.[112] But the contact was again severed in the middle of July 1870, when Cosima obtained a divorce, allowing her to marry Wagner on 25 August 1870, which Liszt learnt about only from the newspapers. Not until the end of September 1871 did Liszt send his daughter a short note. Prior to that neither party seemed to have had anything more to say to the other: the family bonds appeared to have been severed.

LA VIE TRIFURQUÉE
(1869–86)

In the Hofgärtnerei

'A MAJOR CHANGE IN my outward existence should take place next year and bring me closer to Germany again,' Liszt wrote in June 1868. 'I cannot guess how this final chapter in my life will turn out.'[1] At the date in question, the preparations for his return to Weimar were already under way. Ever since Liszt had left for Rome, Carl Alexander had been appealing to his former Kapellmeister to return, even describing that return as 'necessary'. Now, seven years after Liszt had abandoned the town of Goethe and Schiller, he responded to the entreaties of his aristocratic friend. There were several reasons for his willingness to do so now. According to the Liszt scholar Serge Gut, his time in Rome had proved to be a mistake.[2] For a long time Liszt had thought that a career at the Vatican was desirable, and yet it had failed to materialize. As a composer, too, he fell short of his own expectations, for although these years witnessed the composition of a good deal of sacred music, their quality is variable. Liszt had initially lived in the Via Felice before moving to the monastery of the Madonna del Rosario, followed by a spell at the Vatican and, finally, at the monastery of Santa Francesca Romana. All of these moves lent an air of improvisation to his time in the Eternal City and contributed to the fact that he never really felt at home there. In particular, his visit to Karlsruhe in

August 1864 had revived his love of travel. Writing to Carolyne von Sayn-Wittgenstein in 1856, he had described himself as 'half gypsy, half Franciscan',[3] and now it was the gypsy who once again appeared to be setting the tone.

On the other hand, Liszt had no wish to leave Rome permanently: he still felt a bond with the princess and so regular returns to the city went without saying. At the same time, he and his music were eliciting increasing interest from Hungary. In short, Weimar, Rome and Budapest were to be the three focal points of Liszt's existence from now on, encouraging him to describe this period as a 'vie trifurquée', a trifurcate life. From the winter of 1869/70 until his death he spent a certain amount of time almost every year in each of these three cities, even developing a kind of rhythm: the spring and summer months were generally spent in Weimar, the autumn and winter in either Rome or Budapest. The Altenburg was no longer available, and so Liszt had to find a new base that was both imposing and yet in keeping with his well-known modesty. Carl Alexander finally made available a building known as the Hofgärtnerei at the western entrance to the park that lies on the banks of the Ilm, where the Marienstraße turns into the Belvederer Allee. It dates from 1798/9. Liszt's first-floor apartment consisted of a bedroom, a dining room, servants' quarters and a large music salon that was divided into two by means of a pair of heavy curtains in the Hungarian national colours of red, white and green. Liszt himself described the room in a letter to Carolyne von Sayn-Wittgenstein:

There are beautiful rugs everywhere; four tiled stoves from Berlin, French windows, curtains made from valuable fabric over both the windows and the doors, matching furniture, three bronze pendulum clocks, several bronze candelabra with three candles each, six or eight Carcel lamps, two mirrors in gilded frames, and silverware, glasses and porcelain for six. I've been told that the grand duchess and the princesses personally chose the rugs and curtains and so on. The fact of the matter is that this apartment is 'Wagnerian' in its luxury, something that the good people of Weimar were really not accustomed to.[4]

Liszt even had a housekeeper at his disposal, Pauline Apel, who as a young girl had already served Carolyne at the Altenburg in Weimar and who now ran the Hofgärtnerei. She was the tutelary deity of the house and an indispensable part of Liszt's life for the next seventeen years.

Carolyne left Liszt in no doubt that she thought very little of his visits to Weimar and Budapest, having only mockery and contempt for his belated love of his fatherland, and seeing Weimar in a negative light following the evaporation of her dreams there. But she was also afraid that the constant travel between all three cities would undermine the health of the now sixty-year-old Liszt. Her fears were not entirely unfounded, when we recall that Budapest is 750 miles away from Rome by land and that railway journeys were far from an enjoyable pastime at that date in their development. But Carolyne also felt instinctively that during his extended absences from Rome Liszt was no longer subject to her influence and supervision. If she wanted to maintain her control over him, she was dependent on reports from third parties.

'I am entrusting Liszt to you,' Carolyne wrote to Henriette von Schorn in early January 1869.[5] The widow of Ludwig von Schorn, who was well known in his day as a writer on art history, Henriette had been born in 1807 and was a member of Weimar's social establishment. Carolyne had got to know her during her time at the Altenburg. Her role was now that of Carolyne's informant in Weimar. Initially this role left her feeling a little uncomfortable:

> Tell me honestly, my dear princess, if I am giving you too much information about these trifles, but I am judging them by my own standards, namely, everything that contributes in any way to the wellbeing of those who are dear to us is of interest.[6]

This attitude was entirely to Carolyne's liking since she wanted to know everything possible about Liszt: how he felt, who had visited him, how long the person in question stayed, who else was in the town and so on. There was not a single scrap of gossip that she did not want to know about. When Henriette von Schorn died in the middle of May 1869, her twenty-eight-year-old daughter Adelheid took over the task of keeping an eye on Liszt. She lived opposite the Hofgärtnerei at 2 Belvederer Allee, from where she had an unimpeded view of the property. And yet it would be an injustice to describe her as a go-between or as a mere purveyor of tittle-tattle designed to show the composer in a poor light, for it is clear from her numerous letters, which she published many years later, that Adelheid was genuinely concerned about Liszt. Richard Voß has described her as an 'altogether unique personality who looked like the abbess of a Russian convent, even wearing that institution's decorative and highly effective costume'.[7]

One member of Liszt's new entourage in Weimar was Baroness Olga von Meyendorff, who was born into the old Russian aristocracy in 1837, the daughter of Prince Mikhail Gorchakov. Her uncle Alexander served as his country's foreign minister and chancellor. She was twenty when she married the diplomat Felix von Meyendorff. Liszt had known the couple since being introduced to them in Rome in the autumn of 1863. Olga was a beautiful young woman, quite apart from the fact that she played the piano, and so Liszt was happy to spend time with her. When Felix von Meyendorff succeeded Apollonius von Maltitz as attaché at the Russian Embassy in Weimar in 1867, Olga and Liszt lost sight of each other. Three years later the career diplomat was appointed Russian ambassador at the Baden court in Karlsruhe, but in early 1871 events took a tragic turn when he died unexpectedly, leaving the thirty-three-year-old Olga to take care of their four small sons. Not knowing how to manage, she turned to Liszt and asked him if he would mind if she were to settle in Weimar. He appeared to have no objections to her renewed presence in the town. But when she fell in love with him, Liszt became coy, leaving her unimpressed: 'One day I hope that you will not refuse to listen properly to my confession, which I should have given you on the very first day, and it will undoubtedly relieve you of the pressure that wrongly weighs on your far too scrupulous conscience.'[8]

Is it possible that Liszt had a moment of weakness? We simply do not know. Even during his lifetime there were rumours that he and Olga were lovers. Theirs was a complex relationship. Liszt valued their exchange of intellectual ideas, admiring the beautiful baroness's exceptional erudition and undoubtedly falling prey to her exotic charm. Olga polarized opinions: 'Her face is pallid and her hair dark,' recalled one of Liszt's piano pupils, Amy Fay.

> She makes an impression of icy coldness and at the same time of tropical heat. [...] I shall never forget the supercilious manner in which the Countess took out her eye-glass and looked me over as I passed her one day in the park. [...] She waited till I got close up, then deliberately put up this glass and scrutinised me from head to foot, then let it fall with a half-disdainful, half-indifferent air, as if the scrutiny did not reward the trouble.[9]

In Weimar she was a highly controversial figure known as the 'black cat' on account of her propensity to show her claws at any given moment. Almost all of Liszt's female pupils found themselves at odds with a woman who liked to be addressed as 'Your Excellency' and was inordinately jealous, looking askance at all the other young women in the abbé's entourage. Having taken rooms at 1 Belvederer Allee, next door to Adelheid von Schorn, she too was in a position to keep an eye on the goings on in the Hofgärtnerei, allowing her to torment Liszt with the constant reproach that he was cultivating too close a relationship with his female pupils. He was generally required to lunch and dine with her, and if Liszt invited guests to attend his Sunday morning concerts in the Hofgärtnerei or to visit him on other occasions, Olga von Meyendorff made sure that she too was on the guest list.

One wonders why Liszt put up with such behaviour from a woman who could easily have been his daughter. Clearly he felt mysteriously drawn to women who were strong, complicated and even neurotic – the group includes not only the boundlessly egocentric Marie d'Agoult but also the eccentric Carolyne von Sayn-Wittgenstein. Olga von Meyendorff reminded many of Liszt's contemporaries of the princess – not outwardly, for they were too dissimilar in their appearance, but in terms of their strength and dominance and the psychological pressure they were both able to exert on Liszt. It is unsurprising, therefore, that neither woman had a good word to say about the other: while Olga went out of her way to snub her rival in Rome, Carolyne mocked the baroness as Liszt's 'Russian muse' and made fun of her attempts 'to act the part of Leonore' – a reference to Goethe's *Torquato Tasso*, in which Leonora von Este taunts and torments the eponymous poet.[10]

His Majesty Holds Court

According to Adelheid von Schorn, 'there was a matinee concert every Sunday morning between 11 and 1'.[11] The Hofgärtnerei quickly became a social and artistic meeting place in Weimar as Liszt invited well-known and as yet unknown artists to perform with him. Famous musicians such as the violinist Ede Reményi, the pianist Anton Rubinstein and the singer Pauline Viardot-García were among his guests, as were his ever-growing number of pupils. Grand Duke Carl Alexander rarely missed a matinee, while other guests included old and new friends such as councillor Carl Gille, Adelheid von Schorn and Olga von Meyendorff. Artists rubbed shoulders with politicians, writers with scholars, composers with painters. Years earlier Carl Alexander had been obliged to maintain a diplomatic distance on account of the 'Wittgenstein Affair', but now he did everything in his power to enjoy the company of a valued friend. Even in his first year back in Weimar, Liszt's presence brought a new lustre to the sleepy backwater, a lustre also due to his activities as a teacher. Three times a week he taught up to twenty pupils in his salon in the Hofgärtnerei, including the thirty-year-old Amy Fay, who arrived in Weimar from Chicago at the end of April 1873. Thanks to the letters she wrote to her parents, we can form a good impression of life in Weimar at this time.

'There isn't a piano to be had in Weimar for love or money,' Fay noted shortly after her arrival in the town.[12] Weimar was full of young musicians, she was told, all of whom were so keen to audition for Liszt that they had bought up all the available instruments. Not even in the surrounding area had she succeeded in finding a piano, and it required a trip to Leipzig, over sixty miles away, to run one to ground. Her previous teachers had been Carl Tausig and Theodor Kullak, two pianists of considerable stature in their field. But she already sensed that her lessons with Liszt would run along different lines when she saw her idol at a performance in the Weimar Theatre, where he was sitting in a box and holding court, his back turned demonstratively to the stage, while he chatted to a small group of women.

As a rule, Liszt's pupils would gather at three in the afternoon in the Hofgärtnerei salon or, if the weather was fine, in grounds in front of the building. Once Liszt had finished his afternoon nap, he would appear at the window or go straight into his salon, where an unassuming table stood on which students placed the scores they wanted to study with him. After greeting his pupils, he would go over to the table, leaf through the pile of scores and then single one out at random, asking who was performing it. The relevant person then had to play the piece. The selection process seemed arbitrary, and no one could be certain what might appeal to Liszt. There were, however, certain works that he would not hear in any circumstances, including Tausig's arrangement of Bach's Organ Toccata in D minor and his own Second Hungarian Rhapsody, which he felt had been played far too often for its own good.

Liszt did not give private lessons on a one-to-one basis but taught an entire class, which meant that not everyone present was able to play in the course of the lesson. But we know from the diaries of another of Liszt's pupils, August Göllerich, that between four and eight students would be able to play during any one class. The number depended on the pieces in question, on the length of the lesson and, not least, on Liszt's mood at the time. The other students were then passive listeners. Liszt's method was very similar to that of the masterclasses that enjoy widespread popularity today: he was convinced that a musician could benefit merely from listening to a performance and that public teaching created a climate in which every student could be a source of inspiration to the others in the class, an approach that was very much in advance of its time.

Amy Fay soon discovered that Liszt was no ordinary teacher:

> But Liszt is not at all like a master, and cannot be treated like one. He
> is a monarch, and when he extends his royal sceptre you can sit down
> and play to him. You never can ask him to play anything for you, no

matter how much you're dying to hear it. If he is in the mood he will play; if not, you must content yourself with a few remarks.[13]

This anecdote affords further proof of the fact that Liszt was not interested in teaching in the traditional sense of the term. For him, it was almost a charismatic process: 'That is the way Liszt teaches you. He presents an *idea* to you, and it takes fast hold of your mind and sticks there.'[14] This approach worked only with those students who had a vivid imagination, whose technique was flawless and who were already able to express themselves on the piano. With less talented pupils and with beginners, Liszt's method was pitifully inadequate, leading him to lose his temper and become disagreeable and unjust, as Amy Fay was able to observe at first hand: 'He is the most amiable man I ever knew, though he *can* be dreadful, too, when he chooses, and he understands how to put people outside his door in as short a space of time as it can be done.'[15]

Liszt himself admitted that he had no talent when it came to imparting 'the rules of execution, interpretation and expression, which is why I can communicate my ideas only through personal contact'.[16] Hans von Bülow was well aware of the limitations of his former teacher and father-in-law, dismissing Liszt as a poor teacher, mocking the 'Weimar School for Misses' and maliciously noting that 'His Majesty' was 'good for anything apart from educating the young'.[17]

The Cossack

'In affairs of the heart one must think oneself lucky if they end well,' Liszt once told his pupil August Göllerich,[18] striking a mischievous note that might well provide the key to the following events, except that on this occasion Liszt's latest dalliance ended far from well. The affair involved a Cossack countess who was in fact no such thing, and it also involved drug abuse, a revolver hidden in a handbag, mortified feelings, disappointed love, a foiled attempt on Liszt's life and, last but not least, a series of what purported to be kiss-and-tell memoirs. But one thing at a time.

In the middle of 1869, while Liszt was in Rome, another female student joined his class. The young woman went by the name of Olga Janina and claimed to be not only a Cossack but also a genuine countess – although she was in fact neither. Even the name she had given herself was invented – in reality she was called Olga Zielińska and was born in Lviv in Galicia on 17 May 1845 to well-to-do parents. Her father, Ludwik Zieliński, owned a ceramics factory, two mills and a brandy distillery in the town of Lubyczy some fifty miles away. Olga was eighteen when she married her first husband, Karol Janina Piasecki, with whom she had a daughter, Hélène. From the outset, their relationship appears to have been an unhappy one, and it was not long before the couple separated. Olga took over her husband's second name, from then on calling herself Olga Janina. The legend was born.

It seems clear from all that we know about her that Olga Janina was a talented musician. Her first teacher was her mother, but in 1853 she took lessons in Lubyczy with Wilhelm Blodek, a pupil of the famous Alexander Dreyschock. In 1865 she moved to Paris, where she spent eighteen months perfecting her technique with Henri Herz, returning to her native Poland in 1867. Then, in April 1869, she heard Liszt perform in Vienna. It proved a revelation, prompting her to write to her new idol asking him to take her on as his pupil. If Liszt had suspected the problems she was to cause him, he would scarcely have invited her to Rome.

Olga Janina quickly became the main topic of conversation in Liszt's entourage. Even outwardly, she was a striking figure who dressed like a man, preferring trousers and jackets to elegant French outfits, tasteful blouses, skirts and fashionable hats. The sculptor Josef von Kopf recalled that she was 'small, vivacious in her speech, quick in her movements, passionate, excitable and quick-tempered – she was a great piano-player. With her wide mouth, turned-up nose, close-cropped hair, she made an impression of no great beauty.' Kopf was disinclined to believe that blue blood coursed through her veins: 'Polish women were all reputed to be countesses whenever they travelled abroad.'[19] Not only did she smoke cigars, but she often turned up for Liszt's piano classes with a revolver in her handbag, spreading fear and terror among his other pupils. As an additional accessory she was also known to carry a dagger whose point was said to be poisoned. In short, Olga Janina was not a woman to be crossed. Already eccentric and hysterical by nature, she also suffered from substance abuse, especially the opium that was popular in high society at this time. She carried around with her a bag containing various narcotics and poisons. Ferdinand Gregorovius was introduced to Olga Janina at a time when she 'had left her children [sic] as a result of her headstrong passion for Liszt and became his pupil. She is a small, witty, foolish person who is completely mad about Liszt'.[20]

Olga Janina was obsessed by Liszt, her infatuation having something destructive about it. According to Josef von Kopf, 'She was terribly jealous of the Master, and for her rivals, of whom there were dozens, she felt a violent hatred.'[21] She followed Liszt everywhere: nowadays she would be accused of stalking him.

One wonders how the situation got so out of hand and why Liszt ever agreed to spend time with such a woman, rather than casting her adrift much sooner. Here we can only speculate. But it has to be said at the outset that Olga Janina was hugely talented as a pianist and Liszt must have instinctively recognized her artistic potential. 'She played like a demon,' recalled Nadine Helbig. 'I shall never forget how she played the first Mephisto Waltz at the first lesson.'[22] And the abbé in Liszt must have felt something approaching Christian compassion: he was aware of Olga Janina's neurotic personality and of her addiction to drugs and had heard that she had already made one attempt on her own life. He may well have asked himself if it would have been a Christian act to turn away a woman who was clearly in search of help.

But Liszt would also have been drawn to Olga Janina as a woman. After all, she was well educated, quick in the uptake and clever, all qualities that invariably attracted him. Moreover, she resembled her predecessor, Carolyne von Sayn-Wittgenstein, in that she, too, came from what is now the Ukraine. Both women were fanatical in their love, independent in their thinking and unconventional in their appearance. Both the princess and the self-styled countess loved bizarre behaviour – both of them smoked cigars – and both surrounded themselves with an aura of exoticism. Perhaps Olga reminded Liszt of Carolyne, the woman whom he had once loved. This is certainly possible.

Liszt offered his new student his help whenever he could. At the end of May 1870 she accompanied her teacher to Weimar, where he took part in a festival to commemorate the centenary of Beethoven's birth and conducted a performance of his festival cantata *On the Beethoven Centenary* for soloists, chorus and orchestra. She was also a member of his entourage during the months that he spent in Hungary in the summer of 1870, when the Franco-Prussian War broke out. France's army was hopelessly outnumbered and suffered a crushing defeat at Sedan in the Ardennes on 1 September 1870, leading to the arrest of Napoleon III and the proclamation of the French Republic. Metz capitulated in October, Paris – which had been under siege since September – at the end of January 1871. Liszt's sympathies were with the French, a loyalty inspired in no small part by the fact that he was related through marriage to Émile Ollivier, the French minister of justice and head of the government at this time. Having no desire to be in Germany throughout this period, he was grateful for an invitation to spend time in Hungary with one of his friends in that country, Baron Antal Augusz, who lived in Szekszárd, a small town some ninety miles to the south of Budapest. Here he remained for almost nine months, his longest stay in his native Hungary since his childhood.

Throughout the autumn of 1870 Liszt received numerous visitors, among them the violinist Ede Reményi, Liszt's pupil Sophie Menter and the composers François Servais, Ödön von Mihalovich and Mihály Mosonyi. Another guest was Olga Janina, who appeared at a charity concert on behalf of the local Women's Association on 25 September and who gave a gala dinner for Liszt at one of the town's hotels in the middle of October. When Liszt celebrated his fifty-ninth birthday on 22 October, the whole town turned up to acclaim him. Antal Augusz's villa was illuminated, and Liszt appeared at the window as if he were some monarch receiving his subjects' accolade. 'Long live Franz Liszt!' the townsfolk assembled in the street cheered as soon as they saw him. There followed a gala concert in the course of which Olga Janina performed a *Lohengrin* paraphrase. And the evening ended with a banquet for 130 invited guests. By the end of December Olga was in Pest with Liszt, but after that date we lose all trace of her, at least for the immediate present.

Olga Janina's life appears to have taken a decided turn for the worse during the winter of 1870/71, when her father died and her financial problems increased. Without his allowance she was unable to continue her expensive lifestyle, including travel and the use of drugs. During the spring of 1871 she tried her fortune in the casino at Baden-Baden, an act of desperation that ended in disaster. Thereafter she is known to have given recitals in Warsaw and Russia. From this period, too, dates Liszt's only surviving letter to her, which he wrote on 17 May 1871, her twenty-sixth birthday, addressing it to 'Madame Olga Janina (née Comtesse Zielinska)' in Warsaw:

> Did you feel my soul's affectionate embrace on *17 May*? That soul is sad unto death, and my peace will come only from my most bitter bitterness ('Ecce in pace amaritudo mea amarissima!['])).
>
> Why go on about the 'alms of anger and hatred'? Here beside me I have the two red exercise books with the gold star that you brought to me at the *Villa d'Este*. They tell a very different story. Do not give the lie to them but follow *this* star, which shines for you in my heart.
>
> You do well not to *exploit* your very rare and admirable musical talent but put it to good use. But in order not to vitiate its deployment, you must learn to control your whimsy and tetchiness, qualities that are not acceptable in good society and which are no less contrary to my own wishes than they are to the dignity of your character.
>
> Your salamander-like nature and your ability to work like a black guarantee you a noble rank in art. Is it possible that in spite of your conscience's outcry, you might renounce that title and that the shameful pleasures of the hurly-burly and of all the 'degradations' bound up with your pharmaceutical accoutrements, with revolvers and other sickening nonsense, might engulf you?
>
> Let me say no and no again. And allow me to shake and kiss your hand.
>
> F. L.
>
> I await your news from Russia.[23]

This was a remarkable birthday greeting, vacillating, as it did, between the tender protestations of love and a reprimand. Liszt was clearly keen to appeal to Olga's better nature, mentioning her capriciousness and her drug addiction, which he dismisses as 'pharmaceutical accoutrements' ('attirail de pharmacie'). What Olga needed, however, was not warm words but hard cash. Had she written asking for money ('aumône de colère, de haine'), a request that Liszt had turned down?

Olga Janina left for New York in July 1871, but the events that unfolded there remain, for the most part, a mystery. Since Liszt evidently took great care to destroy all her letters to him and since the whereabouts of her unpublished papers remain unknown, we are reduced to supposition and hearsay, but it seems that Liszt encouraged her to give concerts in the New World and in that way to earn some money as quickly as possible. None the less, a question mark is in order here since Liszt was not given to making hasty recommendations, especially in the present case, where they amount to a flight into exile. Moreover, Liszt himself had never been to the United States and had no first-hand experience of the country's musical scene. Last but not least, the concert season was already drawing to a close when Olga Janina arrived in New York, leaving her with few opportunities to earn any money. All in all, it would have been difficult to recommend this trip to her with a good conscience. If Liszt really did advise her to go to New York, then it looks suspiciously like an attempt to get rid of her. Perhaps he hoped she would forget him in America, in which case he was being inordinately naïve.

Given the circumstances, it was inevitable that Olga Janina's tour of America should turn out to be a fiasco. Her own account reads as follows:

I had written to X . . . [Liszt] and day after day I awaited his answer.
His answer came.
There is a kind of love that resembles the cowardly devotion of a dog to its gutless master. The letter was implacable.
This masterpiece of calculated coldness and cruelty I took to heart, rereading it twenty times by way of consolation.
I was able to silence my sense of indignation whenever I was able to judge things properly, as I was able to do at certain times.

I wrote a humble and gentle letter to my master and begged him to send me some loving words that would be my support and strength.

What had I done except to love and admire and defend him? What was I now to do, so far from him, except to make a super-human effort to overcome my feelings and help to disseminate his works!

Another month went by:

It is impossible to describe my sufferings while I waited for the month of November and for a reply to my second letter.

My sufferings clouded my mind. There were moments when, overwhelmed by grief, I cried out to God.

X . . . did not reply.

Finally Olga lost her nerve.

I wrote to him again on 1 October. I begged him to send me the alms of a few gentle words, even if these words were a lie.

On 12 November I finally received these words:

'The violence of your feelings disturbs my peace of mind, which is one of the preconditions of my existence. Permit me, therefore, to inform you that I shall decline to accept any more of your strange ravings at least until such time as you understand that no one who fails to observe God's laws can ever hope to find happiness.

'You also need to reconcile yourself to your fate, which is the product, moreover, of your various acts of imprudence.'[24]

These lines certainly sound authentically Lisztian, so it is entirely possible that Olga Janina is quoting Liszt verbatim here. Seething with rage, she even issued scarcely veiled threats against him, prompting his New York publisher, Julius Schuberth, to warn his client to be on his guard against a woman who was morbidly hysterical and not someone to be trifled with, since she was obsessed by the idea of avenging the aforementioned 'masterpiece of calculated coldness and cruelty'. Liszt reported on these events in a letter to Carolyne von Sayn-Wittgenstein, explaining that at the end of October Olga Janina had sent him a telegram from New York: 'Leaving this week to pay you back for your letter.'

Liszt was shocked, but what could he do? Although he could have reported the matter to the police, it was unclear where Olga might be lying in wait for him – in Rome or Weimar or Pest? Liszt decided to keep his nerve. Time passed, and it is entirely possible that he had already forgotten the matter when events suddenly came to a head on Saturday, 25 November 1871, the day on which Olga Janina stormed into Liszt's apartment in Pest, brandishing not only a revolver but also several vials of poison. As Liszt explained to Carolyne:

> It seems that Mme Janina had informed her friends and acquaintances of her resolution to come to Pest and to kill both me and herself. She did indeed enter my room, armed with a revolver and several bottles of poison – accessories that she had already waved in my face on two occasions last winter.

Beside herself with fury, Olga had threatened to kill Liszt and then take her own life. Her visit was interrupted by the arrival of Ödön von Mihalovich and Antal Augusz, whom Liszt asked to leave as he wanted to deal with Olga on his own.

Once Mihalovich and Augusz had gone, Liszt apparently spent several hours alone with Olga Janina. According to his letter to Carolyne, he told Olga 'very calmly': 'What you are planning to do is wicked, Madame. I beg you to desist from it, although I have no way of stopping you.'[25] The situation escalated when Olga opened one of the bottles of poison that she had brought with her and swallowed its contents, before writhing on the floor in apparent agony. But the whole scene was an act, and in the end Liszt was able to pacify his former student. He took her to her hotel early the following morning, where a doctor declared the liquid harmless. Mihalovich and Augusz then insisted that she leave Pest without delay, or they would take legal steps against her. She left for Paris on 27 November.

One wonders why Liszt did not call the police and why he behaved towards Olga Janina in such a remarkably indulgent manner. Justifying himself to Carolyne, he explained that 'I protested forcefully against intervention by the police, which would in any case have been futile, because Mme Janina was perfectly capable of firing her revolver before the police had time to handcuff her.'[26] Liszt's concern was undoubtedly justified, and yet there was a further reason for his reticence: he was afraid that the 'Janina Affair' would become public knowledge – Olga's arrest would have led to police enquiries that could hardly have passed unnoticed. The whole affair was so embarrassing to him that he preferred to draw a veil over it. Only a few days after the would-be attempt on his life, he wrote to Carolyne: 'Once again I entreat you not to speak about it – not even to me – because I am keen, as far as possible, to forget this crisis which, thanks to my guardian angel, has not turned into a catastrophe or a public scandal.'[27] In a letter to Olga von Meyendorff Liszt referred evasively to a 'spectre' that had suddenly appeared: 'Spare me the pain of a more detailed account.'[28] For the present Liszt was able to prevent the affair from becoming public knowledge, but it was still far from resolved. The worst was yet to come.

Revenge is Sweet

Olga Janina settled in Paris, where she gave the occasional recital, even lecturing on Liszt's music in the spring of 1873, but all the while secretly plotting her revenge. The first product of her hatred appeared the following year in the form of a book, *Souvenirs d'une cosaque*. The next two years saw the publication of a further three titles: *Souvenirs d'un pianiste*, which was intended to be read as Liszt's fictional rebuttal of the earlier volume; *Les amours d'une cosaque par un ami de l'abbé 'X'*; and *Le roman du pianiste et de la cosaque*. All four were written by Olga, for all that the reader looks in vain for her name on their title pages. The *Souvenirs d'une cosaque* were ostensibly written by one Robert Franz, a name that can hardly have been chosen at random as the real Robert Franz, who was born in 1815, was one of Liszt's most loyal friends. In a particularly malicious sideswipe, Franz now saw himself as the author of a deeply defamatory piece of pulp fiction. The *Souvenirs d'un pianiste* were published anonymously, a ploy designed to give the impression that Liszt himself had written this new book by way of a riposte to Robert Franz's lampoon. For her last two tomes Olga Janina used the pseudonym Sylvia Zorelli.

Over a total of 1,050 pages the Cossack recounts what purports to be the story of her love life. Liszt features as 'the pianist' or the ominous 'abbé X' – Olga Janina made no real attempt to disguise her victim's identity. It is hard to gauge the autobiographical value of these four books, which contain frequent repetitions, numerous contradictions and many events that are clearly invented. Olga's imagination was plainly at work when she claimed to have been brought up in a family castle and to have killed wolves with her bare hands when still a girl. Elsewhere we read that she studied in Kiev and that she kept a tiger as a pet at this time, regularly taking it with her to the Kiev Conservatory, where on one occasion it bit the director.[29] All of this is clearly nonsense, and Olga's fabrications would long ago have been dismissed as the self-important posturings of a disturbed personality were it not for the fact that Liszt plays a major role in them, turning them into best-sellers. The *Souvenirs d'une cosaque*, for example, were reprinted thirteen times.

What do Olga Janina's memoirs have to tell us about her relations with Liszt? Here, too, their value is limited, since many of the events that she describes – if they took place at all – have only two eyewitnesses: Liszt and Olga herself. Most of their content can no longer be validated since Liszt never expressed himself in detail on the subject. Be that as it may, Olga Janina proved exceptionally skilful in striking Liszt's most vulnerable spot: his vanity. She describes him as a narcissistic, self-preening fop and as an arrogant and mendacious hypocrite who never showed his true face to his fellow human beings. His religious beliefs were a sanctimonious affectation; the truth of the matter was that he was an old goat. 'On Good Friday and Easter Saturday he spent the entire afternoon in church,' Olga wrote. 'Prostrating himself before Christ's grave, he shed countless tears and beat his breast. The whole city wept in edification.' But Liszt then went straight from church to

Olga's private apartment, and all thoughts of spiritual edification were forgotten:

> Proudly, he held his head aloft, his eyes glowed with passion. He took me in his arms and kissed me. No Christian has ever celebrated the resurrection of his Saviour in a better way.
>
> 'You see, my darling,' he said to me, 'there is no better way of salving one's conscience.'
>
> I understood that he would repent periodically.
>
> [. . .] This belittled him in my eyes, and yet I loved him so much that all the scorn, the hatred and the revulsion that had formerly swollen my heart as a result of such hypocrisy were now resolved in bitter sadness.
>
> Perhaps this man believed in the heavenly efficacy of these pitiful acts of treachery.[30]

Olga Janina is known to have visited Liszt at the Villa d'Este in Tivoli, a particularly piquant detail inasmuch as this was the summer residence of Cardinal Gustav Adolf zu Hohenlohe. But Liszt allegedly had no consideration for his God-fearing host. 'I can resist you no longer,' Liszt is said to have sighed, drawing Olga into his arms, after which she claims the two of them spent the night together.[31]

Olga Janina was keen not only to undermine Liszt's credibility and moral integrity but also to expose him to public ridicule and rob him of his honour, her actions amounting to a public execution. It mattered not a whit whether the scenes she describes in Weimar's church, in her own apartment or in Liszt's private rooms in Tivoli took place in the way she claims or whether the whole thing was a figment of her frenzied imagination. Far greater was the impact of the images Olga conjured up: they confirmed many contemporaries' view of Liszt, for she was adept at appealing to existing prejudices, namely, that the abbé was incapable of keeping his hands to himself, that his religious beliefs had no substance and that he was a vainglorious actor.

What made matters worse was that the scandal surrounding Olga Janina was by no means the only one to attach itself to the elderly abbé.

August Stradal, who was a pupil of both Bruckner and Liszt, reports an anecdote passed on to him by Bruckner:

> I met Liszt in St Michael's Square and he invited me to accompany him to Bösendorfer's. We'd taken only a few steps along the Herrengasse when a women threw herself at Liszt and cried out in a loud voice: 'My dearest Franz, when are we finally going to get married?' Liszt was highly agitated and, seizing me by the arm, said: 'Bruckner, let's be on our way, it's a poor madwoman.'[32]

The woman in question was Hortense Voigt, a by no means unknown figure in Vienna. She wrote letters to her idol that began, 'My passionately loved fiancé, my sweet and affectionate Franz.'[33] She was clearly disturbed, and yet Bruckner seems to have believed her. 'Goodness me,' he exclaimed to Stradal, 'your master must have been a Don Juan.'[34] Anecdotes like this one found a responsive audience and afforded further proof of the Latin proverb 'Semper aliquid haeret' – if enough mud is flung at a victim, some of it will stick.

But let us return to La Janina. In an attempt to rub salt into Liszt's wounds, she proceeded to send copies of her books to a number of his closest friends. Revenge is sweet. It must have caused Liszt particular pain and embarrassment to know that Grand Duke Carl Alexander received a copy inscribed to him. However, Liszt initially betrayed no reaction and even refused to acknowledge the existence of her books. Only when he started to receive more and more letters from acquaintances, asking him how he planned to respond, did Liszt finally react by writing two rejoinders, one of which was penned before he had read the *Souvenirs d'une cosaque*, the other some time afterwards.

> I have not yet read the *Souvenirs* in question; but from what I have heard about them the writer delights in making me look both ridiculous and odious. She and her friends are free to behave as they think fit – or otherwise; I can only greet certain scandals with a discreet silence, preferring not to sink into the mire but leaving to others the responsibility for debasing themselves. That *la Cosaque* should

surpass the learned *Nélida* in decrying me and in raining down blows on me is a matter of some indifference; each of them has in the past written me numerous impassioned letters on the nobility of my character and the integrity of my feelings. In this I shall not contradict them, but shall continue to prize sincerely their remarkable and brilliant talents as artists, writers and inventors, while regretting that they should turn those talents so energetically against my poor self. This last volume will serve as a final warning, I hope, against my mistake in tolerating the artificial excitement of artists who handle contraband goods and the blaze of intrusive passion . . .

By his own lights, Liszt's second statement is unusually sharply worded, although this is entirely understandable in the circumstances: he, too, wanted to avenge himself by portraying Olga as a deceitful, malicious and money-grubbing viper, as a sickly courtesan and, in the final analysis, as a prostitute:

La Cosaque, an interloper like *Nélida*, but an incendiary, prowled for whole nights around my lodgings in Rome. My great wrong lies in my having let myself finally be taken in by her make-believe eccentric heroism and by her babble, which, admittedly, is not devoid of wit or of a disconcerting kind of eloquence; she has, moreover, astonishing energy in her work and a very rare talent as a pianist. Assuredly, I should have sent her packing immediately after her first avowal of love and not have yielded to the silly temptation of imagining that I could be of use to her in any way. Little snakes of this kind can only be tamed by riding in coaches with powdered footmen and by flaunting their shame in lodgings adorned with fantastic furniture and tropical plants.[35]

Carolyne von Sayn-Wittgenstein was not satisfied with Olga's stigmatization, and even before Liszt had picked up his copy of the *Souvenirs d'une cosaque*, she had written to him to say that she 'prayed to God that reading the book does not cause you as much pain as it has caused me'.[36] This was unequivocal. Carolyne had her own very clear ideas on the cause of the scandal. According to Lina Ramann, she was firmly convinced – and she justified her conviction psycho-logically – that if Cosima had not betrayed Bülow, neither the Cossack affair nor Meyendorff's Leonore games would have occurred at all. He [Liszt] had been so desperate at the time that a change had taken place in him, paralysing him as a composer.[37]

Carolyne's harsh reaction to Liszt's daughter was unjust, for Cosima can hardly be blamed for her father's behaviour. In a long letter to Eduard Liszt, Carolyne expressed herself more clearly, writing half in French and half in her stilted German and attempting to sum up Liszt's relations with the opposite sex. 'For ten years in succession he led an abstemious lifestyle. Both in Weimar and in Rome. But he is weak, and if a woman wants to control him, he cannot resist her.' The first woman to turn Liszt's head during this time was allegedly the soprano Emilie Merian-Genast, who had

wrenched him out of the almost sagacious, intellectual life that had become a habit with him – and ten years later Janina did the same! When Meyend[orff] turned up later, she found that all of Liszt's moral constraints had been lifted. Yet these can still be restored.

But Carolyne felt that on her own she would not be able to restore Liszt's sense of morality. 'He must undergo an inner process of repentance. I cannot help him in this since I am the one who has been insulted.' It was Eduard, she went on, who was the right person to bring Liszt back to the path of virtue. It was pointless to appeal to the catechism: 'He confesses conscientiously. But he will easily receive absolution for his sins, which are in fact not very numerous.' Rather, Eduard should appeal to Liszt's dignity as a man of honour. 'It is this that is his most sensitive spot. Tell him that the world knows very well that Janina's pamphlet is full of untruths, but people are saying that only trivial details are wrong.' He should make it clear that for Liszt to flaunt his affairs in public was tantamount to insulting her, Carolyne. 'Tell him that the world, which treats a married man's infidelities with indulgence, does not forgive such misdemeanours.' And again: 'Tell him that the world would have forgiven all his secret infidelities but that it refuses to condone the public lack of respect for a woman whom he fully accepted and whose husband he should have been.'

Carolyne then came to arguably the most important part of her letter. Instead of admiring Liszt's work, both the general public and the press were making far too much fuss about his character, 'which was never entirely blameless'. People had marvelled at his escapades and praised his elegant lifestyle:

> I have seen through this – that he thinks his happiness lies with women throws light on this view of him as a person and turns him into the stuff of legend! As a result he clings only to what gives a man the right to compromise a woman in order to gain the prestige of good fortune.

Carolyne ended by asking Eduard to maintain total secrecy: 'You can surmise what you like, but you cannot tell him about me. Otherwise he will see in you only my delegate hauling him over the coals in my name.'[38]

Largely overlooked by writers on Liszt, this letter is explosive in its impact. First, it is clear that Carolyne von Sayn-Wittgenstein was in no doubt that Liszt's affairs with Olga Janina, Emilie Merian-Genast and Olga von Meyendorff were sexual in nature. We might also add Agnes Street-Klindworth to this list, except that it is entirely possible that in her ivory tower in Rome Carolyne was unaware of this long-term liaison. Certainly Liszt's older biographers were wrong to idealize these relationships and treat them as platonic friendships underpinned by a strict sense of morality. Carolyne paints a picture of a man who even in old age was receptive to erotic charms and sexual charisma. Her analysis was implacable – essentially she was describing an elderly Casanova or an ageing Don Juan who derived his feelings of self-worth from the luck he had with women.

Carolyne's plenipotentiary in Weimar, Adelheid von Schorn, proposed a radically different view that portrayed Liszt in the transfiguring light of an ascetic. 'I have never seduced a young woman,' he is reported to have told her. 'I know this statement to be true,' Schorn confirmed, although she can hardly have been present on each occasion, quite apart from the implausibility of Liszt's ever offering such a confession. And what about 'older women', the cynic is tempted to ask. Here, too, Schorn had an explanation:

> It was often with a sense of horror that I saw just how attractive Liszt was to the opposite sex. And this did not end as he grew older. It was almost painful to note that there were still women who regarded the old man, in desperate need of peace and quiet, as desirable prey. But just as Liszt, in spite of everything, saw only the best in every woman, so he refused to be misled whenever they importuned him.[39]

Schorn's account provided Liszt's later hagiographers with their point of departure, allowing them to create a legend by desexualizing him and turning him into the mere victim of women in search of love. Carolyne knew better.

Liszt's earlier life had been full of scandals of one kind or another. Many faded away like dew on an April morning, while others, such as *Nélida*, proved to be a source of considerable embarrassment. The affair surrounding Olga Janina revealed another quality, not only leaving Liszt deeply shaken but confronting him with a vision of himself as a man who was inwardly divided. 'I have a long struggle ahead of me,' he wrote to Carolyne in January 1871,

> until I defeat my old and wild-eyed enemy, who is not the imp of polite conversation but the demon of arousal and extreme emotions. Knowing it, as I do, from the many times that it has laid me low, I now avoid all occasions when it could easily overwhelm me – and I hope to triumph over it completely thanks to the grace of God, which I pray for every day.[40]

The Dear Family

'My very dear friend,' Wagner began his letter to Liszt on 18 May 1872. It was more than four years since the two men had last seen each other, and much had happened in the meantime – too much, one is tempted to add, so that any rapprochement now seemed out of the question. But Wagner here took the first step and invited Liszt to attend the forthcoming ceremony marking the laying of the foundation stone of his planned theatre in Bayreuth:

> Cosima maintains that you would not come, even if I were to invite you. This is a disappointment that we should have to endure, as we have had to endure so much else! But I cannot forbear to invite you. And what is it that I call out to you when I say 'Come'? You entered my life as the greatest man to whom I have ever been privileged to address myself on terms of intimate friendship; you slowly moved away from me, perhaps because I had become less close to you than you were to me. In your place there came your innermost being, born anew, and it was she who fulfilled my yearning desire to know you close to me. Thus you live before me and within me in perfect beauty, and we are as one beyond the grave itself.[41]

It must be asked if Wagner's approach was serious. Was he really anxious to be reconciled with his father-in-law? Or was he merely trying to persuade another prominent guest of honour to lend further lustre to the ceremony on 22 May? Whatever the answer, Wagner's words proved effective, and although Liszt did not attend the ceremony, he wrote a letter notable for its genuine affection. 'Sublime, dear friend,' he began. 'Deeply shaken by your letter, I cannot thank you in words. But I earnestly hope that all the considerations that keep me away will vanish and that we shall see each other again soon.'[42]

The letter was delivered in person by Olga von Meyendorff, who on handing it over evidently permitted herself a number of less than respectful remarks, giving the Wagners the impression that she was speaking for Liszt and that the mood in Weimar was not conducive to a resumption of the former good relations between the two parties. Wagner was dismayed and annoyed, and his anger found expression in a tirade directed at Adelheid von Schorn. On being introduced to her, he had initially struck a jocular tone, but when he discovered that she had travelled to Bayreuth from Weimar, the mood abruptly changed.

At that point Wagner let go of my hand, turned on his heel and walked away. It was not an agreeable moment – I did not know if I should leave or remain. But it lasted no more than an instant, and the connection then became clear to me. Wagner's reaction was directed not at my own person but at Liszt. [...] The fact that Liszt had not come had deeply offended him, and it was I who had to pay the price.[43]

Nerve ends had been exposed, and when a female acquaintance suggested that Cosima travel to Weimar on her own to visit her father, her brusque response was that she would 'do this only along with Wagner – either a complete reunion, or none at all'.[44] Proud as she now was, she was afraid that Liszt would once again reproach her for her past behaviour, and she had no wish to appear before her father merely to ask favours of him. The closer the date drew, the greater became her unease. 'Unsatisfactory discussion with R.', she noted in her diary at the end of August 1872; 'great misgivings, this journey seems to us foolhardy – God knows what we shall decide; whichever way, we shall feel apprehensive.'[45] But once the misunderstandings caused by Olga von Meyendorff had been resolved, nothing stood in the way of the visit any longer.

The Wagners arrived in Weimar on the evening of 2 September 1872. 'My father well and pleased, pleasant time together in the Russischer Hof.'[46] During the days that followed they spent a good deal of time together, and at table Wagner tried to break the ice by cracking various jokes and succeeded in lightening the mood. Liszt even delighted his daughter by playing works by Bach, Beethoven and Chopin and excerpts from Wagner's operas: 'He talks a lot about old times, when together we bought fruit in the market in Berlin – and the old feelings of familiarity are recaptured.'[47]

But within twenty-four hours she noticed that something was not right and that her father had 'had to pay for having shown his great affection for me yesterday'.[48] It seems to have been the ubiquitous Olga von Meyendorff who had exacted this penance from him, and we can easily imagine her reproaching Liszt for the fact that Wagner was a scoundrel, Cosima an adulteress, poor Hans the injured party and much else along similar lines. But the baroness was merely saying what the princess was thinking, reminding Liszt of the fact that it was Carolyne who was standing in the way of any reconciliation with the Wagners. Cosima had no idea about any of this and simply did not understand why her father was suddenly so reserved and even dismissive. Saddened, the Wagners returned to Bayreuth on 6 September: 'I depart in sorrow – it is not the separation which pains me, but the fear of entirely losing touch.'[49]

When Carolyne learnt of the family reunion, she reacted with typical fury, showering Liszt with malice-filled letters in which she launched a series of intemperate attacks on Wagner and his *Ring* cycle. She regarded Wagner as a heretic, the incarnation of the Antichrist who posed a threat to Liszt's salvation. As she explained to Liszt in mid-September 1872, the two men must follow different paths in life:

> One step is enough to decide between the path that leads to the right and the one that leads to the left. This step involves your presence or absence at the *Ring* in Bayreuth. You can be as certain of this as if it were Providence itself that were speaking to you. You want this because you like it and because it inspires you. You want it whatever the cost – and in wanting it you trample my heart underfoot. In the depths of your consciousness there is a voice that is undoubtedly telling you this. You sense that once you are there, you could easily box your own ears for being there. With all the fame of your genius, you would commit an act of blatant frivolity with the most beautiful and greatest action of your life by going over from the camp of Christ, whose sacred watchword you have espoused, to the adherents of Buddha, whose anti-Christian dogma Wagner preaches and whose flag he has raised on his theatre! And you know that it is not harsh words that issue from my mouth and that if Cosima were to come to me – and perhaps some misfortune or other will persuade her to do so –, she will find my door, my arms and my heart open. Love means something very different from getting involved in something that is neither good nor holy.[50]

This was unequivocal. Carolyne had never come to terms with her failed marriage to Liszt, and ever since she had been attempting to bind him to her by means of her wayward view of Christianity. However much she may have been concerned for Liszt's spiritual welfare, her pious appeal was also an attempt to exert power over her former companion. She demonized the 'pagan' Wagners since she was afraid that as a result of their influence, Liszt might drift even further away from her, and when Liszt finally announced that he was planning to visit Bayreuth on his birthday, 22 October, she pulled out all the stops:

> To see your birthday celebrated by those who deny Jesus Christ in word and deed and who commit acts of evil while professing to do good – this will one day be a painful chapter in your life since you will have to tell yourself that you provoked these celebrations by visiting Bayreuth at this very time.[51]

In spite of Carolyne's contumely, Liszt initially refused to be swayed, and Wagner and his family were just sitting down to lunch on 15 October when their maidservant announced that 'the Herr Doktor' was 'just coming up the steps'. Both parties were delighted to see each other again, and in the course of the next six days Liszt played an active part in the family's daily life, attending church in the morning before taking breakfast with the Wagners, then visiting the site of the new festival theatre or undertaking excursions in the surrounding area. Guests were often invited round in the evening, when Liszt would even play the piano. His father-in-law's visit even inspired Wagner to propose a rhyming toast: 'A noble spirit and a good Christian, long live all things Lisztian!'[52]

Father and daughter used the opportunity afforded by their meeting to discuss the situation in detail:

> Long talk with my father; Princess Wittgenstein is tormenting him on our account – he should flee from Wagner's influence, artistic as well as moral, should not see me again, his self-respect demands this, we murdered Hans from a moral point of view, etc. I am very upset that my father should be tormented like this – he is so tired and is always being so torn apart! Particularly this wretched woman in

Rome has never done anything but goad him – but he does not intend to give me and us up.[53]

But Cosima was also relieved, because she was no longer afraid that her father was planning to reject her – it was Carolyne, she now realized, who was spreading poison about the Wagners. Even after his confession, however, the princess's shadow still hung over the reunion, for Liszt was evidently reluctant to remain in Bayreuth for his birthday. Perhaps fearing another reprimand or wanting to avoid any further unpleasantness, he left for Regensburg on the morning of 21 October and celebrated his sixty-first birthday alone there.

His ongoing war of attrition with Carolyne left him no peace, and at the end of October he wrote to her: 'I should add that I really do not know who could have told you that Cosima and Wagner have "disavowed Jesus Christ" and are now proclaiming themselves atheists. Not a single word on their part would justify such an assumption.' There is something almost touching about Liszt's attempts to defend the Wagners against their critic in Rome:

> There is no doubt that Wagner makes no claim to be numbered among Orthodox and God-fearing Christians, but is that a reason to lump him together with the army of Godless non-believers? [. . .] But you presumably regard me as a poor witness in these matters, which are beyond my feeble understanding.

At the end of his long letter Liszt seems to have sensed that he was wasting his time trying to salvage his own honour:

> Your flight of fancy has taken you to loftier regions, while I myself remain behind in the stony valley of ordinary art which lives from day to day. Here, in thought, I often seek your help and support, while sensing that I have lost that help and, acquiescing in my fate, none the less admiring you from the very depths of my heart.[54]

Liszt wrote these lines at Horpács Castle near Ödenburg (now Sopron close to Hungary's western border with Austria), where he was spending a few days with his friend, Count Imre Széchényi, and where he used the occasion to visit the nearby village of Raiding. 'Since my last visit twenty-four years ago no perceptible changes have taken place in the house where I was born,' he reported to Eduard Liszt. 'The peasants recognized me at once, they paid their respects at the inn and rang the church bells when we left.'[55] In the middle of November he retired to his place of refuge in Pest, which was in the process of being merged with Buda to form the city of Budapest. He then spent the next five months giving concerts and recitals and taking part in charity events.

Festive Strains

Among the highlights of the spring of 1873 was the first complete performance of Liszt's oratorio *Christus* in Weimar's Municipal Church on 29 May. The event marked the culmination of what had been a lengthy journey for its composer, for Liszt had expressed a desire to set Christ's life to music as early as 1853, but for a long time he had made no progress on the project, not least because he lacked a suitable libretto. The poet Georg Herwegh, Liszt's secretary Peter Cornelius and even Carolyne von Sayn-Wittgenstein had all tried their hand at the task, but in vain, and in the end it was Liszt himself who compiled a libretto based on excerpts from the Bible and passages from the Catholic liturgy, completing the mammoth work in 1868. Over fourteen numbers, Liszt describes the life of our Lord, beginning with the Annunciation and Christ's birth and ending with the Passion and Resurrection. Other high points include the Three Wise Men, the Beatitudes and the entry into Jerusalem. On the other hand, he eschewed the device of the Evangelist narrator used, among others, by Bach. The music begins by striking a contemplative, pastoral note but as the work proceeds it becomes more complex and more modern, ending after three hours with a 'Resurrexit' that provides the magisterially orchestrated composition with a powerful apotheosis.

The church was completely full when Liszt took his place on the podium at six o'clock that Thursday evening. Many friends and acquaintances had travelled to Weimar for the occasion, including Richard and

Cosima Wagner and Cosima's eldest daughter, Daniela. 'I was again standing in the chancel, not far from Liszt,' Adelheid von Schorn recalled.

> We all felt that the performance was by no means flawless. Liszt had conducted only the final rehearsals [. . .] – neither the choir nor the orchestra was used to a conductor laying his baton aside for minutes at a time, resulting in several instances where the performance almost fell apart. Wagner's presence in the nave added further to the pressure on the performers.[56]

Liszt gave the impression of a man whose thoughts were elsewhere that day, and he was certainly aware that the work was inadequately rehearsed. But in spite of the adverse circumstances the audience reacted enthusiastically, even if the Wagners' assessment was mixed. Back in Bayreuth, Cosima wrote a long and appreciative letter to her father, whereas her diary entry is far more reserved:

> Remarkable, peculiar impression, best summed up in the words R. said to me in the evening: 'He is the last great victim of this Latin-Roman world.' During the very first bars R. said to me, 'He conducts splendidly, it will be magnificent.' [. . .] R.'s reaction covers all extremes, from ravishment to immense indignation, in his attempt to do it both profound and loving justice.[57]

It is strange that Wagner described his father-in-law as a 'victim'. And the fact that he felt a sense of indignation during the performance speaks volumes. But only Cosima's diaries report this reaction. In their dealings with Liszt the Wagners preferred to put on a brave face and to kowtow to the composer. When they caught scent of a rumour that the conductor Hans Richter had made unflattering remarks about Liszt, Cosima lost no time in putting pen to paper: as 'Wagner's disciple', Richter should 'speak out vigorously' for her father 'in word and deed'.[58] There were good reasons for the Wagners to adopt this attitude. The attempt at a rapprochement was, of course, a delicate bloom that required careful cultivation, but Liszt was also needed to help sponsor the Bayreuth Festival. To that extent the Wagners' concern for Liszt was also a wise investment for the future. Business and morality had always been two sides of the same coin in the Wagner household, so it is hardly surprising that Cosima drew on all her powers of persuasion in inviting her father to the topping-out ceremony in Bayreuth. Liszt's presence, it was calculated, would be the best possible advertisement for the inchoate undertaking. Although Liszt had other plans, he finally sent word to his daughter that he would attend the ceremony.

The weather was fine and the town was filled with flags and bunting when the shell of the theatre on Bayreuth's Green Hill was consecrated on 2 August 1873 to the strains of the march from *Tannhäuser*. The local dean intoned a few lines of his own composition, after which Wagner himself declaimed a poem that he had cobbled together at the very last minute. Liszt was treated as a family member for the duration of his ten-day visit, undertaking excursions with his grandchildren during the daytime and making music in the evening.

The autumn of 1873 found Liszt back on the road, but by early October he had returned to Rome after a train journey lasting sixty-four hours. Two years had passed since his last visit to the Eternal City, in November 1871. In spite of his lengthy absence he seemed not especially interested in the place, and the weeks he spent there appear to have been more of a courtesy call than a matter that was close to his heart. 'I haven't looked much round in Rome,' he told Olga von Meyendorff, 'and do not feel at all inclined to seek out its historical and artistic grandeurs and marvels. Most of my hours are spent in talking with Princess W[ittgenstein].'[59] To Carolyne's dismay he was able to spend only three weeks in the city, after which he set off for Budapest.

When he arrived in Budapest in early November, Liszt had only a vague idea of what awaited him during the coming days. Central to these events was a gala marking the fiftieth anniversary of his first concert appearance. In fact the date was of only symbolic significance since Liszt had first performed in Eisenstadt in September 1819. But the organizers clearly wanted some more prestigious point of reference and so they declared his famous farewell concert in Vienna in April 1823 as the start of his career. The festivities were organized by a Liszt Jubilee Committee under the chairmanship of Archbishop Lajos Haynald, who in his promotional material described Liszt as a 'compatriot' and a 'great son' of the 'Hungarian nation'.[60] In this way the tone was set for a series of events designed not only to mark an important milestone in Liszt's career but also to celebrate Hungary's greatness as a nation. Liszt was consciously appropriated as a Hungarian, even though he had spent only a very short period of his life in the country. But that was of no importance here.

Even the opening ceremony was spectacular: early on the morning of 8 November two regimental bands assembled in the Fischplatz beneath the windows of Liszt's rooms on the top floor of the proposed Royal Academy of Music and serenaded him, while countless admirers and curious onlookers streamed into the square, shouting 'Éljen! Ferenc Liszt!' (Long live Liszt). The artistic high point of the festivities was a performance of *Christus*, and the festival ended with a banquet at the Hotel Hungária. Among the two hundred guests, Liszt glimpsed many friends who had travelled to Budapest from all over Europe, together with local dignitaries and emissaries from Vienna and Weimar. In his speech Archbishop Haynald declared that 'formerly Liszt came to the nations, whereas now it is the nations that come to him'.[61]

The country was in a state of acute Lisztomania, and there seemed to be no end in sight. Liszt was in constant demand. He visited Gran, attended a performance of his 'Gran' Mass in Pressburg and on 28 November was even received at a private audience with Emperor Franz Joseph in Budapest.

By the beginning of 1874 Liszt was in Vienna for a charity concert. Twenty-eight years had passed since his last appearance in the capital. The news of his comeback spread like wildfire, and tickets were sold out almost as soon as they went on sale. Among the audience on 11 January was Vienna's leading music critic, Eduard Hanslick, who seemed to be infected by the general enthusiasm, noting that even at the age of sixty-two Liszt 'still plays the most difficult music with the ease and freshness of youth' and was able to induce a paroxysm of frenzy in his listeners. It was with some astonishment that Hanslick observed that even when dressed in an abbé's cassock Liszt was still just as capable of charming his audience as he had been during his years as a virtuoso. A consummate showman, he flirted with his audience, regaling them with wonderful music and with an equally impressive spectacle:

> Sometimes he plays from notes, at other times from memory, putting on and taking off his spectacles accordingly. Sometimes his head is bent forward attentively, sometimes thrown back boldly. All this has the utmost fascination for his listeners – particularly female listeners. It has always been one of Liszt's characteristics to prove effective in his great art by drawing on all manner of lesser arts. [. . .] Several hundred strong, the audience applauded, shouted, cheered, rose to its feet, recalled the master again and again, indefatigably. The latter, in turn, with the quiet, friendly, gracious bearing of the habitual conqueror, let it be known that he, too, was not yet tired.

Hanslick concluded, laconically, that Liszt was 'a darling of the gods indeed'.[62]

Duty and Obedience

Liszt had spent over six months in Hungary when he left Budapest in the middle of May 1874. Normally he spent the spring months in Weimar, but this year was different, and for the first time in his 'vie trifurquée' he seemed keen to avoid the city of Goethe and Schiller. As early as March he had written to Carolyne von Sayn-Wittgenstein:

> I have no idea how they have got wind of the fact that I may not be returning to Weimar, but for the last two weeks I have been receiving letters from the town announcing the preparations for yet more jubilee celebrations. Loën, Frau Helldorf and others are urging me to tell them when I shall be coming back. To such an unambiguous question I was bound to offer an unambiguous answer 'that I shall not be returning at all'. In my reply to Loën I even quoted

a complacently melancholic remark by Bismarck: 'And so I have made the discovery that one is growing tired in the sand and recognizing one's impotence.'

Not only were Olga von Meyerdorff and Liszt's other friends in Weimar unsettled by this news, so too was Grand Duke Carl Alexander, who expressed his surprise at the absence of this famous resident and showed clear signs of bewilderment in asking for the reasons for Liszt's decision. As Liszt explained in his letter to Carolyne: 'He wrote to me in January, an interesting letter that I am forwarding to you herewith and that I did not consider merited a reply (not least because I did not want to tell him too soon that it was already too late).' Only when Carl Alexander intervened once again, this time striking a note of some pique, did Liszt deign to address a few lines to him. He was annoyed. 'A number of circumstances and individuals are both nuisances and a pain in the neck,' he concluded his letter to the princess. 'To become stuck in their talons and claws is a foolish martyrdom that is ridiculous rather than praiseworthy.'[63]

Liszt also vented his annoyance in a letter to Olga von Meyendorff: 'Are you also aware of the real pain which Their Royal Highnesses have caused me – perhaps unconsciously? – during my three last stays in Weimar? They have never once mentioned the Princess to me.' Liszt's absence was intended to make it unmistakably clear that he disagreed with the Weimar court's continuing ostracism of Carolyne. In the present situation, it was Liszt's 'absolute duty' to go to Rome, 'and it is entirely of my own accord, without anyone else "prescribing" it, that I go there.'[64]

It was not with a light heart that Liszt left for Rome, for he was concerned about Carolyne. 'The princess is physically and, worse, morally sick,' he told his daughter Cosima. Her life, he went on, had lost its sense of direction. For fifteen years she had endured an 'intolerably provisional' existence that was causing her constant difficulties, while a number of magnificent items of furniture were languishing in storage in Weimar. It was now time to take some organizational decisions: 'These decisions are extremely urgent; she continues to resist taking them, but I hope to persuade her to do so, not in eight days, but in eight months.'[65]

Liszt had taken on a lot. He arrived in Rome on 21 May and, as so often, he stayed at a hotel close to the princess's apartment, visiting her every day, talking to her and playing the piano for her. Only on one point did he make no progress: when he suggested that she might travel with him to Weimar to sort out a number of pressing financial matters, she refused outright, explaining to Adelheid von Schorn:

> You have no idea how fifteen years of living on my own and of being absorbed in my work have made me anxious and impractical. I shall never be able to leave Rome on my own. – I might have managed to travel to Siena, a four-hour journey from here – but not to cross the Alps![66]

It cannot be claimed that Carolyne was unwilling to make the trip: she simply did not have it in her any longer. Her letter reveals a great fear of life that she was already feeling, even though she was only in her mid-fifties.

Liszt was familiar with the strange behaviour of his former partner and knew all about her many whims, which he generally accepted with a smile. But now more was at stake than eccentricity and theatrical gestures – Carolyne, after all, could have played the part of the 'comic old lady' in a comedy by Beaumarchais. Her 'physical and moral sickness' was now manifesting itself in her increasing isolation. Initially she had still been able to leave her apartment to go shopping, to attend concerts or to visit museums, but with the passage of time she went out only after dark, driving round the surrounding area in a carriage, only rarely alighting. As we have already noted, she had a morbid fear of leaving Rome and spent even the hot summer months in her cave-like apartment, even though she received numerous invitations to move to cooler climes. On one occasion she visited the Villa d'Este but by the following day had found her unfamiliar surroundings unbearable. Apart from these psychological constraints, there were also a number of physical infirmities that now restricted her movements.

After Liszt had spent a good two weeks with the princess in Rome, he withdrew to his refuge at the spectacularly beautiful Villa d'Este in Tivoli and composed *Die heilige Cäcilia*, a tribute to the patron saint of music scored for mezzo-soprano, chorus and orchestra, and *The Bells of Strasbourg*, a setting of lines from Longfellow's *Golden Legend* for soloists, chorus and orchestra. From time to time he received visits from friends, including one in June from Hans von Bülow, but otherwise he led a secluded existence. His peace and quiet were suddenly shattered in the middle of September, when he received a call for help from Rome: Carolyne was said to be seriously ill and he was required to come at once. He found her in a pitiful state. 'In addition to her other ills,' he informed Olga von Meyendorff, the princess had also 'caught the Roman fever.'[67] It is possible that Carolyne had contracted malaria many years earlier and that it had proved to be a recurring problem. Liszt saw to the patient's needs as best he could, but when her condition had still not improved after a week, he went to see her daughter Marie in Duino near Trieste and they agreed that her mother needed full-time care. She was lonely and helpless and at the mercy of her servants: someone must take charge of the situation. Help was soon found in the person of Adelheid von Schorn, now thirty-three years old and friendly with Carolyne since her childhood. Having been in regular contact with her throughout that time, she knew exactly what to expect.

Adelheid arrived in Rome on 7 December, and it is thanks to her reminiscences that we are so well informed about Carolyne's eccentric life in the Via del Babuino:

> The princess undermined her own health most of all by her unnatural lifestyle. She refused to believe the doctors who observed a regular pulse and would not have believed a thermometer if such things had existed at that time; she lay in her bed for weeks on end, and for months she cut herself off from fresh air, so that, far from regaining her strength, she grew increasingly weak.[68]

Whenever Liszt called, arguments would break out, and it was impossible to reach agreement even on what to read in the day's newspaper.

> She invariably believed that nothing that people said to her or that appeared in print was true. [. . .] She clung to the conviction that if

someone said a thing was black, then it must be white. She would then say: 'That's what it's like in the big wide world.' Liszt often struggled to overcome this belief, saying that sometimes things that people said to each other or that they read in print were in fact true.[69]

Even Liszt's work as a composer proved to be a bone of contention, with Carolyne often finding fault with his music, describing his transcriptions as 'childish nonsense' that should not be taken seriously and challenging him to write something that in her eyes would be truly great. 'Since she had not been able to possess him,' Adelheid von Schorn speculated, 'she wanted to keep him for the world of music, in other words, she wanted him to pursue the course that she alone considered to be the right one.'[70]

This course was that of church music. Carolyne wanted Liszt to devote his entire life to the Church. He was, she claimed, merely wasting his valuable time in Weimar and Budapest. Instead, he should live in Rome or Tivoli and write music to the greater glory of God. As she was pleased to point out, he had not written a major work since *Christus*. Such criticisms must have caused Liszt considerable pain, especially given that he was doing all in his power to be Carolyne's 'umilissimo sclavissimo'. He spent the summer of 1874 working on a large-scale religious work that was intended to find favour with the princess, but in the event his *Legend of St Stanislaus* remained unfinished, in spite of numerous attempts to complete it. 'Believe me,' he had told a friend in 1865, 'I would willingly forgo all the cheering and all the enthusiasm if I could produce one truly creative work.'[71] Now, ten years later, his self-doubts increased to the point of resignation, and a composer whom Carolyne had wanted to be a latter-day Palestrina had to admit 'that we are all useless servants. To imagine that God needs our empty phrases in literature or music or elsewhere seems to be foolish and blasphemous.'[72] Carolyne simply refused to accept that if Liszt was already a comical saint as an abbé, then he was completely miscast as a latter-day Palestrina. To lead a life of seclusion devoted to sacred music alone was not for Liszt – even as a cleric he remained a man of the world, needing outside stimuli that included occasional forays into the brilliant world of the

salons of Europe. In this regard Adelheid von Schorn proved a percep-
tive observer: 'Whenever he was in the mood to write serious works,
then he himself was pleased, but the mood was not always there.'[73] It was
as simple as that.

New Challenges

Once Carolyne's state of health had improved, Liszt left Rome in early
February 1875 and returned to Budapest, where a shock awaited him:
his apartment had been broken into and its contents stolen. Although
the thieves were quickly apprehended, there was no trace of the items of
value that had been taken and that included an expensive silver wreath
that Liszt had once been given in Amsterdam. And that was by no means
the end of his annoyance, for worrying news reached him from Bayreuth
that Wagner's plans to found his own festival had run into financial
difficulties. Wagner urgently needed to raise some extra capital, otherwise the festival announced for the following year would be placed at
serious risk. For better or worse, Wagner set out on a brief concert tour,
the proceeds of which were earmarked for the festival coffers. In March,
concerts were planned in Vienna and Budapest, although it was for a
long time far from clear whether the venture would be profitable at all.
In Budapest ticket sales proved particularly sluggish, a state of affairs
due in no small part to anti-German propaganda. When Liszt learnt
that the organizers were facing a fiasco, he stepped in and offered his
services. It was an astute move, for Liszt was famous in Budapest, and no
concert at which he appeared could possibly be ignored. Within a short
time, all the tickets had been sold.

The programme on 10 March 1875 began with the world première of
Liszt's cantata, *The Bells of Strasbourg*, which he himself conducted, after
which he took the solo part in Beethoven's Fifth Piano Concerto under
the direction of Hans Richter. The concert ended with excerpts from the
Ring conducted by Wagner. Reporting on the previous day's rehearsal,
Cosima noted in her diary that her father 'absolutely overwhelms us with
the way he plays the Beethoven Concerto – a tremendous impression!
Magic without parallel – this is not playing, it is pure sound. R. says it

annihilates everything else.'[74] On the morning of the actual concert Liszt suffered a cut to one of the fingers on his right hand, prompting a concerned friend to advise him to cancel his appearance, but Liszt would hear of no such thing, saying that he would play the work without the injured finger. He carried it off, and the 3,000 listeners were ecstatic. And yet their enthusiasm was directed only at Liszt as a performer, not at *The Bells of Strasbourg* or at Wagner's contribution, which remained no more than a *succès d'estime*. It was as a pianist that Liszt enchanted the masses.

The Wagners did not really feel at their ease in Budapest: 'On the whole a very dismal impression of Hungary as a country,' Cosima confided in her diary,

> it seems to be heading for complete dissolution. Within the administration robbery is a matter of course, and then the delusions of grandeur – it is not permitted to speak a word of German. Life is appallingly expensive; no middle class, only an inflated, uncultivated aristocracy. The musical situation just as dismal, my father is barred from everything, from any activity – he is in fact a complete stranger here.[75]

This was less than the whole truth, for Liszt was currently taking on an entire new series of duties and challenges in his native country – although these tasks were not always a source of pleasure for him. Two years earlier the Hungarian parliament had agreed to found a Royal Academy of Music with its headquarters in Budapest, an ambitious project, with Liszt – Hungary's best-known musician and a man well respected throughout the length and breadth of Europe – as the president of the new institution. Those responsible for the project appealed to Liszt's amour-propre and national pride – invariably a way of enlisting his services – and prevailed on him to offer them his help. If he had really had an opportunity to turn down the post, then that time had already passed. To a certain extent he had been caught unawares, as he informed the princess in February 1873:

> The problem is that if the academy survives, it will be a millstone round my neck. The noose will follow, and the officials will take

good care to tighten it. Even so – as I have already told you – I cannot withdraw without being accused of cowardice. And so I am asking my guardian angel to shine a light on me and sustain me.[76]

Liszt was officially named president of the Academy of Music at the end of March 1875, but it was not until 14 November that the institution finally opened its doors. Perhaps symbolically, it opened in his absence, for by then Liszt was already back in Rome. He had advocated a broadly based curriculum, but since funding was tight, the lessons were initially limited to the piano and theory, and it was only with the passage of time that the range of subjects on offer increased. The new president was also the professor of piano, but apart from the use of a service flat he received no remuneration for either post.

The first year of study was already almost over when Liszt began giving lessons in March 1876. Within a month he had again left Budapest, not returning until the middle of October. During the second term, he taught for four months, but in later years he rarely remained for more than two or three months in the city. In addition to his teaching commitments he also took part in charity events and attended recitals by his students. Since his service flat was in the Academy itself, he had little peace and quiet even within his own four walls. Count Albert Apponyi, an acquaintance of Liszt's at this time, recalled much later that 'In the evening, I would often meet a little group of friends there from the Budapest world of music. Sometimes they had come to supper, which at Liszt's always consisted of cold dishes, and which he called "cold treatment".[77]

Finding himself at the heart of the city's social life was hardly a novel experience for Liszt, still less can it have been disagreeable. Indeed, he positively enjoyed the attention he received. And yet it sometimes became too much for him – he was, after all, in his mid-sixties when he took over as president of the Academy. He described a typical day to his biographer Lina Ramann:

I spend at least four hours every day writing letters: then paying visits both social and non-social and correcting proofs. On weekday afternoons several hours of piano lessons with a dozen students, some of whom are masterly; in the evening, I sometimes attend concerts and play whist to relax. I can barely apply myself to my own work here.[78]

By his own work, Liszt meant his work as a composer, which almost always suffered as a result of his other commitments. 'Liszt is going to Weimar to rest and to compose because he can never find the time to do so in Budapest,' wrote one local newspaper, hitting the nail on the head. 'He is always having to attend dinner, suppers, soirées and concerts, in other words, all the honours that are being showered on him are proving fatal.'[79]

Liszt generally put on a brave face when writing to the princess. Although he sometimes mentioned all the correspondence he had to deal with, including, of course, his voluminous letters to Carolyne herself, he never complained. There were good reasons for this, since she regarded his visits to Budapest as a sheer waste of time: 'He has become a piano teacher there,' she told Eduard Liszt, striking a caustic note before adding sarcastically, 'A fine and major appointment!' She was concerned about Liszt's reputation in the world, and it seemed to her unworthy of the 'new Palestrina' that he was merely giving piano lessons. The fact that he was no longer under her control in Budapest and Weimar and might even have been teaching young women was a further reason for her disquiet, to which she referred obliquely: 'Pest and Weimar are very deleterious for him. Real poison! – physically because of the excessively cold climate and morally – for many reasons!'[80]

Liszt's constant commuting between Rome, Weimar and Budapest took up an enormous amount of time and also proved physically draining, quite apart from the fact that his work at the Budapest Academy prevented him from composing. He could barely concentrate on large-scale works as each day was taken up with other matters. On the other hand, he was doing all of this voluntarily, not having been obliged to assume the presidency of the Academy or even to renounce a salary. His willingness to help others – to take a charitable view of the subject – was a part of his personality. That he was very often the victim of his own

LA VIE TRIFURQUÉE 265

goodness is another story. Apponyi aptly summed up the situation when he wrote that 'Liszt was plagued by talented and untalented musicians who sought his advice and help, for the gift of ridding himself of the failures was never his.'[81]

Bayreuth

'Without being hypocritical, I cannot grieve for her following her death any more than I could during her lifetime,' Liszt wrote to Carolyne von Sayn-Wittgenstein in the middle of March 1876, commenting on the death of Marie d'Agoult on the 5th. 'Mme d'Agoult had a taste, and even a passion, for all that was false – except in certain moments of ecstasy whose memory she could later no longer abide!'[82] The countess's final years were marked by her progressive physical decline. Her 'spleen' had refused to leave her in peace, so that even as early as the winter of 1860/61 Claire de Charnacé had been convinced that her mother was mentally ill. She was delusional and suffered from severe depression, even toying with thoughts of suicide. One day she would be reduced to a state of total lethargy, scarcely able to move, while on the next she would be tormented by terrible panic attacks, when she would become aggressive, lashing out and sometimes having to be placed in a strait-jacket. She spent long periods in clinics and sanatoria, but it would be wrong to suggest that she was locked away on a permanent basis. Whenever her demons left her in peace, she enjoyed moments of lucidity and was able to lead an active social life and pursue her literary career. In 1866, for example, she published a book on Goethe and Dante and completed the first part of her memoirs.

But now, in March 1876, Marie d'Agoult was dead. Liszt refused to be reconciled to her memory, preferring to shower her with scorn and contempt. 'It remains a mystery to me how your mother managed to fritter away her fortune,' he sneered in a letter to Cosima:

But I assume that the volume of her memoirs that has been edited and revised by Ollivier will be a success. She read thirty or so pages from it to me in Paris in 1866. At that date the title was not yet agreed on. The memoirist herself was particularly keen on 'Poetry and Truth', except that thanks to Goethe this title already had certain associations. In the course of our conversation I finally suggested 'Posturing and Lies', which was too close to the truth to be accepted.[83]

Cosima's grief was equally muted:

> Had she been less gifted, she could undoubtedly have led a more harmonious life, but since she could never have admitted as much to me and right up to the end continued arrogantly to deny all personal sufferings, I shall assume, rather, that it was easy for her to have to do this.[84]

In the spring of 1876 Cosima Wagner had no time for mournful thoughts, for preparations were by now well under way for the first Bayreuth Festival. Stage rehearsals began on 3 June, and Liszt arrived in the small town in Upper Franconia on 1 August. When he had attended the preliminary rehearsals the previous year, the Green Hill had still resembled a building site, but now Otto Brückwald's theatre could be admired in all its beauty and technical boldness. Ludwig II, too, turned up for the dress rehearsals in early August. He undoubtedly deserved an ovation since he alone had made the Bayreuth Festival possible, but he no longer cared to meet his own people, preferring to alight from a special train in the open country-side at dead of night. In other respects, too, he behaved in a distinctly odd way and whenever he was driven through the streets of the town insisted on having the curtains drawn in his carriage. Three days later he left as conspiratorially as he had arrived but returned incognito in late August. Among other heads of state to descend on the town were Kaiser Wilhelm and his wife and Dom Pedro II of Brazil, not to mention King Karl I of Württemberg, Grand Duke Carl Alexander of Saxe-Weimar, Grand Duke Friedrich Franz III of Mecklenburg-Schwerin and representatives of the Austro-Hungarian monarchy. Also present were not only Liszt but Saint-Saëns, Bruckner and Tchaikovsky and, among painters, Franz von Lenbach, Adolph von Menzel, Anton von Werner and Hans Makart. Actors, poets, scientists and journalists were also among the audience.

Bayreuth was ill prepared for this onslaught. The town had few hotel rooms at its disposal, so that most visitors had to find board and lodging with local families whose homes lacked the creature comforts to which they were otherwise accustomed. The absence of water closets proved troublesome to many a count. Liszt's friend Count Apponyi recalled that he always had to carry around four keys with him: 'The first was the front-door key, the second the key to my rooms, the third gave access to the adjoining flat, – it was necessary whenever one wanted to use the fourth.'[85] There was total chaos in the inns and guesthouses, Tchaikovsky recalled, with empty seats being fought over, although plates and bowls were generally empty: 'Throughout the whole duration of the Festival, food forms the chief interest of the public; the artistic representations take a secondary place. Cutlets, baked potatoes, omelettes – all are discussed much more eagerly than Wagner's music.'[86]

But Tchaikovsky's strictures did not apply to Wahnfried, where Liszt had one of the guest rooms. Here in the Wagners' elegant villa there was no shortage of food. Instead, reception gave way to reception, banquet to banquet. One of the frequent guests was the soprano Lilli Lehmann, who was singing one of the Rhine daughters. During this summer of 1876 she had ample opportunity to observe the abbé at close quarters: 'It is remarkable what a relative stranger Liszt remained to me,' she mused:

> It may have been because he was either claimed by the family at 'Wahnfried', or, especially in '76, was obliged to be almost exclusively with those visitors, who, as patrons, brought money to the enterprise, and who took him by storm and did not allow him to have a free moment. Perhaps the cause is also to be found in the numerous pretty women, young and old, who dogged his footsteps, accompanied him to and from church, who appeared like little beauty plasters at his side, and who seemed to be as indispensable to the great man as sun and air.[87]

Elsewhere in her memoirs she recalls Liszt holding court at Wahnfried: 'Around him stood all the pretty women, about whom he spun, who enchained him, to whom he threw kisses, laughter, regard, and love in

tones, with whom he played as with children, but who did not understand him.' By this date Liszt was sixty-four, but in spite of his cassock he
evidently still exuded an erotic fascination irresistible to women: 'They
all coquetted with him, and – shall I say it? – he with them.'[88] But it is
also clear from Lilli Lehmann's account that Liszt had a function to
perform in Bayreuth – entertaining the Festival's patrons and keeping
them in a good mood.

On 18 August a banquet was held in the restaurant next to the theatre;
the five hundred or so guests seated at long tables included two of Liszt's
friends, Adelheid von Schorn and Count Apponyi, as well as his pupil
Berthold Kellermann and his French colleague Camille Saint-Saëns.
Among the speakers were the Liberal Reichstag deputy Franz Duncker,
who, to the embarrassment of everyone present, announced that no one
could know 'what posterity would think of it all, but the *striving* was
worthy of recognition'.[89] Wagner too rose to his feet and proposed a toast
to his father-in-law: 'Here is the man who first had faith in me at a time
when no one had heard of me and without whom you would probably
not have heard a note of my music, my dear friend – Franz Liszt.' The
two men stepped closer to one another and embraced, leading to hearty
applause and cries of 'Three cheers!' Moved in turn, Liszt replied:

> I am grateful to my friend for acknowledging me in a way that
> does me great honour and I remain devoted to him in deepest
> reverence – most humbly; just as we bow before the genius of Dante,
> Michelangelo, Shakespeare and Beethoven, so I bow before the
> genius of the Master.[90]

However well meant their words of mutual praise, the summer of 1876
witnessed the beginning of a chain of events that was to prove highly
unpleasant for Liszt, for in Wagner's entourage he was increasingly
treated as a facilitator for the great Richard and reduced to the status of
a servant of the Bayreuth demigod. The fact that Liszt, two years older
than Wagner, was arguably the greatest pianist of the nineteenth century
and a brilliant composer was soon lost sight of by the Wagnerian
community. Once, when Lilli Lehmann was singing Liszt's setting of

Goethe's 'Kennst du das Land', Wagner unexpectedly entered the room and listened to the rest of the song:

> Then, with his head thrown back, a bearing that gave him the appearance of great self-consciousness, he strode rather stiffly through the drawing-room with a bundle of music under his arm, and turned, before leaving, to Frau Cosima. 'Really, my dear,' he said, 'I did not know that your father had written such pretty songs; I thought he had rendered service only in fingering for piano playing. On the whole, the poem about the blooming lemon trees always reminds me of a funeral messenger.' Whereupon he imitated the gestures of a funeral attendant carrying lemons. Frau Cosima had to receive, with a laugh, what was not pleasant for either her or me to hear.[91]

Liszt was almost painfully anxious not to be the centre of attention in Bayreuth and not to steal Wagner's thunder by getting in his way. When Lina Ramann asked him if he could obtain dress rehearsal tickets for her, he declined, saying that he 'needed to avoid submitting requests for rehearsal tickets', since he

> had already had trouble with a number of friends to whom I was able to say only that they should either appeal directly to Wagner or approach some Bayreuth patron or one of the artists, but not *mea parvitas*, since I am required to show the strictest discretion.[92]

Carolyne had seen this coming. In her hatred of the Wagners, she was in any case convinced that Liszt would merely be exploited by his family, and since she knew that he would not write openly and honestly to her on the subject, she asked Adelheid von Schorn to spy on him for her. Everything that Adelheid saw and heard and that 'the newspapers do not report' was to be written down.[93] And she went on to add that in her reports Adelheid should ignore the 'general outlines', effectively stating that she was interested only in the scandal and gossip. Whatever Adelheid reported, Carolyne showered Liszt with reproaches, telling him that Bayreuth and the Wagners were bad for his health, and much else besides. This time, however, Liszt parried her attacks, writing to say that he did not deserve such a letter and striking a note of self-assurance: 'After today's letter I shall not be returning to Rome.'[94] Only now did Carolyne realize what she had done and wrote again by return of post, attempting to placate her former lover, but in vain. Liszt remained obdurate. His absence from Rome was the keenest weapon that he could use against Carolyne. Not until August 1877 did he return to the Eternal City.

The argument that erupted in September 1876 was only the temporary nadir of a development that had started some time earlier. As Liszt told Cosima, he had struggled years earlier to reduce his dealings with the princess 'to the most important points in our lives',[95] implying that he now granted his former partner only a minor role in his existence. As if keen to underline this fact, he now made a point of spending Holy Week and Easter Day 1877 in Bayreuth.

Liszt evidently felt at home in Wahnfried. After attending church in the morning, he would work on the proofs of his latest compositions and deal with his correspondence, after which he devoted himself to his family and enjoyed his new proximity to the Wagners and to his five grandchildren. Daniela was now seventeen and going through a difficult stage in her adolescence, but she was already a talented young pianist who from time to time was allowed to perform for her grandfather. In return he dedicated to her his *Arbre de Noël*, a collection of twelve delightful impressions completed the previous year. On Easter Sunday Cosima arranged a party for around one hundred guests: 'It comes off very well, since my father is kind enough to play (*Saint François de Paule marchant sur les flots*) and R. is in good spirits.'[96] The next day, too, Wagner was in a good mood and to celebrate his father-in-law's name day gave him a copy of his autobiography, *My Life*, with a rhyming quatrain by way of a dedication: 'Dear Saint Francis! / You're my man! This / Life is yours. I / Give it gladly.' Liszt was touched and by way of thanks sat down at the Wahnfried piano and played his monumental Sonata in B minor. 'A lovely, cherished day,' Cosima noted in her diary, 'on which I can thank Heaven for the comforting feeling that nothing – no deeply tragic parting of the ways, no malice on the part of others, no differences in character – could ever separate us three.'[97] The 'malice on the part of others' was clearly a reference to the machinations of the princess. Her influence on Liszt was now broken. And yet Cosima had no idea how her father really felt.

Nuages Gris

Nuages gris – 'Grey Clouds' – is the title of a piano miniature that may well reflect Liszt's state of mind during the final decade of his life. True, he led a privileged life that he divided between Hungary, Italy and Germany. He was surrounded by friends, pupils and admirers, as well as being loved and reconciled with his family, giving the impression to superficial observers that all was well with his life. Yet clouds increasingly cast a pall over his existence. Writing to Olga von Meyendorff in September 1876, he admitted that 'sometimes sadness envelops my soul like a shroud.'[98] By this he meant not the vague melancholy and low spirits that occasionally affect many people but bouts of deep depression: 'I am desperately sad and completely incapable of finding a single ray of happiness.'[99] He also complained of insomnia, which in turn led to all manner of physical ailments, and sometimes he was so lethargic that, unable to work, he spent the whole day in bed, scarcely able to write even the briefest of letters. All in all, he felt 'extremely tired of living', and only his faith in God prevented him from taking his own life.[100]

This was more or less the mood in which Liszt returned to the Villa d'Este in late August 1877. For days on end he sat in the park with its fountains and centuries-old cypresses, which cast a magical spell on him. In particular, the archaic beauty of the trees would not let him go. 'I have spent the whole of the last three days beneath the cypresses!' he told Carolyne. 'I was as if possessed by this idea and was incapable of thinking of anything else – not even of the Church – their ancient boles left me no peace, and I listened to the singing and weeping of their branches with their cloak of evergreen needles!'[101] During the late summer of 1877 he wrote five piano pieces to which he later added another two and published as the third volume of his *Années de pèlerinage*. No fewer than two of these pieces were devoted to these cypress

trees and both were subtitled 'Threnody'. They are sombre and melancholy sound pictures of devastating hopelessness. Even Liszt himself
was surprised by such a degree of sadness, as he wrote to Olga von
Meyendorff: 'These pieces are hardly suitable for drawing rooms and
are not entertaining, nor even dreamily pleasing. When I publish them
I'll warn the publisher that he risks selling only a few copies.'[102]

The fourth piece in the set is titled 'Les jeux d'eaux à la Villa d'Este'
and is an atmospheric masterpiece, its music rippling along, while the
impressionistic tone-colours and arabesque-like figures capture the play
of the fountains. All in all, however, these works represent an exception
in Liszt's late oeuvre, for many of the pieces that date from the final
decade of his life are filled with a sense of deep melancholy. Miniatures
such as *Nuages gris, La lugubre gondola* and *Unstern* anticipate music
that was not to be written until many decades later. Their textures grow
increasingly atomized, their harmonic writing often bordering on
atonality. In the *Bagatelle sans tonalité* of 1885 the experimental nature
of the piece is already encapsulated in its title. Other works such as the
late Mephisto Waltzes and the *Csárdás macabre* are demonically convul-
sive caprices. But Liszt also spent this period revising earlier works and
publishing them in new versions. 'I've recently written a couple of piano
pieces,' he told his friend Alexander Wilhelm Gottschalg, 'and I've also
revised a number of older works. Correcting and improving one's earlier
self is the proper job for one's old age.'[103]

No less remarkable is the sacred music from this period. *Via Crucis*
(1878) is a series of meditations on the fourteen Stations of the Cross for
soloists, chorus and organ (it also exists in a version for piano solo) and
attests to a musical asceticism that was found to be shockingly modern
even at the time of its composition. Liszt had reached the end of his life,
and his late music remains moving even today in terms of its extreme
austerity.

But the works of Liszt's old age also include a number of titles that
recall the brilliant and delightful compositions of earlier decades.
Anyone listening to the brief nocturne *En rêve*, for example, might think
they could hear Chopin's shade scurrying past, while the *Quatre valses
oubliées* seem to breathe the spirit of the French salons. And yet these

memories had long since faded in Liszt's mind, with the result that the music, too, sounds somehow faded: the first and third of the *Valses oubliées* end with monophonic melodies that appear to point the way ahead to an uncertain future. But we could just as well claim that they point the way to the twentieth century. Carolyne, too, realized that Liszt's music was a link between Romanticism and modernity:

> People do not yet understand his genius – and they understand it far less than they do in the case of Wagner's genius for Wagner is a reaction against the present, whereas Liszt has cast his spear much further into the future. – Many generations will pass before he is fully understood.[104]

Carolyne was to be proved right: the works of Liszt's final years threw open the door on the modern age, and composers such as Bartók, Schoenberg and Alban Berg drew on his music for many of their ideas and stimuli. Writing in 1911, for example, Schoenberg noted that 'his effect has perhaps been greater, through the many stimuli he left behind for his successors, than Wagner's has been'.[105] And the great Lisztian Ferruccio Busoni wrote that 'the harmony of a revolutionary lies within the calm hand of a ruler', adding: 'We are all descended from him radically, without excepting Wagner, and we owe to him the lesser things that we can do. César Franck, Richard Strauss, Debussy, the penultimate Russians, are all branches of his tree.'[106]

For his part, Wagner had only words of contempt for his father-in-law's ascetic late style. In November 1882, for example, Cosima noted in her diary: 'Late in the evening, when we are alone, R. talks about my father's latest compositions, which he finds completely meaningless, and he expresses his opinion sharply and in much detail.'[107] The matter clearly obsessed Wagner, for a few days later he worked through one of the pieces in Liszt's collection *Arbre de Noël*: 'When I ask him to address his remarks about it to my father himself, he says, "That would be cruel."'[108] On another occasion Wagner even spoke of the 'budding insanity' of Liszt's most recent compositions, adding that he would 'find it impossible to develop a taste for their dissonances'.[109] Although Liszt was only two years older than Wagner, by the end of their lives they were separated by entire worlds in terms of their musical language.

In the Augean Stables

'Only once was I fortunate enough to hear Liszt play,' recalled Emil Sauer, who studied with Liszt in Weimar from May 1884.

> And the reader will forgive my lack of embarrassment when I say that my joy was muted. [...] In spite of my lively imagination and with the best will in the world I found what was on offer far too meagre to allow me to share the ecstasy of the faithful. [...] The only thing that I found really worth noting was the dumb play of his face and eyes, together with the pose afforded by a markedly classical posture. It was not a pianistic feat but a histrionic performance of the first order.[110]

It must remain an open question whether Liszt's playing was really as sobering as Sauer's account insists. After all, the septuagenarian pianist may well have felt out of sorts and Sauer may have caught him on a bad day: great artists cannot always perform to their highest standards. This conjecture may receive some support from the fact that we know from other sources that even in old age Liszt could still cast a spell on his audiences. If the then twenty-one-year-old felt so disillusioned, then this was the result of the way in which even poor performances at the Hofgärtnerei were greeted with hollow and wholly uncritical adulation.

In his autobiography Sauer paints a vivid portrait of the sycophantic atmosphere that characterized Liszt's entourage, providing us with an insight into an additional, and less laudable, aspect of the elderly composer's life. But how reliable is his account? The answer must be: completely. For not only is his version of events confirmed by other eyewitness accounts but in 1901, when he published his memoirs, he was one of the leading pianists in Europe and had no need to score points at his mentor's expense.

However modern Liszt's concept of his masterclasses may have been, his teaching method resembled 'lectures that anyone could attend or miss as the fancy took them'.[111] These classes were held in the afternoon and were attended not only by musicians but also by Liszt's friends and by representatives of the Weimar court, including even the grand duke himself, as well as other more or less illustrious individuals, with the result that it was not always easy to tell where a teaching class ended and a social event began. Nor was it only musical qualifications that provided an entrée to Liszt's classes, for flattery and cosmopolitan airs and graces also played a part here until finally the door to the Hofgärtnerei was thrown open to phoneys and lickspittles. Liszt proved susceptible to their praise – vanity had always been his Achilles' heel. As he grew older, his need for adulation and homage seems to have increased.

On the other hand, many leading artists attended Liszt's piano classes: Hans von Bülow, Carl Tausig, Eugen d'Albert, Sophie Menter, Alfred Reisenauer and August Stradal – to name only some of them – all worked with Liszt, in some cases over a period of several years. All can be described as Liszt's pupils. But the list also includes students whom we know had no business being in his classes.[112] Pianists who had already failed to make an impression at traditional conservatories took advantage of Liszt's well-known antipathy towards such institutions and used flattery to pass themselves off as misprized geniuses. Bülow is said to have coined the malicious witticism: 'No one in the entire world plays as badly as they do in Weimar in July and August.'[113]

It is no wonder, therefore, that Sauer could scarcely believe his eyes and ears when he found himself in a position to study Liszt's 'system' at first hand. 'The salon was full of people who manifestly did not belong there and who did not even known why they had in fact come.' Sauer was reminded of a vanity fair. Each of the students in the class was keen to enjoy Liszt's proximity and to attract his attention, with the result that 'genuine' pianists such as Reisenauer and Sauer might be thrust aside by sycophants and charlatans. 'What pained me most of all was that the elderly gentleman seemed blind or unduly responsive to the very worst of these flatterers, who threw themselves at him with their "dear master here, dear master there". Indeed, it shocked me that he was weak enough to take any pleasure in flattery so effusive as to be offensive.'[114]

Weimar now resembled a fashionable spa with Liszt's visits to the town marking the high point of the season, when the otherwise sleepy backwater was barely recognizable any longer. Visitors came and went, and the hotels were all booked up. The town was full of young pianists, budding composers and pushy publishers whose only aim was to make contact with Liszt. Sauer referred to them as idlers and even as parasites.

These idlers fell into two groups: pretty young women seeking to turn Liszt's head and blasé youths who had recourse to the most refined arts of flattery to ingratiate themselves with the 'Old Man'.[115] There were no limits to what such sycophants would do. One Dutch pupil – Sauer unfortunately does not mention his name – would even drag himself out of bed at break of day in order to attend early Mass and 'melt Liszt's heart with his piety',[116] while the young women adopted an even more sophisticated approach, not a few of them regarding Liszt as what Adelheid von Schorn describes as 'desirable prey'.[117] Good-looking young women already had an inherent advantage:

> Wearing a black velvet jacket, the Master made his way through a
> bevy of languishing maidens, slowly shuffling up and down from the
> grand piano to his desk. Sometimes he would bow low in homage to
> one of the lovely ladies, who was treated to a longer or shorter
> greeting depending on her outward appearance.[118]

Liszt was idolized by his female fans as if he were a pop star, and glorified in often grotesque ways. Berthold Kellermann reports that on one occasion Liszt's admirers slipped into his bedroom and siphoned off some water that had been left standing in a bowl, filling little phials with the precious elixir, which they carried next to their hearts.[119] Another pupil practised Liszt's *Dante* Sonata in his rooms, evidently keen to invest his performance with the greatest possible authenticity: 'He had previously placed a live cat in the stovepipe leading to the tiled stove and lit the stove. The pitiful screaming of the poor cat was meant to give him a clearer idea of the torments of Hell!'[120]

Liszt's daily round in Weimar in the 1870s and '80s began with his rising at four in the morning and going to church without first taking breakfast. This was an inviolable part of his routine, even if he had retired late the previous evening and had only a few hours' sleep. At five he drank a cup of strong coffee laced with cognac and consumed a few dry rolls. He then worked until lunch at one o'clock. According to Kellermann: 'The food was good and nourishing, albeit simple. During the meal he drank a glass of wine or diluted cognac in the French manner, a drink he enjoyed very much. He then smoked – indeed, he always smoked whenever he was not eating or sleeping.'[121]

There were lessons on three afternoons every week, and they usually lasted until around six, but if Liszt was not invited out in the evening, some of his pupils would remain longer and keep him company while he played cards. His housekeeper, Pauline Apel, would serve a frugal supper accompanied by beer. As a result it was often very late at night before the party broke up and it was not unusual for Liszt and his guests to repair to one of the hotels in the town, where they continued to drink large quantities of alcohol. It was frequently one in the morning before they all went their separate ways.

'Here I have to touch on one of the darker aspects of Liszt's life,' Adelheid von Schorn recalled a little demurely. 'And this was his love of stiff drinks.'[122] Another of Liszt's pupils, Felix Weingartner, was less diplomatic and had no hesitation in describing Liszt as a 'confirmed alcoholic'.[123] Liszt had been a heavy drinker all his life and, according to Adelheid von Schorn, he needed alcohol 'as a tonic'. Indeed, he 'felt tired without this stimulant'.[124] By the end of his life Liszt appears to have lost control, and by July 1882 his American pupil Carl Lachmund was noting in his diary that Liszt was getting through a bottle of cognac, two or three bottles of wine and even a quantity of absinthe every day.[125] Even during his classes he would repeatedly slip away to his bedroom for a quick drink.[126] In the light of such vast quantities of alcohol and of Liszt's addictive behaviour, it is difficult to contradict Weingartner's assessment of the situation. Adelheid von Schorn, finally, observed Liszt drinking during the morning: mostly it followed some minor annoyance or other. Liszt himself placed his own interpretation on the problem: 'I know that cognac is my own worst enemy but I can't manage without it for long.'[127]

A teacher – especially a charismatic figure like Liszt – should set a good example, and yet one gains the impression that Liszt failed to maintain the necessary reserve when dealing with his students. He told the young Berthold Kellermann quite categorically: 'A musician has to smoke.' When Kellermann admitted to being a non-smoker, Liszt got out a large cigar and taught Kellermann how to smoke. 'From then on he was always giving me cigars, morning, noon and night, Virginia and Havana cigars.' On one occasion the twenty-five-year-old had practised more than usual. ' "For your playing you'll receive a cigar and a glass of wine," said Liszt, pouring me a glass and personally cutting a cigar for me.'[128] Following in their mentor's footsteps, two of Liszt's most famous pupils, Alfred Reisenauer and Arthur Friedheim, became alcoholics in turn. Reisenauer once drank thirteen pints of beer in three hours. At the time in question – July 1883 – he had just turned nineteen.

Emil Sauer observed these drinking bouts with horror, convinced as he was that it was a dangerous superstition to think that alcohol was conducive to particularly fiery piano playing. Indeed, he had seen for himself how within only a matter of a few years alcohol could destroy all that had been achieved during decades of hard and serious work.[129] We cannot of course blame Liszt for Reisenauer's and Friedheim's alcohol dependency, as it requires more to become addicted than simply a teacher's bad example, and yet Liszt's lack of reserve in his dealings with his pupils throws a strange light on his activities as a teacher. Clara Schumann, whose attitude to her colleague became markedly critical in later life, noted in her diary following Liszt's death:

> He was a great piano-virtuoso, but a dangerous model for the young to imitate. Almost all the rising pianists imitated him, but they lacked his mind, his genius, his delicacy of touch, so that now we have nothing but great masters of technique and a number of caricatures.[130]

The 'idlers' among Liszt's pupils had a natural enemy in Hans von Bülow. When Liszt was away on tour or was prevented from giving lessons,

Bülow would occasionally take his masterclasses, lessons that were much feared because Bülow lacked the qualities that Liszt possessed in abundance: patience and kindness. One such class took place in the middle of June 1880. Kellermann was in no doubt that the lazier among his fellow students faced terrible retribution. 'Let's cleanse the Augean stables,' Bülow had cheerfully exclaimed when the two men had bumped into each other in the street.[131] Bülow began by addressing the assembled class:

> Ladies and gentlemen, let's not forget that the Master was born in 1811 or that he is the very embodiment of kindness and leniency, so let's not abuse him in such a hair-raising way. You in particular, ladies, believe me, most of you are destined for the myrtle rather than the laurel.[132]

Sheer terror was reflected in the eyes of many of those present, and some lost their nerve and fled the room, while others were roundly humiliated by Bülow. Then barely twenty years old, Dory Petersen had elected to play Liszt's virtuoso Hugo-inspired study *Mazeppa*, which tells how a young man in seventeenth-century Poland is tied to the saddle of a horse and driven out into the steppes until he is finally rescued. It seems as if Dory Petersen stumbled her way through the piece, her evocation of the hero's wild ride across the barren landscape leaving much to be desired and prompting Bülow to explode: 'You bring only one quality to this piece, your own equine nature.'[133] Not content with insulting her in this way, he then shouted after the distraught young woman: 'I hope never to see you again. You should be swept out of here – not with the broom, but with the handle.'[134] And he continued in much the same vein: 'You're completely hopeless. You've no right to continue to annoy the Master.'[135] After two hours, those students who had not already fled were reduced to nervous wrecks. Writing afterwards to his daughter Daniela, Bülow continued to make abusive remarks:

> You can be certain that Fräulein D. P. would have been scared off by one or more of the other scarecrows in her class – by Fräulein

Schmalhansen [sic], for example, a protégée of the Empress of all Teutons – and that the abbé's music salon will continue to be a junk shop.[136]

Bülow was regarded as an excellent, if strict, teacher, and yet his whole approach had nothing to do with piano lessons but was an attempt to intimidate and drive away the idlers in the class. He told Adelheid von Schorn that he was 'merely doing the same favour to Liszt as I do to my poodle when ridding it of fleas'. The writer added that 'while he was saying this, he ran around my room, rubbing his hands with glee'.[137] It is unlikely that Bülow's purges served any useful purpose, for when Liszt discovered from Kellermann what had happened, he told the latter: 'Bülow was quite right, but he was too hard on them. If you see these people this evening at the Sächsischer Hof, tell them to wait until Bülow has left and then to come back here.'[138]

The Fall

Saturday, 2 July 1881 began like any other day. We can assume that Liszt attended church, just as he did every day, then, following breakfast, got on with his work. But an unfortunate accident then took place. We cannot be certain exactly what happened, but it appears that Liszt made an awkward movement on the steps at the front of the Hofgärtnerei and, losing his balance, fell. Initially it seemed as if the seventy-year-old abbé had been fortunate. The local doctor, Richard Brehme, found only a cut on the right thigh, but as a precaution he asked his famous colleague, Richard Volkmann from Halle, to examine the patient. Volkmann was regarded as an authority on compound fractures, spinal injuries and all manner of orthopaedic complaints. An initial examination revealed that Liszt had sustained bruising to his legs, toes and ribs. But it also became clear that Liszt was suffering from a whole series of other ailments that he had evidently ignored. Liszt hated being ill, but what he hated even more was talking about illness, especially his own. 'People aren't ill,' he used to say in this context. But it was now clear that Liszt was suffering from dropsy, asthma, a cataract of the left eye and chronic heart disease.[139]

Brehme ordered his patient to remain in bed and to give up alcohol. Liszt reacted as he generally did to illness, regarding the whole episode as a minor inconvenience that would soon pass. But on this occasion the situation was more serious, and he had to spend the next two months in bed.

Adelheid von Schorn described his fall as the beginning of the end – 'in short, he became a different person both physically and mentally. He put on weight, his face was often bloated, his legs were always swollen, and his beautiful, delicate hands acquired a sickly appearance.' His character, too, began to change: he quickly became irritable and could no longer control his temper 'so that he became abusive to innocent strangers'. In a word, 'all these signs of old age first appeared in the summer of 1881 and grew worse with each passing year'.[140]

Bülow and his daughter Daniela happened to be in Weimar during the first week of July. Father and daughter had not seen each other for twelve years but had agreed to meet at Liszt's home in Weimar. As a result of Liszt's accident, their reunion was a sombre occasion. The Bülows decided to remain longer than they had originally planned in order to look after Liszt. 'Weimar sad,' Bülow wrote to his colleague Karl Klindworth. 'Grand Master growing visibly more infirm! (esp. mentally) vermin around him also growing both quantitatively and in terms of its negative quality.'[141] Now twenty, Daniela saw to her grandfather's needs, reading to him and keeping him company, while Bülow assumed responsibility for Liszt's piano classes. The news that Bülow would be taking over spread like wildfire, causing fear and terror among those pupils who had enjoyed the dubious pleasure of his lessons the previous year. One of Liszt's pupils, Emma Großkurth, recalled the 'feeling of apprehension' that gripped the class: 'It was as if a great hawk had swept down among us. Several tried to flutter to cover; to the further end of the salon, or behind the curtains that divided the rooms.' One after another, Bülow humiliated each of his victims in turn, until their ordeal was finally over.[142]

Lina Schmalhausen, too, tried to make good her escape, but Bülow, whom we have already found ridiculing her by renaming her 'Schmalhansen' in his letter to Daniela, implying limited abilities, called her back with the cold-blooded calculation of an executioner: 'No, it is you I wish to hear first.' Lina Schmalhausen struggled with the metre and appears to have made a poor impression. Bülow listened to her for a while before exploding with rage: 'I have heard it said that there are people who cannot count three; but you cannot count *two*.'[143] Lina Schmalhausen naturally felt mortified and, gathering together her music, fled from the room. But if Bülow had hoped she would leave the Hofgärtnerei once and for all, he was to be disabused, for she wrote to Liszt, complaining about Bülow and claiming that he had made her look ridiculous in the eyes of the rest of the class. Her pride, she went on, prevented her from returning for any more lessons. Liszt responded by apologizing to her and inviting her to return to the Hofgärtnerei after Bülow had left. His reaction cannot be explained merely by his legendary good nature: there must be other reasons why he kowtowed to Lina Schmalhausen and effectively showed up Bülow. It is worth examining these reasons in greater detail.

We have little reliable information relating to Lina Schmalhausen's career. She was born in Berlin in 1864, received piano lessons from an early age and was only eleven when she became a pupil of Theodor Kullak, a virtuoso pianist famous in his own day. In Berlin she once had the good fortune to perform in the presence of Kaiser Wilhelm and evidently left a good impression since Wilhelm's wife, Augusta, took the young pianist under her wing. It was even rumoured that Augusta had provided Lina with a personal letter of recommendation, granting its subject an entrée into high society. It also seems to have been Augusta's letter that allowed Lina to gain access to the Hofgärtnerei in Weimar, for she joined Liszt's class in the summer of 1879, when she was still only fifteen years old. As for her musical qualities, the evidence seems to be entirely negative. Carl Lachmund, relying on hearsay, describes her as 'an amateurish pupil',[144] while August Stradal recalled that it was impossible to make music with her since 'her execution was completely unrhythmical and she even omitted whole bars'.[145] A performance of Liszt's A major Piano Concerto at the Allgemeiner Deutscher Musikverein's Festival in May 1885 turned out to be a fiasco, Schmalhausen again proving incapable of keeping time with the music or with the orchestra at the rehearsal, with the outcome that at the concert itself the conductor, Felix Mottl, performed the orchestra part on a second piano and at difficult passages played so loudly that Lina Schmalhausen's part could no longer be heard.[146] Even in the wake of this disaster, Liszt continued to treat her with remarkable indulgence.

It has often been rumoured that the two of them were lovers, a view taken even by Emil Sauer, who reports the following remarkable scene in his autobiography. An American male pupil had just been sent packing when it was Lina Schmalhausen's turn:

> Apart from a passable mask, she brings to the performance an old Liszt arrangement that she has dug up and that even the composer himself has forgotten, but with this touching show of piety she buys herself the right to torment us for half an hour, while Liszt, indulgence incarnate, responds with a transfigured smile, occasionally resting his hands on her shoulders, ignoring all the wrong notes and rhythmic distortions and allowing his piece to be murdered, while frequently interjecting 'Nice'. Fräulein Schmalhausen bangs away at the keyboard more mercilessly and more maliciously than the American youth, but she knows the value of mischievous dimples, she knows how to excavate forgotten works and so she is endured.[147]

There is no doubt that Lina Schmalhausen loved and worshipped her 'Master'. She travelled with him, helped him to run his household in Budapest and took care of his needs, including food and clothing. She also organized his correspondence and ensured that he was surrounded by the creature comforts of a regular home. During the final years of his 'vie trifurquée', Lina represented a constant. Liszt was always susceptible to all forms of attention and he enjoyed the young woman's company, clearly sharing a certain intimacy in the form of an affectionate glance, an embrace or a kiss on the forehead. Sometimes they even secretly held hands. Whether there was anything more we simply do not know. Liszt's friends looked askance at Lina. After all, none of them had forgotten the affair with the self-styled Cossack countess Olga Janina. Was Lina perhaps another fraudster? 'She's no Cossack', Lina Ramann said in the summer of 1883, 'but I can't help recall a comment that he made to me years ago during a conversation about "La Cosaque": "The mistake that I made was in trusting her. I can't guarantee that I shan't be consumed by passion all over again." '[148]

Caution certainly seemed to be called for, not least because a man as trusting as Liszt could easily be exploited. It seems that Lina Schmalhausen was always short of money, and Liszt often gave her a few marks to sort out her most pressing needs, but this was still insufficient. Necessity, as we know, is the mother of invention, and Lina proved especially inventive, in particular by making money out of her influence over the elderly composer. A European celebrity like Liszt was constantly pestered by publishers, composers, pianists and piano builders. Every leading manufacturer at this time wanted to give Liszt a piano, for, however expensive their gifts, they could then claim quite truthfully that the most famous living pianist played on one of their instruments. Liszt turned down most of the instruments that he was offered, mainly for reasons of space: his apartments in Weimar, Budapest and Rome were all relatively small and already crammed full of pianos. He was also on friendly terms with Carl Bechstein, the head of the firm of piano manufacturers that bore his name, so that if Liszt needed a new piano for the Hofgärtnerei, he had only to ask his friend for one.

Another manufacturer who tried in vain to persuade Liszt to take one of his instruments was Rudolf Ibach from Schwelm near Wuppertal. But then he got to know Lina Schmalhausen, whom he supported and encouraged in various ways, lending her money, offering her the free use of pianos in Weimar and at her parents' home in Berlin and occasionally recommending her to concert promoters. Lina thanked him by providing him with information relating to the Hofgärtnerei. It was Lina who finally persuaded Liszt to replace his existing Höhle piano with one of Ibach's instruments. It was important to her, she told Rudolf Ibach, 'that you should get to know me from a better side, and so I have done everything in my power to persuade the Master to dispose of Höhle's upright and install an Ibach in its place'.[149] Liszt accepted the offer. Lina Schmalhausen's reward was a credit note to the value of three hundred marks.

Liszt's other pupils viewed Lina Schmalhausen with envy and jealousy. After all, she had permanent access to their beloved 'Master', quite apart from the fact that she had never been particularly well liked. She was a troublemaker and a gossip – Lachmund called her 'Fräulein Telltale' – who combined local tittle-tattle with malice to produce a toxic mix of calumny and bile that she delighted in retailing to Liszt. Her most implacable enemy was the aforementioned Dory Petersen, who was scarcely able to contain her jealousy of her rival. The two women had initially been friends, but in the end they fell out over their attempts to outdo each other in their show of affection for Liszt, and when Lina fell foul of the law in the spring of 1884, Dory thought her chance had come to deal with her rival once and for all.

Lina Schmalhausen had slipped a length of lace into her shopping basket without paying for it, or so a shop assistant claimed. The accused protested her innocence and even confided in Liszt, who believed her – the only person to do so. Even Lina's own mother regarded her daughter as a common-or-garden thief.[150] With great difficulty Liszt and his friend Carl Gille persuaded the authorities not to pursue the matter. Only then did Dory discover what had happened and, regardless of the embarrassment it might cause Liszt, went to the owner of the haberdasher's shop and prevailed on him to sign a statement that she had already drawn up, accusing Lina of theft. The statement was circulated among Liszt's other pupils. When Liszt learned about Dory's coup, he was furious and wrote her a sternly worded letter: 'After recent events with the Schmalhausen family, you will understand it if I receive no further visits from you. The whole affair was fomented by you out of sheer malice and continued in the same spirit.'[151] He wrote again a few weeks later to say that he would refuse to see Dory again unless she and Lina were reconciled.[152]

Liszt did not even abandon Lina when she was caught stealing from him: his housekeeper, Pauline Apel, claimed to have 'seen Telltale come into the boudoir, open the drawer, thrust her hand hastily into it, and as quickly again close the drawer. But when she told the Meister what she had seen, he would not listen.'[153]

Very real problems with alcohol, declining health, bouts of depression and female pupils who stole from him or who became involved in unseemly squabbles – worries and incidents such as these cast a pall over Liszt's final years. And it was again Hans von Bülow who summed up the situation: 'Lina Schmalhausen – most edifying!' he fulminated in a letter to Karl Klindworth: 'When I met him at the station, Arthur Friedheim told me about the whole scandal. How sad for our Master's dignity.'[154]

La lugubre gondola

For the first few months following his accident in July 1881 Liszt needed constant help. According to Hans von Bülow, 'His helplessness and physical (and, unfortunately, mental) infirmity are getting worse by the day, so that a real misfortune might befall him if he were left to his own devices.'[155] In Weimar there were enough friends and admirers to take care of him, but who would accompany him on his planned visit to Rome in the autumn? Cosima Wagner, who was particularly concerned about her father at this time, decided that Daniela should go with him. Liszt was fond of his granddaughter and the idea appealed to him. Daniela, now twenty-one, agreed after initially hesitating. Adelheid von Schorn expected them to arrive in Rome in the middle of October. 'I was shocked when I saw him,' she later recalled. 'He looked pale and bloated. His hands and feet were swollen and he had put on a lot of weight.' In total Liszt spent some three and a half months in Rome, occupying two rooms with a balcony at the Hotel Alibert, which was only a stone's throw away from Carolyne's apartment in the Via del Babuino. 'Mostly he sat at his desk and worked, often falling asleep as he sat there,' Adelheid von Schorn recalled. 'In the evening he generally played cards – but sometimes he gave us the pleasure of sitting down at the piano and playing.'[156]

On 22 October 1881 Liszt turned seventy. Although he did not want any celebrations, the German ambassador in Rome insisted on organizing a gala concert at the Palazzo Caffarelli. Admittedly, Liszt was pleased at the friendly gesture but would none the less have preferred to spend the day alone. More than a hundred telegrams and letters arrived at his hotel that day, congratulating him on his birthday, with the porter continually announcing the arrival of further good wishes. The many messages raised Liszt's spirits, as he wrote to inform Ludwig Bösendorfer in Vienna:

> In order to express this mood, I wrote several pages of music, but no letters. My disinclination to write letters is becoming an illness with me. Would you be kind enough to ask my friends in Vienna to forgive me? I fully expect to live long enough to provide them with better proof of my affection than words.[157]

Liszt's pupil Arthur Friedheim was also staying at the Hotel Alibert and took on the role of private secretary and dealt not only with Liszt's birthday greetings but, as far as possible, with his mentor's other voluminous correspondence.

During his weeks in Rome, Liszt's health improved markedly, enabling him to announce that he would be leaving for Budapest in January 1882, but when Carolyne heard about his plans she sounded the alarm: it was inconceivable to her that in his present condition Liszt should want to exchange the mild Italian climate for freezing temperatures and possibly even snow. But her constant complaints about Budapest and its allegedly terrible academy fell on deaf ears, with the result that she turned for support instead to Liszt's former pupil, Kornél Ábrányi. The journey to Hungary would be harmful to Liszt's health, she insisted, 'but if you wish to hasten his death, then you should allow him to travel to Pest in winter'. In the circumstances, she continued, 'Liszt's journey to Pest and his sojourn in the city would be an act of patriotic suicide.'[158]

However justified Carolyne's worries may have been, her letter was wildly exaggerated, giving Ábrányi the impression that Liszt was close to death. As was only to be expected, the news of the Master's ostensibly precarious state of health spread quickly, and all the major Hungarian newspapers reported as much. Adelheid von Schorn lost no time in going to see the princess: something had to be done to deny the rumours. But Carolyne would hear no such thing: it was she herself, she freely admitted, who had put the rumour into circulation in order to prevent

Liszt from leaving. Liszt was furious at his former partner's unsolicited meddling, but he refused to abandon his plans and left Rome at the end of January 1882.

'I am afraid that your grandfather is again overdoing it,' Hans von Bülow wrote to Daniela on 6 May 1882, 'even though he needs to keep moving for the sake of his health, and the sleep that he enjoys during performances of his works has proved to be an effective tonic.'[159] During the following months, Liszt spent a good eight weeks in Budapest and another eight in Weimar, but otherwise he was constantly on the move, spending longer or shorter periods of time in Vienna, Florence, Venice, Bratislava, Kalocsa, Brussels, Antwerp, Dornburg, Jena, Freiburg im Breisgau, Baden-Baden and Zurich.

By the middle of July we find the septuagenarian Liszt in Bayreuth, which was preparing for the world première of Wagner's new opera, *Parsifal*. As usual, Liszt stayed at Wahnfried and took an active part in family life. He also entertained the Wagners' guests, attended the final rehearsals and played whist in the evening. On the eve of the first performance, Wagner held a banquet for some four hundred guests, describing the event as a 'love-feast'. The courses moved slowly, recalled Carl Lachmund, and when Wagner, who was aware of his father-in-law's aversion to making speeches, noticed that Liszt had got to his feet to stretch his legs, he teased him by asking him to address the multitude. Liszt shook his head in bemusement, whereupon Wagner turned to the other guests and, shrugging his shoulders, exclaimed: 'It is nothing, my ladies and gentlemen.'[160] All laughed. After the next course Wagner rose to his feet and this time spoke at length, praising his artists and addressing Liszt personally. Unfortunately the text of his speech has not survived, but we do know from Lachmund's account that Wagner gave 'deep-felt thanks to his great friend'. Cosima even described his toast as 'wonderful'.

The curtain rose – or, this being Bayreuth, parted down the middle – at four o'clock on the afternoon of 26 July 1882. The mood was somewhat dampened by torrential rain, while Wagner was in a particularly tetchy frame of mind, complaining not only about the many sightseers who lined the route to the theatre but also about many aspects of the performance, as Cosima noted in her diary:

The first act goes more or less according to his wishes, it is just the large amount of 'play acting' he finds displeasing. When, after the second act, there is much noise and calling, R. comes to the balustrade, says that though the applause is very welcome to his artists and to himself, they had agreed, in order not to impinge on the impression, not to take a bow, so that there would be no 'curtain calls'. After our meal R. and I are together in our box! Great emotion overwhelms us. But at the end R. is vexed by the silent audience, which has misunderstood him; he once again addresses it from the gallery, and when the applause then breaks out and there are continual calls, R. appears in front of the curtain and says that he tried to assemble his artists, but they were by now half undressed.[161]

In spite of these vexations, the sixteen performances between then and the end of August were a great artistic and financial success.

Liszt had been in close contact with the Wagners for much of the year, and at the end of August he also attended the wedding celebrations of his granddaughter Blandine and the Italian Count Biagio Gravina. Before returning to Weimar to continue his teaching, he promised to spend a few weeks with the Wagners in Venice, where they were planning to pass the winter. Travelling via Zurich and Milan, he arrived in Venice on 19 November 1882. Cosima and the children collected him from the station, while Wagner waited for his father-in-law at home. The Wagners were staying at the Palazzo Vendramin-Calergi, one of the city's most beautiful buildings from the time of the Italian High Renaissance. Located on the Grand Canal, it included a garden wing – the Ala bianca – that had been built around 1614. Here Wagner and his retinue occupied some fifteen rooms: apart from Wagner and Cosima, there were also four children (Blandine had moved to Sicily following her wedding), Siegfried's tutor Heinrich von Stein, a governess for the girls and several servants. Numerous friends and acquaintances paid court on a regular basis. Wagner had set aside a suite of rooms for Liszt, where the abbé could withdraw and work in peace. As at the Hofgärtnerei and Wahnfried, they met to perform music, read to each other and converse. Liszt reported on his daily routine in a letter to Olga von

Meyendorff: 'For dinner (two o'clock) and supper (eight o'clock) we are nine at table. [...] Some music, but not too much, before or after supper. Somewhat for my sake, the evening usually ends with two or three games of whist.'[162]

Wagner had undoubtedly been looking forward to Liszt's visit, but even on the day of his arrival in Venice, Cosima was already expressing her concern in her diary: 'For all the cordiality on both sides, it is hard to get a conversation going.'[163] Liszt's visit seemed to tax Wagner's strength. Although only sixty-nine, Wagner was seriously ill and often complained about chest spasms that would nowadays be diagnosed as angina pectoris. His curmudgeonly mood led to numerous violent outbursts that not infrequently centred on poor Liszt. Sometimes he was annoyed that his father-in-law was late for supper, on other occasions he took offence at Liszt's piano playing, or else he complained about his alleged lack of humour. More than once Liszt's music was the object of Wagner's criticism. Even the fact that Cosima and her father spoke French was enough to darken Wagner's mood. And so the days went by. On Christmas Eve Wagner booked the Teatro La Fenice for a private function and performed his early Symphony in C major with a local amateur orchestra – the piece had last been heard almost fifty years earlier. At the end of the performance Wagner's friends and all the musicians who were present drank a toast to mark Cosima's forty-fifth birthday. 'Then R. murmurs in my father's ear, "Do you love your daughter?" My father looks startled. "Then sit down at the piano and play." My father does so at once, to everybody's cheering delight.'[164]

From his rooms at the Palazzo Vendramin-Calergi Liszt had a view of the Grand Canal and could occasionally see funeral gondolas shrouded in black glide past through the mists of the lagoon, a disturbingly beautiful sight that inspired him to write *La lugubre gondola*, a moving threnody that recreates the morbid atmosphere of those December days in Venice. The piece, which exists in multiple versions, later acquired a sad notoriety as it appears to anticipate Wagner's death. Indeed, Liszt himself was not entirely blameless in this regard, for he admitted to one of his publishers, 'As if by way of a premonition I wrote this elegy in Venice six weeks before Wagner's death.'[165] It is entirely possible, therefore, that Wagner heard his own funeral music being written.

Liszt left Venice on 13 January 1883. Exactly a month later Wagner suffered a fatal heart attack at the Palazzo Vendramin-Calergi, precipitating a bizarre lament on Cosima's part, the circumstances of which make curious reading even today. Time and again she returned to the body, lying down beside it or on top of it, kissing and stroking it. She even spent a night in bed with the corpse. Elsewhere in the building there were ghostly goings on during the hours and days after Wagner's death. A local doctor, Friedrich Keppler, and the *Parsifal* designer Paul von Joukowsky, helped to embalm the body, while the sculptor Augusto Benvenuti prepared a death mask. Bayreuth's financial administrator, Adolf von Groß, travelled from Bayreuth to arrange the repatriation of the body.

It would have been a simple matter to send a telegram to Budapest, but it appears that no one thought of informing Liszt about Wagner's passing. Twenty-four hours later Liszt still had no idea what had happened in Venice and was sitting at his desk when his publisher Ferdinand Táborszky rushed into his study with the news. 'Nonsense!' was Liszt's initial reaction. 'He'll live all the longer: I'd be the first person to know!' He could not conceive that his own daughter would keep him in the dark. But when he finally realized that Táborszky was telling the truth, he sank back into his chair, stammering: 'Him today, me tomorrow!'[166] Liszt then cabled to Venice and offered his help, but his offer fell on deaf ears. Cosima's daughter Daniela, who was currently keeping a diary, noted on 16 February: 'Grandpa wanted to come and accompany us, but at Mama's wishes we urged him not to.'[167]

Wagner was buried in the garden at Wahnfried on Sunday, 18 February 1883 in a ceremony attended by only close family and friends. Liszt was absent, presumably persona non grata. During the months that followed, he made a number of attempts to contact Cosima, but she thwarted every one of them, living a completely secluded life accessible only to her children. For the 1883 revival of *Parsifal*, everything remained as it was and the twelve performances, planned by Wagner the previous winter, went ahead as scheduled. 'I shan't be coming to Bayreuth this year,' Liszt wrote to his godchild, Franz von Liszt, 'on account of my daughter's venerable seclusion in her sublime mourning.'[168] Cosima's behaviour struck him as disagreeable if not downright embarrassing, so much so, indeed, that he sought refuge in abstract excuses, telling Olga von Meyendorff, for example, that 'Between her [Cosima] and me there are bonds and dates far removed from ordinary relations.'[169] But when Liszt laid aside the mask of self-control, it became clear to what extent he was hurt by Cosima's rejection. 'While he was in Pest, Liszt wanted to visit his daughter in Bayreuth,' Lina Ramann was told by Adelheid von Schorn, 'but she turned down his visit. Liszt was beside himself when he received her letter – I'd never seen him like it. After that he consumed more cognac than before, and there were times when it was almost impossible to get along with him.'[170]

When the Bayreuth Festival reopened its doors in 1884, Cosima played a more active role, while adopting a decidedly shrewd approach to her new self-appointed mission in life. After all, she knew that her only claim to assume such a task was the fact that she had been married to Wagner but, making a virtue of necessity, she invested her widow-hood with an element of pathos and ensured that the love and respect formerly felt for the 'Meister' were now transferred to her as the 'Meisterin'. She arranged for a booth to be erected at the side of the stage and surrounded it with black curtains. There she would sit, score in hand, and follow the action onstage through a slit. She did not speak and permitted no one to speak to her but wrote down her corrections, suggestions and orders on slips of paper that were then passed on by her assistants.

Liszt returned to Bayreuth that summer. In advance of his visit Daniela was given the disagreeable task of making it clear to her grand-father that he would be unable to stay at Wahnfried. Until then he had invariably stayed at the family villa, but there was ostensibly no longer room for him there. Daniela recommended a furnished apartment on the ground floor of a house owned by the regional forestry commis-sioner, Ludwig Frölich, and his wife Emma in the nearby Siegfriedstraße (now the Wahnfriedstraße). Liszt spent four weeks in Bayreuth. 'Half the days are taken up by rehearsals,' he told Olga von Meyendorff. 'I have attended all those for orchestra. A stand with a lamp, and the score, has been set up for me in the first row of seats.'[171]

Liszt's grandson and Blandine's son, Daniel Ollivier, also attended that summer's Bayreuth Festival. 'His grandfather, whom he had not seen since 1878, seemed to him to be tired and fatter, but still extremely interesting,' Marie-Thérèse Ollivier informed Carolyne von Sayn-Wittgenstein.

> He hasn't met his aunt [Cosima], although on one occasion he happened to catch a glimpse of her emaciated figure in the garden. It also seems that she met Liszt in the corridors of the theatre. He addressed a few words to her but she reacted with only a ghostly silence. 'Non è finita la commedia [The show must go on]!'

It is all too easy to imagine the grotesque situation, with Liszt chancing upon his daughter and attempting to speak to her, only for her to walk straight past him in silence. Practically everything was grotesque – and unworthy of Wagner – during these months of high summer, with Cosima hiding in her onstage booth and issuing commands, while her own father sat in the auditorium like some subordinate assistant director not taken particularly seriously and even ridiculed. According to Marie-Thérèse Ollivier, 'To the Holy Family's immense indignation, Liszt – either from tiredness or boredom – often fell asleep during the culminating apotheosis of each of the acts. This is what is known as spiritual withdrawal.'[172]

Liszt occasionally met his grandchildren, being especially keen to support Daniela. Now twenty-four years old, the oldest of Cosima's daughters had to stand in for her mother on official occasions, doing the honours at the elegant receptions that were held at Wahnfried as usual, while her mother generally sulked in her rooms on the top floor of the villa. As a man of the world, Liszt was able to provide his granddaughter with words of advice, including the appropriate way to serve food:

> Once a week you should serve tea and the usual pastries to guests of your choice at Wahnfried; then, at around ten, sandwiches with red

and white wine – no champagne – and finally ice ad libitum. And since we are fortunate to be in Bavaria, you can also serve beer for afternoon tea.[173]

The Poodle Begs

Liszt began 1886 with a New Year's Day prediction: 'You'll see that this will be an unlucky year for me because it starts on a Friday.'[174] August Göllerich did not attach much importance to his mentor's prognostication, for on the one hand he knew how superstitious Liszt was, while on the other hand the seventy-four-year-old composer was in remarkably good shape. He had been back in Rome since the end of October, and the mild Italian climate had left him visibly refreshed. His old friend Malwida von Meysenbug wrote to Daniela to report that he was 'looking remarkably well: it's extraordinary how well he has recovered, especially when I think of the time when you were here with him'.[175] When Liszt left the Eternal City on 21 January, no one imagined that he would never see Rome again. He travelled via Florence and Venice to Budapest, where he remained until the middle of March. Again it was to prove his last stay in the city. Indeed, his itinerary in 1886 resembled nothing so much as a farewell tour. He visited Vienna, Liège and Antwerp, was a frequent guest in Paris and for the first time since 1841 crossed the English Channel, one of his English pupils, Walter Bache, having long been urging him to return to Britain. Not entirely sure what to expect there, he thought it wise to make clear his limitations: 'It seems to be the intention to put me in front of a piano in London. Publicly I cannot agree to this since my fingers, now seventy-five years old, are no longer fit for purpose, and Bülow, Saint-Saëns, Rubinstein and you, dear Bache, can play my compositions much better than little old me, decrepit as I now am.'[176]

Liszt arrived in London on 3 April 1886 to find that Bache had arranged a veritable Liszt Festival for him. The full-length *Legend of St Elizabeth* was performed twice and there were also piano recitals and orchestral concerts. On 7 April Liszt was received at Windsor Castle. He had last seen Queen Victoria in Bonn in August 1845, and after such a period of time both parties were keen to be reacquainted. Victoria noted in her diary afterwards:

> After luncheon we went to the Red Drawing-room, where we saw the celebrated abbé Liszt, whom I had not seen for 43 years [*sic*], and who, from having then been a very wild phantastic looking man, was now a quiet benevolent looking old Priest, with long white hair, and scarcely any teeth. We asked him to play, which he did, several of his own compositions. He played beautifully.[177]

Liszt also performed on a number of other occasions, notably at a farewell banquet at Westwood House on 18 April. He thanked his English friends by playing piano works by Beethoven, Weber, Cramer and Bach as well as his own Schubert-based *Soirées de Vienne*. All in all, the London festival was a triumphant success.

By the end of April we find Liszt in Paris, where the *Legend of St Elizabeth* was performed in his presence at the Trocadéro. When the final note had died away, the 7,000-strong audience began to cheer. Liszt's triumphs on the Thames and on the Seine proved that even in old age he was still capable of casting a spell on people and bringing happiness to them through his music. He was regarded as the greatest pianist of his age and was loved and idolized all over the world. The previous year an American concert promoter had presented himself and offered him the fabulous sum of two million marks for a tour of the United States. Apparently, Liszt would have had to play only a single piece. But he found the offer risible: 'What am I supposed to do with two million marks at the age of seventy-four? Am I expected to play *Erlkönig* three hundred times in America? An old poodle no longer sits on its hindquarters and begs.'[178] He had already bade an inner farewell to piano playing. 'If only my tiresome piano playing were finally over!' he complained to his biographer, Lina Ramann. 'It has long since become a form of animal cruelty for me. And so Amen to that!'[179]

Perhaps recent events had fuelled his amour-propre and filled him with pride, or perhaps the wounds that Cosima had dealt him through her behaviour following Wagner's death had not yet healed, but Liszt was determined to give Bayreuth a wide berth that summer and felt absolutely no desire to meet his family. He told his pupil August Göllerich: 'No, this time I'm not going there, I'm tired of being their lapdog!'[180] Unfortunately things worked out differently.

Cosima turned up unannounced in Weimar on 18 May 1886. Liszt had not seen his daughter since their ghostly encounter in Bayreuth in the summer of 1884, an encounter that could hardly be described as a meeting. But now Cosima begged her father to come to Bayreuth, where his granddaughter Daniela would be getting married that summer. She hoped Liszt could be the guest of honour, and he could remain in the town until the official opening of the festival. And so it went on. It is entirely possible that Daniela was genuinely looking forward to seeing her grandfather in Bayreuth, but it is no less true that Cosima was calculating on being able to use her father's reputation to drum up publicity for the festival. After all, she reckoned, he had managed to fill vast halls in London and Paris – why not also the Bayreuth Festspielhaus? The programme that summer was to include not only further performances of *Parsifal* but also – for the first time – *Tristan und Isolde*. This last-named work represented a serious risk, and it was doubtful if sufficient tickets would be sold, so Cosima needed all the publicity she could get. Flying in the face of Carolyne's explicit wishes, the 'poodle' consented to attend: 'Liszt is doing surprisingly well considering his promise to attend the performances in Bay[reuth], a promise that left me beside myself with fury as it is tantamount to tempting fate!'[181]

The Last Journey

Bayreuth was in a festive mood when Liszt arrived in the town on 1 July 1886, although the excitement was directed less at him than at his twenty-five-year-old granddaughter Daniela von Bülow and her fiancé Henry Thode, who was her elder by three years. It went without saying that the wedding of a Wagner was a social event of the first order in Bayreuth, and the preparations were correspondingly complex. Cosima in particular had her hands full, planning not only the family celebrations but also the annual festival. 'Liszt arrived,' the *Tristan* conductor, Felix Mottl, noted in his diary that Thursday. 'Frau Wagner after the rehearsal. In tears! Can't control herself. Hugs me! Went really well! In the evening Liszt. – Frau W[agner]: "Even one's dearest concern strikes one as ridiculous if it is unconnected with the festival!"'[182] Did Cosima really see her father as a ridiculous irrelevance? It is entirely possible. Certainly, she seems to have regarded his visit with mixed feelings, for although she and her children set great store by their famous kinsman's presence in the town, they were unwilling or unable to accommodate the old man within their own four walls. But perhaps he too was relieved not to have to stay with the other wedding guests at Wahnfried. Whatever the answer, he again put up at the Frölichs in the nearby Siegfriedstraße. 'Madame la Conseillère des Forêts', as he addressed his landlady with all due courtesy, had prepared rooms for him on the ground floor. There he could be on his own and enjoy some peace and quiet.

The civil ceremony took place at Wahnfried on 3 July. 'Everything passed off well in Bayreuth,' Liszt reported to Carolyne a few days later.

> On Saturday evening, following the signing of the marriage contract, there was a *ricevimento* in Wahnfried for more than eighty guests. The mayor, who is a family friend, gave a brief but highly fitting speech: the local dignitaries and the out-of-town artists, singers and instrumentalists who are already working on the preparations for *Parsifal* made up the guest list and found ample to fortify themselves at an excellent buffet with plenty of cold dishes.[183]

The church service followed the next morning. The Protestant church was filled with wedding guests and countless onlookers. Afterwards the bride's mother had invited around thirty guests to lunch in the Festspielhaus restaurant. Among those accorded this honour was the conductor Felix Weingartner:

> Frau Wagner was dressed for it as usual, in a long flowing widow's robe, but for that occasion it was not black, but a dull grey. A kind of subdued joy temporarily lightened her deep mourning. She was a

woman who understood to perfection how to be impressive. All those present including myself admired her taste in having selected that dress which, although essentially a widow's garment, was yet perfectly suitable to a wedding; the way she bore herself was also admirable.[184]

Only Daniela's father, Hans von Bülow, was absent: 'Everyone knows that I cannot attend the wedding in Bayreuth!!!' he mocked. 'May God give the members of the third generation less grief in their domestic lives!'[185]

Cosima Wagner hoped her father would remain in Bayreuth until the festival opened on 23 July, since his presence, she calculated, would grant the preparations a patent of nobility and provide something of a tourist attraction in the town as it filled with visitors. But Liszt had other plans, and on the day after Daniela's wedding he left for Luxembourg, where the Hungarian painter Mihály Munkácsy and his wife Cécile had invited him to spend a few days at their castle at Colpach. Although Liszt had promised to return for the opening of the 1886 Bayreuth Festival, Cosima reacted angrily, her brief conversation on the subject being recorded by Felix Mottl: 'Frau Wagner says to Daniela, whom Bülow will be seeing: "My father's departure annoys me. I hope your own father will be a source of greater pleasure." "That's hardly likely," says Daniela.'[186]

Travelling by train, Liszt arrived in Luxembourg on the evening of 5 July 1886 and was collected from the station by his pupil Bernhard Stavenhagen.[187] After a brief delay during which the station manager presented his illustrious guest with a floral bouquet and served refreshments in the waiting room, Liszt continued on his way to Colpach. This final part of the journey was particularly difficult since Liszt and Stavenhagen first had to travel by train to Arlon in Belgium and then make their way by coach to their final destination. The comparatively short distance of thirty miles took a good five hours to complete. But Liszt was able to rest when he reached the Munkácsys' castle. During the mornings he and Stavenhagen dealt with the inevitable correspondence, after which he played whist or went for walks in the surrounding park.

But he also caught a bad cold in Colpach, reporting on it to Olga von Meyendorff in a letter dated 17 July:

> To my physical condition, already so pleasant, has now been added these five days a most violent cough which plagues me day and night. To comfort me, the doctor says that this type of cough is very tenacious. So far, neither cough medicine nor infusions, nor mustard plasters, nor foot-baths have rid me of it.[188]

In short, Liszt was already ill when he attended a concert in his honour at the Luxembourg Casino on the evening of 19 July. Cécile Munkácsy had asked her guest to play a number of piano pieces after the official part of the programme was over. He agreed even though his chill was causing him a lot of difficulties. The large audience was not a little surprised when, after the final orchestral work, a grand piano was rolled on to the stage and Liszt sat down at it. He played his first *Liebestraum*, a Chopin arrangement and the sixth of his *Soirées de Vienne*. This brief appearance was to be Liszt's farewell to the piano. After that he no longer performed in public. One eyewitness reports that he was not well and that his 'audience sat around him in a reverential circle, captivated by the spell of his playing. In order to counter the artist's difficulty in breathing, Frau Munkácsy from time to time held a handkerchief soaked in a strong perfume in front of his face.'[189] He was enthusiastically acclaimed. The next morning Liszt and Stavenhagen set out for Bayreuth via Frankfurt. The Munkácsys had urged him not to travel but to wait until his cold was cured. But Liszt refused, saying that he had promised his daughter that he would go and that he had to keep his word. To make matters worse a carriage window was left open during the night-time journey – a fellow traveller had insisted on it – and Liszt's cough grew steadily worse. By the time that he arrived in Bayreuth on 21 July 1886, he was already gravely ill.

Danse macabre

The events that unfolded in Bayreuth over the next two weeks were undignified in the extreme. They amounted to a tragedy, a bizarre and morbidly grotesque dance of death that even today leaves us shaken and profoundly moved. We are well informed about these terrible events thanks to various reliable sources that include the memoirs of Felix Weingartner, the diaries of Felix Mottl, letters written by the Wagner family and other documents that allow us to reconstruct Liszt's final days in painful detail. The most important source is undoubtedly the diary of Liszt's pupil Lina Schmalhausen, which has only recently become available.[190] For the biographer, such a find is invaluable. The diary that Lina Schmalhausen kept between 22 July and 3 August 1886 revolves around a single theme and its countless variants: Liszt's long and painful death. Even so, we need to adopt a critical stance when dealing with this diary, since Lina levels such serious reproaches and accusations against the people in Liszt's immediate entourage – above all the members of the Wagner family – that we must begin by questioning the document's reliability.

As we have already noted, Lina Schmalhausen was a controversial figure in Liszt's inner circle, and the more she found herself excluded from it, the more she kept a watchful and suspicious eye on the composer. In her letters to friends and acquaintances, she not infrequently paints a portrait of Liszt as a lonely man ill treated by the heartless and uncomprehending people around him. The reasons for this seem obvious: her own star was to shine all the more brightly as that of Liszt's one true confidante. To take a single example: Liszt marked his seventy-fourth birthday in Innsbruck on 22 October 1885. Among those present on that occasion were not only Lina Schmalhausen but also three of Liszt's other pupils, Bernhard Stavenhagen, István Thomán and Conrad Ansorge. In short, Liszt was by no means alone, quite apart from the fact that his presence in the town could not be kept a secret, with the local male-voice choir even serenading the composer. Even so, the accounts of these birthday celebrations differ considerably from one another. In a letter to his colleague August Göllerich, Conrad Ansorge noted that

> You're bound to find it interesting to hear what Fräulein Schmalhausen had to say in a letter to Fräulein Stahr. She wrote – and I am quoting literally – that 'The Master spent his birthday more or less on his

own in Innsbruck without any congratulations (!). I'd been to see the music committee and got them to serenade him in the evening. The Master felt extremely relaxed in Innsbruck & remained there for 5 days. Later we were joined by Stavenhagen, Ansorge & Thomán, who had coming looking for the Master.' (sic!) In fact she and I bought presents together for the Master's birthday, and in the evening, during the serenade, Stavenhagen & I took the Master outside to talk to the singers. She wrote this 3 or 4 days later from Rome; so it can't have been forgetfulness, since too short a period of time had elapsed (before she wrote her letter).[191]

Lina was evidently jealous of Stavenhagen and the others, hence her decision to draw a discreet veil over their presence. Her letter's recipients, Anna and Helene Stahr, were to form the impression that only the faithful Lina was looking after poor Liszt. What light does this throw on her diary? We certainly need to tread carefully whenever Liszt's other pupils are mentioned for they are clearly described in consciously negative terms. But in spite of this her account of the events surrounding Liszt's death has a ring of truth to it, not least because it can be confirmed by other sources. Let us start our search on 22 July 1886.

The day in question was a Thursday. That morning Lina went to see Liszt at the Frölichs, where he had again taken rooms. She was shocked when she saw him: 'The Master looked as if he were suffering a great deal and coughed terribly.'[192] Lina, August Göllerich and Liszt's manservant Mihály ('Miska') Kreiner saw to the patient's needs, kept him company while he played whist – his favourite card game – and read to him. But they had to keep breaking off 'because the Master continually coughed, and his whole body shook violently. His head became blood-red and he probably spat out four handkerchiefs of phlegm during two hours.'[193]

Once a day – generally first thing in the morning – Cosima Wagner called on her ailing father and remained for about an hour, drinking coffee. He initially took his meals with the Wagners at Wahnfried, but when his condition continued to deteriorate, Cosima sent round food to the Frölichs. Since Liszt was suffering from problems with his teeth and gums, he was unable to eat the veal fillets, cutlets and steaks that Cosima provided. Mostly, he poked at his food with a fork and ate a few mouthfuls of rice. He had in any case very little appetite. 'If only I had fallen ill somewhere else,' he is said to have exclaimed in his despair, 'but to have to be ill right here, amid all this clamour, is really too stupid.'[194] He attended the opening night of *Parsifal* on 23 July and two days later, this time accompanied by Weingartner, was present at the first performance of *Tristan und Isolde*. Throughout the entire evening he held a handkerchief in front of his mouth in an attempt to stifle his coughing.

Even though he was gravely ill, Liszt continued to receive visitors – too many, we may say with hindsight. And they all insisted on talking to him, which was hardly conducive to his recovery. Even now, etiquette was uncommonly important to him, as Weingartner recalled:

> He was lying in an armchair and had a thick blanket over his knees. He was freezing in spite of the July heat. When the visit of a countess was announced, he snatched the blanket away and rose to his feet. 'But Master, don't get up!' I called out in some concern and seized his feverishly hot hands. But he refused my advice and quickly changed his comfortable lounge suit for his cassock and received his visitor with all his innate royal gallantry.[195]

On 25 July Cosima sent her own doctor, Carl Landgraf, to examine Liszt, and afterwards Lina Schmalhausen stopped him in the hallway. How was the Master? And what could be done for him? Landgraf sought to reassure her, telling her that there was as yet no danger. 'The doctor left, and I had a distasteful feeling about him; he seemed to me to be an unscrupulous old dandy who did not understand the Master's illness.' When she returned to the salon, Liszt said to her: 'Lina, I am approaching my end. The doctor doesn't understand me. I have no confidence in him. He always says it's already getting better. My God, then I should feel cured already, but I feel that every day I am getting worse.' Lina tried to reassure him: he should receive fewer visitors and look after himself, otherwise he would contract pneumonia, prompting Liszt to say: 'I thought that I had already had it for a long time.'[196]

The Wagners were evidently unaware of quite how ill Liszt was. But for Cosima his illness could not have come at a worse time since the festival had opened the previous week and everything now revolved around Wagner. Whereas Cosima had previously begged her father to attend the performances in Bayreuth, he was now simply a nuisance. Although she continued to visit him every morning and although his grandchildren, too, occasionally looked in on him, that was all. When Miska turned up at Wahnfried for the broth that the doctor had ordered for his patient, he was turned away with the words that broth would only be served twice a week.[197]

Felix Mottl's diary entry for 27 July 1886 reads: 'Tremendous fuss. Liszt ill.'[198] The previous evening his condition had worsened perceptibly and there could no longer be any doubt that his cold had turned to pneumonia. With that his fate seemed sealed, for such an illness in a man who would soon be seventy-five was essentially incurable. Penicillin would have helped, but this was not developed until 1938. Cosima turned up at the Frölichs' house as usual that morning. Lina left the room, but without Liszt's noticing, and the affectionate remarks that he continued to address to her were heard, instead, by Cosima, who was appropriately embarrassed. The relationship between her elderly father and a young woman who could have been his granddaughter struck her as unseemly, and when she left, she walked straight past Lina without saying a word. Instead, she informed Miska that Liszt was to receive no more visitors, and that included Lina Schmalhausen and Liszt's other pupils. Her intervention was to prove fatal, since she was now too preoccupied with the festival to be able to care for a patient as sick as her father. And yet there was no lack of people eager to help. Adelheid von Schorn, too, offered to look after Liszt, but Cosima declined her offer, signalling her determination 'to assume sole responsibility for her father's care, together with her daughters'.[199]

Lina and Miska happened to meet Emma Frölich in the street on 29 July. Liszt's landlady was furious and complained that Cosima had had a bed set up in an adjoining room in order to spend the nights there. She had even carried her own linen across the road but, Frau Frölich went on, it was all an empty show designed to impress the neighbours. In any case, Cosima never arrived until midnight, and she had no idea how her father was feeling since she always locked her bedroom door. 'Yes, I believe that as well,' Lina reports Frau Frölich saying. 'They would be content; they are heartless toward the old gentleman. I can't sleep at night. My bedroom is above that of the old gentleman, and his moaning and rattling cuts me to the quick, and I don't even know him. Last night he groaned terribly.'[200]

The situation did not improve in the course of the day. It is unclear if Eva and Isolde were hopelessly out of their depth or whether they simply had no desire to look after their grandfather, but they restricted themselves to quietening him down. Lina had slipped into the house and hidden in an adjacent room, from where she heard Liszt asking to get out of bed. Eva – 'this monster of a grandchild' – answered in a cutting tone:

'Grandpapa, I beg you, don't be so *childish* as to want to get up in your condition. I don't understand you.' The Master: 'But at least until my bed is made. You can't believe how sore I am.' Eva in a mocking tone: 'Just wait until Mama arrives. She will tell you what you have to do.'[201]

Meanwhile, the Bayreuth Festival was going ahead as usual, which Lina Schmalhausen found hard to fathom: 'The Wagners today were attending a performance of *Parsifal*. There they were moved by a puppet theatre, while the living Amfortas was here, struggling with death on his sickbed.'[202]

Initially it seemed as if Liszt would have a restful night on 30/31 July. Lina had found a place to conceal herself in the garden, from where she had a clear view of his ground-floor room. Carl Landgraf arrived at around 23:30, followed by Cosima Wagner a good thirty minutes later. She and the doctor spoke briefly, after which she went to bed and put out the light, without looking in on her father. The doctor, too, went home. Liszt's breathing was laboured. Miska sat in an armchair beside him, dozing. Then, at two in the morning, disaster struck. Liszt suddenly shouted: 'Air! Air!' He was suffocating and in unspeakable pain. This attack lasted half an hour, Liszt's screams and groans being audible throughout the neighbourhood. He finally collapsed and sank into a coma. Only now did Cosima send for Landgraf. When the latter finally arrived ninety minutes later, he thought Liszt was already dead but then administered 'Hoffmann's drops' – a mixture of alcohol and ether – so that Liszt recovered consciousness. His death throes continued.

Cosima Wagner now realized that caring for a sick patient was beyond her, and so early on the morning of 31 July – literally at the eleventh hour – she engaged the services of a nurse, whose task was to make the dying man as comfortable as possible. 'The Master has fallen ill with pneumonia, which is following its usual course,' Liszt's servant Mihály Kreiner wrote in a matter-of-fact tone to Alexander Wilhelm Gottschalg, by which he meant that Liszt's condition was incurable and that they should say their goodbyes.[203] Liszt's children and a few close friends such as Anna and Helene Stahr were allowed to visit him one last time. 'He really is dying,' wrote Mottl in his diary.

> A sick lion! Magnificent with his white hair against the red upholstery. With him again this afternoon. Very weak & no strength. Groaning a lot. 'Poor, dear Master! Est-ce que vous êtes fatigué?' Fr. Wagner asked him. 'Je ne sais pas!' were the last words I heard him speak.[204]

Carl Landgraf returned in the early evening, this time accompanied by Richard Fleischer, a well-known professor of medicine from Erlangen. Together they took Liszt's pulse, while the Wagners' factotum, Bernhard Schnappauf, tried to relieve the patient's suffering by applying compresses to his calves and chest. There was nothing more they could do.

> Daniela, Isolde, Eva, and Siegfried now left. Siegfried went over to Wahnfried and sat on an upstairs windowsill and read. (This child had the heart to sit quietly upon a windowsill pursuing his novel while his grandfather was in the throes of death.) Around 8:30 P.M. a cozy dinner was offered at Wahnfried. Stavenhagen was invited to join them.[205]

Lina Schmalhausen was still at her post when at around eleven o'clock Liszt was given two injections in the region of the heart. These may have been camphor, which Schnappauf had obtained from the local chemist. Lina claims to have recognized the characteristic smell through the window, which had been propped open. The consequences were dramatic: Liszt's body rose up violently and was convulsed by violent spasms. At around a quarter past eleven, the groaning suddenly stopped, the doctors leaned over Liszt and confirmed that he was dead.

'Cosima knelt down in front of the bed (from this position I could observe her face). She was completely calm; not the slightest trace of emotion was visible on her marble face,' we read in Lina Schmalhausen's account. 'She continued to kneel in front of the bed for another ten minutes, folded her hands, and prayed. Isolde entered, knelt down in front of the bed, embraced her mother, and went out again.'[206] Lina was initially unsure what to make of all this, especially since no words were exchanged. Neither mother, daughter nor the two doctors spoke. The silence was eerie. Once Isolde and the two doctors had left the room, Cosima lay diagonally across Liszt's lower limbs, then, after a while, went to sit in the chair at the foot of the bed and again folded her hands. She then fell asleep, her head nodding back and forth and up and down. From time to time she would wake up, only to doze off again. When morning came, Lina left the Frölichs' garden since she was afraid of being discovered there. She felt relieved as she thought that Liszt had received a sedative injection and that he had spent the night asleep. Any other interpretation seemed impossible. The thought that Liszt was dead and that Cosima had simply fallen asleep beside her dead father seemed so absurd that she assumed the Master was still alive.

POSTLUDE

'DR. LISZT DIED IN the night,' Weingartner was informed by his Swabian maid on the morning of 1 August. He dressed and made his way to the house of mourning, which was already seething with activity. Bernhard Schnappauf and Miska had draped the room in black and decorated it with flowers. Liszt's body had already been laid on a bier. At its head – significantly – was a bust of Wagner, at its foot a crucifix. Weingartner described the scene: 'His face had fallen in and his hair had been smoothed down – he looked a little old man, and it was hard to recognize in his lifeless body the man he had been so shortly before, the man who had created the "Faust" and the "Dante" symphonies.'[1]

By now Lina Schmalhausen had learnt the news from her landlady. She found it hard to grasp what had happened, since only a few hours earlier she thought that Liszt had fallen into a restful sleep. When she arrived at the house, a Catholic priest was blessing the body. 'Not one of the three granddaughters nor Siegfried shed a single tear. Cold, without the slightest trace of melancholy, they stood around the deathbed.'[2] Cosima had also refused to allow her father – an abbé – to receive the last rites, a decision that the priest found inexplicable.

But the dance of death was not yet over. Since Cosima was unwilling to have her father's body in Wahnfried – she had arranged for an official supper to be held there that evening – the body was simply left at the Frölichs'. According to Schnappauf, 'Frau Fröhlich [sic] expressed her disapproval of the fact that the body was being laid out in her house without so much as a by your leave.'³ Her annoyance increased when a large crowd of onlookers gathered outside the house. Even on his bier Liszt remained a tourist attraction. 'The public now arrived en masse,' Lina noted in her diary. 'The inhabitants of Bayreuth brought along their three- and four-year-old children in their arms. Few of them were sincere in their grief. They were mostly driven by curiosity.'⁴ When the body began to putrefy on account of the high temperature and Isolde became ill with the smell, Frölich finally lost his temper, laying into Schnappauf and ordering him to remove the body forthwith as he and his wife had other tenants and had no wish for an epidemic to break out within their four walls. Unless Liszt's body was taken away, he would call the police. 'I immediately hurried off to find Frau Cosima,' Schnappauf recalled. 'She was still in bed. I told her what had happened and was instructed to transfer the body to Wahnfried once it had been placed in a coffin and the coffin had been sealed.' Cosima dressed quickly and accompanied Schnappauf back to the Frölichs'. Franz Liszt's mortal remains were finally collected in an ordinary handcart. 'Frau Cosima took the feet and I took the head. The coffin was wheeled into Wahnfried through a side entrance and placed on an improvised trestle in the hall, where it was covered in black material taken from the room's existing decor.'⁵

Liszt was buried in Bayreuth's municipal cemetery on Tuesday, 3 August 1886. It would not be inaccurate to describe the funeral as a combination of state occasion and social spectacle. The deceased's closest friends and family members met at Wahnfried at ten in the morning. Liszt's friend of many years' standing, Olga von Meyendorff, fainted and had to be revived with a glass of red wine. A priest again blessed the body, after which the cortège set off for the cemetery headed by a delegation from the volunteer fire brigade followed by an imposing carriage festooned with flowers. After it came the local clergy, three precentors and Miska Kreiner, who carried Liszt's numerous orders on a velvet cushion. Then came the catafalque with its gilded coffin. 'We, his latest pupils and friends, were his pall-bearers,' Weingartner recalled. 'Low clouds hung down, creating a bleak impression, but there was only light rain.'[6] Immediately behind the coffin came the Wagner family – Siegfried Wagner and Henry Thode were on foot, while Cosima Wagner and her daughters rode in a carriage. Behind them walked representatives of the various German courts, the town council, the regional council, the officer corps, the festival artists and thousands of townspeople. Bayreuth was in mourning. According to the local paper, the *Bayreuther Tagblatt*, 'All of the gas lamps were lit and, draped with black crepe, they shed a sombrely muted glow that added to the mood of grief.'[7] Half an hour later the cortège reached the cemetery, where, following the service, the local mayor, Theodor Muncker, and Liszt's old friend, Carl Gille, both gave moving speeches.

A Requiem Mass was held the next day in the town's Catholic church where, at Cosima Wagner's behest, Bruckner, who had been in Bayreuth since 24 July, performed an improvisation on *Parsifal*. 'The church was full of artists,' Lina Ramann noted in her diary. 'They breathed a sigh of relief when he began as they expected something highly artistic and worthy of Liszt. Unfortunately it wasn't to be.' Bruckner's playing was 'monotonous, endless, wearisome. When Liszt's pupils, unable to conceal their dismay, asked him why he had not based his improvisations on a theme from one of Liszt's own compositions, he replied that unfortunately he did not know any – they should have given him one.' To make matters worse, the church choir sang a number of simple occasional compositions, while the rest of the interminable service was made up of nasal chanting by three priests.

It was above all Liszt's many friends and pupils who were dismayed at such a service. Almost as bad was the fact that the Wagner family did not attend. 'A Requiem Mass or a reception for the German crown prince – that was the alternative they faced.'[8] The Wagners showed no other signs of mourning – quite the opposite in fact. According to Weingartner, 'Everything was made to look – as if on purpose – that Franz Liszt's passing was not of sufficient importance to dim the glory of the Festival even temporarily by a veil of mourning.'[9] Nothing was allowed to disrupt Cosima's inscenation of Wagner's legacy, and so life went on as usual in Bayreuth. On the evening of the Requiem Mass she held another of her soirées at Wahnfried. Even her favourite conductor,

Felix Mottl, was repulsed by the spectacle: 'Wahnfried. Food. In the entrance hall there was still the smell of mortality emanating from Liszt's dead body!'[10]

The lack of respect that was shown to Liszt in death proved a rallying call for those contemporaries who were already critical of the Wagner family and of Bayreuth. They wondered why Liszt had been buried in a town where he had never lived and where he had died more or less by chance. The answer was simple: Cosima Wagner wanted it so. Even so, family reasons were secondary. Now in sole charge of the Bayreuth Festival, she regarded the deceased celebrity as a kind of relic or, worse, a trophy. Bayreuth was the epicentre of Wagnerolatry, and she reckoned that Liszt's grave could be effortlessly integrated into the local cult: Liszt was another jewel in Wagner's crown.

In implementing her plan, Cosima skilfully took advantage of a certain confusion concerning her father's final wishes, a confusion to which he himself had contributed. His will of 1861 had failed to mention where he wanted to be buried, and in the years that followed he had made only contradictory remarks on the subject: in 1863 he had expressed the wish to be interred in Rome, whereas three years later he had spoken of Blandine's grave in the Maritime Cemetery at Saint-Tropez. Tivoli and Hungary had also been mentioned. At the end of November 1869, finally, he had written to Carolyne von Sayn-Wittgenstein: 'I want no other resting place for my body than the cemetery that is in use in the place where I die, nor do I want any other church service apart from a silent Mass (not a sung Requiem) in the parish church.'[11]

But Cosima Wagner cannot have known of the existence of this letter. Instead, she appealed to Liszt's manservant Mihály Kreiner, who on the day of Liszt's death had hastened to inform her that his master had always wanted to be buried in the town where he died. But Miska did Liszt a disservice inasmuch as the latter's instructions dated from a time when his circumstances were very different. In November 1869 Cosima and Hans von Bülow had not yet got divorced, and Liszt's relations with his daughter and with Wagner were not yet as fraught as they were to become soon afterwards. Above all, Bayreuth's bizarre cult of Wagner had not yet been initiated. Seventeen years later his exclamation 'If only I had fallen ill somewhere else' suggests that he would not have agreed with the decision to bury him in Bayreuth. But why did he not make other arrangements during the final days of his life? The reason is as banal as it is human: he was simply too physically frail to do so.

During the months that followed there were attempts to spirit Liszt away from Bayreuth. Grand Duke Carl Alexander of Saxe-Weimar wanted his prominent subject to be buried in Weimar, while Carolyne von Sayn-Wittgenstein demanded that his mortal remains be transferred to Hungary. Only the previous year she had expressed her fears that some misfortune might befall her former partner, writing to the theologian Ignaz von Döllinger in her stilted German in October 1885:

> Liszt has arrived in Munich with a recurrence of his illness. At his age and in spite of his strong but exhausted constitution, anything could pose a danger to him. I know no one in Munich who is truly Catholic, and so I am writing to you, dear sir, to ask you to find some pretext to send an intelligent man of the cloth. Enthusiasm for his religious music would be a good excuse.

Carolyne demonstrated positively clairvoyant abilities when she wrote that

> If some misfortune were to befall him, I should like to remind you that in Pest he belongs to the third order of the Franciscans and that he has often expressed the wish to be buried there in the habit of the Franciscan order. [. . .] His wish is to be buried at five in the morning like a poor Franciscan – without pomp and ceremony. I could never forgive myself if this beautiful wish, expressed in the form of his last will and testament, were not to be fulfilled.[12]

This letter was written in October 1885. When Carolyne learnt of Liszt's death the following summer, she suffered a stroke and never left her bed after that. Even so, she continued to feel that it was shameful that a man with whom she had spent nearly forty years of her life should find his final resting place in Bayreuth. When she was shown the Bayreuth newspapers for the period of Liszt's death, her reaction was one of shock and anger:

> Not once is Liszt's illness mentioned, as in a bathing resort where illness and death are hushed up in order to arouse no painful sensitivities among the other bathers. [. . .] Then, the fact that he was a Catholic is kept quiet, or kept dark. Every reader will think that he was buried in this nest of atheists by some free-thinking Protestant clergyman! In the issue of 11 August you can see that she who for three years would not see her own father was staying ten days later in a public house called 'The Gaiety'![13]

'She' was Cosima Wagner. Although Carolyne left no stone unturned in her attempts to have Liszt's remains removed from this 'nest of atheists', she found an obstinate adversary in Cosima, remaining obdurate even when Grand Duke Carl Alexander objected in no uncertain terms to Bayreuth as Liszt's final resting place. Without referring to Carolyne by name, Cosima answered coolly that she was again happy to trust in Miska's statement. This was unequivocal. The battle over Liszt's grave was undoubtedly also a battle between two powerful women. Perhaps this was Cosima's attempt to be avenged on her old adversary and to punish her for all that she had suffered as a young woman.

Carolyne von Sayn-Wittgenstein survived Liszt by only seven months, dying in Rome on 8 March 1887. Her daughter, Marie von Hohenlohe, described her mother's final days:

> The first day she still spoke with a certain animation. I found her very short of breath, her face and hands were badly swollen, but nothing suggested that her end was close. Her doctor gave me to understand that her illness would be long and painful. By the following day she had a very high temperature, which rose rapidly within only a few days. She was not aware that she was dying. Her death was peaceful, she passed away during her sleep at one in the morning without any death throes.[14]

Carolyne von Sayn-Wittgenstein was buried in the Campo Santo Teutonico in Rome. Her death did not leave Cosima unmoved. 'The princess's death left a deep impression on me,' she admitted to Adolf von Groß. 'In life she caused me a lot of pain, but she also awakened great feelings in me & brought me the most unique experiences.'[15] Cosima had won the battle of wills. Carolyne had 'failed utterly', Cosima informed her daughter, Daniela. 'I really believe that her defeat over the transfer of Grandpapa's remains dealt her a blow from which she was unable to recover. She had to submit and with that she died.'[16]

One hundred and thirty years have passed since Liszt's death. What remains is a dazzling picture of a fascinating individual who, coming from the poorest background, conquered the whole of Europe. Liszt was a brilliant pianist, a great composer and a genuine superstar. Crowned heads of state paid court to him, women threw themselves at his feet and others lost their reason. For years at a time Europe was gripped by a highly infectious strain of Lisztomania.

As a person, Liszt was a contradictory character: he was arrogant, vain and possessed of a great talent for drama, earning vast sums of money and living like a lord, while at the same time donating generously to charitable causes. Fundamentally he was a modest man. He was also deeply religious and even entered the minor orders, while never caring a whit for questions of sexual morality. He was a ladies' man whose affairs were the stuff of legend.

How can these opposites be reconciled? The observer sometimes has the feeling that the 'real Liszt' lies hidden behind a whole series of masks. Were the flirtatious goings on of the young snob in Paris in the 1830s not just as much a disguise as the abbé's cassock forty years later? But what if the 'real Liszt' never existed and it was only those apparently irreconcilable opposites that constituted his personality?

Liszt once said: 'In life one must decide whether to conjugate the verb "to have" or the verb "to be".'[17] He clearly opted for the second of these alternatives.

NOTES

Abbreviations (see also Unpublished Sources)

AEM   Archiv des Erzbistums München und Freising
BNF   Bibliothèque nationale de France
BSB   Bayerische Staatsbibliothek München
GSA   Goethe- und Schiller-Archiv, Weimar
NAB   Nationalarchiv der Richard-Wagner-Stiftung, Bayreuth
ÖNB   Österreichische Nationalbibliothek, Vienna
ÖSA   Österreichisches Staatsarchiv, Vienna
SBB   Staatsbibliothek zu Berlin, Preußischer Kulturbesitz
SHB   Katholisches Dompfarramt Sankt Hedwig, Berlin
THA   Thüringisches Hauptstaatsarchiv, Weimar
VMA   Bibliothèque municipale de Versailles

Prologue

1. Klaus Umbach, *Geldschein-Sonate: Das Millionenspiel mit der Klassik* (Frankfurt, 1994), 27–8.
2. Eliza Wille, *Erinnerungen an Richard Wagner: Mit 15 Briefen Richard Wagners* (Zurich, 1982), 64.
3. Nike Wagner, 'Sich in die Unsterblichkeit spielen', *Der Tagesspiegel* (2 January 2011).
4. Richard Wagner, *Sämtliche Briefe*, ed. Gertrud Strobel, Werner Wolf, Werner Breig and others (Leipzig, 1967–2000 and Wiesbaden, 1999–), xi.282 (letter from Richard Wagner to Hans von Bülow, 7 October 1859).
5. Cosima Wagner, *Die Tagebücher*, ed. Martin Gregor-Dellin and Dietrich Mack, 2 vols (Munich and Zurich, 1976–7), ii.166; trans. Geoffrey Skelton as *Cosima Wagner's Diaries*, 2 vols (London, 1978–80), ii.140 (entry of 29 August 1878).
6. Nicholas Kenyon, *Simon Rattle: From Birmingham to Berlin* (London, 2002), 315.

Chapter One · Childhood and Adolescence

1. *Pressburger Zeitung* (22 October 1811), 2.
2. August Heinrich Hoffmann von Fallersleben, *Mein Leben: Aufzeichnungen und Erinnerungen*, 6 vols (Hanover, 1868), i.36.

3. See Ernő Békefi, 'Franz Liszt: Seine Abstammung – seine Familie', in *Franz Liszt: Beiträge von ungarischen Autoren*, ed. Klára Hamburger (Budapest, 1978), 23.

4. Gerhard J. Winkler, 'Adam Liszt: Charakterstudie eines Vaters', *Franz Liszt: Ein Genie aus dem pannonischen Raum*, ed. Wolfgang Gürtler and Susanne Klement (Eisenstadt, 1986), 60–61 (letter from Adam Liszt to Prince Nicholas Esterházy, July 1819).

5. Ibid., 63–4 (letter from Adam Liszt to Prince Nicholas Esterházy, 13 April 1820).

6. *Pressburger Zeitung* (28 November 1820), 1.

7. Carl Czerny, *Erinnerungen aus meinem Leben*, ed. Walter Kolneder (Strasbourg, 1968), 27.

8. Eduard Hanslick, *Geschichte des Concertwesens in Wien* (Vienna, 1869), 223–4.

9. Czerny, *Erinnerungen* (note 7), 28.

10. *Allgemeine musikalische Zeitung* (22 January 1823), cols 52–3.

11. Ibid., col. 53.

12. See Alan Walker, *Franz Liszt: The Virtuoso Years 1811–1847* (London and New York, 1983), 81–5.

13. Czerny, *Erinnerungen* (note 7), 29.

14. ÖSA, StK Wissenschaft, Kunst und Literatur 11-2-16 (letter from Adam Liszt to Klemens Wenzel von Metternich, 4 August 1823).

15. ÖSA, StK Wissenschaft, Kunst und Literatur 11-2-16 (Franz Joseph von Bretfeld's letter of recommendation, 8 August 1823).

16. GSA 59/105,4 (letter from Adam Liszt to Ludwig Hofer, 20 March 1824).

17. See Walker, *Franz Liszt: The Virtuoso Years* (note 12), 92.

18. GSA 59/105,4 (letter from Adam Liszt to Ludwig Hofer, 20 March 1824).

19. Franz Liszt, *Frühe Schriften*, ed. Rainer Kleinertz (Wiesbaden, 2000), 34 ('De la situation des artistes').

20. ÖNB, Autogr. 31/65-4 (letter from Ferdinando Paer to Klemens Wenzel von Metternich, 28 October 1823).

21. GSA 59/105,4 (letter from Adam Liszt to Ludwig Hofer, 20 March 1824).

22. Alphonse Martainville, 'Concert du jeune Liszt', *Le Drapeau Blanc* (9 March 1824).

23. GSA 59/105,4 (letter from Adam Liszt to Ludwig Hofer, 20 March 1824).

24. Serge Gut, *Franz Liszt* (Sinzig, 2009), 23.

25. La Mara, 'Aus Franz Liszts erster Jugend: Ein Schreiben seines Vaters mit Briefen Czernys an ihn', *Die Musik*, v/13 (1905/6), 26 (letter from Carl Czerny to Adam Liszt, 5 November 1824).

26. Ibid., 22 (letter from Carl Czerny to Adam Liszt, 3 April 1824).

27. La Mara, *Klassisches und Romantisches aus der Tonwelt* (Leipzig, 1892), 260 (letter from Adam Liszt to Carl Czerny, 14 August 1825).

28. Ibid., 258 (letter from Adam Liszt to Carl Czerny, 14 August 1825).

29. Ibid., 258–9 (letter from Adam Liszt to Carl Czerny, 14 August 1825).

30. See Nicolas Dufetel and Malou Haine (eds), *Franz Liszt: Un saltimbanque en province* (Lyons, 2007).

31. Detlef Altenburg and Rainer Kleinertz (eds), *Franz Liszt: Tagebuch 1827* (Vienna, 1986), 13.

32. Lina Ramann, *Franz Liszt. Als Künstler und Mensch*, 3 vols (Leipzig 1880–94), i.97.

33. Klára Hamburger (ed.), *Franz Liszt: Briefwechsel mit seiner Mutter* (Eisenstadt, 2000), 41 (letter from Franz Liszt to Anna Liszt, 24 August 1827).

34. La Mara (ed.), *Franz Liszt's Briefe*, 8 vols (Leipzig, 1893–1905), vii.82 (letter from Franz Liszt to Carolyne von Sayn-Wittgenstein, 26 August 1874).

Chapter Two · Rehearsing and Studying

1. Franz Liszt, *Frühe Schriften*, ed. Rainer Kleinertz (Wiesbaden, 2000), 92; trans. Charles Suttoni as *An Artist's Journey: Lettres d'un bachelier ès musique 1835–1841* (Chicago, 1989), 16 (letter from Liszt to George Sand, January 1837).

2. August Göllerich, *Franz Liszt* (Berlin, 1908), 161.
3. La Mara (ed.), *Franz Liszt's Briefe*, 8 vols (Leipzig, 1893–1905), i.4–5 (letter from Liszt to Monsieur de Mancy, 23 December 1829).
4. Alan Walker, *Franz Liszt: The Virtuoso Years 1811–1847* (London and New York, 1983), 134–5.
5. Wilhelm von Lenz, *The Great Piano Virtuosos of Our Time* (New York, 1899), 15–17.
6. Lina Ramann, *Franz Liszt. Als Künstler und Mensch*, 3 vols (Leipzig, 1880–94), i.113.
7. Liszt, *Frühe Schriften* (note 1), 92; Engl. trans., 17.
8. Ramann, *Franz Liszt* (note 6), i.144.
9. Ibid., i.153.
10. See Ralph P. Locke, 'Liszt's Saint-Simonian Adventure', *19th Century Music*, iv (1981), 209–27.
11. David Cairns (ed.), *The Memoirs of Hector Berlioz* (London, 1969), 138.
12. Bronislas Édouard Sydow (ed.), *Correspondance de Frédéric Chopin*, 3 vols (Paris, 1981), ii.93 (letter from Liszt, Chopin and Auguste Franchomme to Ferdinand Hiller, 20 June 1833).
13. Meirion Hughes (ed.), *Liszt's Chopin* (Manchester, 2010), 85.
14. Serge Gut and Jacqueline Bellas (eds), *Franz Liszt – Marie d'Agoult: Correspondance* (Paris, 2001), 448 (letter from Liszt to Marie d'Agoult, 9 December 1839).
15. Heinrich Heine, *Sämtliche Schriften*, ed. Klaus Briegleb, 6 vols (Munich, 1995), i.577.
16. La Mara, *Franz Liszt's Briefe* (note 3), i.7 (letter from Liszt to Pierre Wolff, 2 May 1832).
17. Auguste Boissier, *Liszt pédagogue: Leçons de piano données par Liszt à Mademoiselle Valérie Boissier à Paris en 1832* (Paris, 1993), 56–7 (24 February 1832).
18. Ibid., 46 (14 February 1832).
19. Ibid., 22 (16 January 1832).
20. Béla Bartók, *Essays*, selected and edited by Benjamin Suchoff (Lincoln, NE, and London, 1976), 451–2 ('Liszt's Music and Today's Public').
21. Hans Christian Andersen, *A Poet's Bazaar*, trans. Charles Beckwith, 3 vols (London, 1846), i.50–54.
22. Max Weber, *Economy and Society: An Outline of Interpretive Sociology*, trans. Guenther Roth and Claus Wittich (Berkeley, 1978), 241.
23. Heine, *Sämtliche Schriften* (note 15), v.533–4 ('Lutetia').
24. Robert Bory, 'Diverses lettres inédites de Liszt', *Schweizerisches Jahrbuch für Musikwissenschaft*, iii (1928), 5–25, esp. 12 (letter from Liszt to Valérie Boissier, 31 May 1833).
25. Charles F. Dupêchez (ed.), *Mémoires, souvenirs et journaux de la Comtesse d'Agoult*, 2 vols (Paris, 1990), i.299–300.
26. Ibid., i.67–8.
27. Ibid., i.72–3.
28. Ibid., i.134.
29. Ibid., i.182.
30. Ibid., i.172.
31. Ibid., i.196.
32. Ibid., i.292.
33. Gut and Bellas, *Correspondance* (note 14), 143 (undated letter from Liszt to Marie d'Agoult, [late May or early June 1834]).
34. Ibid., 149 (undated letter from Liszt to Marie d'Agoult, [3 or 10 June 1834]).
35. Ibid., 104 (undated letter from Liszt to Marie d'Agoult, [between January and April 1834]).
36. Dupêchez, *Mémoires* (note 25), i.311–13.
37. Gut and Bellas, *Correspondance* (note 14) 192–3 (undated letter from Liszt to Marie d'Agoult, [15 December 1834]).
38. Ibid., 196 (undated letter from Liszt to Marie d'Agoult, [4 January 1835]).

39. Charles F. Dupêchez (ed.), *Marie de Flavigny, comtesse d'Agoult: Correspondance générale*, 3 vols (Paris, 2003-5), i.267 (letter from Marie d'Agoult to Charles d'Agoult, 26 May 1835).
40. Dupêchez, *Mémoires* (note 25), i.232n.

Chapter Three · Années de pèlerinage

1. Klára Hamburger (ed.), *Franz Liszt: Briefwechsel mit seiner Mutter* (Eisenstadt, 2000), 61 (letter from Franz Liszt to Anna Liszt, 4 June 1835).
2. Charles F. Dupêchez (ed.), *Mémoires, souvenirs et journaux de la Comtesse d'Agoult*, 2 vols (Paris 1990), i.320.
3. Ibid., i.328.
4. Ibid., i.330-31.
5. Hamburger, *Franz Liszt: Briefwechsel mit seiner Mutter* (note 1), 80 (undated letter from Franz Liszt to Anna Liszt, [November(?) 1835]).
6. See Günther Protzies, 'Studien zur Biographie Franz Liszts und zu ausgewählten seiner Klavierwerke in der Zeit der Jahre 1828-1846' (PhD diss., Bochum, 2004), 54.
7. Hamburger, *Franz Liszt: Briefwechsel mit seiner Mutter* (note 1), 88 (letter from Franz Liszt to Anna Liszt, 17 January 1836).
8. Dupêchez, *Mémoires* (note 2), ii.118 (9 June 1837).
9. Hamburger, *Franz Liszt: Briefwechsel mit seiner Mutter* (note 1), 93 (undated letter from Franz Liszt to Anna Liszt, [March 1836]).
10. Serge Gut and Jacqueline Bellas (eds), *Franz Liszt - Marie d'Agoult: Correspondance* (Paris, 2001), 211 (letter from Liszt to Marie d'Agoult, 23 April 1836).
11. Ibid., 218-20 (letter from Liszt to Marie d'Agoult, 29 April 1836).
12. Ibid., 224 (letter from Liszt to Marie d'Agoult, 1 May 1836).
13. Ibid., 227 (letter from Liszt to Marie d'Agoult, 2 May 1836).
14. See Protzies, 'Studien zur Biographie Franz Liszts' (note 6), 190-2.
15. 'Virtuosität gegen Virtuosität oder Liszt gegen Thalberg', *Allgemeine musikalische Zeitung* (15 February 1837), 106-8.
16. Gut and Bellas, *Correspondance* (note 10), 265 (letter from Liszt to Marie d'Agoult, 13 February 1837).
17. Ibid., 276 (letter from Liszt to Marie d'Agoult, 23 February 1837).
18. Ibid., 323-4 (undated letter from Liszt to Marie d'Agoult, [May 1838]).
19. Dupêchez, *Mémoires* (note 2), ii.123 (14/15 June 1837).
20. Ibid., ii.140 (10 August 1837).
21. Ibid., ii.142-3 (20 August 1837).
22. Ibid., ii.147 (9 September 1837).
23. Hamburger, *Franz Liszt: Briefwechsel mit seiner Mutter* (note 1), 114 (undated letter from Franz Liszt to Anna Liszt, [*c*. 22 October 1837]).
24. Ibid., 114 (undated letter from Franz Liszt to Anna Liszt, [*c*. 22 October 1837]).
25. Ibid., 118 (undated letter from Franz Liszt to Anna Liszt, [late November 1837]).
26. Dupêchez, *Mémoires* (note 2), ii.151 (22 October 1837).
27. Ibid., ii.165-6 (after 20 March and before 24 March 1838).
28. Ibid., ii.178-81 (10-19 July 1838).
29. Ibid., ii.252.
30. Ibid., ii.247.
31. Berthold Litzmann (ed.), *Clara Schumann: Ein Künstlerleben*, 3 vols (Leipzig, 1902-8), i.199; trans. Grace E. Hadow as *Clara Schumann: An Artist's Life*, 2 vols (London and Leipzig, 1913), i.149 (diary entries of 12-18 April 1838).
32. Gut and Bellas, *Correspondance* (note 10), 315-16 (letter from Liszt to Marie d'Agoult, 18 April 1838).
33. Ibid., 321-2 (letter from Liszt to Marie d'Agoult, 28 April 1838).
34. Dupêchez, *Mémoires* (note 2), ii.250-1.

35. Ibid., ii.182 ([August 1838]).
36. Ibid., ii.194–5 (3–5 January 1839).
37. Gut and Bellas, *Correspondance* (note 10), 383 (letter from Marie d'Agoult to Liszt, 23 October 1839).

Chapter Four · Living like a Lord

1. La Mara (ed.), *Franz Liszt's Briefe*, 8 vols (Leipzig, 1893–1905), i.25 (letter from Franz Liszt to Cristina Belgiojoso, 4 June 1839).
2. Serge Gut and Jacqueline Bellas (eds), *Franz Liszt – Marie d'Agoult: Correspondance* (Paris, 2001), 740 (letter from Franz Liszt to Marie d'Agoult, 6 January 1841).
3. Charles F. Dupêchez (ed.), *Mémoires, souvenirs et journaux de la Comtesse d'Agoult*, 2 vols (Paris, 1990), ii.13.
4. Marcel Herwegh, *Au printemps des dieux: Correspondance inédite de la Comtesse Marie d'Agoult et du poète Georges Herwegh* (Paris, 1929), 64 (letter from Marie d'Agoult to Georg Herwegh, 24 March 1844).
5. Gut and Bellas, *Correspondance* (note 2), 413 (letter from Marie d'Agoult to Franz Liszt, 19 November 1839).
6. Ibid., 425 (letter from Franz Liszt to Marie d'Agoult, 24 November 1839).
7. Ibid., 754 (letter from Marie d'Agoult to Franz Liszt, 18 January 1841).
8. Ibid., 444 (letter from Franz Liszt to Marie d'Agoult, 6 December 1839).
9. Ibid., 446 (letter from Franz Liszt to Marie d'Agoult, 6 December 1839).
10. Ibid., 409 (letter from Franz Liszt to Marie d'Agoult, 15 November 1839).
11. Ibid., 460 (letter from Franz Liszt to Marie d'Agoult, 19 December 1839).
12. Quoted from Alan Walker, *Franz Liszt: The Virtuoso Years 1811–1847* (London and New York, 1983), 325–6.
13. The caricature is reproduced in Robert Bory, *La vie de Franz Liszt par l'image* (Paris, 1936), 100.
14. Franz von Schober, *Briefe über F. Liszt's Aufenthalt in Ungarn* (Berlin, 1843), 43–4.
15. Gut and Bellas, *Correspondance* (note 2), 484 (letter from Franz Liszt to Marie d'Agoult, 6 January 1840).
16. Ibid., 532 (letter from Franz Liszt to Marie d'Agoult, 22 February 1840).
17. Ibid., 527 (letter from Franz Liszt to Marie d'Agoult, 16 February 1840).
18. Ibid., 533 (letter from Franz Liszt to Marie d'Agoult, 22 February 1840).
19. Ibid., 430 (letter from Marie d'Agoult to Franz Liszt, 27 November 1839).
20. Ibid., 490–1 (letter from Franz Liszt to Marie d'Agoult, 13 January 1840).
21. Ibid., 511 (letter from Franz Liszt to Marie d'Agoult, 4 February 1840).
22. Ibid., 530 (letter from Marie d'Agoult to Franz Liszt, 21 February 1840).
23. Ibid., 542 (letter from Marie d'Agoult to Franz Liszt, 28 February 1840).
24. Ibid., 518 (letter from Marie d'Agoult to Franz Liszt, 10 February 1840).
25. Ibid., 513 (letter from Marie d'Agoult to Franz Liszt, 5 February 1840).
26. Ibid., 560 (letter from Franz Liszt to Marie d'Agoult, 20 March 1840).
27. Berthold Litzmann (ed.), *Clara Schumann: Ein Künstlerleben*, 3 vols (Leipzig, 1902–8), i.416; trans. Grace E. Hadow as *Clara Schumann: An Artist's Life*, 2 vols (London and Leipzig, 1913), i.287 (letter from Robert Schumann to Clara Wieck, 22 March 1840).
28. Ibid., i.419–20; Engl. trans., i.289–90 (letter from Robert Schumann to Clara Wieck, 25 March 1840).
29. Ibid., i.416; Engl. trans., i.288 (letter from Robert Schumann to Clara Wieck, 22 March 1840).
30. Gut and Bellas, *Correspondance* (note 2), 613 (letter from Franz Liszt to Marie d'Agoult, 19 June 1840).
31. Ibid., 757–8 (letter from Franz Liszt to Marie d'Agoult, 21 January 1841).
32. Ibid., 763 (letter from Franz Liszt to Marie d'Agoult, 25 January 1841).

33. See Hans Rudolf Jung (ed.), *Franz Liszt in seinen Briefen* (Berlin, 1987), 78 (letter from Franz Liszt to Franz von Schober, 30 April 1841).

34. Gut and Bellas, *Correspondance* (note 2), 808 (undated letter from Franz Liszt to Marie d'Agoult, [May 1841]).

35. Charles F. Dupêchez (ed.), *Marie de Flavigny, comtesse d'Agoult: Correspondance générale*, 3 vols (Paris, 2003–5), iii.564 (letter from Marie d'Agoult to Charles-Augustin de Sainte-Beuve, 16 August 1841).

36. Dupêchez, *Mémoires* (note 3), ii.254.

37. Gut and Bellas, *Correspondance* (note 2), 848–9 (letter from Marie d'Agoult to Franz Liszt, 10 August 1841).

38. Karl August Varnhagen von Ense, *Tagebücher*, ed. Ludmilla Assing, 15 vols (Berlin, Zurich and Hamburg, 1861–1905, R1972), i.385–6.

39. Adalbert Cohnfeld, 'Aus Berlin', *Abend-Zeitung* (13 April 1842), col. 704.

40. Karl Schorn, *Lebenserinnerungen: Ein Beitrag zur Geschichte des Rheinlands im neunzehnten Jahrhundert*, 2 vols (Bonn, 1898), i.278.

41. Adolf Brennglas [i.e. Adolf Glaßbrenner], 'Franz Liszt in Berlin: Eine Komödie in drei Acten', *Berlin wie es ist und – trinkt*, 2 vols (Leipzig, 1835–50), i/14.13–14.

42. Heinrich Heine, *Sämtliche Schriften*, ed. Klaus Briegleb, 6 vols (Munich, 1995), v.533–4.

43. Ludwig Rellstab, *Franz Liszt: Beurtheilungen, Berichte, Lebensskizze* (Berlin, 1842), 37.

44. Gut and Bellas, *Correspondance* (note 2), 878 (letter from Franz Liszt to Marie d'Agoult, 25 January 1842).

45. See Julius Kapp, *Liszt und die Frauen* (Leipzig, 1911).

46. Dupêchez, *Mémoires* (note 3), ii.333 (letter from Marie d'Agoult to Marie von Czettritz-Neuhaus, 27 August 1846).

47. Gut and Bellas, *Correspondance* (note 2), 1095–6 (undated letter from Marie d'Agoult to Franz Liszt, [9–11 April 1844]).

48. Ibid., 1097 (letter from Franz Liszt to Marie d'Agoult, 11 April 1844).

49. Herwegh, *Au printemps des dieux* (note 4), 75 (letter from Marie d'Agoult to Georg Herwegh, 28 May 1844).

50. Dupêchez, *Mémoires* (note 3), ii.31–2.

51. Ibid., ii.34–5.

52. Gut and Bellas, *Correspondance* (note 2), 1117 (letter from Franz Liszt to Marie d'Agoult, 2 February 1846).

53. Klára Hamburger (ed.), *Franz Liszt: Briefwechsel mit seiner Mutter* (Eisenstadt, 2000), 150–1 (letter from Franz Liszt to Anna Liszt, 9 August 1844).

54. Ibid., 153 (letter from Franz Liszt to Anna Liszt, 26 August 1844).

55. Gut and Bellas, *Correspondance* (note 2), 1099 (undated letter from Franz Liszt to Marie d'Agoult, [April 1844]).

56. Ibid., 1113 (letter from Marie d'Agoult to Franz Liszt, 3 June 1845).

57. Hamburger, *Franz Liszt: Briefwechsel mit seiner Mutter* (note 53), 174–5 (letter from Franz Liszt to Anna Liszt, 3 May 1845).

58. Max von Waldberg (ed.), *Cosima Wagners Briefe an ihre Tochter Daniela von Bülow 1866–1885* (Stuttgart, 1933), 111 (letter from Cosima Wagner to Daniela von Bülow, 10 January 1881).

59. Paul Pretzsch (ed.), *Cosima Wagner und Houston Stewart Chamberlain im Briefwechsel 1888–1908* (Leipzig, 1934), 99 (letter from Cosima Wagner to Houston Stewart Chamberlain, 17 April 1889).

60. NAB (undated letter from Cosima Liszt to Franz Liszt).

61. Hamburger, *Franz Liszt: Briefwechsel mit seiner Mutter* (note 53), 395 (letter from Anna Liszt to Franz Liszt, 27 November 1846).

Chapter Five · Weimar

1. Serge Gut and Jacqueline Bellas (eds), *Franz Liszt – Marie d'Agoult: Correspondance* (Paris, 2001), 1161 (letter from Franz Liszt to Marie d'Agoult, 20 February 1847).
2. For more on Carl Alexander, see Angelika Pöthe, *Carl Alexander: Mäzen in Weimars 'Silberner Zeit'* (Cologne, 1998).
3. Eduard Hanslick, *Geschichte des Concertwesens in Wien* (Vienna, 1869), 348.
4. La Mara (ed.), *Briefwechsel zwischen Franz Liszt und Carl Alexander* (Leipzig, 1909), 8 (letter from Franz Liszt to Carl Alexander, 6 October 1846).
5. Eduard Genast, *Aus Weimars klassischer und nachklassischer Zeit: Erinnerungen eines alten Schauspielers* (Stuttgart, 1919), 269.
6. See Alan Walker, *Franz Liszt: The Weimar Years 1848–1861* (London, 1989), 26–34.
7. Malwida von Meysenbug, *Der Lebensabend einer Idealistin* (Berlin, 1903), 89–90.
8. SBB, Nachl. Sayn-Wittgenstein (letter from Peter Iwanowsky to Carolyne Iwanowska, 20 January 1836).
9. The later documents annulling the marriage are reproduced in Alan Walker and Gabriele Erasmi (eds), *Liszt, Carolyne, and the Vatican: The Story of a Thwarted Marriage* (Stuyvesant, 1991), 2.
10. See Alexander Lungu, *Der in Canon 1103 des Codex Iuris Canonici von 1983 enthaltene Ehenichtigkeitsgrund* (Berlin, 2009), esp. 12–14.
11. SBB, Nachl. Sayn-Wittgenstein (undated letter from the Marquis de la Tigrière to Carolyne von Sayn-Wittgenstein).
12. La Mara, *An der Schwelle des Jenseits: Letzte Erinnerungen an die Fürstin Carolyne Sayn-Wittgenstein* (Leipzig, 1925), 19.
13. Klára Hamburger (ed.), *Franz Liszt: Briefwechsel mit seiner Mutter* (Eisenstadt, 2000), 215 (letter from Franz Liszt to Anna Liszt, 5 September 1847).
14. Ibid., 219 (letter from Franz Liszt to Anna Liszt, 12–14 November 1847).
15. Ibid., 408 (letter from Anna Liszt to Franz Liszt, 9 December 1847).
16. See Hans Rudolf Jung (ed.), *Franz Liszt in seinen Briefen* (Berlin, 1987), 108 (letter from Franz Liszt to Franz von Schober, 22 April 1848).
17. Daniela von Bülow's note is reproduced in Wolfram Huschke, *Franz Liszt: Wirken und Wirkungen in Weimar* (Weimar, 2010), 31.
18. For more on the history of the Altenburg, see Jutta Hecker, *Die Altenburg: Geschichte eines Hauses* (Berlin, 1988); and Walker, *Franz Liszt: The Weimar Years* (note 6), 74–87.
19. La Mara, *An der Schwelle des Jenseits* (note 12), 26.
20. Marie von Bülow (ed.), *Hans von Bülow: Briefe und Schriften*, 8 vols (Leipzig, 1895–1908), i.478 (letter from Franziska von Bülow to Marie Isidore von Bülow, November 1852).
21. GSA 59/191 (letter from Carolyne von Sayn-Wittgenstein to Franz Liszt, 18 September 1856).
22. ÖNB, Autogr. 299/46–51 (undated letter from Pius Richter to Josef Proksch).
23. See Anon., *Staats-Handbuch für das Großherzogthum Sachsen-Weimar-Eisenach 1851* (Weimar, 1851), 39–40.
24. See Anon., *Staats-Handbuch für das Großherzogthum Sachsen-Weimar-Eisenach 1859* (Weimar, 1859), 71–2.
25. Decree of the Lord Chamberlain's Office, 17 December 1851, reproduced in Peter Raabe, *Liszts Leben* (Tutzing, 1968), 104–5.
26. See Alexander Wilhelm Gottschalg, *Franz Liszt in Weimar und seine letzten Lebensjahre* (Berlin, 1910), 54.
27. Hanjo Kesting (ed.), *Franz Liszt – Richard Wagner Briefwechsel* (Frankfurt, 1988), 126–7 (letter from Franz Liszt to Wagner, 2 September 1850).
28. Richard Wagner, *Sämtliche Briefe*, ed. Gertrud Strobel, Werner Wolf, Werner Breig and others (Leipzig, 1967–2000, and Wiesbaden, 1999–), iv.190 (letter from Richard Wagner to Franz Liszt, 20 November 1851).

29. Richard Wagner, *Mein Leben*, ed. Martin Gregor-Dellin (Munich, 1976), 426; trans. Andrew Gray as *My Life*, ed. Mary Whittall (Cambridge, 1983), 413 (rewritten).
30. GSA 59/137,2 ('Großherzogl. Sächs. Kreisgericht zu Weimar betr. einer Anzeige gegen den Hofkapellmeister Dr. Liszt hier wegen Beleidigung 1849/1850').
31. David Cairns (ed.), *The Memoirs of Hector Berlioz* (London, 1969), 411–12.
32. Hamburger, *Franz Liszt: Briefwechsel mit seiner Mutter* (note 13), 231 (undated letter from Franz Liszt to Anna Liszt [February/March 1849]).
33. Adelheid von Schorn, *Zwei Menschenalter: Erinnerungen und Briefe aus Weimar und Rom* (Stuttgart, 1913), 67.
34. Bülow, *Hans von Bülow: Briefe* (note 20), i.235–6 (letter from Hans von Bülow to Franziska von Bülow, 2 September 1850).
35. Wagner, *Sämtliche Briefe* (note 28), viii.204 (letter from Richard Wagner to Hans von Bülow, 29 November 1856).
36. Friedrich von Bernhardi (ed.), *Aus dem Leben Theodor von Bernhardis*, 9 vols (Leipzig, 1893–7), ii.106 ('Unter Nikolaus I. und Friedrich Wilhelm IV.: Briefe und Tagebuchblätter aus den Jahren 1834–1857') (diary entry of 15 November 1851).
37. Schorn, *Zwei Menschenalter* (note 33), 349 (letter from Carolyne von Sayn-Wittgenstein to Adelheid von Schorn, 9 November 1882).
38. Cairns, *Memoirs of Berlioz* (note 31), 484–5.
39. GSA 59/190 (letter from Carolyne von Sayn-Wittgenstein to Franz Liszt, 27 May 1855).
40. GSA 59/189 (letter from Carolyne von Sayn-Wittgenstein to Franz Liszt, 25 July 1853).
41. Peter Cornelius, *Literarische Werke*, ed. Carl Maria Cornelius, Edgar Istel and Adolf Stern, 4 vols (Leipzig 1904–5), i.187–8 (diary entry of 3 December 1854).
42. Bülow, *Hans von Bülow: Briefe* (note 20), i.437 (letter from Hans von Bülow to Franziska von Bülow, 23 May 1852).
43. La Mara (ed.), *Franz Liszt's Briefe*, 8 vols (Leipzig, 1893–1905), iv.58 (letter from Franz Liszt to Carolyne von Sayn-Wittgenstein, 1 February 1851).
44. Ibid., iv.115 (undated letter from Franz Liszt to Carolyne von Sayn-Wittgenstein, [10 May 1851]).
45. Raabe, *Liszts Leben* (note 25), 255 (letter from Carolyne von Sayn-Wittgenstein to Franz Liszt, 11 July 1853, not included in La Mara's edition).
46. GSA 59/191 (letter from Carolyne von Sayn-Wittgenstein to Franz Liszt, 18 September 1856).
47. La Mara, *Franz Liszt's Briefe* (note 43), iv.126 (letter from Franz Liszt to Carolyne von Sayn-Wittgenstein, 22 June 1852).
48. Bernhardi, *Aus dem Leben Theodor von Bernhardis* (note 36), ii.103; Engl. trans. from Adrian Williams, *A Portrait of Liszt* (Oxford, 1990), 278 (emended) (diary entry of 11 November 1851).
49. Ibid., ii.107; Engl. trans., 280 (diary entry of 24 November 1851).
50. Hamburger, *Franz Liszt: Briefwechsel mit seiner Mutter* (note 13), 226 (letter from Franz Liszt to Anna Liszt, 21 September 1848).
51. Daniel Ollivier (ed.), *Correspondance de Liszt et de sa fille Madame Émile Ollivier 1842–1862* (Paris, 1936), 42 (letter from Blandine Liszt to Franz Liszt, February 1850).
52. Ibid., 43–5 (letter from Franz Liszt to Blandine Liszt, 28 February 1850).
53. Hamburger, *Franz Liszt: Briefwechsel mit seiner Mutter* (note 13), 240 (letter from Franz Liszt to Anna Liszt, 5 October 1850).
54. NAB (undated letter from Blandine Liszt to Franz Liszt, [between 18 August and 17 September 1853]).
55. Ollivier, *Correspondance* (note 51), 83 (letter from Blandine Liszt, to Franz Liszt, 3 July 1852).
56. NAB (letter from Cosima Liszt to Franz Liszt, 25 December 1851).
57. NAB (letter from Cosima and Blandine Liszt to Carolyne von Sayn-Wittgenstein, 3 April 1853).
58. BNF (NAF 25191, 383–8): 'Scène de la vie intime' (20 March 1855).

59. Ollivier, *Correspondance* (note 51), 65 (letter from Franz Liszt to Blandine Liszt, 17 January 1851).

60. THA, Akte 449 (report submitted by Moritz Henzschel and dated 14 May 1852).

61. Bernhardi, *Aus dem Leben Theodor von Bernhardis* (note 36), 138 (diary entry of 10 September 1852).

62. Ibid., 139–40.

63. Ibid.

64. Ibid., 142; see also Walker, *Franz Liszt: The Weimar Years* (note 6), 142–3.

65. THA, Akte 450 (letter from Carolyne von Sayn-Wittgenstein to Maria Pawlowna, 6 January 1853).

66. THA, Akte 450 (letter from Nicholas von Sayn-Wittgenstein to Maria Pawlowna, 26 January 1853).

67. THA, Akte 450 (letter from Nicholas von Sayn-Wittgenstein to Apollonius von Maltitz, 17 February 1853).

68. THA, Akte 450 (letter from Christian Bernhard von Watzdorf to Maria Pawlowna, 15 March 1853).

69. THA, Akte 450 (memorandum drafted by Christian Bernhard von Watzdorf, 18 March 1853).

70. THA, Akte 450 (letter from Franz Liszt to Apollonius von Maltitz, 27 March 1853).

71. THA, Akte 450 (letter from Christian Bernhard von Watzdorf to Maria Pawlowna, 14 April 1853).

72. Carl Maria Cornelius, *Peter Cornelius: Der Wort- und Tondichter*, 2 vols (Regensburg, 1925), i.158.

73. GSA 59/189 (letter from Carolyne von Sayn-Wittgenstein to Franz Liszt, 15 July 1853).

74. For more on Agnes Street-Klindworth, see Pauline Pocknell's admirable preface in Pauline Pocknell (ed.), *Franz Liszt and Agnes Street-Klindworth: A Correspondence 1854–1886* (Hillsdale, 2000).

75. See Alfred Stern, 'Georg Klindworth: Ein politischer Geheimagent des neunzehnten Jahrhunderts', *Historische Vierteljahresschrift*, xxv (1931), 430–58.

76. Heinrich Friedjung, *Der Kampf um die Vorherrschaft in Deutschland 1859 bis 1866*, 6th edn, 2 vols (Stuttgart, 1904–5), ii.569–70.

77. Paul Pretzsch (ed.), *Cosima Wagner und Houston Stewart Chamberlain im Briefwechsel 1888–1908* (Leipzig, 1934), 246 (letter from Cosima Wagner to Houston Stewart Chamberlain, 31 October 1891).

78. Max von Waldberg (ed.), *Cosima Wagners Briefe an ihre Tochter Daniela von Bülow 1866–1885* (Stuttgart, 1933), 233 (letter from Cosima Wagner to Daniela von Bülow, 26 October 1881).

79. Wagner, *Mein Leben* (note 29), 516; Engl. trans., 503 (emended).

80. THA, Akte 450 (letter from Nicholas von Sayn-Wittgenstein to Apollonius von Maltitz, 19 December 1853).

81. THA, Akte 451 (letter from Nicholas von Sayn-Wittgenstein to Apollonius von Maltitz, 18 January 1854).

82. THA, Akte 451 (letter from Christian Bernhard von Watzdorf to Maria Pawlowna, 10 March 1854).

83. THA, Akte 451 (letter from Nikolai Tomau to Apollonius von Maltitz, 25 March 1854).

84. Cornelius, *Peter Cornelius: Der Wort- und Tondichter* (note 72), i.157.

85. Schorn, *Zwei Menschenalter* (note 33), 71.

86. Cornelius, *Peter Cornelius: Der Wort- und Tondichter* (note 72), i.157–8.

87. THA, Akte 451 (medical certificate dated 17 November 1854 and signed by Heinrich le Goullon).

88. THA, Akte 452 (letter from Peter von Oldenburg to Maria Pawlowna, 1 July 1855).

89. THA, Akte 452 (letter from Christian Bernhard von Watzdorf to Maria Pawlowna, 2 October 1855).

90. THA, Akte 452 (letter from Marie von Sayn-Wittgenstein to Nicholas von Sayn-Wittgenstein, 28 November 1855).

91. THA, Akte 453 (letter from Nicholas von Sayn-Wittgenstein to Apollonius von Maltitz, 18 January 1856).

92. THA, Akte 453 (memorandum, 14 May 1856).

93. ÖNB, Autogr. 299/46–7 (letter from Pius Richter to Josef Proksch, 28 March 1848).

94. See Walker, *Franz Liszt: The Weimar Years* (note 6), 217.

95. Pocknell, *Franz Liszt and Agnes Street-Klindworth* (note 74), 5 (letter from Franz Liszt to Agnes Street-Klindworth, 11 April 1855).

96. Ibid., 12 (letter from Franz Liszt to Agnes Street-Klindworth, 22 April 1855).

97. Ibid., 36 (letter from Franz Liszt to Agnes Street-Klindworth, 10 June 1855). Pocknell suggests that the 'cabin' was the room that the couple occupied in Düsseldorf.

98. Ibid., 55 (letter from Franz Liszt to Agnes Street-Klindworth, 26 August 1855).

99. GSA 59/190 (letter from Carolyne von Sayn-Wittgenstein to Franz Liszt, 27 May 1855).

100. Pocknell, *Franz Liszt and Agnes Street-Klindworth* (note 74), 5 (letter from Franz Liszt to Agnes Street-Klindworth, 11 April 1855).

101. Hamburger, *Franz Liszt: Briefwechsel mit seiner Mutter* (note 13), 268 (letter from Franz Liszt to Anna Liszt, 13 August 1855).

102. Ibid., 429 (letter from Anna Liszt to Franz Liszt, 18 August 1855).

103. Ibid., 431–2 (letter from Anna Liszt to Franz Liszt, 3 September 1855).

104. Pocknell, *Franz Liszt and Agnes Street-Klindworth* (note 74), 55 (letter from Franz Liszt to Agnes Street-Klindworth, 26 August 1855).

105. La Mara (ed.), *Briefwechsel zwischen Franz Liszt und Hans von Bülow* (Leipzig, 1898), 143 (letter from Franz Liszt to Hans von Bülow, 1 September 1855).

106. Marie von Bülow, *Hans von Bülow in Leben und Wort* (Stuttgart, 1925), 65 (undated letter from Franz Liszt to Franziska von Bülow).

107. Ibid., 67–8 (letter from Hans von Bülow to Franz Liszt, 20 April 1856).

108. SHB (entry in marriage register no. 259/1857).

109. Cosima Wagner, *Die Tagebücher*, ed. Martin Gregor-Dellin and Dietrich Mack, 2 vols (Munich and Zurich, 1976–7), i.28; trans. Geoffrey Skelton as *Cosima Wagner's Diaries*, 2 vols (London, 1978–80), i.33 (entry of 8 January 1869).

110. Bülow, *Hans von Bülow: Briefe* (note 20), iii.107 (letter from Hans von Bülow to Richard Pohl, 17 August 1857).

111. Hans Jürgen Syberberg, *Winifred Wagner und die Geschichte des Hauses Wahnfried 1914–1975* (video interview with Winifred Wagner released by Alexander Verlag of Berlin in 1975 and again in 1995 with ISBN 3-923854-85-4).

112. Berthold Litzmann (ed.), *Clara Schumann: Ein Künstlerleben*, 3 vols (Leipzig, 1902–8), ii.317; trans. Grace E. Hadow as *Clara Schumann: An Artist's Life*, 2 vols (London and Leipzig, 1913), ii.74 (diary entry of 25 May 1854).

113. La Mara, *Franz Liszt's Briefe* (note 43), ii.251 (letter from Franz Liszt to Eduard Liszt, 2 January 1877).

114. Cornelius, *Literarische Werke* (note 41), i.299–300 (undated letter from Peter Cornelius to Carl Cornelius, [late November 1858]).

115. Ibid., i.301 (letter from Peter Cornelius to Susanne Hestermann, 17 December 1858).

116. Ibid., i.304–5 (letter from Peter Cornelius to Carl Cornelius, 19 December 1858).

117. Adelheid von Schorn, *Das nachklassische Weimar unter der Regierungszeit von Karl Alexander und Sophie* (Weimar, 1912), 93.

118. Huschke, *Wirken und Wirkungen in Weimar* (note 17), 267 (letter from Marie zu Hohenlohe-Schillingsfürst to Peter Raabe, 23 August 1918).

119. THA, Akte 456 (letter from Franz Liszt to Carl Alexander, 8 July 1859).

120. THA, Akte 456 (letter from Marie von Sayn-Wittgenstein to Apollonius von Maltitz, 15 July 1859).

121. Hamburger, *Franz Liszt: Briefwechsel mit seiner Mutter* (note 13), 491 (letter from Anna Liszt to Franz Liszt, 11 September 1859).

122. Ibid., 492 (letter from Anna Liszt to Franz Liszt, 18 October 1859).
123. Bülow, *Hans von Bülow: Briefe* (note 20), iii.269 (letter from Hans von Bülow to Felix Draeseke, 8 October 1859).
124. La Mara, *Franz Liszt's Briefe* (note 43), iv.503 (letter from Franz Liszt to Carolyne von Sayn-Wittgenstein, 15 December 1859).
125. Ibid., iv.504 (letter from Franz Liszt to Carolyne von Sayn-Wittgenstein, 15 December 1859).
126. Bülow, *Hans von Bülow: Briefe* (note 20), iii.284 (letter from Hans von Bülow to Joachim Raff, 16 December 1859).
127. NAB (letter from Blandine Liszt to Cosima Wagner, 19 December 1859).
128. Cosima Wagner, *Die Tagebücher* (note 109), i.288–9; Engl. trans., i.274 (entry of 23 September 1870).
129. Ibid., i.386; Engl. trans., i.364 (entry of 8 May 1871).
130. Ibid., ii.679; Engl. trans., ii.611 (entry of 30 January 1881).
131. Cornelius, *Literarische Werke* (note 41), i.438 (letter from Peter Cornelius to Susanne Hestermann, 18 December 1859). 'Mundus vult Schundus' is Liszt's variant of the Latin proverb 'Mundus vult decipi', 'The world wants to be deceived'.

Chapter Six · Rome

1. Howard E. Hugo (ed.), *The Letters of Franz Liszt to Marie zu Sayn-Wittgenstein* (Cambridge, MA, 1953), 122 (letter from Franz Liszt to Marie zu Hohenlohe-Schillingsfürst, 7 April 1860).
2. Pauline Pocknell (ed.), *Franz Liszt and Agnes Street-Klindworth: A Correspondence 1854–1886* (Hillsdale, 2000), 166 (letter from Franz Liszt to Agnes Street-Klindworth, 28 May 1860).
3. Peter Cornelius, *Literarische Werke*, ed. Carl Maria Cornelius, Edgar Istel and Adolf Stern, 4 vols (Leipzig, 1904–5), i.474 (letter from Peter Cornelius to Marie Gärtner, 23 July 1860).
4. Alan Walker, *Franz Liszt: The Weimar Years 1848–1861* (London and New York, 1989), 521–8.
5. THA, Akte 457 (telegram from Franz Liszt to Carl Alexander, 21 October 1860).
6. See Walker, *Franz Liszt: The Weimar Years* (note 4), 528 (letter from Carolyne von Sayn-Wittgenstein to Franz Liszt, 11 January 1861).
7. La Mara, *An der Schwelle des Jenseits: Letzte Erinnerungen an die Fürstin Carolyne von Sayn-Wittgenstein* (Leipzig, 1925), 46.
8. Serge Gut and Jacqueline Bellas (eds), *Franz Liszt – Marie d'Agoult: Correspondance* (Paris, 2001), 1215 (diary entry of 27 May 1861).
9. Ibid., 1216 (diary entry of 31 May 1861).
10. Ibid., 1217 (diary entry of 8 June 1861).
11. Alan Walker, *Franz Liszt: The Final Years 1861–1886* (New York and London, 1997), 29.
12. Cornelius, *Literarische Werke* (note 3), i.629 (letter from Peter Cornelius to Carl Tausig, 6 December 1861).
13. Adelheid von Schorn, *Zwei Menschenalter: Erinnerungen und Briefe aus Weimar und Rom* (Stuttgart, 1913), 82–3.
14. La Mara, *An der Schwelle des Jenseits* (note 7), 48.
15. Richard Voß, *Aus einem phantastischen Leben: Erinnerungen* (Stuttgart, 1922), 89–90.
16. Ibid.
17. For an overview, see Walker, *Franz Liszt: The Final Years* (note 11), 553–4.
18. Schorn, *Zwei Menschenalter* (note 13), 254.
19. See Jesús Martínez de Bujanda (ed.), *Index Librorum Prohibitorum 1600–1966* (Montreal, 2002), 811; see also Hubert Wolf (ed.), *Systematisches Repertorium zur Buchzensur 1814–1917: Indexkongregation* (Paderborn, 2005), 571 and 586.
20. Walker, *Franz Liszt: The Final Years* (note 11), 322–38, esp. 323.

21. Hans Rudolf Jung (ed.), *Franz Liszt in seinen Briefen* (Berlin, 1987), 199–200 (letter from Franz Liszt to Richard Pohl, 18 December 1861).
22. Ferdinand Gregorovius, *Römische Tagebücher*, 2nd edn, ed. Friedrich Althaus (Stuttgart, 1893), 136 (diary entry of 13 April 1862). The identity of Frau von S. is unclear.
23. Marie von Bülow (ed.), *Hans von Bülow: Briefe und Schriften*, 8 vols (Leipzig, 1895–1908), iii.494 (letter from Hans von Bülow to Joachim Raff, 23 September 1862).
24. La Mara (ed.), *Franz Liszt's Briefe*, 8 vols (Leipzig, 1893–1905), ii.32 (letter from Franz Liszt to Eduard Liszt, 19 November 1862).
25. Daniel Ollivier (ed.), *Correspondance de Liszt et de sa fille Madame Émile Ollivier 1842–1862* (Paris, 1936), 294–5 (letter from Blandine Ollivier to Franz Liszt, 25 October 1861).
26. La Mara, *Franz Liszt's Briefe* (note 24), ii.41 (letter from Franz Liszt to Franz Brendel, 18 June 1863).
27. Kurd von Schlözer, *Römische Briefe 1864–1869* (Stuttgart, 1913), 18 (diary entry of 25 March 1864).
28. Pocknell, *Franz Liszt and Agnes Street-Klindworth* (note 2), 217 (letter from Franz Liszt to Agnes Street-Klindworth, 30 August 1863).
29. Schlözer, *Römische Briefe* (note 27), 72 (diary entry of 1 June 1864).
30. Wilhelm von Csapó, 'Aus meinen Erinnerungen', in *Franz Liszt's Briefe an Baron Anton Augusz 1846–1878*, ed. Wilhelm von Csapó (Budapest, 1911), 25–6.
31. Schlözer, *Römische Briefe* (note 27), 72 (diary entry of 1 June 1864).
32. Voß, *Aus einem phantastischen Leben* (note 15), 251.
33. Schlözer, *Römische Briefe* (note 27), 74; Engl. trans. from Adrian Williams, *Portrait of Liszt* (Oxford, 1990), 393–9 (diary entry of 1 June 1864).
34. *Pesti Napló* (30 January 1864), quoted by Desző Legány, 'Liszt in Rom, nach der Presse', *Studia Musicologica Academiae Scientiarum Hungaricae*, xix (1977), 85–107, esp. 98.
35. La Mara, *Franz Liszt's Briefe* (note 24), ii.46 (letter from Franz Liszt to Franz Brendel, 18 July 1863).
36. Adolf Stern (ed.), *Franz Liszts Briefe an Carl Gille* (Leipzig, 1903), 11–12 (letter from Franz Liszt to Carl Gille, 10 September 1863).
37. La Mara, *Franz Liszt's Briefe* (note 24), ii.28 (letter from Franz Liszt to Franz Brendel, 8 November 1862).
38. Schorn, *Zwei Menschenalter* (note 13), 83.
39. Schlözer, *Römische Briefe* (note 27), 187–8 (diary entry of 11 February 1865).
40. Gregorovius, *Römische Tagebücher* (note 22), 177 (diary entry of 27 March 1864).
41. Bülow, *Hans von Bülow: Briefe* (note 23), iv.303 (letter from Hans von Bülow to Richard Pohl, 23 June 1869).
42. La Mara (ed.), *Briefwechsel zwischen Franz Liszt und Carl Alexander* (Leipzig, 1909), 127 (letter from Carl Alexander to Franz Liszt, 8 March 1865).
43. Ibid., 128 (letter from Franz Liszt to Carl Alexander, 31 March 1865). The quotation is from Pascal's *Pensées* of 1670.
44. Gregorovius, *Römische Tagebücher* (note 22), 201 (diary entry of 30 April 1865).
45. Schlözer, *Römische Briefe* (note 27), 211 (diary entry of 25 April 1865).
46. Ibid., 210–11.
47. William Wallace, *Liszt, Wagner and the Princess* (London, 1927), 104.
48. Raphael Molitor, *Vom Sakrament der Weihe: Erwägungen nach dem Pontificale Romanum*, 2 vols (Regensburg, 1938), i.105.
49. Klára Hamburger (ed.), *Franz Liszt: Briefwechsel mit seiner Mutter* (Eisenstadt, 2000), 504 (letter from Anna Liszt to Franz Liszt, 4 May 1865).
50. Richard Wagner, *Das braune Buch: Tagebuchaufzeichnungen 1865 bis 1882*, ed. Joachim Bergfeld (Zurich, 1975), 75; trans. George Bird as *The Diary of Richard Wagner: The Brown Book 1865–1882* (London, 1980), 65 (diary entry of 1 September 1865).
51. La Mara, *Briefwechsel zwischen Franz Liszt und Carl Alexander* (note 42), 132 (letter from Carl Alexander to Franz Liszt, 12 May 1865).

52. Schlözer, *Römische Briefe* (note 27), 211; Engl. trans. from Williams, *Portrait of Liszt* (note 33), 400–1 (diary entry of 25 April 1865).

53. Ibid., 211; Engl. trans., 401 (diary entry of 25 April 1865).

54. Gregorovius, *Römische Tagebücher* (note 22), 313 (diary entry of 26 November 1865).

55. Schlözer, *Römische Briefe* (note 27), 218; Engl. trans. from Williams, *Portrait of Liszt* (note 33), 403 (diary entry of 26 May 1865).

56. Gregorovius, *Römische Tagebücher* (note 22), 320; Engl. trans. from Williams, *Portrait of Liszt* (note 33), 407 (diary entry of 15 February 1866).

57. Ibid., 321–2; Engl. trans., 408 (diary entry of 26 February 1866). The identity of Frau L. is uncertain.

58. Robert Franz [i.e. Olga Janina], *Souvenirs d'une cosaque* (Paris, 1874), 161–2; Engl. trans. from Williams, *Portrait of Liszt* (note 33), 449.

59. Richard Wagner, *Sämtliche Briefe*, ed. Gertrud Strobel, Werner Wolf, Werner Breig and others (Leipzig, 1967–2000, and Wiesbaden, 1999–), xvi.227–9 (letter from Richard Wagner to Hans von Bülow, 9 June 1864).

60. NAB (witness deposition from Anna Mrazek, Munich District Court, 20 May 1914).

61. La Mara, *Franz Liszt's Briefe* (note 24), ii.75 (letter from Franz Liszt to Eduard Liszt, 7 September 1864).

62. Lina Ramann, *Lisztiana: Erinnerungen an Franz Liszt in Tagebuchblättern, Briefen und Dokumenten aus den Jahren 1873–1886/87* (Mainz, 1983), 76.

63. Nicolas Dufetel, 'Liszt et la "propagande wagnérienne": Le projet de deux livres en français sur l'histoire de l'opéra et sur Wagner (1849–1859)', *Acta musicologica*, lxxxii (2010), 263–304, esp. 269.

64. Wagner, *Das braune Buch* (note 50), 88; Engl. trans., 75.

65. Wagner, *Sämtliche Briefe* (note 59), xvi.293 (letter from Richard Wagner to Mathilde Maier, 8 September 1864).

66. Bülow, *Hans von Bülow: Briefe* (note 23), iii.602 (letter from Hans von Bülow to Joachim Raff, 29 September 1864).

67. Wagner, *Das braune Buch* (note 50), 142; Engl. trans., 119.

68. Angelika Pöthe, *Carl Alexander: Mäzen in Weimars 'Silberner Zeit'* (Cologne, 1998), 249–50 (Carl Alexander's diary entry, 30 September 1864).

69. Ibid., 249 (Carl Alexander's diary entry, 29 September 1864).

70. Ibid., 250 (Carl Alexander's diary entry, 1 October 1864).

71. Charles F. Dupêchez, *Marie d'Agoult 1805–1876* (Paris, 1989), 267.

72. Cornelius, *Literarische Werke* (note 3), ii.6 (diary entry of 1 January 1865).

73. Ibid., ii.20 (letter from Peter Cornelius to Carl Hestermann, 17 January 1865).

74. NAB (witness deposition from Anna Mrazek, Munich District Court, 20 May 1914).

75. Bülow, *Hans von Bülow: Briefe* (note 23), iv.24–25 (letter from Hans von Bülow to Carl Gille, 14 April 1865).

76. AEM (baptismal register of St Boniface's Parish Church, Munich).

77. Bülow, *Hans von Bülow: Briefe* (note 23), iv.58 (letter from Hans von Bülow to Carl Gille, 21 August 1865).

78. Wagner, *Das braune Buch* (note 50), 90; Engl. trans., 76 (emended) (diary entry of 24 October 1865).

79. Ibid., 75; Engl. trans., 65 (emended) (diary entry of 1 September 1865).

80. Ibid., 78; Engl. trans., 67 (emended) (diary entry of 4 September 1865).

81. Ibid., 88; Engl. trans., 75 (emended) (diary entry of 11 September 1865).

82. Otto Strobel (ed.), *König Ludwig II. und Richard Wagner: Briefwechsel*, 5 vols (Karlsruhe, 1936–9), i.200 (letter from Richard Wagner to Ludwig II, 16 October 1865).

83. Detta and Michael Petzet, *Die Richard Wagner-Bühne König Ludwigs II.* (Munich, 1970), 72 (letter from Ludwig von der Pfordten to Ludwig II, 1 December 1865).

84. Klára Hamburger (ed.), *Lettres à Cosima et à Daniela* (Sprimont, 1996), 54 (letter from Franz Liszt to Cosima von Bülow, 14 December 1865).

85. Cornelius, *Literarische Werke* (note 3), ii.311–12 (letter from Peter Cornelius to Bertha Jung, 10 December 1865).
86. La Mara, *Franz Liszt's Briefe* (note 24), vi.111–12 (letter from Franz Liszt to Carolyne von Sayn-Wittgenstein, 15 April 1866).
87. James Harding, *Saint-Saëns and His Circle* (London, 1965), 49.
88. L[illie] de Hegermann-Lindencrone, *In the Courts of Memory 1858–1875* (New York and London, 1912), 161–2. (The writer's reminiscences purport to date from June 1867, although Liszt was not in Paris at any point during the whole of 1867.)
89. La Mara, *Franz Liszt's Briefe* (note 24), vi.110–11 (letter from Franz Liszt to Carolyne von Sayn-Wittgenstein, 13 April 1866).
90. Cornelius, *Literarische Werke* (note 3), ii.368 (letter from Peter Cornelius to Bertha Jung, 22 April 1866). Dating back to the Middle Ages, Tribschen was a fortified villa overlooking Lake Lucerne. Wagner called it Triebschen, fancifully arguing that its name derived from the German verb *treiben* ('to drive') and reflected his status as a refugee driven into exile. Most of Wagner's contemporaries adopted this form, whereas later writers have generally reverted to the earlier form Tribschen.
91. Ibid., ii.370–1 (letter from Peter Cornelius to Bertha Jung, 12 May 1866).
92. Ibid., ii.382 (undated letter from Peter Cornelius to Bertha Jung [June 1866]).
93. Bülow, *Hans von Bülow: Briefe* (note 23), iv.145 (letter from Hans von Bülow to Joachim Raff, 26 August 1866).
94. Cornelius, *Literarische Werke* (note 3), ii.382 (undated letter from Peter Cornelius to Bertha Jung, [June 1866]).
95. Bülow, *Hans von Bülow: Briefe* (note 23), iv.143 (letter from Hans von Bülow to Joachim Raff, 26 August 1866).
96. Pauline Pocknell, 'Princess Carolyne von Sayn-Wittgenstein: Correspondence with Franz Liszt's Family and Friends', *Liszt Saeculum*, il (1992), 3–67 and l (1993), 3–45, esp. il (1992), 58–9 (undated letter from Carolyne von Sayn-Wittgenstein to Eduard Liszt, [late July 1866]).
97. Richard Du Moulin Eckart (ed.), *Hans von Bülow: Neue Briefe* (Munich, 1927), 217–18 (letter from Hans von Bülow to Carl Bechstein, 16 February 1867).
98. Pocknell, *Franz Liszt and Agnes Street-Klindworth* (note 2), 257 (letter from Franz Liszt to Agnes Street-Klindworth, 29 May 1867).
99. Richard Pohl, 'Liszts Besuch in Triebschen', *Richard Wagner-Jahrbuch*, ed. Joseph Kürschner (Stuttgart, 1886), 81.
100. Wagner, *Das braune Buch* (note 50), 147; Engl. trans., 124.
101. Strobel, *König Ludwig II. und Richard Wagner: Briefwechsel* (note 82), ii.195 (letter from Richard Wagner to Ludwig II, 12 October 1867).
102. Pohl, 'Liszts Besuch in Triebschen' (note 99), 81.
103. Cosima Wagner, *Franz Liszt: Ein Gedenkblatt von seiner Tochter* (Munich, 1911), 55.
104. Pohl, 'Liszts Besuch in Triebschen' (note 99), 83.
105. Wagner, *Das braune Buch* (note 50), 198; Engl. trans., 167 (emended).
106. Ibid., 200; Engl. trans., 168 (emended).
107. NAB (letter from Cosima Wagner to Marie von Schleinitz, 31 May 1871).
108. VMA, Ms. F 859, 1/3 (letter from Franz Liszt to Cosima von Bülow, 2 November 1868). The present translation is taken from Walker, *Franz Liszt: The Final Years* (note 11), 135–6. Walker was the first scholar to reproduce the letter in its entirety, though excerpts had already appeared in 1970 in Alice Hunt Sokoloff's *Cosima Wagner* details and Margarete Bormann's *Außergewöhnliche Tochter von Franz Liszt* details. The original was reproduced for the first time in the French edition of Walker's study (Paris, 1998), ii.155–6. The Rousseau quotation about the dangers of contempt is from *La Nouvelle Héloïse* (Paris, 1819), ii.363.
109. Bülow, *Hans von Bülow: Briefe* (note 23), iv.418 (letter from Hans von Bülow to Jessie Laussot, 4 July 1870).

110. ÖNB, Autogr. 461/10-1 (letter from Ludwig Hartmann to an unidentified correspondent, 24 August 1869). The pianist Carl Tausig (1841-71) married fellow pianist Seraphine von Vrabél (1840-1931) at the end of 1864. Bülow's correspondence with the piano maker Carl Bechstein (1826-1900) was published by Richard Du Moulin Eckart in 1927, but the letter to which Hartmann refers appears not to have survived.
111. Hanjo Kesting (ed.), *Franz Liszt - Richard Wagner Briefwechsel* (Frankfurt, 1988), 663 (letter from Franz Liszt to Richard Wagner, 22 May 1870).
112. Cosima Wagner, *Die Tagebücher*, ed. Martin Gregor-Dellin and Dietrich Mack, 2 vols (Munich and Zurich, 1976-7), i.233; trans. Geoffrey Skelton as *Cosima Wagner's Diaries*, 2 vols (London, 1978-80), i.222 (entry of 22 May 1870).

Chapter Seven · La vie trifurquée

1. La Mara (ed.), *Franz Liszt's Briefe*, 8 vols (Leipzig 1893-1905), ii.121 (letter from Franz Liszt to Franz Brendel, 17 June 1868).
2. Serge Gut, *Franz Liszt* (Sinzig, 2009), 231.
3. La Mara, *Franz Liszt's Briefe* (note 1), iv.316 (letter from Franz Liszt to Carolyne von Sayn-Wittgenstein, 13 August 1856).
4. Ibid., vi.196 (letter from Franz Liszt to Carolyne von Sayn-Wittgenstein, 17 January 1869).
5. Adelheid von Schorn, *Zwei Menschenalter: Erinnerungen und Briefe aus Weimar und Rom* (Stuttgart, 1913), 119.
6. Ibid., 123 (letter from Henriette von Schorn to Carolyne von Sayn-Wittgenstein, 27 January 1869).
7. Richard Voß, *Aus einem phantastischen Leben: Erinnerungen* (Stuttgart, 1922), 258.
8. Quoted by Julius Kapp, *Liszt: Eine Biographie* (Berlin, 1924), 257. Unfortunately Kapp fails to give a source for this quotation.
9. Amy Fay, *Music-Study in Germany* (London, 1893), 239 (letter of 15 September 1873).
10. Lina Ramann, *Lisztiana: Erinnerungen an Franz Liszt in Tagebuchblättern, Briefen und Dokumenten aus den Jahren 1873-1886/87* (Mainz, 1983), 87.
11. Schorn, *Zwei Menschenalter* (note 5), 120.
12. Fay, *Music-Study* (note 9), 189 (letter of 7 May 1873).
13. Ibid., 200 (letter of 29 May 1873).
14. Ibid., 204 (letter of 6 June 1873).
15. Ibid., 199 (letter of 29 May 1873).
16. Ramann, *Lisztiana* (note 10), 39 (letter from Franz Liszt to Lina Ramann, 30 August 1874).
17. Marie von Bülow (ed.), *Hans von Bülows Leben dargestellt aus seinen Briefen* (Leipzig, 1921), 282 (letter from Hans von Bülow to Jessie Laussot, 19 October 1874).
18. August Göllerich, *Franz Liszt* (Berlin, 1908), 104.
19. Josef von Kopf, *Lebenserinnerungen eines Bildhauers* (Stuttgart, 1899), 370; Engl. trans. from Adrian Williams, *A Portrait of Liszt* (Oxford, 1990), 443.
20. Ferdinand Gregorovius, *Römische Tagebücher*, 2nd edn, ed. Friedrich Althaus (Stuttgart, 1893), 304 (diary entry of 30 January 1870).
21. Kopf, *Lebenserinnerungen* (note 19), 371; Engl. trans. from Williams, *Portrait of Liszt* (note 19), 443.
22. Raphaël Ledos de Beaufort, *Franz Liszt: The Story of His Life* (Boston, 1910), 217.
23. Robert Bory, 'Diverses lettres inédites de Liszt', *Schweizerisches Jahrbuch für Musikwissenschaft*, iii (1908), 5-25, esp. 22 (letter from Franz Liszt to Olga Janina, 17 May 1871). The Latin sentence at the end of the first paragraph is from Isaiah 38:17 ('Behold, for peace I had great bitterness').
24. Robert Franz [i.e. Olga Janina], *Souvenirs d'une cosaque* (Paris, 1874), 261-2.
25. La Mara, *Franz Liszt's Briefe* (note 1), vi.330 (letter from Franz Liszt to Carolyne von Sayn-Wittgenstein, 3 February 1872).
26. Ibid.

27. Ibid., vi.317 (letter from Franz Liszt to Carolyne von Sayn-Wittgenstein, 29 November 1871).
28. William R. Tyler and Edward N. Waters, *The Letters of Franz Liszt to Olga von Meyendorff 1871–1886* (Washington, 1979), 30 (letter from Franz Liszt to Olga von Meyendorff, 1 December 1871).
29. See Alan Walker, *Franz Liszt: The Final Years 1861–1886* (New York and London, 1997), 181.
30. Franz, *Souvenirs d'une cosaque* (note 24), 204–5.
31. Ibid., 174.
32. August Stradal, *Erinnerungen an Franz Liszt* (Berne, 1929), 171–2.
33. Eduard Liszt, *Franz Liszt: Abstammung, Familie, Begebenheiten* (Vienna, 1938), 78.
34. Stradal, *Erinnerungen* (note 32), 172.
35. Bory, 'Diverses lettres inédites' (Note 23), 21–2 (Franz Liszt, 'Extrait d'un carnet de notes'); Engl. trans. from Tyler and Waters, *The Letters of Franz Liszt to Olga von Meyendorff*, 178 (emended).
36. GSA 59/47,1 (undated letter from Carolyne von Sayn-Wittgenstein to Franz Liszt, [1874]).
37. Ramann, *Lisztiana* (note 10), 87.
38. Mária P. Eckhardt and Cornelia Knotik (eds), *Franz Liszt und sein Kreis in Briefen und Dokumenten aus den Beständen des burgenländischen Landesmuseums* (Eisenstadt, 1983), 66–9 (letter from Carolyne von Sayn-Wittgenstein to Eduard Liszt, 30 May 1875).
39. Schorn, *Zwei Menschenalter* (note 5), 191–2.
40. La Mara, *Franz Liszt's Briefe* (note 1), vi.284 (letter from Franz Liszt to Carolyne von Sayn-Wittgenstein, 17 January 1871).
41. Hanjo Kesting (ed.), *Franz Liszt – Richard Wagner Briefwechsel* (Frankfurt, 1988), 663 (letter from Richard Wagner to Franz Liszt, 18 May 1872).
42. Ibid., 664 (letter from Franz Liszt to Richard Wagner, 20 May 1872).
43. Schorn, *Zwei Menschenalter* (note 5), 173–4.
44. Cosima Wagner, *Die Tagebücher*, ed. Martin Gregor-Dellin and Dietrich Mack, 2 vols (Munich and Zurich, 1976–7), i.523; trans. Geoffrey Skelton as *Cosima Wagner's Diaries*, 2 vols (London 1978–80), i.489 (entry of 23 May 1872).
45. Ibid., i.568; Engl. trans., i.529 (entry of 28 August 1872).
46. Ibid., i.570; Engl. trans., i.532 (entry of 2 September 1872).
47. Ibid., i.571; Engl. trans., i.532 (entry of 4 September 1872).
48. Ibid., i.571–2; Engl. trans., i.533 (entry of 5 September 1872).
49. Ibid., i.572; Engl. trans., i.533 (entry of 6 September 1872).
50. GSA 59/205 (letter from Carolyne von Sayn-Wittgenstein to Franz Liszt, 16–19 September 1872).
51. GSA 59/205 (undated letter from Carolyne von Sayn-Wittgenstein to Franz Liszt).
52. Cosima Wagner, *Die Tagebücher* (note 44), i.582; Engl. trans., i.543 (entry of 18 October 1872).
53. Ibid., ii.581; Engl. trans., i.542 (entry of 17 October 1872).
54. See Hans Rudolf Jung (ed.), *Franz Liszt in seinen Briefen* (Berlin, 1987), 234–5 (letter from Franz Liszt to Carolyne von Sayn-Wittgenstein, 29 October 1872).
55. La Mara, *Franz Liszt's Briefe* (note 1), ii.177 (letter from Franz Liszt to Eduard Liszt, 6 November 1872).
56. Schorn, *Zwei Menschenalter* (note 5), 187–8.
57. Cosima Wagner, *Die Tagebücher* (note 44), i.689; Engl. trans., i.640–41 (entry of 29 May 1873).
58. NAB (letter from Cosima Wagner to Hans Richter, 1 June 1873).
59. Tyler and Waters, *The Letters of Franz Liszt to Olga von Meyendorff* (note 28), 98 (letter from Franz Liszt to Olga von Meyendorff, 18 October 1873).
60. A facsimile of this proclamation is reproduced by Walker, *Franz Liszt: The Final Years* (note 29), 270.
61. Quoted by Serge Gut, *Franz Liszt* (Sinzig, 2009), 774.

62. Eduard Hanslick, *Concerte, Componisten und Virtuosen der letzten fünfzehn Jahre 1870–1885* (Berlin, 1886), 124–5; Engl. trans. from Henry Pleasants (ed.), *Eduard Hanslick: Music Criticisms 1846–99* (Harmondsworth, 1963), 110 (emended).

63. GSA 59/89 (letter from Franz Liszt to Carolyne von Sayn-Wittgenstein, 16 March 1874). Baron August Loën was the intendant of the Weimar Court Theatre, while Baroness Thérèse von Helldorf and her husband were close friends of Liszt in the town. The Bismarck quotation comes from a speech that the German chancellor delivered to the lower house on 25 January 1873.

64. Tyler and Waters, *The Letters of Franz Liszt to Olga von Meyendorff* (note 28), 135 (letter from Franz Liszt to Olga von Meyendorff, 27 April 1874).

65. Klára Hamburger (ed.), *Lettres à Cosima et à Daniela* (Sprimont, 1996), 112–13 (letter from Franz Liszt to Cosima Wagner, 11 April 1874).

66. Schorn, *Zwei Menschenalter* (note 5), 196 (letter from Carolyne von Sayn-Wittgenstein to Adelheid von Schorn, 4 June 1874).

67. Tyler and Waters, *The Letters of Franz Liszt to Olga von Meyendorff* (note 28), 158 (letter from Franz Liszt to Olga von Meyendorff, 23 September 1874).

68. Schorn, *Zwei Menschenalter* (note 5), 222–3.

69. Ibid., 217.

70. Ibid., 210.

71. Kurd von Schlözer, *Römische Briefe 1864–1869* (Stuttgart, 1913), 187 (diary entry of 11 February 1865).

72. La Mara, *Franz Liszt's Briefe* (note 1), vii.120 (letter from Franz Liszt to Carolyne von Sayn-Wittgenstein, 28 December 1875).

73. Schorn, *Zwei Menschenalter* (note 5), 210–11.

74. Cosima Wagner, *Die Tagebücher* (note 44), i.901; Engl. trans., i.831 (entry of 9 March 1875).

75. Ibid., i.901; Engl. trans., i.831 (entry of 10 March 1875).

76. La Mara, *Franz Liszt's Briefe* (note 1), vii.9 (letter from Franz Liszt to Carolyne von Sayn-Wittgenstein, 27 February 1873).

77. Albert Apponyi, *Erlebnisse und Ergebnisse* (Berlin, 1933), 68; trans. anonymously as *The Memoirs of Count Apponyi* (New York, 1935), 69.

78. Lina Ramann, *Franz Liszt. Als Künstler und Mensch*, 3 vols (Leipzig, 1880–94), ii.481.

79. Quoted from József Ovári, *Ferenc Liszt: Eine leichtverständliche Biographie des grossen ungarischen Komponisten* (Budapest, 2003), 350.

80. Eckhardt and Knotik, *Franz Liszt und sein Kreis* (note 38), 76 (letter from Carolyne von Sayn-Wittgenstein to Eduard Liszt, 31 October 1877).

81. Apponyi, *Erlebnisse und Ergebnisse* (note 77), 69; Engl. trans., 70.

82. La Mara, *Franz Liszt's Briefe* (note 1), vii.131 (letter from Franz Liszt to Carolyne von Sayn-Wittgenstein, 14 March 1876).

83. GSA 59/455,6 (letter from Franz Liszt to Cosima Wagner, 8 November 1876).

84. NAB (undated letter from Cosima Wagner to Marie von Schleinitz, [March 1876]).

85. Apponyi, *Erlebnisse und Ergebnisse* (note 77), 86; Engl. trans., 89–90.

86. Robert Hartford, *Bayreuth: The Early Years* (London, 1980), 53.

87. Lilli Lehmann, *Mein Weg*, 2nd edn (Leipzig, 1920), 228; trans. Alice Benedict Seligman as *My Path Through Life* (New York and London, 1914), 212–13.

88. Ibid., 235; Engl. trans., 221.

89. Cosima Wagner, *Die Tagebücher* (note 44), i.999; Engl. trans., i.919 (entry of 18 August 1876).

90. Liszt's speech is reproduced by Kapp, *Liszt: Eine Biographie* (note 8), 266.

91. Lehmann, *Mein Weg* (note 87), 228; Engl. trans., 211–12.

92. GSA 59/403 (letter from Franz Liszt to Lina Ramann, 24 July 1876).

93. Schorn, *Zwei Menschenalter* (note 5), 268 (letter from Carolyne von Sayn-Wittgenstein to Adelheid von Schorn, 4 August 1876).

94. La Mara, *Franz Liszt's Briefe* (note 1), vii.155 (letter from Franz Liszt to Carolyne von Sayn-Wittgenstein, 6 September 1876).

95. Hamburger, *Lettres à Cosima* (note 65), 134 (letter from Franz Liszt to Cosima Wagner, 22 February 1877).

96. Cosima Wagner, *Die Tagebücher* (note 44), i.1041; Engl. trans., i.955 (diary entry of 1 April 1877).

97. Ibid., i.1041; Engl. trans., i.956 (diary entry of 2 April 1877).

98. Tyler and Waters, *The Letters of Franz Liszt to Olga von Meyendorff* (note 28), 244 (letter from Franz Liszt to Olga von Meyendorff, 27 September 1876).

99. Ibid., 297 (letter from Franz Liszt to Olga von Meyendorff, 9 November 1877).

100. Ibid., 299 (letter from Franz Liszt to Olga von Meyendorff, 28 November 1877).

101. La Mara, *Franz Liszt's Briefe* (note 1), vii.202 (letter from Franz Liszt to Carolyne von Sayn-Wittgenstein, 23 September 1877).

102. Tyler and Waters, *The Letters of Franz Liszt to Olga von Meyendorff* (note 28), 294–5 (letter from Franz Liszt to Olga von Meyendorff, 14 October 1877).

103. GSA 59/67 (letter from Franz Liszt to Alexander Wilhelm Gottschalg, 25 January 1883).

104. Schorn, *Zwei Menschenalter* (note 5), 195 (letter from Carolyne von Sayn-Wittgenstein to Adelheid von Schorn, 4 June 1874).

105. Arnold Schoenberg, 'Franz Liszt's Work and Being', *Style and Idea: Selected Writings of Arnold Schoenberg*, ed. Leonard Stein and trans. Leo Black (Berkeley, 1975), 445.

106. Ferruccio Busoni, *The Essence of Music and Other Papers*, trans. Rosamond Ley (New York, 1965), 155 and 139.

107. Cosima Wagner, *Die Tagebücher* (note 44), ii.1059; Engl. trans., ii.962 (diary entry of 28 November 1882).

108. Ibid., ii.1062; Engl. trans., ii.965 (diary entry of 2 December 1882).

109. Ibid., ii.1059–60; Engl. trans., 963 (diary entry of 29 November 1882). (These final comments were obliterated in ink by an unknown hand in an attempt to render them illegible. An additional sentence here cannot be recovered at all.)

110. Emil Sauer, *Meine Welt: Bilder aus dem Geheimfache meiner Kunst und meines Lebens* (Stuttgart, 1901), 174.

111. Ibid., 169.

112. A complete list of Liszt's pupils may be found in Walker, *Franz Liszt: The Final Years* (note 29), 249–52.

113. Stradal, *Erinnerungen* (note 32), 112.

114. Sauer, *Meine Welt* (note 110), 165–6.

115. Ibid., 170.

116. Ibid., 173.

117. Schorn, *Zwei Menschenalter* (note 5), 192.

118. Sauer, *Meine Welt* (note 110), 171.

119. Berthold Kellermann, *Erinnerungen: Ein Künstlerleben* (Leipzig, 1932), 51.

120. Ibid., 28. Carl Lachmund tells the same anecdote, although in this case the culprit is named as Carl Tausig: see Alan Walker (ed.), *Living with Liszt from The Diary of Carl Lachmund: An American Pupil of Liszt, 1882–1884* (Stuyvesant, NY, 1998), 107 (diary entry of 5–27 July 1882).

121. Ibid., 33.

122. Schorn, *Zwei Menschenalter* (note 5), 310.

123. Felix Weingartner, *Lebenserinnerungen*, 2nd edn (Zurich, 1928–9), i.164. The passage cited here is missing from Marguerite Wolff's heavily abridged Engl. trans. of 1937.

124. Schorn, *Zwei Menschenalter* (note 5), 311.

125. Walker, *Franz Liszt: The Final Years* (note 29), 412.

126. See Walker, *Living with Liszt* (note 120), 115 (diary entry of 27 July 1882).

127. Schorn, *Zwei Menschenalter* (note 5), 311.

128. Kellermann, *Erinnerungen* (note 119), 21.

129. Emil Sauer, 'The Training of a Concert Pianist', *The Etude: A Monthly Publication for Teachers and Students of the Piano-Forte* (December 1908), 763.

130. Berthold Litzmann (ed.), *Clara Schumann: Ein Künstlerleben*, 3 vols (Leipzig, 1902–8), iii.479; trans. Grace E. Hadow as *Clara Schumann: An Artist's Life*, 2 vols (London and Leipzig, 1913), ii.387 (diary entry of 1 August 1886).

131. Kellermann, *Erinnerungen* (note 119), 25.

132. Marie von Bülow, *Hans von Bülow in Leben und Wort* (Stuttgart, 1925), 273.

133. Ibid.

134. Walker, *Living with Liszt* (note 120), 20.

135. Kellermann, *Erinnerungen* (note 119), 25–6.

136. Richard Du Moulin Eckart (ed.), *Hans von Bülow: Neue Briefe* (Munich, 1927), 594 (letter from Hans von Bülow to Daniela von Bülow, 1 July 1882).

137. Schorn, *Zwei Menschenalter* (note 5), 303.

138. Kellermann, *Erinnerungen* (note 119), 26.

139. See Walker, *Franz Liszt: The Final Years* (note 29), 403–5.

140. Schorn, *Zwei Menschenalter* (note 5), 317.

141. Du Moulin Eckart, *Bülow: Neue Briefe* (note 136), 80 (letter from Hans von Bülow to Karl Klindworth, 14 July 1881).

142. Walker, *Living with Liszt* (note 120), 20.

143. Ibid.

144. Ibid.

145. Stradal, *Erinnerungen* (note 32), 102.

146. Walker, *Living with Liszt* (note 120), 148.

147. Sauer, *Meine Welt* (note 110), 171–2.

148. Ramann, *Lisztiana* (note 10), 212 (diary entry of 18 July 1883).

149. Florian Speer, *Ibach und die Anderen: Rheinisch-Bergischer Klavierbau im 19. Jahrhundert* (Neustadt, 2002), 162 (letter from Lina Schmalhausen to Rudolf Ibach, 31 January 1885).

150. GSA 59/380,3 (undated letter from Lina Schmalhausen to her mother).

151. GSA 59/380,3 (letter from Franz Liszt to Dory Petersen, 8 July 1884).

152. GSA 59/380,3 (letter from Franz Liszt to Dory Petersen, 23 August 1884).

153. Walker, *Living with Liszt* (note 120), 319–20.

154. Du Moulin Eckart, *Bülow: Neue Briefe* (note 136), 122 (letter from Hans von Bülow to Karl von Klindworth, 13 June 1885).

155. Marie von Bülow (ed.), *Hans von Bülow: Briefe und Schriften*, 8 vols (Leipzig, 1895–1908), vi.108 (letter from Hans von Bülow to Franziska von Bülow, 6 November 1881).

156. Schorn, *Zwei Menschenalter* (note 5), 322–3.

157. La Mara, *Franz Liszt's Briefe* (note 1), ii.317 (letter from Franz Liszt to Ludwig Bösendorfer, 8 December 1881).

158. Margit Prahács (ed.), *Franz Liszt: Briefe aus ungarischen Sammlungen 1835–1886* (Kassel, 1966), 419 (letter from Carolyne von Sayn-Wittgenstein to Kornél Ábrányi, 29 December 1881).

159. Du Moulin Eckart, *Bülow: Neue Briefe* (note 136), 586 (letter from Hans von Bülow to Daniela von Bülow, 6 May 1882).

160. Walker, *Living with Liszt* (note 120), 121–2.

161. Cosima Wagner, *Die Tagebücher* (note 44), ii.984; Engl. trans., ii.894 (diary entry of 26 July 1882).

162. Tyler and Waters, *The Letters of Franz Liszt to Olga von Meyendorff* (note 28), 437–8 (letter from Franz Liszt to Olga von Meyendorff, 29 November 1882).

163. Cosima Wagner, *Die Tagebücher* (note 44), ii.1053; Engl. trans., ii.957 (diary entry of 19 November 1882).

164. Ibid., ii.1079; Engl. trans., ii.981 (diary entry of 24 December 1882).

165. La Mara, *Franz Liszt's Briefe* (note 1), ii.381 (letter from Franz Liszt to Ferdinand Táborszky, 8 June 1885).

166. Göllerich, *Franz Liszt* (note 18), 25.

167. NAB (Daniela von Bülow, unpublished diary, February 1883).

168. Jung, *Franz Liszt in seinen Briefen* (note 54), 291 (letter from Franz Liszt to Franz von Liszt, 14 June 1883).

169. Tyler and Waters, *The Letters of Franz Liszt to Olga von Meyendorff* (note 28), 449 (letter from Franz Liszt to Olga von Meyendorff, 20 February 1883).

170. Ramann, *Lisztiana* (note 10), 208.

171. Tyler and Waters, *The Letters of Franz Liszt to Olga von Meyendorff* (note 28), 464 (letter from Franz Liszt to Olga von Meyendorff, 16 July 1884).

172. Anne Troisier de Diaz (ed.), *Émile Ollivier et Carolyne de Sayn-Wittgenstein: Correspondance 1858–1887* (Paris, 1984), 311 (letter from Marie-Thérèse Ollivier to Carolyne von Sayn-Wittgenstein, 12 August 1884).

173. Hamburger, *Lettres à Cosima* (note 65), 211 (letter from Franz Liszt to Daniela von Bülow, 12 July 1884).

174. Göllerich, *Franz Liszt* (note 18), 122.

175. NAB (letter from Malwida von Meysenbug to Daniela von Bülow, 7 December 1885).

176. La Mara, *Franz Liszt's Briefe* (note 1), ii.389 (letter from Franz Liszt to Walter Bache, 11 February 1886).

177. Quoted in Walker, *Franz Liszt: The Final Years* (note 29), 486.

178. Stradal, *Erinnerungen* (note 32), 99.

179. GSA 59/403 (letter from Franz Liszt to Lina Ramann, 2 March 1879).

180. Göllerich, *Franz Liszt* (note 18), 124–5.

181. Troisier de Diaz, *Émile Ollivier et Carolyne de Sayn-Wittgenstein* (note 172), 342 (letter from Carolyne von Sayn-Wittgenstein to Marie-Thérèse Ollivier, 1 June 1886).

182. BSB, Nachl. Mottl (Felix Mottl, diary entry of 1 July 1886).

183. Jung, *Franz Liszt in seinen Briefen* (note 54), 298 (letter from Franz Liszt to Carolyne von Sayn-Wittgenstein, 6 July 1886).

184. Weingartner, *Lebenserinnerungen* (note 123), i.264; Engl. trans., 145.

185. Bülow, *Hans von Bülow: Briefe* (note 155), vii.42 (letter from Hans von Bülow to Eugen Spitzweg, 25 June 1886).

186. BSB, Nachl. Mottl (Felix Mottl, diary entry of 4 July 1886).

187. See Guy May, 'Franz Liszt und Luxemburg', *Nos cahiers: Lëtzebuerger zäitschrëft fir kultur*, iii (1986), 87–122.

188. Tyler and Waters, *The Letters of Franz Liszt to Olga von Meyendorff* (note 28), 500 (letter from Franz Liszt to Olga von Meyendorff, 17 July 1886).

189. Quoted by May, 'Franz Liszt und Luxemburg' (note 187), 115.

190. Lina Schmalhausen's diary first appeared in English as Alan Walker (ed.), *The Death of Franz Liszt: Based on the Unpublished Diary of His Pupil Lina Schmalhausen* (Ithaca, 2002). A German edition of the original diary followed in 2011: Ernst Burger (ed.), *Franz Liszt: Leben und Sterben in Bayreuth* (Regensburg, 2011).

191. ÖNB, Nachl. Göllerich (letter from Conrad Ansorge to August Göllerich, 7 February 1886).

192. Walker, *The Death of Franz Liszt* (note 190), 32 (diary entry of 22 July 1886).

193. Ibid., 39 (diary entry of 22 July 1886).

194. Ramann, *Lisztiana* (note 10), 375.

195. Weingartner, *Lebenserinnerungen* (note 123), i.273–4; this passage is not in Marguerite Wolff's Engl. trans.

196. Walker, *The Death of Franz Liszt* (note 190), 74 (diary entry of 25 July 1886).

197. Ibid., 87 (diary entry of 26 July 1886).

198. BSB, Nachl. Mottl (Felix Mottl, diary entry of 27 July 1886).

199. Schorn, *Zwei Menschenalter* (note 5), 377.

200. Walker, *The Death of Franz Liszt* (note 190), 109–10 (diary entry of 29 July 1886).

201. Ibid., 110 (diary entry of 29 July 1886).

202. Ibid., 127 (diary entry of 30 July 1886).

203. GSA 59/67 (letter from Mihály Kreiner to Alexander Wilhelm Gottschalg, 31 July 1886).

204. BSB, Nachl. Mottl (Felix Mottl, diary entry of 31 July 1886).
205. Walker, *The Death of Franz Liszt* (note 190), 132 (diary entry of 31 July 1886).
206. Ibid., 133 (diary entry of 31 July 1886).

Postlude

1. Felix Weingartner, *Lebenserinnerungen*, 2nd edn (Zurich, 1928–9), i.274–5; trans. Marguerite Wolff as *Buffets and Rewards: A Musician's Reminiscences* (London, 1937), 150.
2. Alan Walker, *The Death of Franz Liszt: Based on the Unpublished Diary of His Pupil Lina Schmalhausen* (Ithaca, 2002), 139.
3. Klára Hamburger, 'Ein unbekanntes Dokument über Franz Liszts Tod', *Studia Musicologica*, xlvi (2005), 403–12, esp. 410.
4. Walker, *The Death of Franz Liszt* (note 2), 139.
5. Hamburger, 'Ein unbekanntes Dokument' (note 3), 411.
6. Weingartner, *Lebenserinnerungen* (note 1), i.275; Engl. trans., 150 (first sentence only).
7. 'Liszt's Begräbnis', *Bayreuther Tagblatt* (4 August 1886).
8. Lina Ramann, *Lisztiana: Erinnerungen an Franz Liszt in Tagebuchblättern, Briefen und Dokumenten aus den Jahren 1873–1886/87* (Mainz, 1983), 364.
9. Weingartner, *Lebenserinnerungen* (note 1), i.276; Engl. trans., 150–1.
10. BSB, Nachl. Mottl (Felix Mottl, diary entry of 4 August 1886).
11. August Göllerich, *Franz Liszt* (Berlin, 1908), 192 (letter from Franz Liszt to Carolyne von Sayn-Wittgenstein, 27 November 1869).
12. BSB, Döllingeriana (letter from Carolyne von Sayn-Wittgenstein to Ignaz von Döllinger, 19 October 1885).
13. Quoted by Julius Kapp, *Liszt: Eine Biographie* (Berlin, 1924), 297 (undated letter from Carolyne von Sayn-Wittgenstein to an unnamed correspondent); Engl. trans. from Alan Walker, *Franz Liszt: The Final Years, 1861–1886* (New York and London, 1997), 521–2 (emended).
14. Anne Troisier de Diaz (ed.), *Émile Ollivier et Carolyne de Sayn-Wittgenstein: Correspondance 1858–1887* (Paris, 1984), 368 (undated letter from Marie von Hohenlohe to Émile Ollivier, [March 1887]).
15. NAB (letter from Cosima Wagner to Adolf von Groß, 11 March 1887).
16. NAB (letter from Cosima Wagner to Daniela Thode, 21 March 1887).
17. Cosima Wagner, *Franz Liszt: Ein Gedenkblatt von seiner Tochter* (Munich, 1911), 117.

BIBLIOGRAPHY

Unpublished Sources

Archiv des Erzbistums München und Freising (AEM)
Baptism register of the Parish of Saint Boniface, Munich, MM 227
Bayerische Staatsbibliothek München (BSB)
Ana 452: Unpublished papers of Felix Mottl
Döllingeriana
Bibliothèque municipale des Versailles (VMA)
Ms F 859: Archives Claire de Charnacé
Bibliothèque nationale de France (BNF)
NAF 25191: Archives Daniel Ollivier
Katholisches Dompfarramt Sankt Hedwig, Berlin (SHB)
Marriage registers
Birth registers
Klassik Stiftung Weimar, Goethe- und Schiller-Archiv (GSA)
Bestand 59: Unpublished papers of Franz Liszt
Nationalarchiv der Richard-Wagner-Stiftung, Bayreuth (NAB)
Österreichische Nationalbibliothek, Vienna, Department of Manuscripts (ÖNB)
Unpublished papers of August Göllerich
Correspondence of various musicians
Österreichisches Staatsarchiv, Vienna, Haus-, Hof- und Staatsarchiv (ÖSA)
StK Wissenschaft, Kunst und Literatur 11-2-16
Staatsbibliothek zu Berlin, Preußischer Kulturbesitz, Department of Manuscripts (SBB)
Unpublished papers of Carolyne von Sayn-Wittgenstein
Thüringisches Hauptstaatsarchiv, Weimar (THA)
Großherzogliches Hausarchiv A XXV, 445–60

Published Sources

Altenburg, Detlef and Rainer Kleinertz (eds), *Franz Liszt: Tagebuch 1827* (Vienna, 1986)
Andersen, Hans Christian, *A Poet's Bazaar*, trans. Charles Beckwith, 3 vols (London, 1846)
Anon., 'Virtuosität gegen Virtuosität oder Liszt gegen Thalberg', *Allgemeine musikalische Zeitung* (15 February 1837), 106–9
—, *Staats-Handbuch für das Großherzogthum Sachsen-Weimar-Eisenach*, vols for 1851 and 1859

—, 'Liszt's Begräbnis', *Bayreuther Tagblatt* (4 August 1886)

Apponyi, Albert, *Erlebnisse und Ergebnisse* (Berlin, 1933); trans. anonymously as *The Memoirs of Count Apponyi* (New York, 1935)

Bartók, Béla, *Essays*, selected and edited by Benjamin Suchoff (Lincoln, NE, and London, 1976)

Beaufort, Raphaël Ledos de, *Franz Liszt: The Story of His Life* (Boston, 1910)

Bernhardi, Friedrich von (ed.), *Aus dem Leben Theodor von Bernhardis*, 9 vols (Leipzig, 1893–7)

Boissier, Auguste, *Liszt pédagogue: Leçons de piano données par Liszt à Mademoiselle Valérie Boissier à Paris en 1832* (Paris, 1993)

Bory, Robert, 'Diverses lettres inédites de Liszt', *Schweizerisches Jahrbuch für Musikwissenschaft*, iii (1928), 5–25

— (ed.), *Liszt et ses enfants Blandine, Cosima et Daniel* (Paris, 1936)

—, *La vie de Franz Liszt par l'image* (Paris, 1936)

Brennglas, Adolf [i.e. Adolf Glaßbrenner], 'Franz Liszt in Berlin: Eine Komödie in drei Acten', *Berlin wie es ist und – trinkt*, 2 vols (Leipzig, 1835–50)

Bujanda, Jesús Martínez de (ed.), *Index Librorum Prohibitorum 1600–1966* (Montreal, 2002)

Bülow, Marie von (ed.), *Hans von Bülow: Briefe und Schriften*, 8 vols (Leipzig, 1895–1908)

— (ed.), *Hans von Bülows Leben dargestellt aus seinen Briefen* (Leipzig, 1921)

—, *Hans von Bülow in Leben und Wort* (Stuttgart, 1925)

Burger, Ernst, *Franz Liszt: Eine Lebenschronik in Bildern und Dokumenten* (Munich, 1986); trans. Stewart Spencer as *Franz Liszt: A Chronicle of His Life in Pictures and Documents* (Princeton, 1989)

—, *Franz Liszt: Die Jahre in Rom und Tivoli* (Mainz, 2010)

— (ed.), *Franz Liszt: Leben und Sterben in Bayreuth* (Regensburg, 2011)

Busoni, Ferruccio, *The Essence of Music and Other Papers*, trans. Rosamond Ley (New York, 1965)

Cairns, David (ed.), *The Memoirs of Hector Berlioz* (London, 1969)

Carter, Gerard and Adler, Martin, *Franz Liszt's Precursor, Sonata of 1849: A Trial Run in the Master's Inner Circle* (Ashfield, Sydney, 2011)

Cohnfeld, Adalbert, 'Aus Berlin', *Abend-Zeitung* (13 April 1842), cols 703–4

Cornelius, Carl Maria, *Peter Cornelius: Der Wort- und Tondichter*, 2 vols (Regensburg, 1925)

Cornelius, Peter, *Literarische Werke*, ed. Carl Maria Cornelius, Edgar Istel and Adolf Stern, 4 vols (Leipzig, 1904–5)

Csapó, Wilhelm von (ed.), *Franz Liszt's Briefe an Baron Anton Augusz 1846–1878* (Budapest, 1911)

Czerny, Carl, *Erinnerungen aus meinem Leben*, ed. Walter Kolneder (Strasbourg, 1968)

Dufetel, Nicolas, 'L'artiste saint-simonien et la bataille pour l'autonomie esthétique', *Musique et utopies*, ed. Bernard Sève (Paris, 2010), 93–109

—, 'Liszt et la "propagande wagnérienne": Le projet de deux livres en français sur l'histoire de l'opéra et sur Wagner (1849–1859)', *Acta musicologica*, lxxxii (2010), 263–304

— and Malou Haine (eds), *Franz Liszt: Un saltimbanque en province* (Lyons, 2007)

Du Moulin Eckart, Richard (ed.), *Hans von Bülow: Neue Briefe* (Munich, 1927)

Dupêchez, Charles F., *Marie d'Agoult 1805–1876* (Paris, 1989)

— (ed.), *Mémoires, souvenirs et journaux de la Comtesse d'Agoult*, 2 vols (Paris, 1990)

— (ed.), *Marie de Flavigny, comtesse d'Agoult: Correspondance générale*, 3 vols (Paris, 2003–5)

Eckhardt, Mária P. (ed.), *Das Album der Prinzessin Marie von Sayn-Wittgenstein* (Weimar, 2000)

— and Cornelia Knotik (eds), *Franz Liszt und sein Kreis in Briefen und Dokumenten aus den Beständen des burgenländischen Landesmuseums* (Eisenstadt, 1983)

Fay, Amy, *Music-Study in Germany* (London, 1893)

Franz, Robert [i.e. Olga Janina], *Souvenirs d'une cosaque* (Paris, 1874)

Friedjung, Heinrich, *Der Kampf um die Vorherrschaft in Deutschland 1859 bis 1866*, 6th edn, 2 vols (Stuttgart, 1904–5)

Genast, Eduard, *Aus Weimars klassischer und nachklassischer Zeit: Erinnerungen eines alten Schauspielers* (Stuttgart, 1919)

Göllerich, August, *Franz Liszt* (Berlin, 1908)

Gottschalg, Alexander Wilhelm, *Franz Liszt in Weimar und seine letzten Lebensjahre* (Berlin, 1910)

Gregorovius, Ferdinand, *Römische Tagebücher*, 2nd edn, ed. Friedrich Althaus (Stuttgart, 1893)

Gut, Serge, *Franz Liszt* (Sinzig, 2009) (a much-expanded German translation of the French original of 1989)

— and Jacqueline Bellas (eds), *Franz Liszt – Marie d'Agoult: Correspondance* (Paris, 2001)

Hamburger, Klára (ed.), *Franz Liszt: Beiträge von ungarischen Autoren* (Budapest, 1978)

— (ed.), *Lettres à Cosima et à Daniela* (Sprimont, 1996)

— (ed.), *Franz Liszt: Briefwechsel mit seiner Mutter* (Eisenstadt, 2000)

—, 'Ein unbekanntes Dokument über Franz Liszts Tod', *Studia Musicologica*, xlvi (2005), 403–12

—, *Franz Liszt: Leben und Werk* (Cologne, 2010)

Hanslick, Eduard, *Geschichte des Concertwesens in Wien* (Vienna, 1869)

—, *Concerte, Componisten und Virtuosen der letzten fünfzehn Jahre 1870–1885* (Berlin, 1886)

Harding, James, *Saint-Saëns and His Circle* (London, 1965)

Hartford, Robert, *Bayreuth: The Early Years* (London, 1980)

Hecker, Jutta, *Die Altenburg: Geschichte eines Hauses* (Berlin, 1988)

Hegermann-Lindencrone, L[illie] de, *In the Courts of Memory 1858–1875* (London and New York, 1912; R1980)

Heine, Heinrich, *Sämtliche Schriften*, ed. Klaus Briegleb, 6 vols (Munich, 1995)

Herwegh, Marcel, *Au printemps des dieux: Correspondance inédite de la Comtesse Marie d'Agoult et du poète Georges [sic] Herwegh* (Paris, 1929)

Hoffmann von Fallersleben, August Heinrich, *Mein Leben: Aufzeichnungen und Erinnerungen*, 6 vols (Hanover, 1868)

Hughes, Meirion (ed.), *Liszt's Chopin* (Manchester, 2010)

Hugo, Howard E. (ed.), *The Letters of Franz Liszt to Marie zu Sayn-Wittgenstein* (Cambridge, MA, 1953)

Huschke, Wolfram, *Franz Liszt: Wirken und Wirkungen in Weimar* (Weimar, 2010)

Jung, Hans Rudolf (ed.), *Franz Liszt in seinen Briefen* (Berlin, 1987)

Kapp, Julius, *Liszt und die Frauen* (Leipzig, 1911)

—, *Liszt: Eine Biographie* (Berlin, 1924)

Kellermann, Berthold, *Erinnerungen: Ein Künstlerleben* (Leipzig, 1932)

Kenyon, Nicholas, *Simon Rattle: From Birmingham to Berlin* (London, 2002)

Kesting, Hanjo (ed.), *Franz Liszt – Richard Wagner: Briefwechsel* (Frankfurt, 1988)

Kopf, Josef von, *Lebenserinnerungen eines Bildhauers* (Stuttgart, 1899)

La Mara, *Klassisches und Romantisches aus der Tonwelt* (Leipzig, 1892)

— (ed.), *Franz Liszt's Briefe*, 8 vols (Leipzig, 1893–1905)

— (ed.), *Briefe hervorragender Zeitgenossen an Franz Liszt*, 3 vols (Leipzig, 1895–1904)

— (ed.), *Briefwechsel zwischen Franz Liszt und Hans von Bülow* (Leipzig, 1898)

—, 'Aus Franz Liszts erster Jugend: Ein Schreiben seines Vaters mit Briefen Czernys an ihn', *Die Musik*, v (1905/6), 15–29

— (ed.), *Aus der Glanzzeit der Weimarer Altenburg: Bilder und Briefe aus dem Leben der Fürstin Carolyne Sayn-Wittgenstein* (Leipzig, 1906)

— (ed.), *Briefwechsel zwischen Franz Liszt und Carl Alexander* (Leipzig, 1909)

—, *An der Schwelle des Jenseits: Letzte Erinnerungen an die Fürstin Carolyne Sayn-Wittgenstein* (Leipzig, 1925)

Legány, Dezső, *Ferenc Liszt and His Country*, 2 vols (Budapest, 1976–92)

—, 'Liszt in Rom, nach der Presse', *Studia Musicologica Academiae Scientiarum Hungaricae*, xix (1977), 85–107

Lehmann, Lilli, *Mein Weg*, 2nd edn (Leipzig, 1920); trans. Alice Benedict Seligman as *My Path Through Life* (New York and London, 1914)

Lenz, Wilhelm von, *The Great Piano Virtuosos of Our Time* (New York, 1899)

Liszt, Eduard von, *Franz Liszt: Abstammung, Familie, Begebenheiten* (Vienna, 1938)

Liszt, Franz, *Frühe Schriften*, ed. Rainer Kleinertz (Wiesbaden, 2000)

Litzmann, Berthold (ed.), *Clara Schumann: Ein Künstlerleben*, 3 vols (Leipzig, 1902–8); trans. Grace E. Hadow as *Clara Schumann: An Artist's Life*, 2 vols (London and Leipzig, 1913)

Locke, Ralph P., 'Liszt's Saint-Simonian Adventure', *19th Century Music*, iv (1981), 209–27

Lungu, Alexander, *Der in Canon 1103 des Codex Iuris Canonici von 1983 enthaltene Ehenichtigkeitsgrund* (Berlin, 2009)

Martainville, Alphonse, 'Concert du jeune Liszt', *Le Drapeau Blanc* (9 March 1824)

May, Guy, 'Franz Liszt und Luxemburg', *Nos cahiers: Lëtzebuerger zäitschrëft fir kultur*, iii (1986), 87–122

Meysenbug, Malwida von, *Der Lebensabend einer Idealistin* (Berlin, 1903)

Molitor, Raphael, *Vom Sakrament der Weihe: Erwägungen nach dem Pontificale Romanum*, 2 vols (Regensburg, 1938)

Ollivier, Daniel (ed.), *Correspondance de Liszt et de sa fille Madame Émile Ollivier 1842–1862* (Paris, 1936)

Ovári, József, *Ferenc Liszt: Eine leichtverständliche Biographie des grossen ungarischen Komponisten* (Budapest, 2003)

Petzet, Detta and Petzet, Michael, *Die Richard Wagner-Bühne König Ludwigs II.* (Munich, 1970)

Pocknell, Pauline (ed.), 'Princess Carolyne von Sayn-Wittgenstein: Correspondence with Franz Liszt's Family and Friends', *Liszt Saeculum*, il (1992), 3–67 and l (1993), 3–45

—— (ed.), *Franz Liszt and Agnes Street-Klindworth: A Correspondence 1854–1886* (Hillsdale, 2000)

Pohl, Richard, 'Liszts Besuch in Triebschen', *Richard Wagner-Jahrbuch*, ed. Joseph Kürschner (Stuttgart, 1886), 78–84

Pöthe, Angelika, *Carl Alexander: Mäzen in Weimars 'Silberner Zeit'* (Cologne, 1998)

Prahács, Margit (ed.), *Franz Liszt: Briefe aus ungarischen Sammlungen 1835–1886* (Kassel, 1966)

Pretzsch, Paul (ed.), *Cosima Wagner und Houston Stewart Chamberlain im Briefwechsel 1888–1908* (Leipzig, 1934)

Protzies, Günther, 'Studien zur Biographie Franz Liszts und zu ausgewählten seiner Klavierwerke in der Zeit der Jahre 1828–1846' (PhD diss., Bochum, 2004)

Raabe, Peter, *Liszts Leben* (Tutzing, 1968)

Ramann, Lina, *Franz Liszt. Als Künstler und Mensch*, 3 vols (Leipzig 1880–94)

—— (ed.), *Franz Liszt: Gesammelte Schriften*, 6 vols (Leipzig 1881–99)

——, *Lisztiana: Erinnerungen an Franz Liszt in Tagebuchblättern, Briefen und Dokumenten aus den Jahren 1873–1886/87* (Mainz, 1983)

Rellstab, Ludwig, *Franz Liszt: Beurtheilungen, Berichte, Lebensskizze* (Berlin, 1842)

Sauer, Emil, *Meine Welt: Bilder aus dem Geheimfache meiner Kunst und meines Lebens* (Stuttgart, 1901)

——, 'The Training of a Concert Pianist', *The Etude: A Monthly Publication for Teachers and Students of the Piano-Forte* (December 1908), 763

Schlözer, Kurd von, *Römische Briefe 1864–1869* (Stuttgart, 1913)

Schober, Franz von, *Briefe über F. Liszt's Aufenthalt in Ungarn* (Berlin, 1843)

Schoenberg, Arnold, 'Franz Liszt's Work and Being', *Style and Idea: Selected Writings of Arnold Schoenberg*, ed. Leonard Stein and trans. Leo Black (Berkeley, 1975), 442–7

Schorn, Adelheid von, *Das nachklassische Weimar unter der Regierungszeit von Karl Alexander und Sophie* (Weimar, 1912)

——, *Zwei Menschenalter: Erinnerungen und Briefe aus Weimar und Rom* (Stuttgart, 1913)

Schorn, Karl von, *Lebenserinnerungen: Ein Beitrag zur Geschichte des Rheinlands im neunzehnten Jahrhundert*, 2 vols (Bonn, 1898)

Speer, Florian, *Ibach und die Anderen: Rheinisch-Bergischer Klavierbau im 19. Jahrhundert* (Neustadt, 2002)

Stern, Adolf (ed.), *Franz Liszts Briefe an Carl Gille* (Leipzig, 1903)

Stern, Alfred, 'Georg Klindworth: Ein politischer Geheimagent des neunzehnten Jahrhunderts', *Historische Vierteljahresschrift*, xxv (1931), 430–58

Stradal, August, *Erinnerungen an Franz Liszt* (Berne, 1929)

Strobel, Otto (ed.), *König Ludwig II. und Richard Wagner: Briefwechsel*, 5 vols (Karlsruhe, 1936–9)

Suttoni, Charles (ed.), *An Artist's Journey: Lettres d'un bachelier ès musique 1835–1841* (Chicago, 1989)

Sydow, Bronislas Édouard (ed.), *Correspondance de Frédéric Chopin*, 3 vols (Paris, 1981)

Troisier de Diaz, Anne (ed.), *Émile Ollivier et Carolyne de Sayn-Wittgenstein: Correspondance 1858–1887* (Paris, 1984)

Tyler, William R., and Edward N. Waters (eds), *The Letters of Franz Liszt to Olga von Meyendorff 1871–1886* (Washington, 1979)

Umbach, Klaus, *Geldschein-Sonate: Das Millionenspiel mit der Klassik* (Frankfurt, 1994)

Varnhagen von Ense, Karl August, *Tagebücher*, ed. Ludmilla Assing, 15 vols (Berlin, Zurich and Hamburg, 1861–1905, R1972)

Vier, Jacques (ed.), *Marie d'Agoult, son mari, ses amis: Documents inédits* (Paris, 1950)

Voß, Richard, *Aus einem phantastischen Leben: Erinnerungen* (Stuttgart, 1922)

Wagner, Cosima, *Franz Liszt: Ein Gedenkblatt von seiner Tochter* (Munich, 1911)

—, *Die Tagebücher*, ed. Martin Gregor-Dellin and Dietrich Mack, 2 vols (Munich and Zurich, 1976–7); trans. Geoffrey Skelton as *Cosima Wagner's Diaries*, 2 vols (London, 1978–80)

Wagner, Nike, 'Sich in die Unsterblichkeit spielen', *Der Tagesspiegel* (2 January 2011)

Wagner, Richard, *Sämtliche Briefe*, ed. Gertrud Strobel, Werner Wolf, Werner Breig and others (Leipzig, 1967–2000, and Wiesbaden, 1999–)

—, *Das braune Buch: Tagebuchaufzeichnungen 1865 bis 1882*, ed. Joachim Bergfeld (Zurich, 1975); trans. George Bird as *The Diary of Richard Wagner: The Brown Book 1865–1882* (London, 1980)

—, *Mein Leben*, ed. Martin Gregor-Dellin (Munich, 1976); trans. Andrew Gray as *My Life*, ed. Mary Whittall (Cambridge, 1983)

Waldberg, Max von (ed.), *Cosima Wagners Briefe an ihre Tochter Daniela von Bülow 1866–1885* (Stuttgart, 1933)

Walker, Alan, *Franz Liszt: The Virtuoso Years 1811–1847* (London and New York, 1983)

—, *Franz Liszt: The Weimar Years 1848–1861* (London and New York, 1993)

—, *Franz Liszt: The Final Years 1861–1886* (New York and London, 1997)

— (ed.), *Living with Liszt from The Diary of Carl Lachmund: An American Pupil of Liszt, 1882–1884* (Stuyvesant, NY, 1998)

— (ed.), *The Death of Franz Liszt. Based on the Unpublished Diary of His Pupil Lina Schmalhausen* (Ithaca, 2002)

—, *Hans von Bülow: A Life and Times* (New York, 2010)

— and Gabriele Erasmi (eds), *Liszt, Carolyne, and the Vatican: The Story of a Thwarted Marriage* (Stuyvesant, 1991)

Wallace, William, *Liszt, Wagner and the Princess* (London, 1927)

Weber, Max, *Economy and Society: An Outline of Interpretive Sociology*, trans. Guenther Roth and Claus Wittich (Berkeley, 1978)

Weingartner, Felix, *Lebenserinnerungen*, 2nd edn (Zurich, 1928–9); trans. Marguerite Wolff as *Buffets and Rewards: A Musician's Reminiscences* (London, 1937)

Wille, Eliza, *Erinnerungen an Richard Wagner: Mit 15 Briefen Richard Wagners* (Zurich, 1982)

Williams, Adrian, *A Portrait of Liszt* (Oxford, 1990)

Winkler, Gerhard J., 'Adam Liszt: Charakterstudie eines Vaters', *Franz Liszt: Ein Genie aus dem pannonischen Raum*, ed. Wolfgang Gürtler and Susanne Klement (Eisenstadt, 1986), 60–76

Wolf, Hubert (ed.), *Systematisches Repertorium zur Buchzensur 1814–1917: Indexkongregation* (Paderborn, 2005)

INDEX

Note on subheadings: Carolyne refers to Carolyne von Sayn-Wittgenstein; Marie refers to Marie d'Agoult

Abdul-Medjid Khan, Sultan 109
Ábrányi, Kornél 287
Agoult, Charles d' 48, 49, 73, 97–8
Agoult, Claire d' *see* Charnacé, Claire de
Agoult, Louise Marie Thérèse d' 48, 50–1
Agoult, Marie d' (*née* Flavigny, *pen name*,
    Daniel Stern) 44–70: first impressions
    of Liszt 45–6; background 46–7;
    marriage and children with Charles
    47–8; depressions 48, 65–6, 85–6;
    jealousy 49–50, 52, 54, 57; tensions
    with Liszt 49–50, 51, 54–5, 66, 67–8,
    69, 73, 74, 82, 85–6, 91–2; death of
    daughter, Louise 50–1; births of
    children with Liszt 52, 54, 55–6, 63,
    65, 69; released from marriage 52; in
    Switzerland with Liszt 53–8, 59; in
    Paris 59–60, 69, 73–5; salons of 60,
    78–9; as joint-writer of article on
    Thalberg 61; in Italy 62–6, 68, 69; on
    Blandine 63, 69; diary 64–5; illness
    67–8; loneliness and guilt 73; relations
    with Anna Liszt 74, 98–9, 110;
    arrangements for children 74, 97–100,
    164–7; affairs 78–80; visits Liszt in
    London 82–3; at Nonnenwerth 84–6;
    missed by Liszt 90; end of relationship
    91–4; writes *Nélida* 94–7, 213, 243,
    246; writing career as Daniel Stern 95;
    compared to Carolyne 111; reunion
    with daughters and Liszt's fury 132–3,
135; Carolyne's opinion of 165;
    opposes Cosima's marriage 168; Liszt's
    later meetings with 183, 206, 213;
    memoirs 213, 265–6; death 265–6
Albert, Eugen d' 275
Album d'un voyageur 53–4
Alexander I, Tsar 159, 181
Alexandra (maidservant) 112–13, 114
Allgemeine musikalische Zeitung
    (journal) 13, 61
Allgemeiner Deutscher Musikverein 173,
    183, 282
Altenburg, Weimar 113–15, 123, 125, 142,
    153, 183: Carolyne's daughter at 146,
    156, 160, 175; Liszt's writings while at
    128; matinées 147; Wagner sheltered
    in 119
Amadeus (play and film) 11
Amsterdam 213–14, 261
ancien régime 10, 32, 135
Andersen, Hans Christian 41–2
Anderson, Janet 112–13, 114, 157
Années de pèlerinage 53–4, 271–2
Ansorge, Conrad 300–1
Antwerp 288, 294
Apel, Pauline 226, 277, 285
Apponyi, Albert 263, 265, 267, 268
Arbre de Noël 270, 273
Arndt, Ernst Moritz 85
Arnim, Bettina von 113
Augsburg 16

Augusta of Saxe-Weimar-Eisenach,
   Princess 282
Augusz, Antal, Baron 234, 238

Bach, Johann Sebastian 40, 248, 252, 295;
   Organ Toccata in D minor 230;
   Weinen, Klagen, Sorgen, Zagen 190–1
Bache, Walter 193, 294
Bagatelle sans tonalité 272
Balzac, Honoré de 60, 82, 96; *Béatrix* 93
Bartók, Béla 41, 273
Basel 52, 53, 155, 216, 217
Basel Conservatory 55
Bayreuth 247, 249: Liszt visits 250–1, 266,
   267–71, 288–9, 292–3, 296–8; Liszt's
   illness, death and burial in 299–312;
   première of *Parsifal* 288–9; *see also*
   Wahnfried
Bayreuth Festival 254, 261, 266–71, 292,
   296–7, 304, 309, 310
Bayreuther Tagblatt 309
Bazard, Saint-Amand 34
Bechstein, Carl 284
Beethoven, Ludwig van 9, 12, 22, 102, 248,
   295: centenary 234; legend of kiss
   planted on young Liszt 13–14; Liszt
   conducts opera of 119; Liszt owns
   piano of 114–15; Liszt's transcriptions
   of music of 40, 63; Piano Concertos
   75, 261–2; Piano Sonata no. 29
   ('Hammerklavier') 59
Belgiojoso, Cristina, Princess 62
Bellagio 63, 64
Bellini, Vincenzo: *Norma* 194
Belloni, Gaëtano 72, 89, 90, 122
Bells of Strasbourg, The 259, 261, 262
Benvenuti, Augusto 291
Béranger, Pierre-Jean de 96
Berg, Alban 273
Berlin: Bülow's performance of B minor
   Piano Sonata 169–70; Daniel's death
   in 176–7; Liszt in 86–91; Liszt's
   daughters in 165–8, 176, 181–2, 183
Berlin Philharmonic 116
Berlioz, Hector 37, 45, 60, 62, 113, 116:
   Carolyne's advice to 126; friendship
   with Liszt 35–6, 155, 182, 206; gala
   events in honour of 162; Liszt falls out
   with 213; Liszt's article on 126–7; on
   Liszt's drunken behaviour 122;
   Benvenuto Cellini 119; *L'enfance du
   Christ* 162; *Harold en Italie* 36, 126–7;
   Symphonie fantastique 35, 36; *Les
   Troyens* 126

Bernard, Laure 98, 132, 133
Bernard, Louise 98, 99, 132, 133
Bernhardi, Theodor von 125, 131, 144,
   145–6
Berry, Marie Caroline Ferdinande Louise
   de Bourbon, Duchesse de 19–20
Berthier, Napoléon, Prince de Wagram
   134
Besançon 26
Bethmann, Marie-Élisabeth *see* Flavigny,
   Marie-Élisabeth de
Biedermeier Age 10
Blodek, Wilhelm 232
Boieldieu, Adrien 17
Boissier, Auguste 39
Boissier, Valérie 39–40
Bonn 85, 295
Bordeaux 25
Bösendorfer, Ludwig 287
Boulogne-sur-Mer 24; Adam Liszt's death
   in 27–8
Bourges, Michel de 63
Brahms, Johannes 113
Bratislava *see* Pressburg
Brehme, Richard 280, 281
Brendel, Franz 172, 191, 194
Bretfeld, Franz Joseph von 15–16
Brno 102
Bruckner, Anton 242, 266, 309
Brückwald, Otto 266
Budapest: formation of 252; Liszt in 225,
   226, 283, 287–8, 294; Liszt Jubilee gala
   254–5; Liszt's apartment burgled 261;
   Royal Academy of Music 262–4;
   Wagner's money-raising concert
   261–2; *see also* Pest
Bülow, Blandine von (daughter of Cosima
   and Hans) 202, 214, 222: marriage
   289
Bülow, Cosima von *see* Wagner, (Gaetana)
   Cosima
Bülow, Daniela von (daughter of Cosima
   and Hans): birth 181–2; on Carolyne's
   relationship with Liszt 112; at *Christus*
   performance 253; marriage 296–8;
   and mother's assignations with
   Wagner 202, 214, 222; as pianist
   270; relationship with Liszt 281,
   286, 291, 292, 293–4; reunion with
   Hans 281
Bülow, Eva Maria von (daughter of Cosima
   and Wagner) 216, 304, 307
Bülow, Franziska von (mother of Hans)
   165–7

Bülow, Hans von: births of daughters 181–2, 202; on Blandine's death 189–90; on Carolyne 124, 129; character 167–8; and Cosima's daughters by Wagner 207–8, 216; conducts Wagner's works 208–9, 218; and Daniel's death 176–7; on life as a bachelor 216; on Liszt as teacher 231; Liszt on ability of 294; on Liszt's Catholicism 196; and Liszt's illness 281, 286, 288; marriage to Cosima 167–9, 172; performs Liszt works 169–70, 208; poor health 167–8, 203, 204, 207, 217; as pupil of Liszt 115, 275; at Stern Conservatory 165, 202; takes Munich court appointment 204–5, 207, 216; as teacher 165, 278–80, 281–2; unable to attend Daniela's wedding 298; visits Liszt in Tivoli 259; in Weimar 113, 115, 183; and wife's affair with Wagner 200–11, 214–17, 218–23

Bülow, Isolde von (daughter of Cosima and Wagner) 202, 207–8, 210, 214, 304, 306, 307, 308

Bulwer, Henry Lytton Earle 78, 79–80

Busoni, Ferruccio 273

Bussmann, Johann Jacob 46

Cadore, Camille de Nompère de Champagny, duc de 217

Carl Alexander of Saxe-Weimar-Eisenach, Grand Duke (*formerly* Crown Prince): accedes to dukedom (1853) 153; and Liszt's burial 311, 312; Liszt's letters to 103, 173, 196–7; and Liszt's Weimar appointment 101–2, 121; reaction to Cornelius opera fiasco and Liszt's resignation 171–2; reaction to Liszt's receiving minor orders 198; subsequent friendship with Liszt 205–6, 224, 225, 229, 242, 257; visits Bayreuth 266; and the 'Wittgenstein Affair' 142, 173, 181, 196–7, 206–7, 229

Carlsbad 130, 150, 156

Carlsbad Decrees (1819) 10

Caterini, Prospero 184

Catholicism: Carolyne and 131, 187; *Christus* oratorio 252–3, 255, 260; Lamennais and 34–5; Liszt's interest in 5, 26–7, 31–2, 131, 191–2, 193–6, 206, 240–1; and marriage 107–8, 143, 144, 161; minor orders 197; Polish 106; renewed influence of Church 32

censorship 10, 32–3

Chamonix 60

'Chapelle de Guillaume Tell, La' 54

Charles X, king of France 32–3

Charnacé, Claire Christine de (*née* d'Agoult) 48, 52, 219, 265

'Chasse-neige' 40

Château de la Moutte 188–90

Cherubini, Luigi 12, 17

Chopin, Frédéric 33, 36–7, 41, 52, 60, 102, 299; Liszt's monograph on 129

Clary, Zénaide Françoise 134

coach travel 25–6, 72

Cohen, Hermann ('Puzzi') 54

Cohnfeld, Adalbert 87

Cologne 85, 163

Colpach Castle 298–9

Comet, Great (1811) 1–2, 5

Como, Lake 63, 65, 69

Conservatoire, Paris 17–18, 57, 61–2

Constantinople 71, 102, 109

Cooper, James Fenimore 85

Cornelius, Carl Maria 150–1

Cornelius, Peter: attempt to set Christ's life to music 252; on the Bülows' marriage 207, 209, 211–12, 214, 215; on Carolyne 128–9, 181; and Daniel Liszt 176; as Liszt's pupil 115; translates Liszt's writings 128; on underappreciation of Liszt 178; visits Weimar 183; *Der Barbier von Bagdad* (première fiasco) 170–2, 178

Corsaire, Le (journal) 31

Cramer, Johann Baptist 295

Croissy, Château de 49, 52

Csapó, Vilmos von 192

Csárdás macabre 272

Czerny, Carl: background 9; impressed with boy Liszt 8–9, 11; Liszt's lessons with 11, 12, 18, 28; teaching methods 9, 39; unease over tour but maintains contact with Liszt's father 14, 23, 24; Vienna reunion with Liszt 67; works 9, 20, 22

Dante Alighieri 118, 265

Dante Sonata 276

Dante Symphony 118, 199

Danube, River: floods 66

Debussy, Claude 273

Degen, Jacob 1, 2

Demellayer, Antoine 56, 63

Denis-Street, Ernest 153, 156, 163

Deux Légendes 209, 212

Diabelli, Anton 12
Didier, Charles 63
Didier, Euphémie 43, 49
Dijon 25, 60
Dingelstedt, Franz von 170–2
Divertimento sur une cavatine de Pacini 62, 76
Döllinger, Ignaz von 187, 311
Don Sanche, ou Le château d'amour 23
Douglas, Mr 193
Drapeau Blanc, Le (journal) 20–1
Dresden 80, 92: uprising 119
Dreyschock, Alexander 232
Dublin 83
Dumas, Alexandre 33–4
Duncker, Franz 268
Düsseldorf music festival 162, 163

École des Beaux-Arts, Paris 95
Edinburgh 83
Eisenstadt 3, 4, 5, 6, 254
Eliot, George 113
Elisavetgrad 109
En rêve 272
Enfantin, Barthélemy-Prosper 34
Érard, Camille 206
Érard, Jean-Baptiste 18–19, 22, 29
Érard, Sébastien 18–19, 22, 24, 29, 40, 58
Érard Frères: pianos 18, 19, 22, 40, 109; salons 59, 62
Esterházy, Michael, Count 7–8
Esterházy, Nicholas II, Prince 2–3, 6–7, 9, 12
Esterházy family 3, 5, 6–8
Études d'exécution transcendante d'après Paganini 9, 40

Faubourg Saint-Germain, Paris 33, 44–5
Faust Symphony 118
Fay, Amy 228, 229–31
Festetics, Leo, Count 76
Festklänge 203
Fétis, François-Joseph 17
'Feux follets' 40
finger exercises 39–40
Flaugergues, Honoré 1
Flavigny, Alexandre, Vicomte de 46
Flavigny, Marie-Élisabeth de (*née* Bethmann) 46, 53, 73
Fleischer, Richard 305
Florence 69, 288
Forman, Miloš 11
Foudras, Isaure de, Comtesse 134
France: July Revolution (1830) 32–3; tours

25–6, 71, 98; *see also* Boulogne-sur-Mer; Paris
Francis of Assisi, St: music depicting 194, 209, 212
Franciscans 3, 209, 311
Franck, César 273
Franco-Prussian War 234
Frankfurt am Main 46–7, 106
Franz, Robert 239–40
Franz Joseph I, emperor of Austria 174, 255
Freiligrath, Ferdinand 85
French language 29, 60, 61, 76, 106, 128
French Revolution 10, 32, 78
Friedheim, Arthur 278, 286, 287
Friedrich August II, king of Saxony 119
Friedrich Franz III, Grand Duke of Mecklenburg-Schwerin 266
Friedrich Wilhelm III, king of Prussia 107
Friedrich Wilhelm IV, king of Prussia 86
Frölich, Emma 292, 297, 301, 303–4, 307–8
Frölich, Ludwig 292, 297, 301, 308
Fulda, bishop of 179, 180

Gabriac, Cathérine de, Marquise 49
Geneva 25, 54–8, 59, 63, 106, 214
Genoa 37, 69
George IV, king of Great Britain 22
German language 2, 4
Germany: tours 71, 85, 86–91, 92, 98; *see also* Bayreuth; Berlin; Munich; Nonnenwerth; Weimar
Gilbert, Elizabeth Rosanna *see* Montez, Maria de los Dolores Porrys y
Gille, Carl 194, 229, 285, 309
Girardin, Émile and Delphine de 95
Glaßbrenner, Adolf 88
Glasgow 83
Gluck, Christoph von 119
Goethe, Johann Wolfgang von 102, 119, 224, 265, 266: *Faust* 35, 118; 'Kennst du das Land' 269; *Torquato Tasso* 118, 172–3, 229
Göllerich, August 230, 231, 294, 296, 300, 301
Gottschalg, Alexander Wilhelm 272, 305
Gounod, Charles 182
Graf, Conrad 67
'Gran' Mass 162–3, 173, 211, 212–13, 255
Grand galop chromatique 76, 103
Grande fantaisie de bravoure sur La clochette de Paganini 40
Grande valse di bravura 56

Grandes études de Paganini 40
Gravina, Biagio, Count 289
Gravina, Blandine *see* Bülow, Blandine von
Great Britain 22–4, 26, 28, 71, 81–4, 294–5
Gregorovius, Ferdinand 187–8, 196, 197, 199, 233
Groß, Adolf von 291, 313
Großkurth, Emma 281
Gut, Serge 23, 224
gypsies 5

Hagn, Charlotte von 91, 93
Halévy, Jacques 182
Hamlet (symphonic poem) 118
Handel, George Frideric 102
Hanover Square Rooms, London 81
Hanslick, Eduard 10, 103, 255–6
Harmonies poétiques et religieuses 103
Hartmann, Ludwig von 222
Haussmann, Georges Eugène 17
Haydn, Franz Joseph 3
Haynald, Lajos 255
Hebbel, Friedrich 113, 175
Heilige Cäcilia, Die 258–9
Heine, Heinrich 21, 33, 37–8, 43, 88–9
Helbig, Nadine 193, 233
Helbig, Wolfgang 193
Henzschel, Moritz 144
Herwegh, Georg 73, 78, 94, 252
Herz, Henri 232
Hiller, Ferdinand 33, 113
Hofer, Ludwig 16, 17, 19, 22
Hoffmann von Fallersleben, August Heinrich 2, 113
Hofgärtnerei, Weimar 225–7, 228, 229, 230, 274, 275, 281–2, 284
Hohenlohe-Schillingsfürst, Chlodwig zu 174–5, 217
Hohenlohe-Schillingsfürst, Gustav Adolf zu 174, 175, 179, 181, 184, 197, 198, 241
Hohenlohe-Schillingsfürst, Konstantin Victor Ernst Emil Karl Alexander Friedrich zu 174–5, 179–80, 181
Hohenlohe-Schillingsfürst, Marie zu *see* Sayn-Wittgenstein, Marie Pauline Antonia von
Hohenzollern-Hechingen, Konstantin zu 183, 205
Höhle piano 284
Horowitz, Vladimir viii
Horpács Castle 251–2
Hotel Alibert, Rome 286–7
Hôtel d'Angleterre, Paris 17
Hôtel de France, Paris 60

Hôtel de Strasbourg, Paris 23
Hotel Zur Stadt Frankfurt, Vienna 104
Hugo, Victor 33, 60, 78
Huit variations 23
Humboldt, Alexander von 113
Hummel, Johann Nepomuk 3, 9, 12, 13, 20, 22, 26
Hungarian language 2
Hungarian Rhapsodies 119, 230
Hungary: Cosima on 262; floods 66, 75; and Great Comet 1–2; Liszt's early concerts and presentation of sabre 75–8; Liszt's 1846–47 tour 102; Liszt's 1870 stay 234; Liszt's increased interest in 226; Liszt's visit with the Bülows 209–10; national pride 75–6, 255; upsurge of interest in Liszt 225, 255; *see also* Budapest; 'Gran' Mass; Pest; Raiding
Hunnenschlacht 118

Ibach, Rudolf, piano of 284
Ideale, Die 118
'Illustrations' 41
Illustrations de L'africaine 195
Innsbruck 300–1
Institut des Demoiselles, Paris 98, 99, 132, 133
Ireland 83
Isnard, Charles 189–90
Isnard, Josephine 189
'Isolde's Love-Death' 204
Italy 63–6, 68, 69; *see also* Rome; Venice
Iwanowska, Pauline 105, 106, 111–12
Iwanowsky, Peter 105, 106–8, 109, 143

Janin, Jules 155, 182, 206
Janina, Olga 200, 231–46, 283
Joachim, Joseph 113, 116
Joukowsky, Paul von 291

Kapp, Julius 38
Karajan, Herbert von viii, ix
Karl I, king of Württemberg 266
Karl August of Saxe-Weimar-Eisenach, Grand Duke 102
Karl Friedrich of Saxe-Weimar-Eisenach, Grand Duke 101–2, 142, 144–5, 153
Karlsruhe 203–4, 224–5, 227
Kaulbach, Wilhelm von 113, 118, 217
Kellermann, Berthold 268, 276, 277, 278, 279, 280
Kempfenhausen 201, 202

Kempis, Thomas à: *De imitationi Christi* 26-7
Keppler, Friedrich 291
Kiev 101, 104-5, 108
Kiev Contract Fair 105
Klindworth, Georg 152-3
Klindworth, Karl 115, 281, 286
Kopf, Josef von 232, 233
Kostenecka, Antoinette 114
Kreiner, Mihály ('Miska') 301, 303, 304, 305, 307, 308, 310, 312
Kreutzer, Rodolphe 17
Kullak, Theodor 229, 282

Laborie, Charlotte 43
'Lac de Wallenstedt, Le' 53
Lachmund, Carl 277, 282, 285, 288
Lagarde, Auguste de, Comte 47
Lamartine, Alphonse de 78, 118, 182
Lamennais, Félicité de 34-5, 53, 96
Landgraf, Carl 302, 304, 305
Lannoy, Heinrich Eduard von 75
Lausanne 60
L'avenir (journal) 34-5
Lavenu, Louis Henry 83, 84
Le Goullon, Heinrich 159
Le Vayer, Renée de Maupéou, Marquise 44-5, 48, 96
Legend of Saint Elizabeth 209, 294, 295
Legend of Saint Stanislaus 260
Legends see *Deux Légendes*
Lehmann, Henri 97
Lehmann, Lilli 267-9
Leipzig 80-1, 172-3
Lenbach, Franz von 266
Lenz, Wilhelm von 32
Lewald, Fanny 113
Lichnowsky, Felix von 112
Liebestraum 299
Liszt, Adam (father): background and career 2-5; and Liszt's musical education 5-11, 14, 17-18; markets Liszt's talents 9-11, 14-17, 19-20, 22, 24, 28; in Paris 17-20; on son's interest in priesthood 27; death 27-30, 31
Liszt, Anna (*née* Lager, mother): background and marriage 4; and birth of son 2, 4, 5; early years in Paris 17, 24-5; in Graz 25, 27, 29; and husband's death 27-8; joins Liszt in Paris 29, 30, 32, 33, 49; and Liszt's affairs 44, 64, 105; and Liszt's rivalry with Thalberg 57; looks after Liszt's children 74-5, 97-9, 100, 132, 133, 134-5, 165, 166, 168, 176, 190; and Marie 74, 98-9, 110; reaction to Liszt's relationship with Carolyne 110, 123; shock at Liszt's receiving minor orders 198; illness and death 206, 212
Liszt, Blandine *see* Ollivier, Blandine-Rachel
Liszt, Cosima *see* Wagner, (Gaetana) Cosima
Liszt, Daniel (son of Liszt and Marie): birth 69; childhood and education 73-4, 97-9, 100, 131-2, 155, 166, 168, 175-6; death 176-8, 190
Liszt, Eduard (uncle) 64, 183, 203, 215, 224-5, 252, 264
Liszt, Franz (1811-86)
  CHARACTERISTICS: appearance x, 32, 183, 187-8; as card player 264, 277, 286, 288, 290, 298, 301; character 11, 45-6, 68, 72, 125, 126, 129-30, 131, 231, 240, 264-5, 281, 313; charisma 41-2, 212, 231; concern with etiquette 111, 302; destructive piano playing 67; dislike of patronization 30; as drinker 30-1, 123, 126, 277-8; improvising abilities 5, 8, 12-13, 19, 22; insomnia and tiredness 271; interest in Catholicism 5, 26-7, 31-2, 131, 191-2, 193-6, 206, 240-1; large hands 40; love of reading 33-4; love of travel 224-5; phases of depression 44, 271-2; showmanship 41-3, 72, 82, 89, 255-6; sight-reading ability 11, 13, 218; as smoker 30-1, 278; style of recitals 71-2; as superstar viii-xi, 86-90; superstitious 294; virtuosity 38-9, 71, 103; women's reaction to 41-2, 43, 68, 87, 88-9, 199-200, 212, 245-6, 256, 267-8, 276
  LIFE: background and birth in Raiding 1-4; childhood 4-28; languages 4-5, 29, 60, 61, 76, 106, 128; early illnesses 4, 7; shows early talent 5; musical studies in Vienna 5-14; as child prodigy 7-8, 10-11, 12-13, 19-21, 23, 26-7, 29; first concerts in Vienna 12-14; 1823 German tour 16-17; with father in Paris 17-22, 23; studies in Paris 17-18; press reviews 20-2, 82, 212-13; organization of tours of Great Britain 22-4, 26, 28, 71, 81-4, 294-5; 1826-27 tours 25-6; religious diary 26; considers priesthood 26-7; and father's death 27-30, 31; as teacher

30–1, 39–40, 54, 55, 115, 153, 192–3, 229–33, 263–4, 275, 277, 278; relationship with Paris society 30–1; unhealthy lifestyle 30–1; early affairs 31, 37, 43–4; rumours of death 31; and Paris revolution 33; and salons 33; and new religious ideas 34–5; relations with other composers 35–7, 80–1; affair with Marie 44–70; rents apartment 49; tensions with Marie 49–50, 51, 54–5, 66, 67–8, 69, 73, 74, 82, 85–6, 91–2; births of children with Marie 52, 54, 55–6, 63, 65, 69; moves to Switzerland 53–9; finances 56, 59, 64, 83, 84, 103–4, 117; rivalry with Thalberg 56–9, 60–2; returns to Paris 58–9; moves to Italy 63–6, 69; concerts in Vienna 66–8, 69, 75; charity concerts 66–7, 68, 75, 105, 193, 197, 234, 252, 255, 263; 'virtuoso years' (1839–47) 71; extensive touring 71–2, 74, 75, 86–91, 92, 98, 102–5, 109; organization of tours 72; private secretary 72, 89; arrangements for his children 74, 97–100, 164–7; illnesses 75, 90, 271; returns to Hungary 75–8; concert in Pest 76–8, 209; revisits Raiding 78, 102, 252; other mistresses 78–9, 90–1, 92–3; and Marie's affairs 78–80; charitable donations 83, 104, 313; visits Nonnenwerth 84–6; end of relationship with Marie 91–4; depicted in Marie's *Nélida* 94–7; as Kapellmeister in Weimar 36, 101–2, 110, 111, 113, 116–17, 120–1, 123; starts affair with Carolyne 101, 105, 109, 110–16, 123–31; reasons for attraction to Carolyne 110–11, 123; Carolyne's efforts to obtain annulment of marriage 113, 142–51, 154, 155, 156–8, 159–61, 163, 164, 173–4, 175, 179–82, 194; library of 114, 135; as conductor of operas 119–20; friendship with Wagner 120, 151, 155, 182, 183, 218, 268–9, 270, 288, 289; conflict with authorities 121–2; writings by 126–7, 128–9; assistant 127–8; correspondence with Carolyne 129–31, 151–2, 155; relations with children 131–42, 155, 165–7; possible children by Carolyne 150–1; affair with Agnes Street-Klindworth 154–5, 156, 163–4, 180–1; later visits to Paris 155–6, 182, 206, 211–13, 294, 295;

workload 162, 263–4, 277, 288; and Cosima's marriage to Hans von Bülow 167–9; Cornelius opera fiasco leads to resignation from Weimar post 170–2, 178; at Leipzig festival 172–3; and Allgemeiner Deutscher Musikverein 173, 183; and son's death 175–8, 190; and grandchildren 181–2, 189, 254, 270, 289, 293–4, 296, 297, 303, 304; Carolyne plans marriage to 182, 183–4; appointed Commander of the Legion of Honour 182; later contact with Marie 183, 206, 213; returns to Weimar 182, 183, 205–6, 225–7, 228, 229, 230, 274–86; joins Carolyne in Rome 183–8; consent for wedding withdrawn 184–5; change in relationship with Carolyne 185, 193, 199; social life in Rome 187, 193; moves to monasteries, receives minor orders and becomes abbé 191–4, 197–8, 199–200, 209, 212; fails to marry Carolyne after death of Sayn-Wittgenstein 196–7; moves into Vatican 197, 224; Karlsrühe concert 203; and Cosima's affair with Wagner 203–10; friendship with Carl Alexander 205–6, 224, 225, 229, 242, 257; and mother's death 206, 212; in Amsterdam 213–14, 261; secretly visits Wagner 217–18; letter to Cosima about Wagner 220–2; and Cosima's marriage to Wagner 223; returns to Weimar 224–31; 'trifurcate life' in Weimar, Rome and Budapest 225; relationship with Olga von Meyendorff 227–9; affair with Olga Janina 231–46; Olga threatens to kill 238–9; Olga's memoirs on 239–41, 242–4; other scandals 241–2, 244–6; at Villa d'Este 241, 258–9, 271–2; Carolyne's letter on sexual infidelities of 244–5; attempts at reconciliation with Wagners 246–51, 253–4; visits to Bayreuth and Bayreuth Festival 250–1, 266, 267–71, 288–9, 292–3, 296–8; later visits to Rome 254, 257–8, 286–7, 294; in Budapest for fiftieth anniversary jubilee 254–5; return visit to Vienna 255–6; decides not to return to Weimar 256–7; and Carolyne's illness 257–8, 261; Budapest apartment broken into 261; performs at Wagner's Budapest concert 261–2; and Royal

Academy of Music 262–4; lack of time for composing 264; reaction to Marie's death 265–6; anger with Carolyne 270, 287–8; increasingly susceptible to flattery 274–5; fall and illnesses 280–1, 286, 287–8; relationship with Lina Schmalhausen 281–6; seventieth birthday 286–7; last visits to Budapest 287–8, 294; continues to travel 288, 294–5; visits Wagners in Venice 289–91; and Wagner's death 290–2; hurt by Cosima's rejection 291–2, 293, 295–6; no longer wishes to play piano 294, 295, 299; seventy-fourth birthday 300–1; persuaded to return to Bayreuth and granddaughter's wedding 296–8; visits Luxembourg and catches cold 298–9; returns to Bayreuth 299; final illness and death 299–308; burial 308–9, 310–13; Requiem Mass for 309
MUSIC: early compositions 12, 23; experimental music 272; Hungarian Rhapsodies 119, 230; influences 5, 33–5, 38–9, 40, 41; later music and link with modernity 272–4; melancholic music 271–2; Mephisto Waltzes 203, 233, 272; musical travel diary 53–4; opera 23; orchestral works xi, 127–8; paraphrases 41, 62, 195, 234; piano concertos 162, 282; piano sonata 169–70, 203, 270; sacred music 162–3, 209, 224, 260–1, 272; symphonic poems 118, 203; transcriptions 36, 40–1, 63, 76, 103, 197, 204, 260; Weimar compositions 117–19; *see also individual compositions*
Liszt, Franz von (cousin and godson) 292
Liszt, Georg Adam (grandfather) 3
Lisztomania 21, 86–90, 199–200, 255, 276
London 14, 15, 16, 22, 23, 26, 81–2, 84, 294–5
Longfellow, Henry Wadsworth: *The Golden Legend* 259
Louis XVIII, king of France 32
Louis-Philippe, duc d'Orléans and king of France 33
Luca, Antonino Saverio de 179, 181
Lucerne 25, 214, 215, 222
Ludwig I, king of Bavaria 92
Ludwig II, king of Bavaria 201–2, 204, 207, 209, 210–11, 214, 216, 217, 266
Lugubre gondola, La 272, 290–1

Luxembourg 298–9
Lviv 109, 232
Lycée Bonaparte, Paris 99, 132
Lyons 25, 56, 58, 59

Maier, Mathilde 204
Makart, Hans 266
Maltitz, Apollonius von 144–5, 147, 148–50, 153, 156, 161, 173–4, 227
Manchester 22–3
marriages of convenience 47
Marseilles 25
Martainville, Alphonse 20–1
Matignon, Angélique-Élisabeth de, Countess 52
Mazeppa 279
Meiningen orchestra 116
Meißner, Alfred 113
Mélodies hongroises 103
Mendelssohn, Felix 33, 80, 86
Menter, Sophie 234, 275
Menzel, Adolph von 266
Mephisto Waltzes 272: First 203, 233
Merian-Genast, Emilie 244, 245
Messager, André 156
Metternich, Klemens Wenzel von 10, 14–16, 17, 18, 67
Meyendorff, Felix von 227
Meyendorff, Olga von: background 227; Carolyne on 229, 244, 245; character 228; and Liszt's funeral 308; Liszt's letters to 239, 254, 257, 271, 272, 289–90, 292, 293, 299; nature of relationship with Liszt 227–9, 245; surprise at Liszt's absence from Weimar 257; and the Wagners 247, 248–9
Meyer, Friederike 204
Meyerbeer, Giacomo 12, 33, 60, 86; *L'africaine* 195
Meysenbug, Malwida von 294
Mickiewicz, Adam 33
middle classes: French 32, 33; Viennese 10
Mihalovich, Ödön von 234, 238
Milan 63–4, 65, 69
Miroir Drolatique, Le 77
Mohilow: Consistory Court 143, 144
Molitor, Raphael 198
Monastery of Santa Francesca Romana 200, 224
Monastery of the Madonna del Rosario, Monte Mario 191–4, 197, 224
Monasterzyska 105, 106

Montez, Maria de los Dolores Porrys y ('Lola') 92
Morelli, Francesco 184
Moscow 91
Mosonyi, Mihály 234
Mottl, Felix 283, 297, 298, 300, 303, 305, 310
Mozart, Wolfgang Amadeus 11, 115, 119: Liszt compared to 16, 18, 20–1
Mrazek, Anna 201, 202, 208
Mrazek, Franz 201, 202
Muncker, Theodor 309
Munich: Bülows in 201–2, 204–5, 207, 210–11, 214, 216–17, 218; Liszt in 14, 15–16, 217, 311; Wagner in 207, 209–11, 218
Munito (performing dog) 30
Munkáczy, Cecile 298, 299
Munkáczy, Mihály 298
music-making, domestic 10
Musikverein, Vienna 67, 102
Musset, Alfred de 50

Napoleon Bonaparte 10, 48, 107
Napoleon III, Emperor 182, 234
Neue Zeitschrift für Musik (journal) 172
New German School 118, 172
Nicholas I, Tsar 113, 147–8, 159, 163
Nicolai, Otto: Die lustigen Weiber von Windsor 162
Nohant 60, 62–3
Nonnenwerth, 84–6, 91–2
Nôtre-Dame de Paris 49
Nuages gris 271, 272

Odessa 109
Okraszewski, Władisław 173–4, 175, 179, 180
Oldenburg, Peter von 160
Ollivier, Blandine-Rachel ('Mouche') (née Liszt, daughter of Liszt and Marie): birth 52, 54, 55–6; childhood 56, 63, 69–70, 73–5, 79, 97–100; lives with Anna Liszt 74–5, 98–9; at Louise Bernard's school 98; reunion with mother and Liszt's fury 132–3, 135; under Mme Patersi's regime 133–42, 164–5; private diary 137–41; reunion with Liszt 155; sent to Berlin 165–7; misses Cosima's wedding 168; marriage 172; and Daniel's death 177; visits Weimar 183; home in France 188; pregnancy and death 189–90; grave 206, 310

Ollivier, Daniel 189, 293
Ollivier, Démosthène 188
Ollivier, Émile 172, 183, 188–90, 206, 212, 234, 265
Ollivier, Marie-Thérèse 293
On the Beethoven Centenary 234
opera 23, 119–20, 170–1: paraphrases 41, 62, 195, 234
opium 233
oratorios 195, 209, 252
orchestral music 127–8
orchestras 116–17
Orpheus 118

Pacini, Giovanni: Niobe 62
Paer, Ferdinando 18, 23
Paganini, Nicolò 37–9, 40, 41
Palais Metternich, Paris 212
Palazzo Barberini, Rome 197
Palazzo Caffarelli, Rome 286
Palazzo Vendramin-Calergi, Venice 289, 290, 291
Palestrina, Giovanni Pierluigi da 195, 260
paraphrases 41, 62, 195, 234
Paris: Adam Liszt and son in 14, 15, 16, 17–22, 23; Anna Liszt joins son in 29, 30, 32, 33, 49; Conservatoire 17–18, 57, 61–2; July Revolution (1830) 32–3; Liszt remains in after father's death 29–52; Liszt returns to 58–9; Liszt's later visits to 155–6, 182–3, 206, 211, 212–13, 294, 295; Olga Janina in 239; Paganini in 38–9; Polish émigrés in 33; salons 33, 44, 45, 47, 60, 61, 62, 78–9; siege of 234; Thalberg in 56–8; travel from 25–6
Patersi de Fossombroni, Louise Adélaide 133–42, 155, 164, 177
Pawlowna, Maria of Saxe-Weimar-Eisenach, Grand Duchess: birthday celebrations 119; and Liszt's salary 117; as Marie von Sayn-Wittgenstein's guardian 146, 156–7, 159; as owner of the Altenburg 114; position as tsar's sister 113, 153; and the 'Wittgenstein Affair' 142, 146, 148, 149, 156–7, 158
Pedro II of Brazil, Dom 266
Pest 66, 76–8, 209, 234, 238, 252; see also Budapest
Petersen, Dory 279, 285
Pfistermeister, Franz Seraph von 210
Pfordten, Ludwig von der 210
Piano Concerto no. 1 in E flat major 162
Piano Concerto no. 2 in A major 282

Piano Sonata in B minor 169–70, 203, 270
pianos: and domestic music-making 10; by Érard Frères 18, 19, 22, 40, 109; gifts of 284; by Ibach 284; Liszt's collection of 115; Liszt's upright at Monte Mario 192, 193–4; as orchestral instrument 40; positioning for recitals 72; weak construction 67
Piasecki, Hélène 232
Pius IX, Pope 181, 193–4, 197–8
Pleyel, Camille 37
Pleyel, Marie 37
Podolia 105–6
Pohl, Richard 169, 187, 217, 218
Polcastro, Countess 65
Polish émigrés 33
Portugal 98
Potocki, Bernard, Count 79, 80
Potter, Cipriani 24
Prague 122
Preller, Friedrich 113
Préludes, Les 118
press: censorship 32–3; reviews 20–2, 82, 212–13
Pressburg (Bratislava) 3, 7–8, 75–6
Pressburger Zeitung (journal) 1, 2, 7–8
Presse, La (journal) 95
programme music 118, 126–7
Prometheus 118
Prunarède, Adèle de la, Countess 43
Psalm XIII, setting of 203
Puzzi *see* Cohen, Hermann

Quatre valses oubliées 272–3

Raff, Joachim 115, 127–8, 177, 204, 215
Raiding 2–5, 6–7, 78, 102, 252
railways 25, 72, 133–4, 254
Rákóczy March (anon), arrangement of 76
Ramann, Lina 32, 34, 243–4, 269, 283–4, 292, 295, 309
Randeckart, Friedrich 117
Rattle, Simon xii–xiii
Ravenna 69
Rechberg, Johann Bernhard von 152
Redoutensaal, Pest 209
Redoutensaal, Vienna 13, 14, 67, 75
Reicha, Antoine 18
Reisenauer, Alfred 275, 278
Reményi, Ede 229, 234
'Réminiscences' 41
Réminiscences de Don Juan 103
Réminiscences de La Juive 56

Réminiscences de Robert le diable 102
Réminiscences des Puritains 56
Reubke, Julius 115
Revue et Gazette Musicale de Paris 60–1, 92
Revue indépendante 95, 97
Rhineland 84–5, 98
Richter, Hans 253, 261
Richter, Pius 115, 162–3
Ricordi, Tito and Giovanni 64
Ries, Ferdinand 5, 13
Rietschel, Ernst 113
Rohrer, Johann 4
Rome: Carolyne decides to move to 180–2; Carolyne's burial in 313; Liszt joins Carolyne in 183–8; Liszt moves to monasteries and receives minor orders 191–4, 197, 200, 224; Liszt moves into Vatican 197, 224; Liszt's regular returns to 225, 226, 227, 243, 254, 257–61, 286–7, 294; Liszt stays away due to anger with Carolyne 270; Marie and Liszt and Daniel's birth in 69, 74; Okraszewski in 173–4, 174, 179; Olga Janina in 200, 231–3
Rossini, Gioachino 23, 33, 60, 62, 182, 206
Rousseau, Jean-Jacques 221
Royal Academy of Music, Hungary 262–4
Royal Society of Musicians, London 22
Rubinstein, Anton 113, 229, 294
Russia: Agnes Street-Klindworth as possible spy 153–4, 163; Carolyne's background and marriage in 101, 105–9, 111–12; Liszt in 71, 90, 91, 101, 102, 104–5, 109; proceedings against Carolyne 157–8, 159–60; renewal of divorce case 173–4

sacred music 162–3, 209, 224, 260–1, 272
Sagan, Duchesse de 146
Saint-Cloud, ordinances of 33
Saint-Cricq, Caroline de 31, 44
Saint-Eustache church, Paris, 211, 212–13
St François d'Assise: La prédication aux oiseaux 194
St François de Paule marchant sur les flots 270
St Hedwig's Church, Berlin 168, 177
Saint-Mars, Jeanne Claire de 134, 135, 138, 164
St Petersburg 90, 91, 107: Consistorial Court 161
Saint-Saëns, Camille 212, 266, 268, 294

Saint-Simon, Claude-Henri de Rouvroy, comte de 34
Saint-Simonists 34, 35
St Stanislaus see Legend of St Stanislaus
Saint-Tropez 188–91, 206
Sainte-Beuve, Charles-Augustin de 33, 34, 78, 85
Salieri, Antonio 9, 11–12, 28
Salle Pleyel, Paris 36
salons, Paris 33, 44, 45, 47, 60, 61, 62, 78–9
Salons Érard 59, 62
Salons Zimmermann 61
Salvagni, Fortunato 192
Sand, George (Amandine-Aurore-Lucile Dupin de Francueil) 50, 52, 60, 62–3, 96
Sauer, Emil 274–6, 278, 283
Sayn-Wittgenstein, (Jeanne-Élisabeth) Carolyne von, Princess (née Iwanowska): background 105–7; Liszt meets 101, 105, 109; appearance 107, 110–11, 123–4, 186; marriage and separation 107–9, 111, 112; Anna Liszt's reaction to 110, 123; moves to Weimar with Liszt 110–15; intellect 111; considered scandalous 123–4, 149–50, 151; as smoker 123, 124, 158; talkativeness 124–5; ambition for Liszt 125–9; strong opinions of 126–9, 144; writing style 128–9, 130; correspondence with Liszt 129–31, 151–2, 155; and arrangements for Liszt's children 133–42, 165–7; efforts to obtain annulment of marriage 113, 142–51, 154, 155, 156–8, 159–61, 163, 164, 173–4, 175, 179–82, 194; possible pregnancies 150–1; as possible target of spying activities 154; visit to Paris 155–6; breaks agreement with Nicholas 156–7; Russian proceedings against 157–8, 159–60; ostracized 158, 172, 257; loses Russian citizenship and exiled 159–60; on Cosima 165, 215; and daughter's marriage 175; blamed for Daniel's death 177–8; moves to Rome 180–8; marriage finally annulled 182; plans marriage to Liszt but papal consent withdrawn 182, 183–5; relationship with Liszt changes 185, 193, 199; apartment in Rome 185–6; belief in spiritualism 186; writings 186–7; continued support for Liszt 195; Liszt fails to marry 196–7; blamed for Liszt's becoming abbé 198;

Liszt's continued bond with 225; dislike of Liszt's stays in Weimar and Budapest 226–7, 260, 264; mocks Olga von Meyendorff 229; Olga Janina's resemblance to 233; hatred of the Wagners 243–4, 249–51, 269–70; on Liszt's sexual infidelities 243–6; attempt to write libretto 252; Liszt's later visits to 254, 257–8, 287–8; illness, isolation and eccentricity 257–8, 259–60; wish for Liszt to write sacred music 260; on Liszt's later music 273; concern for Liszt's health 287–8, 296; and Liszt's burial 311–12; stroke 311; death 312–13; Causes intérieures de la faiblesse extérieure de l'Église en 1870 186–7
Sayn-Wittgenstein, Ludwig von 159
Sayn-Wittgenstein, Marie Pauline Antonia von (later zu Hohenlohe-Schillingsfürst): birth 108; moves to Weimar with mother 110, 112–13, 114, 115; letters 142; and inheritance 143, 145; under Maria Pawlowna's guardianship 146, 156–7, 159; planned marriage to Talleyrand 146–7, 149, 150, 156–7, 159, 160–1; visit to Paris 155; on Weimar court 172; beauty 174; marriage to Prince Konstantin 174–5, 180; on tragic events in Rome 182, 185; and mother's illness 259; on mother's death 312
Sayn-Wittgenstein, Nicholas von, Prince: marriage and separation 107–9, 111, 112; opposition to Carolyne's wish for annulment 113, 143–9; letters 142; new relationship 145; as possible employer of Agnes 154; anger over broken agreement 156–7, 158; tries to prevent daughter's marriage 159, 161; marriage annulment 161, 179, 182; remarriage 161; death 196, 199
Schiller, Friedrich von 118, 224
Schleinitz, Marie von 219
Schloss Belvedere, Weimar 144–5
Schloß Krzyzanowitz, Racibórz 112–13
Schloss Wilhelmsthal 205–6
Schlözer, Kurd von 191, 192, 193, 195, 197, 198, 199
Schmalhausen, Lina 279–80, 281–6: on Liszt's death 300–1, 302, 303, 304, 305–6, 307, 308
Schnappauf, Bernhard 305, 306, 307–8
Schoenberg, Arnold 273

Schorn, Adelheid von: at Bayreuth banquet 268; on Carolyne 124, 158, 185, 259–60; and the Hofgärtnerei 227, 228, 229; on Liszt and serious works 261; on Liszt's drinking 277, 292; on Liszt's illness 281, 286; on Liszt's reaction to Cosima's rejection 292; nurses Carolyne 259; offers to nurse Liszt 303; on performance of *Christus* 253; provides Carolyne with news of Liszt 226–7, 245–6, 269; tries to stop rumours about Liszt's health 287; Wagner's anger with 247–8; on women's attraction to Liszt 245–6, 276

Schorn, Henriette von 226
Schorn, Ludwig von 226
Schrober, Franz von 77–8
Schubert, Franz 12, 41, 63, 76, 102, 295: *Alfonso und Estrella* 119; *Erlkönig* 103, 197
Schuberth, Julius 237
Schumann, Clara 67, 80–1, 113, 169–70, 278
Schumann, Robert 41, 80–1, 169: *Genoveva* 162
science 34
Scotland 83
séances musicales 61
Sechter, Simon 12
Seebach, Friedrich von 114
Semper, Gottfried 113
Sept variations brillantes sur un thème de Rossini 23
Servais, François 234
Sgambati, Giovanni 192–3
Singakademie, Berlin 86
Smetana, Bedřich 113
Soirées de Vienne 295
Sophie, Archduchess of Austria 67, 75
Spain 98
Spontini, Gaspare 86
Stahr, Anna and Helene 301, 305
Starnberg, Lake 201, 202, 204
Stavenhagen, Bernhard 298, 299, 300, 301, 305
Stein, Heinrich von 289
Stern, Daniel *see* Agoult, Marie d'
Stern Conservatory, Berlin 165, 202
Stradal, August 242, 275, 282
Strasbourg 16; *see also* Bells of Strasbourg
Strauss, Richard 273
Street, Charles 163
Street, Georges 156

Street-Klindworth, Agnes 152–5, 156, 163–4, 165, 180–1, 191–2, 217, 245
Stuttgart 16, 217
Sue, Eugène 33, 78
Switzerland 25, 50, 52, 53–8, 59, 60, 98, 211, 214–16; *see also* Basel; Geneva; Lucerne
symphonic poems 118, 203
symphony: considered outdated 118
Széchényi, Imre, Count 252

Táborszky, Ferdinand 291
Talleyrand-Périgord, Charles-Angélique, Baron de 146–7, 149, 150, 156, 159, 160–1, 164, 165, 174, 175
Tasso: lamento e trionfo 118, 172–3
Tausig, Carl 113, 115, 176, 183, 229, 230, 275
Tchaikovsky, Pyotr 266, 267
Thalberg, Sigismond 56–9, 60–2, 96: *Fantaisie sur des motifs de l'opéra La Straniera de Bellini* 57; *Fantaisie sur des thèmes de l'opéra Moïse de Rossini* 62; *Grande fantaisie* 60
Théatre Italien, Paris 20–1, 57, 58, 59
Theiner, Agostino 191
Thermes, Ludemille de 134
Thode, Daniela *see* Bülow, Daniela von
Thode, Henry 296–7, 309
Thomán, István 300, 301
threnody 271–2, 290
Thuringian State Archives 142
Tichatschek, Joseph 113
Tigrière, Marquis de la 108–9
Tivoli 198; *see also* Villa d'Este
Tomau, Nikolai 157–8
Tonkünstlerverein 203
Totentanz 208
transcendental approach 41
transcriptions 36, 40–1, 63, 76, 103, 197, 204, 260
transport *see* coach travel; railways
Tribschen *see* Villa Tribschen
Trocadero, Paris 295

United States: Liszt refuses tour of 295; Olga Janina in 236–8
Unstern 272
Uslar, Constantin von 122

'Vallée d'Obermann' 53
'Valse infernale' *see* Réminiscences de Robert le diable
'Variations' 41
Varnhagen von Ense, Karl August 86–7

Vatican 197–9, 224
Velluti, Giovanni Battista 24
Venice 65–6, 68, 96, 288, 289–91
Verdi, Giuseppe: *Ernani* 119
Via Crucis 272
Viardot-García, Pauline 113, 229
Victoria, queen of Great Britain 82, 295
Vieuxtemps, Henri 113
Vienna: Biedermeier Age 10; Carolyne in
    113; child prodigies 10–11, 14; Daniel
    Liszt in 175–6, 177; domestic
    music-making 10; hotel bill 104; Liszt's
    childhood studies in 6–14; Liszt's early
    concerts in 12–14; Liszt's flood relief
    benefit concerts in 66–8; Liszt's
    further concerts in 69, 75, 78, 102,
    103; Liszt's reappearance at comeback
    concert (1874) 255–6; Liszt's visit in
    1886 294; Maria von Sayn-
    Wittgenstein in 175; population 17;
    Salieri in 11–12
Vienna Congress (1815) 10, 15
Vigny, Alfred de 33
Villa d'Este, Tivoli 241, 258–9, 271–2
Villa Pellet, Kempfenhausen 201–3
Villa Tribschen 214–16, 217–19
'Vision' 40
Voight, Hortense 242
Volkmann, Richard 280
Voß, Richard 185–6, 193, 227

Wagner, (Gaetana) Cosima (*née* Liszt,
    daughter of Liszt and Marie, first
    married to Hans von Bülow): birth 65;
    childhood 69–70, 73–5, 97–100; lives
    with Anna Liszt 74–5, 98–9; reunion
    with mother and Liszt's fury 132–3,
    135; under Mme Patersi's regime
    133–42, 164–5; on Agnes 153; reunion
    with Liszt 155; character 165; sent to
    Berlin 165–7; marriage to Hans von
    Bülow 167–9, 172; and Daniel's death
    175, 176–8; daughters with Bülow
    181–2, 202; affair with Wagner
    200–23; births of children with
    Wagner 202, 205, 207–8, 216, 223;
    travels with Liszt 205–7; in Hungary
    with Hans 209–10; joins Wagner in
    Switzerland 214–19; separation from
    Hans 219–23; disappointment with
    father 219–20, 248–9; Liszt's letter to
    220–2; marries Wagner 223; Carolyne's
    anger with 243–4, 249; rapprochement
    with Liszt 250–4, 289–90; on Liszt's

performance of Beethoven Concerto
    261–2; on state of Hungary 262;
    reaction to mother's death 266;
    arranges party at Bayreuth 270–1; on
    première of *Parsifal* 288–9; in Venice
    289, 290; forty-fifth birthday 290; and
    Wagner's death 291–2; rejection of
    Liszt 291–2, 293, 295–6; and Bayreuth
    Festival xi–xii, 292, 293, 296–7, 298;
    persuades Liszt to return to Bayreuth
    296–7; and Daniela's wedding 296–8;
    anger with Liszt 298; and Liszt's death
    and burial 301–6, 307–11, 312, 313; on
    Carolyne's death 313
Wagner, Eva *see* Bülow, Eva Maria von
Wagner, Isolde *see* Bülow, Isolde von
Wagner, Nike xii
Wagner, Richard: egoism x; musical debt to
    Liszt xii–xiii; admiration of Liszt's
    sight-reading ability 11; Berlioz's envy
    of 36; Liszt's transcriptions of 41; visits
    Liszt at the Altenburg 113; Weimar's
    lack of appreciation of 116, 172; advice
    on Liszt's *Dante* Symphony 118; escape
    to Weimar 119; friendship with Liszt
    120, 151, 155, 182, 183, 218, 268–9,
    270, 288, 289; breakthrough as
    composer 120; on shortcomings of
    Liszt's position at Weimar 121; on
    Carolyne 124–5; Liszt's article on
    128–9; reaction to Liszt's becoming
    abbé 198; debts paid off by Ludwig II
    201; affair with Cosima 200–23; births
    of children with Cosima 202, 205,
    207–8, 216, 223; Liszt's distrust of
    203–4; series of affairs 203–4; settles
    in Munich but instructed to leave 207,
    209–11, 218; anger with Liszt and
    Cosima 210; in Switzerland 211, 214;
    Liszt's secret visit to 217–18; marries
    Cosima 223; attempts at reconciliation
    with Liszt 246–51, 253–4; and
    Bayreuth 247, 249, 250, 254;
    Carolyne's attacks on 249–51; attends
    performance of *Christus* 252–3; and
    Bayreuth Festival 254, 261, 266–7; and
    Budapest concert 261–2; overshadows
    Liszt xi–xii, 268–9; Carolyne on music
    of 273; on Liszt's late music 273–4; and
    première of *Parsifal* 288–9; in Venice
    289–91; illness and anger with Liszt
    290; death 290–1; *Der fliegende
    Holländer* 120; *Lohengrin* 119–20, 234;
    Die Meistersinger von Nürnberg 216,

218; *My Life* 270; *Parsifal* 288–9, 291–2, 296, 302, 304, 309; *Das Rheingold* 128–9; *Rienzi* 92; Symphony in C major 290; *Tannhäuser* 119, 120, 162, 254; *Tristan und Isolde* 173, 204, 208–9, 296, 302

Wagner, Siegfried 223, 289, 305, 307, 309

Wagner Festival, Weimar 120

Wahnfried, Bayreuth 267–8, 270, 288, 291, 293–4, 297, 301, 303, 305, 308, 309–10

Walker, Alan 150, 163, 187

Watzdorf, Christian Bernhard von 148–50, 157, 160

Weber, Carl Maria 102, 295; *Invitation to the Dance* 197; *Konzertstück* 67

Weber, Max 42

Weimar: archives 142–3; Berlioz in 162; bureaucracy and authoritarianism 120–2; diocese 179; Liszt's compositions while at 117–19; Liszt's daughters in 166; Liszt's position as Kapellmeister 36, 101–2, 110, 111, 113, 116–17, 120–1, 123; Liszt's resignation after Cornelius opera fiasco 170–2; Liszt's return to 224–31; Liszt's subsequent boycott of 256–7; Liszt's visits in later life 274–80; Marie von Sayn-Wittgenstein's wedding 175; Nicholas von Sayn-Wittgenstein in 144–5; orchestra 116–17, 120; performance of *Christus* 252; relations with Russia 153–4, 163, 227; right to vote 116–17; Talleyrand in 146–7; Wagner in 119; *see also* Altenburg; Hofgärtnerei

Weimar Theatre 170–1, 230

Weinen, Klagen, Sorgen, Zagen, Variations on 190–1

Weingartner, Felix 277, 297–8, 300, 302, 307, 308–9

Werner, Anton von 266

Wieck, Friedrich 67

'Wilde Jagd' 40

Wilhelm I, Emperor 266, 282

Windsor Castle 22, 294–5

'Wittgenstein Affair' 142–51, 154, 155, 156–8, 159–61, 163, 164, 173–4, 175, 179–82, 194

Woronince 106, 108, 109, 110

Zhitomir: Consistory Court 143–4

Zielińska, Olga *see* Janina, Olga

Zieliński, Ludwik 232, 234–5

Zylinski, Wenceslaus, bishop of Mohilow 179

Printed and bound by CPI Group (UK) Ltd, Croydon, CR0 4YY

18/09/2024

14558719-0001